ROMAN MOSAICS

OR
STUDIES IN ROME AND
ITS NEIGHBOURHOOD

By

HUGH MACMILLAN

Double 9
BOOKS

Roman Mosaics
Or
Studies In Rome And Its Neighbourhood

by **Hugh Macmillan**

ISBN:978-93-58595-67-3

Published by

DOUBLE 9 BOOKS

2/13-B, Ansari Road, Daryaganj
New Delhi – 110002
info@double9books.com
www.double9books.com
Tel. 011-40042856

This book is under public domain

ABOUT THE AUTHOR

Hugh Macmillan (1833-1903) was a Scottish pastor who served as the Free Church of Scotland's General Assembly Moderator in 1897. He wrote a lot about theology and the interaction between God and the natural world. His best-selling book, Bible Teachings in Nature, was published in 15 editions in the UK and the USA and was multilingual. The eldest of Margaret (née Macfarlane) and Alexander Macmillan's nine children, he was born on September 17, 1833, in Aberfeldy. His parents were merchants. He first attended Hill Street Academy in Edinburgh after attending school in Aberfeldy. At the University of Edinburgh, he started studying for an arts degree and then for a medical degree before quitting to join the Free Church of Scotland, which had been founded in 1843. He received his education at New College in Edinburgh. He spent his last years of preaching at Greenock's 70 Union Street. He co-founded the Clan MacMillan Society in 1892 and led it as its Chief from 1892 to 1896. He left his job in 1901. He died on May 24, 1903, at his residence in West Edinburgh, 2 Murrayfield Road, and was laid to rest in Dean Cemetery. The burial is located on its southern wall in the first northern addition, backing up to the original cemetery.

CONTENTS

PREFACE

The title of this book may seem fanciful. It may even be regarded as misleading, creating the idea that it is a treatise like that of Mr. Digby Wyatt on those peculiar works of art which decorate the old palaces and churches of Rome. But notwithstanding these objections, no title can more adequately describe the nature of the book. It is applicable on account of the miscellaneous character of the chapters, which have already appeared in some of our leading magazines and reviews, and are now, with considerable changes and additions, gathered together into a volume. There is a further suitableness in the title, owing to the fact that most of the contents have no claim to originality. As a Roman Mosaic is made up of small coloured cubes joined together in such a manner as to form a picture, so my book may be said to be made up of old facts gathered from many sources and harmonised into a significant unity. So many thousands of volumes have been written about Rome that it is impossible to say anything new regarding it. Every feature of its topography and every incident of its history have been described. Every sentiment appropriate to the subject has been expressed. But Rome can be regarded from countless points of view, and studied for endless objects. Each visitor's mind is a different prism with angles of thought that break up the subject into its own colours. And as is the case in a mosaic, old materials can be brought into new combinations, and a new picture constructed out of them. It is on this ground that I venture to add another book to the bewildering pile of literature on Rome.

But I have another reason to offer. While the great mass of the materials of the book is old and familiar, not a few things are introduced that are comparatively novel. The late Dean Alford made the remark how difficult it is to obtain in Rome those details of interest which can be so easily got in other cities. Guide-books contain a vast amount of information, but there are many points interesting to the antiquarian and the historian which they overlook altogether. There is no English book, for instance, like Ruffini's Dizionario Etimologico-Storico delle Strade, Piazze, Borghi e Vicoli della Città di Roma, to tell one of the origin of the strange and bizarre names of the streets of Rome, many of which involve most interesting historical facts and most romantic associations of the past. There is no English book on the ancient marbles of Rome like Corsi's Pietre Antiche, which describes the mineralogy and source of the building materials of the imperial city, and traces their history from the law courts and temples of which they first formed part to the churches and palaces in which they may now be seen. Every nook in London, with its memories and points of interest, has been chronicled in a form that is accessible to every one. But there is an immense amount of most interesting antiquarian lore regarding out-of-the-way things in Rome which is buried in the transactions of learned societies or in special Italian monographs, and is therefore altogether beyond the reach of the ordinary visitor. Science has lately shed its vivid light upon the physical history of the Roman plain; and the researches of the archæologist have brought into the daylight of modern knowledge, and by a wider comparison and induction have invested with a new significance, the prehistoric objects, customs, and traditions which make primeval Rome and the surrounding sites so fascinating to the imagination. But these results are not to be found in the books which the English visitor usually consults. In the following chapters I have endeavoured to supply some of that curious knowledge; and it is to be hoped that what is given—for it is no more than a slight sample out of an almost boundless store—will create an interest in such subjects, and induce the reader to go in search of fuller information.

Many of the points touched upon have provoked endless disputations which are not likely soon to be settled. Indeed there is hardly any line of study one can take up in connection with Rome which does not bristle with controversies; and a feeling of perplexity and uncertainty continually haunts one in regard to most of the subjects. It is not only in the vague field of the early traditions of the city, and of the medieval traditions of the Church, that this feeling oppresses one; it exists everywhere, even in the more solid and assured world of Roman art, literature, and history. Where it is so difficult to arrive at settled convictions, I may be pardoned if I have expressed views that are open to reconsideration.

I am aware of the disadvantages connected with thus collecting together a number of separate papers, instead of writing a uniform treatise upon one continuous subject. The picture formed by their union must necessarily have much of the artificiality and clumsiness of the mosaic as compared with the oil or water-colour painting. But only in this form could I have brought together such a great variety of important things. And though I cannot hope that the inherent defect of the mosaic will be compensated by its permanence—for books of this kind do not last—yet it will surely serve some good purpose to have such a collocation of facts regarding a place whose interest is ever varying and never dying.

The personal element is almost entirely confined to the first chapter, which deals on that account with more familiar incidents than the others. Twelve years have elapsed since my memorable sojourn in Rome; and many changes have occurred in the Eternal City since then. I have had no opportunity to repeat my visit and to add to or correct my first impressions, desirable as it might be to have had such a revision for the sake of this book. I duly drank of the water of Trevi the night before I left; but the spell has been in abeyance all these years. I live, however, in the hope that it has not altogether lost its mystic power; and that some day, not too far off, I may be privileged to go over the old scenes with other and larger eyes than those with which I first reverently gazed upon them. It needs two visits at least to form any true conception of Rome: a first visit to acquire the personal interest in the city which will lead at home to the eager search for knowledge regarding it from every source; and then the second visit to bring the mind thus quickened and richly stored with information to bear with new comprehension and increased interest upon the study of its antiquities on the spot.

HUGH MACMILLAN.

CHAPTER I - A WALK TO CHURCH IN ROME

I know nothing more delightful than a walk to a country church on a fine day at the end of summer. All the lovely promises of spring have been fulfilled; the woods are clothed with their darkest foliage, and not another leaflet is to come anywhere. The lingering plumes of the meadow-sweet in the fields, and the golden trumpets of the wild honeysuckle in the hedges, make the warm air a luxury to breathe; and the presence of a few tufts of bluebells by the wayside gives the landscape the last finishing touch of perfection, which is suggestive of decay, and has such an indescribable pathos about it. Nature pauses to admire her own handiwork; she ceases from her labours, and enjoys an interval of rest. It is the sabbath of the year. At such a time every object is associated with its spiritual idea, as it is with its natural shadow. The beauty of nature suggests thoughts of the beauty of holiness; and the calm rest of creation speaks to us of the deeper rest of the soul in God. On the shadowed path that leads up to the house of prayer, with mind and senses quickened to perceive the loveliness and significance of the smallest object, the fern on the bank and the lichen on the wall, we feel indeed that heaven is not so much a yonder, towards which we are to move, as a here and a now, which we are to realise.

A walk to church in town is a different thing. Man's works are all around us, and God's excluded; all but the strip of blue sky that looks down between the tall houses, and suggests thoughts of heaven to those who work and weep; all but the stunted trees and the green grass that struggle to grow in the hard streets and squares, and whisper of the far-off scenes of the country, where life is natural and simple. But even in town a walk to church is pleasant, especially when the streets are quiet, before the crowd of worshippers have begun to assemble, and there is nothing to distract the thoughts. If we can say of the country walk, "This is holy ground," seeing that every bush and tree are aflame with God, we can say of the walk through the city, "Surely the Lord hath been here, this is a dreadful place." And as the rude rough stones lying on the mountain top shaped themselves in the patriarch's dream into a staircase leading up to God, so the streets and houses around become to the musing spirit suggestive of the Father's many mansions, and the glories of the City whose streets are of pure gold, in which man's hopes and aspirations after a city of rest, which are baffled here, will be realised. I have many pleasing associations connected with walks to church in town. Many precious thoughts have come to me then, which would not have occurred at other times; glimpses of the wonder of life, and revelations of inscrutable mysteries covered by the dream-woven tissue of this visible world. The subjects with which my mind was filled found new illustrations in the most unexpected quarters; and every familiar sight and sound furnished the most appropriate examples. During that half-hour of meditation, with my blood quickened by the exercise, and my mind inspired by the thoughts of the service in which I was about to engage, I have lived an intenser life and enjoyed a keener happiness than during all the rest of the week. It was the hour of insight that struck the keynote of all the others.

But far above even these precious memories, I must rank my walks to church in Rome. What one feels elsewhere is deepened there; and the wonderful associations of the place give a more vivid interest to all one's experiences. I lived in the Capo le Case, a steep street on the slope between the Pincian and Quirinal hills, situated about three-quarters of a mile from the church outside the Porta del Popolo. This distance I had to traverse every Sunday morning; and I love frequently to shut my eyes and picture the streets through which I passed, and the old well-known look of the houses and monuments. There is not a more delightful walk in the world than that; and I know not where within such a narrow compass could be found so many objects of the most thrilling interest. For three months, from the beginning of February to the end of April, twice, and sometimes four times, every Sunday, I passed that way, going to or returning from church, until I became perfectly familiar with every object; and associations of my own moods of mind and heart mingled with the grander associations which every stone recalled, and are now inextricably bound up with them. With one solitary exception, when the weather in its chill winds and gloomy clouds reminded me of my native climate, all the Sundays were beautiful, the sun shining down with genial warmth, and the sky overhead exhibiting the deep violet hue which belongs especially to Italy. The house in which I lived had on either side of the entrance a picture-shop; and this was always closed, as well as most of the other places of business along the route. The streets were remarkably quiet; and all the circumstances were most favourable for a meditative walk amid such magnificent memories. The inhabitants of Rome pay respect to the Sunday so far as abstaining from labour is concerned; but they make up for this by throwing open their museums and places of interest on that day, which indeed is the only day in which they are free to the public; and they take a large amount of recreation for doing a small amount of penance in the interests of religion. Still there is very little bustle or traffic in the streets, especially in the morning; and one meets with no more disagreeable and incongruous interruptions on the way to church in the Eternal City than he does at home. At the head of the Capo le Case is a small church, beside an old ruinous-looking wall of tufa, covered with shaggy pellitory and other plants, which might well have been one of the ramparts of ancient Rome. It is called San Guiseppe, and has a faded fresco painting on the gable, representing the Flight of the Holy Family into Egypt, supposed to be by Frederico Zuccari, whose own house—similarly decorated on the outside with frescoes—was in the immediate vicinity. From the windows of my rooms, I could see at the foot of the street the fantastic cupola and bell-turret of the church of St. Andrea delle Fratte, which belonged to the Scottish Catholics before the Reformation, and is now frequented by our Catholic countrymen during Lent, when sermons are preached to them in English. It is the parish church of the Piazza di Spagna, and the so-called English quarter. The present edifice was only built at the end of the sixteenth century, and, strange to say, with the proceeds of the sale of Cardinal Gonsalvi's valuable collection of snuff-boxes; but its name, derived from the Italian word Fratta, "thorn-bush," would seem to imply that the church is of much greater antiquity, going back to a far-off time when the ground on which it stands was an uncultivated waste. A miracle is said to have happened in one of the side chapels in 1842, which received the sanction of the Pope. A young French Jew of the name of Alfonse Ratisbonne was discovered in an ecstasy before the altar; which he accounted for by saying, when he revived, that the Virgin Mary had actually appeared to him, and saluted him in this place, while he was wandering aimlessly, and with a smile of incredulity, through the church. This supernatural vision led to his conversion, and he was publicly baptized and presented to the Pope by his godfather, the general of the Jesuits; receiving on the occasion, in commemoration of the miracle, a crucifix, to which special indulgences were attached.

At the foot of the Capo le Case is the College of the Propaganda, whose vast size and plain massive architecture, as well as its historical associations, powerfully impress the imagination. It was begun by Gregory XV., in 1622, and completed by his successor, Urban VIII., and his brother, Cardinal Antonio Barberini, from the plans partly of Bernini and Borromini. On the most prominent parts of the edifice are sculptured bees, which are the well-known armorial bearings of the Barberini family. The Propaganda used to divide with the Vatican the administration of the whole Roman Catholic world. It was compared by the Abbé Raynal to a sword, of which the handle remains in Rome, and the point reaches everywhere. The Vatican takes cognisance of what may be called the domestic affairs of the Church throughout Europe; the College of the Propaganda superintends the foreign policy of the Church, and makes its influence felt in the remotest regions of the earth. It is essentially, as its name implies, a missionary institution, founded for the promotion and guidance of missions throughout the world. Nearly two hundred youths from various countries are constantly educated here, in order that they may go back as ordained priests to their native land, and diffuse the Roman Catholic faith among their countrymen. The average number ordained every year is about fifty. No one is admitted who is over twenty years of age; and they all wear a uniform dress, consisting of a long black cassock, edged with red, and bound with a red girdle, with two bands, representing leading-strings, hanging from the shoulders behind. The cost of their education and support while in Rome, and the expenses of their journey from their native land and back again, are defrayed by the institution. Every visitor to Rome must be familiar with the appearance of the students, as they walk through the streets in groups of three or four, eagerly conversing with each other, with many expressive gesticulations. For the most part they are a fine set of young men, of whom any Church might well be proud, full of zeal and energy, and well fitted to encounter, by their physical as well as their mental training, the hard-ships of an isolated life, frequently among savage races.

An annual exhibition is held in a large hall attached to the college in honour of the holy Magi, about the beginning of January, when students deliver speeches in different languages, and take part in musical performances, the score of which is usually composed by the professor of music in the college. The places of honour nearest the stage are occupied by several cardinals, whose scarlet dresses and silver locks contrast strikingly with the black garments of the majority of the assemblage. The strange costumes and countenances of the speakers, coloured with every hue known to the human family, the novel sounds of the different languages, and the personal peculiarities of each speaker in manner and intonation, make the exhibition in the highest degree interesting. Its great popularity is evinced by the crowds that usually attend, filling the hall to overflowing; and though a religious affair, it is pervaded by a lively spirit of fun, in which even the great dignitaries of the Church join heartily.

The jurisdiction of the Propaganda is independent. The "congregation" of the college is composed of twenty-five cardinals, sixteen of whom are resident in Rome. One of their number is appointed prefect, and has a prelate for his secretary. They meet statedly, once a month, for the transaction of business, in a magnificent hall in the college. Previous to 1851, the affairs of the Roman Catholic Church in England were administered by the Propaganda; our country being included among heretical or heathen lands to which missionaries were sent. But after that memorable year they were transferred to the ordinary jurisdiction of the See of Rome. This movement was the first distinct act of papal aggression, and provoked fierce hostility among all classes of the Protestant community. However some of us may regret that such powerful and well-organised machinery is employed to propagate to the ends of the earth a faith to which we cannot subscribe, yet no one can read the proud inscription upon the front of the edifice, "Collegio di Propagandâ Fide," and reflect upon the grand way in which the purpose therein defined has been carried out, without a sentiment of admiration. At a time when Protestant Churches were selfishly devoted to their own narrow interests, and utterly unmindful of the Saviour's commission to preach the gospel to every creature, this college was sending forth to different countries, only partially explored, bands of young priests who carried their lives in their hands, and endured untold sufferings so that they might impart to the heathen the blessings of Christian civilisation. There is not a region from China and Japan to Mexico and the South Sea Islands, and from Africa to Siberia, which has not been taken possession of by members of this college, and cultivated for the Church. Names that are as worthy of being canonised as those of any saint in the Roman calendar, on account of their heroic achievements, their holy lives, or their martyr deaths, belong to the rôle of the Propaganda. And while sedulously spreading their faith, they were at the same time adding to the sum of human knowledge; many of the most valuable and important contributions to ethnology, geography, philology, and natural science having been made by the students of this college. Pope Pius IX. in his early days, after he had renounced his military career and become a priest, was sent out by the Propaganda, as secretary to a politico-religious mission which Pius VII. organised and despatched to Chili; and in that country his missionary career of two years exhibited all the devotion of a saint.

I had the pleasure of going through the various rooms of this famous institution in the appropriate company of one of the most distinguished Free Church missionaries in India; and was shown by the rector of the college, with the utmost courtesy and kindness, all that was most remarkable about the place. The library is extensive, and contains some rare works on theology and canon law; and in the Borgian Museum annexed to it there is a rich collection of Oriental MSS., heathen idols, and natural curiosities sent by missionaries from various parts of the world. We were especially struck with the magnificent "Codex Mexicanus," a loosely-bound, bulky MS. on white leather, found among the treasures of the royal palace at the conquest of Mexico by Cortes. It is full of coloured hieroglyphics and pictures, and is known in this country through the splendid reproduction of Lord Kingsborough.

But the most interesting of all the sights to the visitor is the printing establishment, which at one time was the first in the world, and had the means of publishing books in upwards of thirty different languages. At the present day it is furnished with all the recent appliances; and from this press has issued works distinguished as much for their typographical beauty as for the area they cover in the mission field. Its font of Oriental types is specially rich. We were shown specimens of the Paternoster in all the known languages; and my friend had an opportunity of inspecting some theological works in the obscure dialects of India. The productions of the Propaganda press are very widely diffused. There is a bookseller's shop connected with the establishment, where all the publications of the institution, including the papal bulls, and the principal documents of the State, may be procured. Altogether the college has taken a prominent part in the education of the world. Its influence is specially felt in America, from which a large number of its students come; the young priest who conducted us through the library and the Borgian Museum being an American, very intelligent and affable. The Roman Catholic religion flourishes in that country because it keeps clear of all political questions, and manifests itself, not as a government, in which character it is peculiarly uncompromising and despotic, but as a religion, in which aspect it has a wonderful power of adaptation to the habits and tastes of the people. The Propaganda rules Roman Catholic America very much in the spirit of its own institutions; and one of the most remarkable social phenomena of that country is the absolute subserviency which the political spirit of unbridled democracy yields to its decrees. The bees of the Barberini carved upon its architectural ornaments are no inapt symbol of the spirit and method of working of this busy theological hive, which sends its annual swarms all over the world to gather ecclesiastical honey from every flower of opportunity.

Passing beyond the Propaganda, we come to a lofty pillar of the Corinthian order, situated at the commencement of the Piazza di Spagna. It is composed of a kind of gray Carystian marble called cipollino, distinguished by veins of pale green rippling through it, like the layers of a vegetable bulb, on account of which it is popularly known as the onion stone. It is one of the largest known monoliths, being forty-two feet in height and nearly five feet in diameter. It looks as fresh as though it were only yesterday carved out of the quarry; but it must be nearly two thousand years old, having been found about a hundred years ago when digging among the ruins of the amphitheatre of Statilius Taurus, constructed in the reign of Cæsar

Augustus on the site now called, from a corruption of the old name, Monte Citorio, and occupied by the Houses of Parliament. When discovered the pillar was unfinished, a circumstance which would indicate that it had never been erected. It was left to Pope Pius IX., after all these centuries of neglect and obscurity, to find a use for it. Crowning its capital by a bronze statue of the Virgin Mary, and disfiguring its shaft by a fantastic bronze network extending up two-fifths of its height, he erected it where it now stands in 1854, to commemorate the establishment by papal bull of the dogma of the Immaculate Conception. It was during his exile at Gaeta, at a time when Italy was torn with civil dissensions, and his own dominions were afflicted with the most grievous calamities, which he could have easily averted or remedied if he wished, that this dogma engrossed the mind of the holy father and his ecclesiastical court. The constitutionalists at Rome were anxiously expecting some conciliatory manifesto which should precede the Pope's return and restore peace and prosperity; and they were mortified beyond measure by receiving only the letter in which this theological fiction was announced by his Holiness. The people cried for the bread of constitutional liberty, and the holy father gave them the stone of a religious dogma to which they were wholly indifferent; thus demonstrating the incompatibility of the functions of a temporal and spiritual sovereign.

The pillar of the Immaculate Conception is embellished by statues of Moses, David, Isaiah, and Ezekiel, with texts from Scripture, and very inferior bronze bas-reliefs of the incidents connected with the publication of the dogma. As a work of art, it is heavy and graceless, with hard mechanical lines; and the figure of the Virgin at the top is utterly destitute of merit. The whole monument is a characteristic specimen of the modern Roman school of sculpture. For ages Rome has been considered the foster mother of art, and residence in it essential to the education of the art-faculty. But this is a delusion. Its atmosphere has never been really favourable to the development of genius. There is a moral malaria of the place as fatal to the versatile life of the imagination as the physical miasma is to health. Roman Catholicism has petrified the heart and the fancy; and a petty round of ceremonies, feasts, and social parties dissipates energy and distracts the powers of those who are not under the influence of the Church. The decadence of art has kept pace with the growing corruption of religion. Descending from the purer spiritual conceptions of former times to grosser and more superstitious ideas, it has given outward expression to these in baser forms. Even St. Peter's, though extravagantly praised by so many visitors, is but the visible embodiment of the vulgar splendour of later Catholicism. The pillar of the Immaculate Conception is not only a monument of religious superstition, but also of what must strike every thoughtful observer in Rome—the decadence of art in modern times as compared with the glorious earlier days of a purer Church. And the art of the sculptor is only in keeping with that of the painter in connection with this dogma. For the large frescoes of Podesti, which occupy a conspicuous place in the great hall of the Vatican, preceding the stanze of Raphael, and depict the persons and incidents connected with the proclamation of the Immaculate Conception, are worthless as works of art, and present a melancholy contrast to the works of the immortal genius in the adjoining halls, who wrought under the inspiration of a nobler faith. No Titian or Raphael, no Michael Angelo or Bramante, was found in the degenerate days of Pio Nono to immortalise what he called the greatest event of his reign.

The square in which the pillar of the Immaculate Conception is situated, along with the surrounding streets, is called the "Ghetto Inglese," for here the English and Americans most do congregate. At almost every step one encounters the fresh open countenances, blue eyes, and fair hair, which one is accustomed to associate with darker skies and ruder buildings. The Piazza di Spagna, so called from the palace of the Spanish ambassador situated in a corner of it, is one of the finest squares of Rome, being paved throughout, and surrounded on every side by lofty and picturesque buildings. In the centre is a quaint old boat-shaped fountain, called Fontana della Barcaccia, its brown slippery sides being tinted with mosses, confervæ, and other growths of wet surfaces. It was designed by Bernini to commemorate the stranding of a boat on the spot after the retiring of the great flood of 1598, which overwhelmed most of Rome. On the site of the Piazza di Spagna, there was, in the days of Domitian, an artificial lake, on which naval battles took place, witnessed by immense audiences seated in a kind of amphitheatre on the borders of the lake. As an object of taste the boat-shaped fountain is condemned by many; but Bernini adopted the form not only because of the associations of the spot, but also because the head of water was not sufficient for a jet of any considerable height. Quaint, or even ugly, as some might call it, it was to me an object of peculiar interest. Its water is of the purest and sweetest; and in the stillness of the hot noon its bright sparkle and dreamy murmur were delightfully refreshing. No city in the world is so abundantly supplied with water as Rome. You hear the lulling sound and see the bright gleam of water in almost every square. A river falls in a series of sparkling cascades from the Fountain of Trevi and the Fontana Paolina into deep, immense basins; and even into the marble sarcophagi of ancient kings, with their gracefully sculptured sides, telling some story of Arcadian times, whose nymphs and naiads are in beautiful harmony with the rustic murmur of the stream, is falling a gush of living water in many a palace courtyard. This sound of many waters is, indeed, a luxury in such a climate;

and some of the pleasantest moments are those in which the visitor lingers beside one of the fountains, when the blaze and bustle of the day are over, and the balmy softness of the evening produce a dreamy mood, to which the music of the waters is irresistibly fascinating.

The most distinguishing feature of the Piazza di Spagna is the wide staircase which leads up from one side of it to the church of the Trinita dei Monti, with its twin towers, through whose belfry arches the blue sky appears. This lofty staircase comprises one hundred and thirty steps, and the ascent is so gradual, and the landing-places so broad and commodious, that it is quite a pleasure, even for the most infirm persons, to mount it. The travertine of which it is composed is polished into the smoothness of marble by constant use. It is the favourite haunt of all the painters' models; and there one meets at certain hours of the day with beautiful peasant girls from the neighbouring mountains, in the picturesque costumes of the contadini, and old men with grizzled beards and locks, dressed in ragged cloaks, the originals of many a saint and Madonna in some sacred pictures, talking and laughing, or basking with half-shut eyes in the full glare of the sun. These models come usually from Cervaro and Saracinesco; the latter an extraordinary Moorish town situated at a great height among the Sabine hills, whose inhabitants have preserved intact since the middle ages their Arabic names and Oriental features and customs.

On this staircase used to congregate the largest number of the beggars of Rome, whose hideous deformities were made the excuse for extorting money from the soft-hearted forestieri. Happily this plague has now greatly abated, and one may ascend or descend the magnificent stair without being revolted by the sight of human degradation, or persecuted by the importunate outcries of those who are lost to shame. The Government has done a good thing in diminishing this frightful mendicancy. But it is to be feared that whilst there are many who beg without any necessity, sturdy knaves who are up to all kinds of petty larceny, there are not a few who have no other means of livelihood, and without the alms of the charitable would die of starvation. The visitor sees only the gay side of such a place as Rome; but there are many tragedies behind the scenes. Centuries of misrule under the papal government had pauperised the people; and the sudden transition to the new state of things has deprived many of the old employments, without furnishing any substitutes, while there is no longer the dole at the convent door to provide for their wants. The whole social organisation of Italy, with its frequent saints' days, during which no work is done, and its numerous holy fraternities living on alms, and its sanctification of mendicancy in the name of religion, has tended to pauperise the nation, and give it those unthrifty improvident habits which have destroyed independence and self-respect. Although, therefore, the Government has publicly forbidden begging throughout the country, it has in some measure tacitly connived at it, as a compromise between an inefficient poor-law and the widespread misery arising from the improvidence of so many of its subjects; the amount of the harvest reaped by the beggars from the visitors to Rome being so much saved to the public purse. And though one does not meet so many unscrupulous beggars as formerly in the main thoroughfares of Rome, one is often annoyed by them on the steps of the churches, where they seem to have the right of sanctuary, and to levy toll upon all for whom they needlessly lift the heavy leathern curtain that hangs at the door. We must remember that mendicancy is a very ancient institution in Italy, and that it will die hard, if it ever dies at all.

The church of the Trinita dei Monti, built in 1494 by Charles VIII. of France, occupies a most commanding position on the terrace above the Spanish Square, and is seen as a most conspicuous feature in all the views of Rome from the neighbourhood. An Egyptian obelisk with hieroglyphics, of the age of the Ptolemies, which once adorned the so-called circus in the gardens of Sallust on the Quirinal, now elevated on a lofty pedestal, dedicated to the Holy Trinity, and surmounted by a cross, stands in front of the church, and gives an air of antiquity to it which its own four hundred years could hardly impart, as well as forms an appropriate termination to the splendid flight of steps which leads up to it. The church is celebrated for the possession of the "Descent from the Cross," a fresco by Ricciarelli, commonly known by the name of Daniel of Volterra, said to be one of the three finest pictures in the world. But the chapel which it adorns is badly lighted, and the painting has been greatly injured by the French, who attempted to remove it in 1817. It does not produce a very pleasing impression, being dark and oily-looking; and the cross-lights in the place interfere with the expression of the figures. We can recognise much of the force and graphic power of Michael Angelo, whom the painter sedulously imitated, in various parts of the composition; but it seems to me greatly inferior as a whole to the better-known picture of Rubens. In another chapel of this church was interred the celebrated painter Claude Lorraine, who lived for many years in a house not far off; but the French transferred the remains of their countryman to the monument raised to him in their native church in the Via della Scrofa.

Adjoining the church is the convent of the Sacred Heart, which formerly belonged to French monks, minims of the order of St. Francis. It suffered severely from the wantonness of the French soldiers who were quartered in it during the French occupation of Rome in the first Revolution. Since 1827 the Convent has been in possession of French nuns, who are all ladies of rank. They each endow the Convent at their initiation with a dowry of £1000; the rest of their property going to their nearest relatives as if they were dead. They spend their time in devotional exercises, in superintending the education of a number of young girls in the higher branches, and in giving advice to those who are allowed to visit them for this purpose every afternoon. The Trinita dei Monti is the only church in Rome where female voices are to be heard chanting the religious services; and on account of this peculiarity, and the fresh sweet voices of the nuns and their pupils, many people flock to hear them singing the Ave Maria at sunset, on Sundays and on great festivals, the singers themselves being invisible behind a curtain in the organ gallery. Mendelssohn found their vespers charming, though his critical ear detected many blemishes in the playing and singing. I visited the church one day. As it is shut after matins, I was admitted at a side door by one of the nuns, who previously inspected me through the wicket, and was left alone, the door being locked behind me. The interior is severely simple and grand, preserving the original pointed architecture inclining to Gothic, and is exquisitely clean and white, as women alone could keep it; in this respect forming a remarkable contrast to the grand but dirty church of the Capuchin monks. I had ample leisure to study the very interesting pictures in the chapels. The solitude was only disturbed by a kneeling figure in black, motionless as a statue behind the iron railing in front of the high altar, or by the occasional presence of a nun, who moved across the transept with slow and measured steps, her face hid by a long white veil which gave her a spirit-like appearance. In the heart of one of the busiest parts of the city, no mountain cloister could be more quiet and lonely. One felt the soothing stillness, lifted above the world, while yet retaining the closest connection with it. It is sweet to leave the busy crowd of various nationalities below, intent only upon pleasure, and, climbing up the lofty staircase, enter this secluded shrine, and be alone with God.

In the Piazza di Spagna some shops are always open on Sundays, especially those which minister to the wants and luxuries of strangers. Rows of cabs are ranged in the centre, waiting to be hired, and groups of flower-sellers stand near the shops, who thrust their beautiful bouquets almost into the face of every passer-by. If Rome is celebrated for its fountains, it is equally celebrated for its flowers. Whether it is owing to the soil, or the climate, or the mode of cultivation, or all combined, certain it is that nowhere else does one see flowers of such brilliant colours, perfect forms, and delicious fragrance; and the quantities as well as varieties of them are perfectly wonderful. Delicate pink and straw-coloured tea-roses, camellias, and jonquils mingled their high-born beauties with the more homely charms of wild-flowers that grew under the shadow of the great solemn stone-pines on the heights around, or twined their fresh garlands over the sad ruins of the Campagna. In the hand of every little boy and girl were bunches for sale of wild cyclamens, blue anemones, and sweet-scented violets, surrounded by their own leaves, and neatly tied up with thread. They had been gathered in the princely grounds of the Doria Pamphili and Borghese villas in the neighbourhood of Rome, which are freely opened to all, and where for many days in February and March groups of men, women, and children may be seen gathering vast quantities of those first-born children of the sun. The violets, especially in these grounds, are abundant and luxuriant, making every space of sward shadowed by the trees purple with their loveliness, like a reflection of the violet sky that had broken in through the lattice-work of boughs, and scenting all the air with their delicious perfume. They brought into the hot hard streets the witchery of the woodlands; and no one could inhale for a moment, in passing by, the sweet wafture of their fragrance without being transported in imagination to far-off scenes endeared to memory, and without a thrill of nameless tenderness at the heart. Some of the bunches of violets I was asked to buy were of a much paler purple than the others, and I was at no loss to explain this peculiarity. The plants with the deep violet petals and dark crimson eye had single blossoms, whereas those whose petals were lilac, and whose eye was of a paler red colour, were double. Cultivation had increased the number of petals, but it had diminished the richness of the colouring. This is an interesting example of the impartial balancing of nature. No object possesses every endowment. Defect in one direction is made up by excess in another. The rose pays for its mass of beautiful petals by its sterility; and the single violet has a lovelier hue, and is perfectly fertile, whereas the double one is pale and cannot perpetuate itself. And the moral lesson of this parable of nature is not difficult to read. Leanness of soul often accompanies the fulfilment of our earthly desires; and outward abundance often produces selfishness and covetousness. The peculiar evil of prosperity is discontent, dissatisfaction with present gain and a longing for more, and a spirit of repining at the little ills and disappointments of life. Humble, fragrant, useful contentment belongs to the soul that has the single eye, and "the one thing needful;" and the more we seek to double our possessions and enjoyments in the spirit of selfishness, the less beautiful and fragrant are we in the sight of God and man, and the less good we do in the world.

From the Piazza di Spagna I passed onward through a long street called the Via Babuino, from an antique statue of a satyr mutilated into the likeness of a baboon, that used to adorn a fountain about the middle of it, now removed. More business is done on Sunday in this street than in any other quarter, with the exception of the Corso. Here a shop full of bright and beautiful flowers, roses, magnolias, hyacinths, and lilies of the valley, perfumed all the air; there a jeweller's shop displayed its tempting imitations of Etruscan ornaments, and beads of Roman pearls, coral, lapis lazuli, and malachite; while yonder a marble-cutter wrought diligently at his laths, converting some fragment of rare marble — picked up by a tourist among the ruins of ancient Rome — into a cup or letter-weight to be carried home as a souvenir.

The Via Babuino opens upon the Piazza del Popolo, the finest and largest square in Rome. In the centre is a magnificent Egyptian obelisk of red Syene granite, about eighty feet in height, carved with hieroglyphics, with four marble Egyptian lions at each corner of the platform upon which it stands, pouring from their mouths copious streams of water into large basins, with a refreshing sound. Perhaps the eyes of Abraham rested upon this obelisk when he went down into Egypt, the first recorded traveller who visited the valley of the Nile; and the familiarity of the sight to the Israelites during their bondage in the neighbourhood may have suggested the wonderful vision of the pillar of cloud by day and of fire by night which regulated their wanderings in the wilderness. God does not paint His revelations on the empty air, but weaves them into the web of history, or pours them into the mould of common earthly objects and ordinary human experiences. Many of the rites and institutions of the Mosaic economy were borrowed from those of the Egyptian priesthood; the tabernacle and its furniture were composed of the gold and jewels of which the Israelites had spoiled the Egyptians; and its form, a tent moved from place to place, accommodated itself to the wandering camp-life of the Israelites. It is not unreasonable, therefore, to suppose that He who appeared to Moses at Horeb, not in some unknown supernatural blaze of glory altogether detached from earth, but in the common fire of a shepherd in the common dry vegetation of the desert, and who made use of the common shepherd's rod which Moses carried in his hand to perform the wonderful miracles before Pharaoh, would also make use of the obelisk of Heliopolis, one of the most familiar objects which met their eye during their captivity, as the pattern of the Shechinah cloud which guided His people in their journey to the land of Canaan. The symbol of the sun that shone upon their weary toil as slaves in the clay-pits beside the Nile, now protected and illumined them in their march as freemen through the desert. What they had probably joined their oppressors in worshipping as an idol, they now beheld with awe and reverence as the token of the overshadowing and overshining presence of the living and true God. That flame-shaped obelisk was the link between Egypt and the Holy Land. The divine effigy of it in the sky of the desert — like the manna as the link between the corn of Egypt and the corn of Canaan—marked the transition from the false to the true, from the old world of dark pagan thought, to the new world of religious light. I need not say with what profound interest such a thought invested the obelisk in the Piazza del Popolo. I was never weary of looking up at its fair proportions, and trying to decipher its strange hieroglyphics—figures of birds and beasts in intaglio, cut clear and deep into the hard granite, and all as bright in colour and carving as though it had been only yesterday cut out of the quarry instead of four thousand years ago. It was my first glimpse into the mysterious East. It made the wonderful story of Joseph and Moses not a mere narrative in a book, but a living reality standing out from the far past like a view in a stereoscope. Every time I passed it—and I did so at all hours—I paused to enter into this reverie of the olden time. The daylight changed it into a pillar of cloud, casting the shadow of the great thoughts connected with it over my mind; the moonlight shining upon its rosy hue changed it into a pillar of fire, illumining all the inner chambers of my soul. Every Sunday it was the cynosure guiding me on my way to church, and suggesting thoughts and memories in unison with the character of the day and the nature of my work. No other object in Rome remains so indelibly pictured in my mind.

From the Piazza del Popolo, three long narrow streets run, like three fingers from the palm of the hand; the Via Babuino, which leads to the English quarter; the famous Corso, which leads to the Capitol and the Forum; and the Ripetta, which leads to St. Peter's and the Vatican. These approaches are guarded by two churches, S. Maria di Monte Santo and S. Maria dei Miracoli, similar in appearance, with oval domes and tetrastyle porticoes that look like ecclesiastical porters' lodges. The name of the Piazza del Popolo is derived, not from the people, as is generally supposed, but from the extensive grove of poplar-trees that surrounded the Mausoleum of Augustus, and long formed the most conspicuous feature in the neighbourhood. The crescent-shaped sides of the square are bounded on the left by a wall, with a bright fountain and appropriate statuary in the middle of it, and a fringe of tall cypress-trees, and on the right by a similar wall, adorned with marble trophies and two columns rough with the projecting prows of ships taken from the ancient temple of Venice and Rome, and rising in a series of terraced walks to the upper platform of the Pincio. At the foot of this Collis Hortulorum, "Hill of Gardens," which was a favourite resort of the ancient Romans, Nero was buried; and in earlier republican times it was the site of the famous Villa of Lucullus, who had accumulated an enormous fortune when general of the Roman army in Asia, and spent it on his retirement from active life in the most sumptuous entertainments and the most prodigal luxuries. Here he gave his celebrated feast to Cicero and Pompey. From Lucullus, the magnificent grounds passed into the possession of Valerius Asiaticus; and while his property they became the scene of a tragedy which reminds one of the story of Ahab and Jezebel and the vineyard of Naboth. The infamous Messalina, the wife of the Emperor Claudius, coveted the grounds of Asiaticus. With the unscrupulous spirit of Jezebel, she procured the condemnation to death of the owner for crimes that he had never committed; a fate which he avoided by committing suicide. As soon as this obstacle was removed out of her way, she appropriated the villa; and in the beautiful grounds abandoned herself to the most shameless orgies in the absence of her husband at Ostia. But her pleasure and triumph were short-lived. The emperor was informed of her enormities, and hastened home to take vengeance. Having vainly tried all means of conciliation, and attempted without effect to kill herself, she was slain in a paroxysm of terror and anguish, by a blow of the executioner's falchion; and the death of Asiaticus was avenged on the very spot where it happened.

The gardens of the Pincio are small, but a fairer spot it would be hard to find anywhere. The grounds are most beautifully laid out, and so skilfully arranged that they seem of far larger extent than they really are. Splendid palm-trees, aloes, and cactuses give a tropical charm to the walks; rare exotics and bloom-laden trees of genial climes, flashing fountains, and all manner of cultivated beauty, enliven the scene; while the air blows fresh and invigorating from the distant hills. From the lofty parapet of the city-wall which bounds it on one side, you gaze into the green meadows and rich wooded solitudes of the Borghese grounds, that look like some rural retreat a score of miles from the city; and from the stone balustrade on the other side you see all Rome at your feet with its sea of brown houses, and beyond the picturesque roofs and the hidden river rising up the great mass of the Vatican buildings and the mighty dome of St. Peter's, which catches like a mountain peak the last level gold of the sunset, and flashes it back like an illumination, while all the intermediate view is in shadow. No wonder that the Pincian Hill is the favourite promenade of Rome, and that on week-days and Sunday afternoons you see multitudes of people showing every phase of Roman life, and hundreds of carriages containing the flower of the Roman aristocracy, with beautiful horses, and footmen in rich liveries, crowding the piazza below, ascending the winding road, and driving or walking round between the palms and the pines, over the garden-paths, to the sound of band music. And thus they continue to amuse themselves till the sun has set, and the first sound of the bells of Ave Maria is heard from the churches; and then they wind their way homewards.

We pass out from the Piazza through the Porta del Popolo, the only way by which strangers used to approach Rome from the north. It was indeed a more suitable entrance into the Eternal City than the present one; for no human being, with a spark of imagination, would care to obtain his first view of the city of his dreams from the outside of a great bustling railway station. But the Porta del Popolo had annoyances of its own that seemed hardly less incongruous. One had to run the gauntlet of the custom-house here, and to practise unheard-of briberies upon the venal douaniers of the Pope before being allowed to pass on to his hotel. And the first glimpse of the city from this point did not come up to one's expectations, being very much like that of any commonplace modern capital, without a ruin visible, or any sign or suggestion of the mistress of the world. The Porta del Popolo almost marks the position of the old Flaminian gate, through which passed the great northern road of Italy, constructed by the Roman censor, C. Flaminius, two hundred and twenty years before Christ, extending as far as Rimini, a distance of two hundred and ten miles. Through that old gate, and along that old road, the Roman cohorts passed to conquer Britain, then a small isle inhabited by savage tribes. Hardly any path save that to Jerusalem has been trodden by so many human feet as this old Flaminian road. The present gate is said to have been designed by Michael Angelo; but it shows no signs of his genius. On the inner side, above the keystone of the arch, is a lofty brick wall in the shape of a horse-shoe, built exclusively for the purpose of displaying in colossal size, emblazoned in stucco, the city arms, the sun rising above three or four pyramidal mountains arranged above each other. The external façade consists of two pairs of Doric columns of granite and marble flanking the arch, whose colour and beauty have entirely disappeared through exposure to the weather. In the spaces between the columns are two statues, one of St. Peter, and the other of St. Paul, of inferior merit, and very much stained and weather-worn. The inscription above the arch, "To a happy and prosperous entrance," seemed a mockery in the old douanier days, when delays and extortions vexed the soul of the visitor, and produced a mood anything but favourable to the enjoyment of the Eternal City. But now the grievances are over. The occupation of the place is gone. The barracks on the left for the papal guards are converted to other purposes; no custom-house officer now meets one at the gate, and all are free to come and go without passport, or bribe, or hindrance. Since I was in Rome this old gateway being found too narrow has been considerably widened by the addition of a wing on each side of the large central arch, containing each a smaller arch in which the same style of architecture is carried out.

On the right as you go out is the remarkable church of Santa Maria del Popolo. It is built in the usual Romanesque style; but its external appearance is very unpretending, and owing to its situation in a corner overshadowed by the wall it is apt to be overlooked. It is an old fabric, eight hundred years having passed away since Pope Paschal II. founded it on the spot where Nero was said to have been buried. From the tomb of the infamous tyrant grew a gigantic walnut-tree, the roosting-place of innumerable crows, supposed to be demons that haunted the evil place. The erection of the church completely exorcised these foul spirits, consecrated the locality, and dispelled the superstitious fears of the people. Reconstructed in the reign of Sixtus IV., about the year 1480, this church has not the picturesque antiquity in this dry climate and clear atmosphere which our Gothic churches in moist England present. Not more widely did the external aspect of the tabernacle in the wilderness, with its dark goat-skin coverings, differ from the interior of the Holy of holies, with its golden furniture, than does the commonplace look of the outside of the church of Santa Maria del Popolo differ from its magnificent interior. It is a perfect museum of sculpture and painting. Splendid tombs of eminent cardinals of the best period of the Renaissance, rare marbles and precious stones in lavish profusion adorn the altars and walls of the chapels; while they are further enriched by beautiful frescoes of sacred subjects from the pencils of Penturicchio and Annibale Caracci. Above the high altar is an ancient picture of the Madonna, with an exceedingly swarthy eastern complexion, which is one among several others in Rome attributed to the pencil of St. Luke the Evangelist, and which is supposed to possess the power of working miracles. One especially magnificent chapel arrests the attention, and leaves a lasting impression—that of the Chigi family, built by Fabio Chigi, better known as Pope Alexander VII. The architecture was planned by Raphael. The design of the strange fresco on the ceiling of the dome, representing the creation of the heavenly bodies, was sketched by him; and he modelled the beautiful statue of Jonah, sitting upon a whale—said to have been carved from a block that fell from one of the temples in the Forum—and sculptured the figure of Elijah, which are among the most conspicuous ornaments of the chapel. This is the only place in which Raphael appears in the character of an architect and sculptor. Like Michael Angelo, the genius of this wonderfully-gifted artist was capable of varied expression; and it seemed a mere accident whether his ideals were represented in stone, or colour, or words. On his single head God seemed to have poured all His gifts; beauty of person, and beauty of soul, and the power to perceive and embody the beauty and the wonder of the world; the eye of light and the heart of fire; "the angel nature in the angel name." And yet amid his fadeless art he faded away; and at the deathless shrines which he left behind the admirer of his genius is left to lament his early death.

Such thoughts receive a still more mournful hue from a touching tomb—touching even though its taste be execrable—which records a husband's sorrow on account of the death of his young wife—a princess of both the distinguished houses of Chigi and Odescalchi—who passed away at the age of twenty, in the saddest of all ways—in childbirth. It goes to one's heart to think of the desolate home and the bereaved husband left, as he says, "in solitude and grief." And though the weeper has gone with the wept, and the sore wound which death inflicted has been healed by his own hand nearly a hundred years ago, we feel a wondrous sympathy with that old domestic tragedy. It is a touch of nature that affects one more than all the blazonry and sculpture around. In this weird church of Santa Maria del Popolo, which seems more a mausoleum of the dead than a place of worship for the living, the level rays of the afternoon sun come through the richly-painted windows of the choir; and the warm glory rests first upon a strange monument of the sixteenth century at the entrance, where a ghastly human skeleton sculptured in yellow marble looks through a grating, and then upon a medallion on a tomb, representing a butterfly emerging from the chrysalis, illumining the inscription, "Ut Phoenix multicabo dies." And this old expressive symbol speaks to us of death as the Christian's true birth, in which the spirit bursts its earthly shell, and soars on immortal wings to God. And the church straightway to the inner eye becomes full of a transfiguration glory which no darkness of the tomb can quench, and which makes all earthly love immortal.

A venerable monastery, tenanted by monks of the order of St. Augustine, is attached to this church, upon whose brown-tiled roofs, covered with gray and yellow lichens, and walls and windows of extreme simplicity, the eye of the visitor gazes with deepest interest. For this was the residence of Luther during his famous visit to Rome. He came to this place in the fervour of youthful enthusiasm; his heart was filled with pious emotions. He knelt down on the pavement when he passed through the Porta del Popolo, and cried, "I salute thee, O holy Rome; Rome venerable through the blood and the tombs of the martyrs!" Immediately on his arrival he went to the convent of his own order, and celebrated mass with feelings of great excitement. But, alas! he was soon to be disenchanted. He had not been many days in Rome when he saw that the city of the saints and martyrs was wholly given up to idolatry and social corruption, and was as different as possible from the city of his dreams. He cared not for the fine arts which covered this pollution with a deceitful iridescence of refinement; and the ruins of pagan Rome had no power to move his heart, preoccupied as it was with horror at the monstrous wickedness which made desolate the very sanctuary of God. When he ascended on his knees the famous Scala Santa, the holy staircase near the Lateran Palace—supposed to have belonged to Pilate's house in Jerusalem, down whose marble steps our Saviour walked, wearing the crown of thorns and the emblems of mock royalty which the soldiers had put upon him—he seemed to hear a voice whispering to him the words, "The just shall live by faith." Instantly the scales fell from his eyes, and he saw the miserable folly of the whole proceeding; and like a man suddenly freed from fetters, he rose from his knees, and walked firm and erect to the foot of the stairs. He could not remain another day in the city. Returning to his monastery, he there celebrated mass for the last time, and departed on the morrow with the bitter words, "Adieu, O city, where everything is permitted but to be a good man!" Ten years later he burnt the Bull of the Pope in the public square of Wittemberg, and all Europe rang with the tocsin of the Reformation. I never passed that venerable monastery without thinking of the austere German monk and his glorious work; and the old well-known motto of the Reformation which had been his battle-cry in many a good fight of faith received new power and meaning from the associations of the place. To the enlightenment received there, paving the way for religious and political liberty throughout Christendom, I owed the privilege of preaching in Rome.

The Presbyterian church—I speak of the past, for since my visit the church has been removed to a more suitable site within the walls—is a little distance farther on, on the opposite side of the street. You enter by a gateway, and find yourself in an open space surrounded with luxuriant hedges in full bloom, and large flowering shrubs, and commanding a fine view of Monte Mario and the open country in that direction, including the meadows where the noble Arnold of Brescia was burnt to death, and his ashes cast into the Tiber. The church is a square, flat-roofed eastern-looking building, in the inside tastefully painted in imitation of panels of Cipollino marble; and on the neat pulpit is carved the symbol of the Scotch Church, the burning bush and its motto, nowhere surely more appropriate than in the place where the Christian faith has been subjected to the flames of pagan and papal persecution for eighteen hundred years, and has emerged purer and stronger. In that simple church I had the privilege of preaching to a large but fluctuating congregation, each day differently composed of persons belonging to various nationalities and denominations, but united by one common bond of faith and love. At stated intervals we celebrated together the touching feast that commemorates our Saviour's dying love, and the oneness of Christians in Him. The wonderful associations of the place lent to such occasions a special interest and solemnity. Surrounded by the ruins of man's glory, we felt deeply how unchanging was the word of God. In a city of gorgeous ceremonials that had changed Christianity into a kind of baptized paganism, we felt it indescribably refreshing to partake, in the beautiful simplicity of our own worship, of the symbols of the broken body and shed blood of our Lord. We seemed to be compassed about with a great cloud of witnesses, apostles, martyrs, and saints, who in the early ages of the Church in this city overcame the world by the blood of the Lamb, and by the word of their testimony, and loved not their lives unto the death. More vividly than anywhere else, we seemed in this place to come to the general assembly and church of the first-born, which are written in heaven, and to the spirits of just men made perfect, and to realise that we were built upon the foundation of the apostles and prophets, Jesus Christ Himself being the chief cornerstone.

On the opposite side of the road is the classic portico that leads to the Borghese Villa. The gate is almost always open; and every person is free to wander at will through the magnificent grounds, upwards of three miles in circuit, and hold picnics in the sunny glades, and pull the wild flowers that star the grass in myriads. On Sunday afternoons multitudes come and go, and a long line of carriages, filled with the Roman nobility and with foreign visitors, in almost endless succession, make the circuit of the drives. The Porta del Popolo becomes too strait for the seething mass of carriages and human beings that pass through it; and it is with difficulty, and some danger to life and limb, that one can force a passage through the gay pleasure-loving crowd. At the Carnival time the ordinary dangers and difficulties are increased tenfold; and the scene presents anything but a Sabbath-like appearance. Nor are the danger and difficulty over when the gate is passed; for the Piazza del Popolo and the streets that lead from it are crowded with carriages and pedestrians going to or returning from the favourite promenade on the Pincian Hill. One runs the gauntlet all the way; meditation is impossible; and the return from church in the afternoon is as different as possible from the morning walk to it. What pleasure can these people derive from the beautiful walks and drives in the Borghese grounds, except perhaps that of seeing and being seen in a crowd? There is no seclusion of nature, no opportunity of quiet thought.

On week-days, at certain hours, one may enjoy the place thoroughly without any distraction, and feel amid the lonely vistas of the woods as if buried in the loneliest solitude of the Apennines. And truly on such occasions I know no place so fascinating, so like an earthly Eden! The whole scene thrills one like lovely music. All the charms of nature and art are there focussed in brightest perfection. The grounds are gay with starry anemones, and billowy acacias crested with odorous wreaths of yellow foam, dark and mysterious with tall ilexes, cypresses, and stone-pines, enlivened by graceful palms and tender deciduous trees, musical with falling and glancing waters, and haunted by the statues of Greek divinities that filled men's minds with immortal thoughts in the youth of the world — dimly visible amid the recesses of the foliage. The path leads to a casino in which sculpture and painting have done their utmost to enrich and adorn the apartments. But the result of all this prodigal display of wealth and refinement is exceedingly melancholy. It would be death to inhabit these sumptuous marble rooms when their coolness would be most agreeable; and the witchery of the shadowy wood paths and bowers in their summer perfection can be enjoyed only at the risk of catching fever. Man has made a paradise for himself, but the malaria drives him out of it, and all its costly beauty is almost thrown away. Only during the desolation of winter, or the fair promise and half-developments of spring, can one wander safely through the place. The sting of the serpent is in this Eden. Cursed is the ground for man's sake in the fairest scene that his industry, and genius, and virtue can make for himself; but cursed with a double curse is the ground that he makes a wilderness by his selfishness and wickedness. And this double curse, this fatal Circean spell, has come upon these beautiful grounds in common with all the neighbourhood of Rome because of ages of human waste and wrong-doing. How striking a picture do they present of all earth's beauties and possessions, which promise what they cannot fully accomplish, which give no rest for the head or home for the heart, and in which, when disposed to place our trust, we hear ever and anon the warning cry, "Arise and depart, for this is not your rest, for it is polluted, for it will destroy you with a sore destruction." And not without significance is the circumstance that such a lesson on the vanity of all earthly things should be suggested by what one sees over against the house of prayer. It illustrates and emphasises the precept which bids the worshipper set his affections on things above, so that the house of God may become to him the very gate of heaven.

From the entrance of the church, through a long suburb, you trace the old Flaminian road till it crosses the Tiber at the Ponte Molle, the famous Milvian Bridge. It is strange to think of this hoary road of many memories being now laid down with modern tramway rails, along which cars like those in any of our great manufacturing towns continually run. This is one of the many striking instances in which the past and the present are incongruously united in Rome. You see on the right side of the road a picturesque ridge of cliffs clothed with shaggy ilexes and underwood, overhanging at intervals the walls and buildings. It was formed by lava ejected from some ancient volcano in the neighbourhood; and over it was deposited, by the action of acidulated waters rising through the volcanic rock, a stratum of travertine or fresh-water limestone. Not far off is a mineral spring called Acqua Acetosa, much frequented by the inhabitants on summer mornings, which may be considered one of the expiring efforts of volcanic action in the neighbourhood. The Milvian Bridge is associated with most interesting and important historical events. The Roman citizens, two hundred years before Christ, met here the messengers who announced the defeat of Asdrubal on the Metaurus at the end of the second Punic war. Here the ambassadors of the Allobroges implicated in Catiline's conspiracy were arrested by order of Cicero. And from the parapets of the bridge the body of Maxentius, the rival pagan emperor, was hurled into the Tiber, after his defeat by Constantine in the great battle of Saxa Rubra, which took place a little distance off. Visitors to the Vatican will remember the spirited representation of this battle on the walls of Raphael's Stanze, designed by the immortal master, and executed by Giulio Romano, the largest historical subject ever painted. By the tragic details of this battle, men and horses being entangled in the eddies of the river, the Christians were reminded of the destruction of Pharaoh and his host in the Red Sea, and the consequent deliverance of Israel. The victory on the side of Constantine led to the total overthrow of paganism, and put an end to the age of religious persecution. On this memorable day the seven-branched golden candlestick which Titus had taken from the temple of Jerusalem, according to tradition, was thrown into the Tiber, where it lies under a vast accumulation of mud in the bed of the river. It would thus seem as if the Jewish religion, too, of which the golden candlestick was the most expressive symbol, had come finally to an end in this triumph of Christianity. Of the monuments by which the great battle was commemorated one still survives near the Colosseum, the well-known triumphal arch of Constantine, which is at once a satire upon the decay of art at the time, and the halting of the new emperor between the two religions, containing, as it does, pagan figures and inscriptions mixed up incongruously with Christian ones.

We gaze with deep interest upon the serene violet sky which broods over the Milvian Bridge, and which still seems to the fancy to glow with the consciousness of the ancient legend, when we remember that it was in that sky, while on his march to the battle, Constantine saw, surmounting and outshining the noonday sun, the wondrous vision of the flaming cross, with the words "In this conquer," which assured him not only of victory in the approaching engagement, but of the subsequent universal ascendancy of Christianity throughout the world. This vision, which in all probability was only a parhelion, exaggerated by a superstitious and excited imagination, produced a crisis in the life of Constantine. He adopted the Christian faith immediately afterwards, and introduced the cross as the standard of his army; and in the faith of the visionary cross he marched from victory to victory, until at last he reigned alone as head of the Church and Emperor of the world, and brought about relations between Church and State which seemed to the historian Eusebius to be no less than the fulfilment of the apocalyptic vision of the New Jerusalem. Beyond this scene stretches to the faint far-off horizon the desert Campagna; a dim, misty, homeless land, where the moan of the wind sounds ever like the voice of the past, and the pathos of a vanished people breathes over all the scene; with here and there a gray nameless ruin, a desolate bluff, or a grassy mound, marking the site of some mysterious Etruscan or Sabine city that had perished ages before Romulus had laid the foundations of Rome. From the contemplation of these wide cheerless wastes beyond the confines of history, peopled with shadowy forms, with whose long-buried hopes and sorrows no mortal heart can now sympathise, I turn back to the fresh, warm, human interests that await me in the Rome of to-day; feeling to the full that from home to church I have passed through scenes and associations sufficient to make a Sabbath in Rome a day standing out from all other days, never to be forgotten!

CHAPTER II - THE APPIAN WAY

It was the proud boast of the ancient Romans that all roads led to their city. Rome was the centre and mistress of the world; and as the loneliest rill that rises in the bosom of the far-off mountain leads, if followed, to the ocean, so every path in the remotest corner of the vast empire conducted to the great gilded column in the Roman Forum, upon which all distances without the walls were marked. To the Romans the world is indebted for opening up communications with different countries. They were the great engineers and road-makers of antiquity. This seems to have been the work assigned to them in the household of nations. Rome broke down the barriers that separated one nation from another, and fused all distinctions of race and language and religion into one great commonwealth. And for the cohesion of all the elements of this huge political fabric nothing could have been more effectual than the magnificent roads, by which constant communication was kept up between all parts of the empire, and armies could be transported to quell a rising rebellion in some outlying province with the smallest expenditure of time and strength. In this way the genius of this wonderful people was providentially made subservient to the interests of Christianity. At the very time that our Lord commissioned, with His parting breath, the apostles to preach the gospel to every creature, the way was prepared for the fulfilment of that commission. The crooked places had been made straight, and the rough places smooth. Along the roads which the Romans made throughout the world for the march of their armies and the consolidation of their government, the apostles, the soldiers of the Prince of Peace, marched to grander and more enduring victories.

Of all the roads of ancient Rome the Via Appia was the oldest and most renowned. It was called by the Romans themselves the regina viarum, the "queen of roads." It was constructed by Appius Claudius the Blind, during the Samnite War, when he was Censor, three hundred and thirteen years before Christ, and led from Rome to Capua, being carried over the Pontine Marshes on an embankment. It was afterwards extended to Brindisi, the ancient seaport of Rome on the Adriatic, and became the great highway for travellers from Rome to Greece and all the eastern provinces of the Roman Empire. A curious link of connection may be traced between the modern

Italian expression, when drinking to a person's health on leaving home, "far Brindisi," and the distant termination of the Appian Way, suggestive, as of old, of farewell wishes for a prosperous journey and a speedy return to the parting guest. The way was paved throughout with broad hexagonal slabs of hard lava, exactly fitted to each other; and here and there along its course may still be seen important remains of it, which prove its excellent workmanship. This method of constructing roads was borrowed by the Romans from the Carthaginians, and was tried for the first time on the Appian Way, all previous roads having been formed of sand and gravel. The greatest breadth of the road was about twenty-six feet between the curbstones; and on both sides were placed, at intervals of forty feet, low columns, as seats for the travel-worn, and as helps in mounting on horseback. Distances of five thousand feet were marked by milestones, which were in the form of columnar shafts, elevated on pedestals with appropriate inscriptions. The physical wants of the traveller were provided for at inns judiciously disposed along the route; while his religious wants were gratified by frequent statues of Mercury, Apollo, Diana, Ceres, Hercules, and other deities, who presided over highways and journeys, casting their sacred shadow over his path. Some of the stones of the pavement still show the ruts of the old chariot-wheels, and others are a good deal cracked and worn; but they are sound enough, probably, to outlast the modern little cubes which have replaced them in some parts. A road formed in this most substantial manner for about two hundred miles, involving cuttings through rocks, filling up of hollows, bridging of ravines, and embanking of swamps, must have been an arduous and costly feat of engineering. Appius Claudius is said to have exhausted the Roman treasury in defraying the expenses of its construction. It was frequently repaired, owing to the heavy traffic upon it, by Julius, by Augustus, Vespasian, Domitian, Nerva, and very thoroughly by the Emperor Trajan. In some parts, where the soft ground had subsided, a second pavement was laid over the first; and in the Pontine Marshes we observe traces of no less than three pavements superimposed above each other to preserve the proper level.

For a considerable distance outside the Porta Capena, where it commenced, the Appian Way was lined on both sides with tombs belonging to patrician families. This was the case, indeed, with all the other roads of Rome that were converted into avenues of death owing to the strenuous law which prohibited all interments within the walls; but the Appian Way was specially distinguished for the number and magnificence of its tombs. The most illustrious names of ancient Rome were interred beside it. At first the sepulchres of the heroes of the early ages were the only ones; but under the Cæsars these were eclipsed by the funereal pomp of the freedmen, the parasites and sycophants of the emperors. At first the tombs were built of volcanic stone, the only building material found in the neighbourhood; but as Rome became mistress of the world, and gathered the marbles and precious stones of the conquered countries into its own bosom, and as wealth and luxury increased, the tombs were constructed altogether of or cased on the outside with these valuable materials. And this circumstance gives us a clue to the age of the different monuments.

The custom of bordering the main approaches of the city with sepulchral monuments was, in all likelihood, derived from the Etruscans, to whom the Romans owed many of their institutions. These monuments were usually structures of great beauty and elegance. Some of them were fashioned as conical mounds, on the slopes of which trees and parterres of flowers were planted; others were built after the model of graceful Grecian temples; others were huge circular masses of masonry; and others were simple sarcophagi with lids, resting on square elevated pedestals. Most of them were adorned with busts and statues of the departed, with altars, columns, and carvings. What these tombs were in their prime, it is difficult for us to picture; but even their remains at the present day produce the conviction that no grander mode of approach to a great city could have been devised.

It would seem to us altogether incongruous to line our public roads with tombs, and to transact the business and pursue the pleasures of the living among the dead. All our ideas of propriety would be shocked by seeing a circus for athletic games beside a cemetery. But the ancient Romans had no such feeling. They buried their dead, not in lonely spots and obscure churchyards as we do, but where the life of the city was gayest. One of the grandest of their sepulchral monuments was placed beside one of the most frequented of their circuses. The last objects which a Roman beheld when he left the city, and the first that greeted him on his coming back, were the tombs of his ancestors and friends; and their silent admonition did not deepen the sadness of farewell, or cast a shadow upon the joy of return. Many of the marble sarcophagi were ornamented with beautiful bas-reliefs of mythical incidents, utterly inconsistent, we should suppose, with the purpose for which they were designed. Nuptials, bacchanalian fêtes, games, and dances, are crowded upon their sculptured sides, in seeming mockery of the pitiable relics of humanity within. They treated death lightly and playfully, these ancient Romans, and tried to hide his terror with a mask of smiles, and to cover his dart with a wreath of flowers.

Why is it that we Christians look upon death with feelings so widely different? Why, when life and immortality have been brought to light in the gospel, are the mementoes of mortality more painful and saddening to us than they were to these pagans who had no hopes of a resurrection? It seems a paradox, but the Christianity which has brought the greatest hope into the world has also brought the greatest fear. By increasing the value of life, our religion has increased the fear of death. By quickening the conscience, it has quickened the imagination; and that death which to the man conscious only of a physical existence is the mere natural termination of life, to the nature convinced of sin is a violent breach of the beautiful order of the world, and the gate to final retribution. The ancient Roman was but a child in spiritual apprehension, and therefore as a child he surrendered his happy pagan life as thoughtlessly as the weary child falls asleep at the end of its play. No terrors of futurity darkened his last hours; he had his own turn at the feast of life, and as a satisfied guest he was content to depart and make room for others. As cheerfully as he had formerly begun his ordinary journeys from Rome through a street of tombs, so now he took the last journey, he knew not whither, through the valley of the shadow of death, and feared no evil; not because a greater Power was with him to defend him, but because for him no evil except the common pangs of dissolution existed. All that he cared for in death was that he should not be altogether separated from the presence and the enjoyments of human life, from the haunts where he had been so happy. He wished to have his tomb on the public thoroughfare, that he might "feel, as it were, the tide of life as it flowed past his monument, and that his mute existence might be prolonged in the remembrance of his friends." I may observe that the Roman custom of bordering the public roads with tombs gives a significance to the inscriptions which some of them bore, — such as, Siste, viator — Aspice, viator, "Stop, traveller" — "Look, traveller"; a significance which is altogether lost when the same inscriptions are carved, as we have often seen them, on tombstones in secluded country churchyards where no traveller ever passes by, and hardly even friends come to weep.

Modern Rome is unlike all other European cities in this respect, that a short distance beyond its gates you plunge at once into a desert. There is no gradual subsidence of the busy life of the gay metropolis, through suburban houses, villages, and farms, into the quiet seclusion of the country. You pass abruptly from the seat of the most refined arts into the most primitive solitude, where the pulse of life hardly beats. The desolation of the Campagna, that green motionless sea of silence, comes up to and almost washes the walls of the city. You know that you are in the immediate neighbourhood of a teeming population; but you might as well be a hundred miles away in the heart of the Apennines, for any signs of human culture or habitation that you perceive within the horizon. There is no traffic on the road; and only at rare intervals do you meet with a solitary peasant, looking like a satyr in shaggy goat-skin breeches, and glaring wildly at you from his great black eyes as he crosses the waste. Far as the eye can see there is nothing but a melancholy plain, studded here and there with a ruin, and populous only with the visionary forms of the past; and its tragic beauty prepares your mind for passing into the solemn shadow of the great Niobe of cities. But it was not thus in the brilliant days of the Empire. For fifteen miles beyond the walls the Appian Way stretched to the beautiful blue Alban hills, through a continuous suburb of the city, adorned with all the charms of nature and art, palatial villas and pleasure-gardens, groves and vineyards, temples and far-extending aqueducts. These homes and fashionable haunts of the living were interspersed in strange association with the tombs of the dead. Through the gate a constant stream of human life passed in and out; and crowds of chariots and horsemen and wayfarers thronged the road from morning to night.

It is only seventeen years since the true point of commencement of the Appian Way was discovered. For a long time the Porta Capena by which it left Rome was supposed to be situated outside of the present walls, in the valley of the Almo. But Dr. Parker, at the period indicated, making some excavations in the narrowest part of the valley between the Coelian and Aventine hills, came upon some massive remains of the original wall of Servius Tullius, and in these he found the true site of the Porta Capena. This discovery, confirming the supposition of Ampère and others, cleared up much that was inexplicable in the topography of this part of Rome, and enabled antiquarians to fix the relative position of all the historical spots. The Via Appia is thus shown to have extended upwards of three-quarters of a mile within the present area of the city, over the space between the wall of Servius Tullius and the wall of Aurelian. And this is still further confirmed by the discovery, three hundred years ago, of the first milestone of the Appian Way in a vineyard, a short distance beyond the modern gate of St. Sebastian, marking exactly a Roman mile from that point to the site of Dr. Parker's discovery. This milestone now forms one of the ornaments on the balustrade at the head of the stairs of the Capitol.

The Appian Way shared in the vicissitudes of the city. After the fall of the Western Empire, about the beginning of the sixth century, when it was finally repaired by Theodoric, it fell into desuetude. The people, owing to the unsettled state of the country, were afraid to move from home. A grievous apathy took possession of all classes; agriculture was neglected, and the drains being stopped up, the line of route was inundated, and the road, especially on the low levels, became quite impassable. For centuries it continued in this state, until it was overgrown with a marshy vegetation in the wet places, and covered with turf in the dry. About a hundred years ago Pope Pius VI. drained the Pontine Marshes, and restored other parts of the road, and made it available as the ordinary land-route from Rome to Naples. But it was left to Pio Nono to uncover the road between Rome and Albano, which had previously been confounded with the Campagna, and was only indicated by the double line of ruined tombs. After three years of hard work, and an expenditure of £3000, the part most interesting to the archæologist—namely, from the third to the eleventh milestone—was laid bare, its monuments identified as far as possible, and a wall of loose stones built on both sides, to protect it from the encroachments of the neighbouring landowners. And now the modern traveller can walk or ride or drive comfortably over the very pavement which Horace and Virgil, Augustus and Paul traversed, and gaze upon the ruins of the very objects that met their eyes.

Taking our departure from the site of the Porta Capena, we are reminded that it was at the Porta Capena that the survivor of the Horatii met his sister, who had been betrothed to one of the Curiatii, and who, when she saw her brother carrying the cloak of her dead lover, which she had wrought with her own hand, upbraided him in a passion of tears for his cruelty. Enraged at the sight of her grief, Horatius drew his sword and stabbed her to the heart, crying, "So perish the Roman maiden that shall weep for her country's enemy!" The tomb of the hapless maiden long stood on the spot. It was at the Porta Capena also that the senate and people of Rome gave to Cicero a splendid ovation on his return from banishment. Numerous historical buildings clustered round this gate—a temple of Mars, of Hercules, of Honour and Virtue, and a fountain dedicated to Mercury, described by Ovid; but not a trace of these now remains.

On the left, at the back of the Coelian Hill, is a valley covered with verdure, wonderfully quiet and rural-looking, though within the walls of a city. In this valley once stood the famous grove where Numa Pompilius had his mysterious interviews with the nymph Egeria. A spring still bubbles forth beside a cluster of farm-buildings, which is said to be the veritable Fountain of Egeria. The temple of the Muses, who were Egeria's counsellors, was close by; and the name of the gate of the city, Porta Capena, was in all likelihood a corruption of Camena, the Latin name for Muse, and was not derived, as some suppose, from the city of Capua. The spot outside the present walls, formerly visited as the haunt of the fabled nymph, before the discovery of the site of the Capena gate fixed its true position—beautiful and romantic as it is—was only the nymphæum of some Roman villa, used as a place of retirement and coolness in the oppressive heat of summer. Of all the legends of Rome's earliest days, none is more poetical than that which speaks of the visits of Numa to this mysterious being, whose counsels in these sacred shades were of such value to him in the management of his kingdom, and who dictated to him the whole religious institutions and civil legislation of Rome. Whatever historical basis it may have, the legend has at least a core of moral truth. It illustrates the necessity of solitude and communion with Higher Powers as a preparation for the solemn duties of life. All who have influenced men permanently for good have drawn their inspiration from lonely haunts sacred to meditation—ever since Moses saw the burning bush in the desert, and Elijah bowed his strong soul to the majesty of the still small voice at Horeb.

The romance of the grove of Egeria was, however, dispelled when the valley was turned into a place of imprisonment for the Jews. Domitian drove them out of the Ghetto, and shut them up here, with only a basket and a wisp of hay for each person, to undergo unheard-of privations and miseries. The Horticultural Gardens, where the shrubs and plants are grown that ornament the public squares and terraces of the city, now occupy the site of the celebrated grove. The shrill scream of the railway whistle outside the gate, and the smell of the gas-works near at hand—these veritable things of the present century—are fatal to all enchantments, and effectually dissipate the spell of the muses and the mystic fragrance of the Egerian solitude. But wonderful is the persistence of a spring in a spot. Continually changing, it is the most changeless of all things. For ever passing away, it is yet the most steadfast and enduring. Derived from the fleeting vapour—the emblem of inconstancy—it outlasts the most solid structure of man, and continues to well up its waters even when the rock beside it has weathered into dust. The Fountain of Egeria flows to-day in the hollow of the Coelian Hill as it flowed nigh three thousand years ago, although the muses have fled, and the deities Picus and Faunus, which Numa entrapped in the wood of the Aventine, have gone back to their native skies with Jupiter; and Mammon and Philosophy have exorcised that unseen world which once presented so many beauties and wonders to the imagination of man.

A little farther on to the right, a side path, called the Via Antonina, leads up to the stupendous ruins of the Baths of Caracalla, a mile in circumference, and covering a space of 2,625,000 square yards. The walls, arches, and domes of massive brickwork hanging up in the sky,—the fragments of sculpture and splendid mosaic pavements belonging to these baths,—produced a deeper impression upon my mind than even the ruins of the Colosseum. With the form and majesty of the Colosseum, owing to its compactness and unity, pictures and other representations have made us familiar from infancy, so that it excites no surprise when we actually visit it; but the Baths of Caracalla cannot be pictorially represented as a whole, on account of their vast variety and extent, and therefore we come to the spectacle wholly unprepared, and are at once startled into awe and astonishment. Notwithstanding the wholesale pillage of centuries, enough in the way of chambers and baths, marble statues, pillars, and works of art, still remains in this mountainous mass of masonry to witness to the unparalleled luxury by which the strength of the Roman youth was enervated, and the foundations of the empire sapped. Shelley wrote on the summit of one of the arches his "Prometheus Unbound;" and certainly a fitter place in which to seek inspiration for such a theme could not be found.

Beyond the Baths, on the same side of the road, is the most interesting little church of the two saints Nereus and Achilles, Christian slaves who suffered martyrdom in the reign of Diocletian. It is supposed that the Nereus whose body reposes in this ancient church is the person referred to by St. Paul in his greetings to the Roman saints at the close of his Epistle — "Salute Nereus, and his sister, and Olympas, and all the saints which are with them." Bolland, in his Acts of the Saints, mentions that he was a servant in the household of Flavia Domitilla, niece of the celebrated Christian lady of the same name, whose mother was the sister of the Emperor Domitian, and whose two sons were intended to succeed to the imperial throne. This younger Domitilla, although so nearly related to the imperial family, was banished to the island of Pontia, because of her refusal to sacrifice to idols. Her two Christian servants, Nereus and Achilles, accompanied her in her exile, and were afterwards burned alive, along with their mistress, at Terracina, and their ashes deposited in the same resting-place. It is a remarkable circumstance that this church and the catacomb where they were buried at first, should have borne the names of the lowly slaves instead of the name of their illustrious mistress, who was as distinguished by her Christian faith as by her rank. Time brought to these noble martyrs a worthy revenge for their ignoble fate; for when their ashes were taken from the catacomb to this church in the year 524, they were first carried in triumph to the Capitol, and made to pass under the imperial arches, on which was affixed the inscriptions "The Senate and the Roman people to Santa Flavia Domitilla, for having brought more honour to Rome by her death than her illustrious relations by their works." "To Santa Flavia Domitilla, and to the saints Nereus and Achilles, the excellent citizens who gained peace for the Christian republic at the price of their blood." Jeremy Taylor, in his splendid sermon on the "Marriage-ring," has a touching reference to the legendary history of Nereus. The church dedicated to the honour of these Christian slaves has many interesting associations. It stands upon the site of a primitive Christian oratory, called Fasciola, because St. Peter was said to have dropped there one of the bandages of his wounds on the way to execution. And its last reconstruction, retaining all the features of the old architecture with the utmost care, was the pious work of its titular cardinal, Cæsar Baronius, the celebrated librarian of the Vatican, whose Ecclesiastical Annals may be called the earliest systematic work on Church History. The church has an enclosed choir, with two ambones or reading-desks in it, surrounding the altar, as was the custom in the older Christian churches. The mosaics on the tribune representing the "Transfiguration" and "Annunciation" are more than a thousand years old, and are interesting besides as the first embodiments in art of these sacred subjects. Behind the high altar is the pontifical chair, supported by lions, with a Gothic gable, on which Gregory the Great was seated when he delivered his twenty-eighth Homily, a few sentences of which are engraved on the marble.

Beyond the church of Sts. Nereus and Achilles, on the opposite side, where the ground rises thirty or forty feet above the level of the road, there is a rude inscription above the door of a vineyard, intimating that the Tomb of the Scipios is here. This is by far the most interesting of all the monuments on the Appian Way. It was the mausoleum of a long line of the most illustrious names in Roman history—patriots and heroes, whose virtues and honours were hereditary. Originally the sepulchre stood above ground, and the entrance to it was by a solid arch of peperino, facing a cross-road leading from the Appian to the Latin Way; but the soil in the course of ages accumulated over it, and buried it out of sight. It was accidentally discovered in 1780, in consequence of a peasant digging in the vineyard to make a cellar, and breaking through a part of the vaulted roof of the tomb. Then was brought suddenly to light the celebrated sarcophagus of plain peperino stone, which contained the remains of the Roman consul, Lucius Scipio Barbatus, after having been undisturbed for nearly twenty-two centuries. Several other sarcophagi belonging to members of the family were found at the same time, along with two busts, one of which is supposed to be that of the poet Ennius, the friend and companion of Scipio Africanus, whose last request on his deathbed was that he might be buried by his side. Pliny remarks that the Scipios had the singular custom of burying instead of burning their dead; and this is confirmed by the discovery of these sarcophagi. I found the mausoleum to consist of a series of chambers and approaches to them, excavated in the solid tufa rock, not unlike the labyrinthine recesses of the catacombs. The darkness was feebly dispelled by the light of wax tapers carried by the guide and myself; and the aspect of the narrow, low-browed passages and chambers was gloomy in the extreme. Here and there were Latin inscriptions attached to the different recesses where the dead had lain; but they were only copies, the originals having been removed to the Vatican, where the sarcophagus of Lucius Scipio Barbatus and the bust of the poet Ennius may now be seen.

The very bones of the illustrious dead have been carried off, and after a series of adventures they are now deposited in a beautiful little monument in the grounds of a nobleman near Padua. The gold signet-ring of Scipio Africanus, with a victory in intaglio on a cornelian stone, found in the tomb of his son, who was buried here, is now in the possession of Lord Beverley. It must be remembered, however, that Scipio Africanus, the most illustrious of his family, and the noblest of all the Roman names, was not interred in this mausoleum. A strange mystery hung over the manner of his death and the place of his burial even in Livy's time. Some said that he died at Rome, and others at Liternum. A fragment of an inscription was found near the little lake at the latter place, beside which he resided during the dignified exile of his later years, which contained only the words—"... ta Patria ... ne ..." Antiquarians have filled out this sentence into the touching epigraph recorded by Livy, which Scipio himself wished to be put upon his tomb: "Ingrata Patria, ne ossa quidem, mea habes," "My ungrateful country, thou hast not even my bones." Empty as the tomb of the Scipios looks, no one can behold it without feelings of profound veneration. The history of the most heroic period of ancient Rome is linked with this tomb; and all the romance of the Punic Wars, of Hannibal and Hasdrubal, pass before the mind's eye, as one gazes upon the desecrated chambers where the son and relatives of the great conqueror had reposed in death.

Within a short distance of the tomb of the Scipios are the most celebrated of all the Columbaria of Rome. Previous to the fifth century of Rome, the bodies of the dead were buried entire, and deposited in sarcophagi; but after that period cremation became the universal custom. The ashes and calcined bones were preserved in ollæ, or little jars like common garden flower-pots, made of the same kind of coarse red earthenware, with a lid attached. These jars were deposited in rows of little niches sunk in the brickwork all round the walls of the tomb, resembling the nests in a pigeon-house; hence the origin of the name. One tomb was thus capable of containing the remains of a large number of persons; no less than six thousand of the freedmen of Augustus being deposited in the Columbarium which bears their name. The entrance to these sepulchral chambers was from the top, descending by an internal stair; and the passages and walls were usually decorated with frescoes and arabesques, illustrating some mythical or historical subject. The names of the dead were carved on marble tablets fixed above the pigeon-holes containing the ashes. Columbaria being only used for dependents and slaves, were generally erected near the tombs of their masters; and hence all along the Appian Way we see numerous traces of them side by side with the gigantic monuments of the patrician families. The Columbaria near the tomb of the Scipios are three in number, and contain the cinerary urns of persons attached to the household of the emperors from the reign of Augustus up to the period of the Antonines, when the system of burying the bodies entire was again introduced. The last discovered Columbarium is the most interesting of the group. Being only thirty-three years exposed, the paintings on the walls and the vases are remarkably well preserved. This tomb contains the ashes of the dependents of Tiberius, the contemporary of our Lord. One pigeon-hole is filled with the calcined bones of the court buffoon, a poor deaf and dumb slave who had wonderful powers of mimicry, and used to amuse his morose master by imitating the gesticulations of the advocates pleading in the Forum. Another pigeon-hole contains the remains of the keeper of the library of Apollo in the imperial palace on the Palatine. A most pathetic lamentation in verse is made by one Julia Prima over the ashes of her husband; and an inscription, along with a portrait of the animal, records that beneath are the remains of a favourite dog that was the pet of the whole household — a little touch of nature that links the ages and the zones, and makes the whole world kin. The whole of this region, called Monte d'Oro, for what reason I know not, seems to have been a vast necropolis, in which not only Columbaria for their slaves and freedmen were built by the great patrician families, but also family vaults for the wealthier middle classes were constructed and sold by speculators, just as in our modern town cemeteries.

Very near the modern gate of the city the road passes under the so-called Arch of Drusus. It consists of a single arch, whose keystone projects on each side about two feet and a half beyond the plane of the frontage; and is built of huge solid blocks of travertine, with cornices of white marble, and two composite columns of African marble on each side, much soiled and defaced, which are so inferior in style to the rest of the architecture that they are manifestly later additions. The whole monument is much worn and injured; but it is made exceedingly picturesque by a crown of verdure upon the thick mass of soil accumulated there by small increments blown up from the highway in the course of so many centuries. It was long supposed that Caracalla had barbarously taken advantage of the arch to carry across the highway at this point the aqueduct which supplied his baths with water. But the more recent authorities maintain that the arch itself, so far from being the monument of Drusus, was only one of the arches built by Caracalla in a more ornamental way than the rest, as was commonly done when an aqueduct crossed a public road. This theory does away at one fell stroke with the idea so long fondly cherished that St. Paul must have passed under this very arch on his way to Rome, and that his eye must have rested on these very stones upon which we gaze now. It is hard to give up the belief that the stern old arch, severe in its sturdiness and simplicity as the character of the apostle himself, did actually cast its haunted shadow over him on the memorable day when, a prisoner in chains in charge of a Roman soldier, he passed over this part of the Appian Way, and it signalised a far grander triumph than that for which it was originally erected. We should greatly prefer to retain the old idea that under that arch Christianity, as represented by St. Paul, passed to its conquest of the whole Roman world; and passed too in character, the religion of the cross, joy in sorrow, liberty in bonds, strength in weakness, proclaiming itself best from the midst of the sufferings which it overcame.

Immediately beyond the Arch of Drusus is the Gate of St. Sebastian, the Porta Appia of the Aurelian wall, protected on either side by two semicircular towers, which from their great height and massiveness have a most imposing appearance. They are composed of the beautiful glowing brick of the ancient Roman structures, and rest upon a foundation of white marble blocks, evidently taken from the Temple of Mars, which once stood close by, and at which the armies entering Rome in triumph used to halt. The gateway was greatly injured in the sixth century during the Gothic War, but was repaired by Belisarius; or, as some say, by Narses. The most remarkable incident connected with it since that period was the triumphal entry into the city of Marco Antonio Colonna, after the victory of Lepanto over the Turks and African corsairs in 1571. This famous battle, one of the few great decisive battles of the world, belongs equally to civil and ecclesiastical history, having checked the spread of Mohammedanism in Eastern Europe, and thus altered the fortunes of the Church and the world. The famous Spanish poet Cervantes lost an arm in this battle. The ovation given to Colonna by the Romans in connection with it may be said to be the last of the long series of triumphal processions which entered the Eternal City; and in point of splendour and ceremony it vied with the grandest of them,—prisoners and their families, along with the spoil taken from the enemy, figuring in it as of old. A short distance outside the gate, the viaduct of the railway from Civita Vecchia spans the Appian Way, and brings the ancient "queen of roads" and the modern iron-way into strange contrast,—or rather, I should say, into fitting contact; for there is a resemblance between the great works of ancient and modern engineering skill in their mighty enterprise and boundless command of physical resources, which we do not find in the works of the intermediate ages.

Beyond the viaduct the road descends into a valley, at the bottom of which runs the classic Almo. It is little better than a ditch, with artificial banks overgrown with weeds, great glossy-leaved arums, and milky-veined thistles, and with a little dirty water in it from the drainings of the surrounding vineyards. And yet this disenchanted brook figures largely in ancient mythical story. Ovid sang of it, and Cicero's letters mention it honourably. It was renowned for its medicinal properties, and diseased cattle were brought to its banks to be healed. The famous simulacrum, called the image of Cybele,—a black meteoric stone which fell from the sky at Phrygia, and was brought to Rome during the Second Punic War, according to the Sybilline instructions,—was washed every spring in the waters of the Almo by the priests of the goddess. So persistent was this pagan custom, even amid the altered circumstances of Christianity, that, until the commencement of the nineteenth century, an image of our Saviour was annually brought from the Church of Santa Martina in the Forum and washed in this stream. In the valley of the Almo the poet Terence possessed a little farm of twenty acres, given to him by his friend Scipio Æmilianus.

After crossing the Almo, two huge shapeless masses of ruins may be seen above the vineyard walls: that on the left is said to be the tomb of Geta, the son of the Emperor Severus, who was put to death in his mother's arms by order of his unnatural brother. Geta's children and friends, to the number, it is said, of twenty thousand persons, were also put to death on the false accusation of conspiracy; among whom was the celebrated jurist Papinian, who, when required to compose a defence of the murder—as Seneca was asked by Nero to apologise for his crime—nobly replied that "it was easier to commit than to justify fratricide." But so capricious was Caracalla that he soon afterwards executed the accomplices of his unnatural deed, and caused his murdered brother to be placed among the gods, and divine honours to be paid to him. It was in this more humane mood that the tomb whose ruins we see on the Appian Way was ordered to be built. The tomb on the right-hand side of the road is a most incongruous structure as it appears at present, having a circular medieval tower on the top of it, and a common osteria or wine-shop in front; but the old niches in which statues or busts used to stand still remain. It was long supposed to be the mausoleum of the Scipios; but it is now ascertained to be the sepulchre of Priscilla, the wife of Abascantius, the favourite freedman of Domitian, celebrated for his conjugal affection by the poet Statius. Covered with ivy and mural plants, the monument has a very picturesque appearance.

The road beyond this rises from the valley of the Almo, and passes over a kind of plateau. It is hemmed in on either side by high ugly walls, shaggy with a profusion of plants which affect such situations. The wild mignonette hangs out its pale yellow spikes of blossoms, but without the fragrance for which its garden sister is so remarkable; and the common pellitory, a near ally of the nettle, which haunts all old ruins, clings in great masses to the crevices, its leaves and ignoble blossoms white with the dust of the road. Here and there a tall straggling plant of purple lithospermum has found a footing, and flourishes aloft its dark violet tiara of blossoms; while bright tufts of wall-flower send up their tongues of flame from an old tomb peering above the wall, as if from a funeral pyre. The St. Mary thistle grows at the foot of the walls in knots of large, spreading, crinkled leaves, beautifully scalloped at the edges; the glazed surface reticulated with lacteal veins, retaining the milk that, according to the legend, flowed from the Virgin's breast, and, forming the Milky Way in mid-heaven, fell down to earth upon this wayside thistle. Huge columns of cactuses and monster aloes may be seen rising above the top of the walls, like relics of a geologic flora contemporaneous with the age of the extinct volcanoes around. But the most curious of all the plants that adorn the walls is a kind of ivy which, instead of the usual dark-greenish or black berries, bears yellow ones. This species is rare, but here it occurs in profusion, and is as beautiful in foliage as it is singular in fruit. The walls themselves, apart from their floral adorning, are very remarkable, and deserving of the most careful and leisurely study. They are built up evidently of the remains of tombs; and numerous fragments of marble sarcophagi, pillars, inscriptions, and rich sculpture are imbedded in them, suggestive of a whole volume of antiquarian lore, so that he who runs may read.

On the right of the road, in a vineyard, are several Columbaria belonging to the family of Cæcilius, an obscure Latin poet, who was a predecessor of Terence, and died one hundred and sixty-eight years before Christ; and on the left are the Columbaria of the freedmen of Augustus and Livia, divided into three chambers. These last when discovered excited the utmost interest among antiquarians; but they are now stripped of all their contents and characteristic decorations, and the inscriptions, about three hundred in number, are preserved in the museums of the Capitol and Vatican. On the same side of the road, in a vineyard, a Columbarium was discovered in 1825 belonging to the Volusian family, who flourished in the reign of Nero; one of whose members, Lucius Volusius, who lived to the age of ninety-three, was extolled on account of his exemplary life by Tacitus.

On the same plateau is the entrance to the celebrated Catacombs of St. Calixtus. It is on the right-hand side of the road, about a mile and a quarter from the present gate, and near where stood the second milestone on the ancient Appian Way. A marble tablet over the door of a vineyard shaded with cypresses points it out to the visitor. The rock out of which this and all the Roman Catacombs were hewn seems as if created specially for the purpose. Recent geological observations have traced in the Campagna volcanic matter produced at different periods, when the entire area of Rome and its vicinity was the seat of active plutonic agency. This material is of varying degrees of hardness. The lowest and oldest is so firm and compact that it still furnishes, as it used to do, materials for building; the foundations of the city, the wall of Romulus, and the massive blocks on which the Capitol rests, being formed of this substance. Over this a later stratum was deposited called tufa granolare, consisting of a similar mechanical conglomerate of scoriæ, ashes, and other volcanic products, but more porous and friable in texture. It is in this last formation, which is so soft that it can be easily hollowed out, and yet so solid that it does not crumble, that the Catacombs are invariably found. There is something that appeals strongly to the imagination in the fact that the early Christians should have formed the homes of their dead and the haunts of their faith in the deposit of the terrible volcano and the stormy sea! The outbursts of the Alban volcanoes were correlated in God's scheme of providence with the outbursts of human fury long ages afterwards; and the one was prepared as a means of defence from the other, by Him who maketh His ministers a flaming fire.

The Catacombs were specially excavated for Christian burial, — tombs beneath the tombs of the Appian Way. Unlike the pagans, who burned the bodies of their dead, and deposited, as we have seen, the ashes in cinerary urns which took up but little space, the Christians buried the bodies of their departed friends in rock-hewn sepulchres. They must have derived this custom from the Jewish mode of interment; and they would wish to follow in this the example of their Lord, who was laid in an excavated tomb. Besides, it was abhorrent to their feelings to burn their dead. Their religion had taught them to value the body, which is an integral part of human nature, and has its own share in the redemption of man. Their mode of sepulture therefore required larger space; and as the Christians grew and multiplied, and more burials took place, they extended the subterranean passages and galleries in every direction. It is computed that upwards of six millions of the bodies of the early Christians were deposited in the Catacombs. The name which these rock-hewn sepulchres first received was cemeteries, places of sleep; for the Christians looked upon their dead as only asleep, to be awakened by the trump of the archangel at the resurrection. And being used as burial-places, the Catacombs became the inalienable property of the Christians; for, according to Roman law, land which had once been used for interment became religiosus, and could not be transferred for any other purpose. It was long supposed that the Catacombs were subsequently made use of as places of abode, when persecution drove the Christians to seek the loneliest spots; but this idea has been dispelled by a more careful examination of them. There can be no doubt, however, that they were employed as places of religious meeting. Numerous inscriptions found in them touchingly record that no Christian worship could be performed in the imperial city without the risk of discovery and death; and therefore the members of the

Christian flock were obliged to meet for worship in these dreary vaults. The passages in some places were expanded into large chambers, and there divine service was performed; not only for the benefit of those who came to bury their dead, but also for those who resided in the city, and were Christians in secret.

Passing from the roughly-paved road into the vineyard where the Catacombs of St. Calixtus are situated, the first objects that caught my eye were the dark, gaunt ruins of a tomb and a chapel of the third century, now wreathed and garlanded with luxuriant ivy. Beside these ruins I descended into the Catacombs by an ancient staircase, at the foot of which my guide provided me with a long twisted wax taper, calculated to last out my visit. A short distance from the entrance, I came to a vestibule surrounded with loculi or rock-hewn graves. The walls were plastered, and covered with rude inscriptions, scratched with a pointed iron instrument. These were done by pilgrims and devotees in later ages, who had come here—many of them from distant lands—to pay their respects at the graves of the saints and martyrs. Two of these pilgrims, from the diocese of Salzburg, visited these Catacombs in the eighth century, and left behind an account of their visit, which has afforded a valuable clue to Cavaliere de Rossi in his identification of the chambers and graves. Passing from this open space, I soon reached a sepulchral chapel, lined with the graves of the earliest popes—many of them martyrs—who were buried here for about a century, from the year 200 to the year 296 of our era. The gravestones of four of them have been found, with inscriptions in Greek. A beautiful marble tablet by Pope Damasus, who died in 384, stands where the altar of the chapel originally stood, and records the praises of the martyrs whose remains lay in the neighbouring chambers; ending with a wish that he himself might be buried beside them, only he feared that he was unworthy of the honour. This good Pope, like an older "Old Mortality," made it a labour of love, to which he consecrated his life, to rediscover and adorn the tombs which had been hidden under an accumulation of earth and rubbish during the fearful persecution of Diocletian.

From this chapel of the Popes I came through a narrow passage to a wider crypt, where the body of St. Cæcilia was laid after her martyrdom in her own house in Rome, in the year 224. There is a rude painting of this saint on the wall, clothed with rich raiment, and adorned with the jewels befitting a Roman lady of high station. And at the back of a niche, where a lamp used to burn before the shrine of the saint, is painted a large head of our Saviour, with rays of glory around it shaped like a Greek cross. This is said to be the oldest representation of our Lord in existence, and from it all our conventional portraits have been taken. Doubts have, however, been thrown upon this by others, who assert that all the paintings in this chamber are not older than the seventh century. After this, I wandered on after my guide through innumerable narrow galleries hewn out of the soft reddish-brown rock, and opening in all directions; all lined with horizontal cavities for corpses, tier above tier, in which once were crowded together old and young,—soldiers, martyrs, rich and poor mingling their dust together, as in life they had shared all things in common. Here social distinctions were abolished; side by side with the obscure and unknown slave were some of the most illustrious names of ancient Rome. These shelves are now empty, for nearly all the bones and relics of the dead have been removed to different churches throughout Europe. Even the inscriptions that were placed above each grave—on marble tablets—have been taken away, and now line the walls of the museums of St. John Lateran and the Vatican. A few, however, remain in their place; and I know nothing more affecting than the study of these. For the most part, they are very short, containing only the name and date; sometimes only an initial letter or a rudely-drawn cross, indicating that it was a time of sore trial, when such hurried obsequies were all that the imminent danger allowed. Sometimes I came upon a larger record—such as, "Thou sleepest sweetly in God;" "In the sleep of peace."

But the most touching of all the inscriptions were those which were scratched rudely in a few places on the walls by visitors to the tombs of their fellow-Christians. The survivors came often to weep over the relics of the dead. Here a husband records the virtues of a beloved wife; there, a son invokes the precious memory of a pious father or mother; and all of them express their calm resignation and unshaken hope. One inscription especially struck me. It was very rude, and almost obliterated, for seventeen hundred years had passed over it. It was a husband's lamentation over a dead wife: "O Sophronia! dear Sophronia! thou mayest live?—Thou shalt live!" How eloquently did that rough, faded scrawl, over a long-forgotten grave, speak of the human fear that perhaps his wife was lost to him for ever—"Thou mayest live?" and of the noble faith that triumphed over it—"Thou shalt live!" Nothing affects and astonishes one more in these inscriptions than this calm, assured confidence that death was but a profound sleep,—a rest unspeakably grateful after such a weary life of awful suffering,—and that they should see their beloved ones again. It was a literal realisation of the words of the Epistle to the Hebrews: "And others were tortured, not accepting deliverance; that they might obtain a better resurrection." They surrendered all that life holds dear, and life itself, from loyalty to the God of truth, knowing whom they had believed, and persuaded that He would keep that which they had committed to Him against the great day. They made their family ties so loyal and sacred, that their human love, in the higher love of Christ Jesus, endured for evermore. In many of the crypts, the emblems of martyrdom are roughly denoted by a sword, an axe, or by faggots and fire. What sorrowful scenes must have taken place in these dreary passages, as the mangled forms of parent, child, brother, or friend were stealthily brought in from the bloody games in the Flavian amphitheatre, or from the cruel tortures of the prison-house, to their last dark, narrow home along the very path I was now treading!

A number of rude paintings ornament the walls of the chapels, which repeat over and over again the simple symbols of the Christian faith, and the touching stories of the Bible. The ark of Noah; Daniel in the lions' den; the miracle of Cana; the raising of Lazarus—are among the most common of these frescoes. And they are deeply interesting, as showing that down in these dim and dreary vaults, which presented such a remarkable contrast to the lovely violet sky and the grand architectural magnificence above ground, among men who cared little for the things of time and sense, because life itself had not a moment's security, were nevertheless nourished thoughts of ideal beauty and unearthly grandeur, which afterwards yielded such glorious fruit in the Christian art of Italy. The frescoes of the Catacombs are the feeble beginnings of an artistic inspiration which culminated in the "Last Supper" of Leonardo da Vinci, and the "Transfiguration" of Raphael.

The anchor of hope, the olive-branch of peace, and the palm-branch as the sign of victory and martyrdom, were seen everywhere. The fish, whose Greek name is formed by the initial letters of the titles of our Lord, was carved on the marble tablets and sarcophagi as the anagram of the Saviour; and an Orante, or female figure praying, was represented as the symbol of the Church. The most common of all the figures, however, was that of the Good Shepherd carrying the lost sheep on His shoulders, or leaning on His staff while the sheep were feeding around Him. And a most touching figure it is, when we think of the circumstances of those who carved or painted it in these gloomy aisles. It was into no green pastures, and beside no still waters, that the Good Shepherd led His flock in those awful days, but into waste and howling wildernesses, where their feet were bruised by the hard stones, and their flesh torn by the sharp thorns, and all the storms of the world beat fiercely upon them. But still He was their Good Shepherd, and in the wilderness He spread a table for them, and in the valley of the shadow of death they feared no evil, for He was with them, and His rod and staff comforted them.

I wish I could express adequately the emotions which filled my breast while wandering through these Catacombs. Save for the feeble glimmer of my own and the guide's lamp, I was in total darkness,—a darkness that might be felt. Not a sound broke the awful silence except the echo of our footsteps in the hollow passages. Not a trace or a recollection of life recalled me from the thought of absolute impenetrable death around. Each passage seemed so like the other, and the ramifications were so endless and bewildering, that but for the presence of my guide I should inevitably have lost myself. Horrible stories of persons who had gone astray in the inextricable maze, and wandering about in the empty gloom till they perished of exhaustion and starvation, recurred to my mind; and my imagination, intensified by the silence and darkness, vividly realised their sufferings. There is indeed no chill or damp in these labyrinths, and the atmosphere is mild and pleasant, but still the gloom was most oppressive. And yet a deep gratitude fills the soul; for the light there shone in darkness, and it was this very darkness that preserved our religion, when it ran the risk of being extinguished. These fearful subterranean passages were the furrows in which were planted the first germs of the Christian religion, — in which they were long guarded in persecution as the seed-corn under the frost-bound earth in winter, to spring up afterwards when summer smiled upon the world, and yield a glorious harvest to all nations.

On the opposite side of the Appian Way, in a vineyard, is the Catacomb of Pretextatus, which is almost as extensive as that of St. Calixtus, and hardly less interesting. It is especially remarkable for a large square crypt, inlaid with brick and plaster, and covered with very fine frescoes and arabesques of birds and foliage. The bodies of St. Januarius, Agapetus, and Felicissimus, who suffered martyrdom in the year 162, were interred in this Catacomb; and two churches, at a subsequent period, were erected over it in honour of the three saints who suffered martyrdom with St. Cæcilia. Recent explorations have brought to light, in a separate part of this Catacomb, curious paintings and inscriptions which have been referred to the mysteries of Mithras — an Oriental worship of the Sun — introduced into Rome about a century before Christ, and which was celebrated in caves. When Christianity became popular, and was threatening the overthrow of polytheism, an attempt was made to counteract its influence in the reign of Alexander Severus, who himself came from the East, by organising this worship. The two systems of religion became, therefore, mixed up together for a while; and hence it is not uncommon to find in pagan sepulchres symbols and arrangements of a Christian character, and in Christian Catacombs Mithraic features. The funeral monuments of those who were converted to Christianity in the earliest ages of the Church indicated the transition between the two religions. We find upon their tombs pagan symbols, which ceased to be identified with pagan worship, and became mere conventional ornaments.

We have other evidences along the Appian Way of the eclectic revival of paganism at this time. When alluding to the classic stream of the Almo, I spoke of the associations of the worship of Cybele. This naturalistic cult was introduced from Phrygia, and its orgiastic rites and nameless infamies had a horrible fascination for an age of decaying faith. And not far from the mounds of the Horatii and Curiatii there is a monument, probably of the age of Trajan, with a bas-relief portrait, dedicated to the memory of one Usia Prima, a priestess of Isis; this worship, with its painful initiations and splendid ritual, being imported from Egypt in the second century. But although this Neo-paganism appealed more to the passions of men than the sunny humanistic worship of older times, and for a time inspired the most frenzied enthusiasm, it failed utterly to resuscitate the decaying corpse of the old religion. Great Pan was hopelessly dead!

At a short distance on the same side of the road is the Catacomb of Sts. Nereus and Achilles, which contained the remains of these saints, and are interesting to us as the most ancient Christian cemetery in the world. The masonry of the vestibule is in the best style of Roman brickwork; and the frescoes on its walls, representing Christ and His apostles, the Good Shepherd, Orpheus, Elijah, etc., indicate a period of high artistic taste. This Catacomb contains the oldest representation extant of the Virgin and Child receiving the homage of the Wise men from the East, supposed to date from the end of the second century, and was often made use of in support of Roman Mariolatry. Several days might be profitably spent by the antiquarian in investigating the contents of the different tiers of galleries; while the geologist would find matter for interesting speculation in the partial intrusion of the older lithoid tufa here and there into the softer and more recent volcanic deposits in which the passages are excavated, and in which numerous decomposing crystals of leucite may be observed. On the same side of the way, farther on, is the Jewish Catacomb, the tombs of which bear Jewish symbols, especially the seven-branched golden candlestick, and are inscribed, not with the secular names and occupations of the occupants, but with their sacred names, as office-bearers of the synagogue, rulers, scribes, etc. The inscriptions are not in Hebrew, but in Greek letters. It is supposed that in this Catacomb were interred the bodies of the Jews who were banished to the valley of Egeria by Domitian.

About a quarter of a mile beyond the Catacombs you come to a descent, where there is a wide open space with a pillar in the centre, and behind it the natural rock of a peculiarly glowing red colour, overgrown with masses of ivy, wall-flower, and hawthorn just coming into blossom. Below the road, on the right, is a kind of piazza, shaded by a grove of funereal cypresses; and here is the church of St. Sebastian, one of the seven great basilicas which pilgrims visited to obtain the remission of their sins. It was founded by Constantine, on the site of the house and garden of the pious widow Lucina, who buried there the body of St. Sebastian after his martyrdom. This saint was a Gaulish soldier in the Roman army, who, professing Christianity, was put to death by order of Diocletian. The body of the saint is said to repose under one of the altars, marked by a marble statue of him lying dead, pierced with silver arrows, designed by Bernini. The present edifice was entirely rebuilt by Cardinal Scipio Borghese; and nothing remains of the ancient basilica save the six granite columns of the portico, which were in all likelihood taken from some old pagan temple. It was from the nave of this church that the only Catacomb which used to be visited by pilgrims was entered; all the other Catacombs which have since been opened being at that time blocked up and unknown. Indeed it was to the subterranean galleries under this church that the name of Catacomb was originally applied.

In the valley beneath St. Sebastian, on the left, is a large enclosure, covered with the greenest turf, and reminding one more, by its softness and compactness, of an English park than anything I had seen about Rome. Here are the magnificent ruins of what was long known as the Circus of Caracalla; but later investigations have proved that the circus was erected in honour of Romulus, the son of the Emperor Maxentius, in the year 311. It is the best preserved of all the ancient Roman circuses, and affords an excellent clue to the arrangements of such places for chariot races and the accommodation of the spectators. The external walls run on unbroken for about a quarter of a mile. In many places the vaults supporting the seats still remain. The spina in the centre marking the course of the races, on either end of which stood the two Egyptian obelisks which now adorn the Piazza Navona and the Piazza del Popolo, though grass-grown, can be easily defined; and the towers flanking the extremities, where the judges sat, and the triumphal gate through which the victors passed, are almost entire. It would not be difficult, with such aids to the imagination, to conjure up the splendid games that used to take place within that vast enclosure; the chariots of green, blue, white, and red driving furiously seven times round the course, the emperor and all his nobles sitting in the places of honour, looking on with enthusiasm, and the victor coming in at the goal, and the shouts and exclamations of the excited multitude. On the elevated ground behind the circus is a fringe of olive-trees, with a line of feathery elms beyond; and rising over all, the purple background of the Sabine and Alban hills. It is a lonely enough spot now; and the gentle hand of spring clothes the naked walls with a perfect garden of wild flowers, and softens with the greenest and tenderest turf the spots trodden by the feet of so many thousands. In the immediate vicinity of the circus are extensive ruins, visible and prominent objects from the road, consisting of large fragments of walls and apses, dispersed among the vineyards and enclosures.

By far the best-known monument on the Appian Way is the Tomb of Cæcilia Metella. It is a conspicuous landmark in the wide waste, and catches the eye at a long distance from many points of view. It is as familiar a feature in paintings of the Campagna almost as the Claudian Aqueduct. This celebrity it owes to its immense size, its wonderful state of preservation, and above all to the genius of Lord Byron, who has made it the theme of some of the most elegant and touching stanzas in Childe Harold. Nothing can be finer than the appearance of this circular tower in the afternoon, when the red level light of sunset, striking full upon it, brings out the rich warm glow of its yellow travertine stones in striking relief against the monotonous green of the Campagna. It is built on a portion of rising ground caused by a current of lava which descended from the Alban volcano during some prehistoric eruption, and stopped short here, forming the quarries on the left side of the road which supply most of the paving-stone of modern Rome. The Appian Way was here lowered several feet below the original level, in order to diminish the acclivity; and the mausoleum was consequently raised upon a substructure of unequal height corresponding with the inclination of the plane of ascent. It was originally cased with marble slabs, but these were stripped off during the middle ages for making lime; and Pope Clement XII. completed the devastation by removing large blocks which formed the basement, in order to construct the picturesque fountain of Trevi. A large portion of the Doric marble frieze, however, still remains, on which are sculptured bas-reliefs of rams' heads, festooned with garlands of flowers. Usually the bas-reliefs are supposed to represent bulls' heads; and the name of Capo de Bove (the "head of the ox"), by which the monument has long been known to the common people, is said to be derived from these ornaments. But a careful examination will convince any one that they are in reality rams' heads; and the vulgar name of the tomb was obviously borrowed from the armorial bearings of the Gaetani family, consisting of an ox's head, affixed prominently upon it when it served them as a fortress in the thirteenth century. Pope Boniface VIII., a member of this family, added the curious battlements at the top, which seem so slight and airy in comparison with the severe solidity of the rest of the structure, and are but a poor substitute for the massive conical roof which originally covered the tomb. Nature has done her utmost for nigh two thousand years to bring back this monument to her own bosom, but she has been foiled in all her attempts, — the travertine blocks of its exterior, though fitted to each other without cement, being as smooth and even in their courses of masonry as when first constructed, and almost as free from weather-stains as if they had newly been taken from the quarry. Only on the broad summit, where medieval Vandals broke down the noble pile and desecrated it by their own inferior workmanship, has nature been able to effect a lodgment; and in the breaches of this fortress, which is but a thing of yesterday as compared with the monument, and yet is far more ruinous, she has planted bushes, trees, and thick festoons of ivy, as if laying her quiet finger upon the angry passions of man, and obliterating the memory of his evil deeds by her own fair and smiling growth.

The sepulchral vault in the interior was not opened till the time of Paul III., about 1540, when a beautiful marble sarcophagus, adorned with bas-reliefs of the chase, was found in it, which is supposed to be that which stands at the present day in the court of the Palazzo Farnese. This is likely to be true, for it is well known that this Pope, who was a member of the Farnese family, unscrupulously despoiled ancient Rome of many of its finest works of art in order to build and adorn his new palace. A golden urn containing ashes is said to have been discovered at the same time; but if so, it has long since disappeared. On a marble panel below the frieze an inscription in bold letters informs us that this is the tomb of Cæcilia Metella, daughter of Quintus Metellus, — who obtained the sobriquet of Creticus for his conquest of Crete, — and wife of Crassus. She belonged to one of the most haughty aristocratic families of ancient Rome, whose members at successive intervals occupied the highest positions in the state, and several of whom were decreed triumphs by the senate on account of their success in war. Her husband was surnamed Dives on account of his enormous wealth. He is said to have possessed a fortune equal to a million and a half pounds sterling; and to have given an entertainment to the whole Roman people in a time of scarcity, besides distributing to each family a quantity of corn sufficient to last three months. Along with Julius Cæsar and Pompey, he formed the famous first Triumvirate. While the richest, he seems, notwithstanding the above-mentioned act of munificence, to have been one of the meanest of the Romans. He had no steady political principle; he was actuated by bitter jealousy towards his colleagues and rivals; and that unsuccessful expedition which he undertook against the Parthians, in flagrant violation of a treaty made with them by Sulla and renewed by Pompey, and which has stamped his memory with incapacity and shame, was prompted by an insatiable greed for the riches of the East. On the field he occupied himself entirely in amassing fresh treasures, while his troops were neglected. The manner of his death, after the defeat and loss of the greater part of his army, was characteristic of his ruling passion. Tempted to seek an interview with the Parthian general by the offer of the present of a horse with splendid trappings, he was cut down when in the act of mounting into the saddle. His body was contemptuously buried in some obscure spot by the enemy, and his hands and head were sent to the king, who received the ghastly trophies while seated at the nuptial feast of his daughter, and ordered in savage irony molten gold to be poured down the severed throat, exclaiming, "Sate thyself now with the metal of which in life thou wert so fond."

There is one incident connected with this most disastrous campaign upon which the imagination loves to dwell. Publius, the younger son of Crassus, born of the woman who lay in this tomb before us, after earning great distinction in Gaul as Cæsar's legate, accompanied his father to the East, and was much beloved on account of his noble qualities and his feats of bravery against the enemy. While endeavouring to repulse the last fierce charge of the Parthians, he was wounded severely by an arrow, and finding himself unable to extricate his troops, rather than desert them he ordered his sword-bearer to slay him. When the news of his son's fall reached the aged father, the old Roman spirit blazed up for a moment in him, and he exhorted his soldiers "not to be disheartened by a loss that concerned himself only." In this last triumph of a nobler nature he disappears from our view; and he who built this magnificent monument to the mother of his gallant son had himself no monument. More fortunate than her husband, whose evil manners live in brass, — less fortunate than her son, whose virtues have been handed down for the admiration of posterity, — Cæcilia Metella has left no record of her existence beyond her name. All else has been swallowed up by the oblivion of ages. Whether her husband raised this colossal trophy of the dust to commemorate his own pride of wealth, or his devoted love for her, we know not. He achieved his object; but he has given to his wife only the mockery of immortality. The substance has gone beyond recall, and but the shadow, the mere empty name, remains.

Built up against this monument are the remains of the castle in which the Gaetani family long maintained their feudal warfare, with fragments of marble sculpture taken from the tomb incorporated into the plain brick walls. And on the other side of the road, in a beautiful meadow, covered with soft green grass, are the ruins of a roofless Gothic chapel, showing little more than a few bare walls and gables built of dark lava stones, with traces of pointed windows in them, and the spring of the groined arches of the roof. Like the fortress, the chapel has few or no architectural features of interest. It is very unlike any other church in Italy, and reminds one of the country churches of England. What led the Gaetanis to adopt this foreign style of ecclesiastical architecture is a circumstance unexplained. Altogether it is a most incongruous group of objects that are here clustered together — a tomb, a fortress, and a church — and affords a curious illustration of the bizarre condition of society at the time. An extraordinary echo repeats here every sound entrusted to it with the utmost distinctness. It doubtless multiplied the wailings of the mourners who brought to this spot two thousand years ago the ashes of the dead; it sent back the rude sounds of warfare which disturbed the peace of the tomb in the middle ages; and now it haunts the spot like the voice of the past, "informing the solitude," and giving a response to each new-comer according to his mood.

Beyond the tomb of Cæcilia Metella the Appian Way becomes more interesting and beautiful. The high walls which previously shut in the road on either side now disappear, and nothing separates it from the Campagna but a low dyke of loose stones. The traveller obtains an uninterrupted view of the immense melancholy plain, which stretches away to the horizon with hardly a single tree to relieve the desolation. Here and there on the waste surface are fragments of ruins which speak to the heart, by their very muteness, more suggestively than if their historical associations were fully known. The mystic light from a sky which over this place seems ever to brood with a sad smile more touching than tears, falls upon the endless arches of the Claudian Aqueduct that remind one, as Ruskin has finely said, of a funeral procession departing from a nation's grave. The afternoon sun paints them with ruby splendours, and gleams vividly upon the picturesque vegetation which a thousand springs have sown upon their crumbling sides. They lead the eye on to the Alban Hills, which form on the horizon a fitting frame to the great picture, tender-toned, with delicate pearly and purple shadows clothing every cliff and hollow, like "harmonies of music turned to shape."

I shall never forget my first walk over this enchanted ground. The day was warm and bright, though a little breeze, like the murmur of a child's sleep, occasionally stirred the languid calm. April had just come in; but in this Southern clime spring, having no storms or frosts to fear, lingers in a strange way and unfolds, with slow, patient tenderness, her beauties; not like our Northern spring, which rushes to verdure and bloom as soon as the winter snows have disappeared. And hence, though the few trees along the road had only put forth their first leaves, tender and flaccid as butterfly's wings, the grass was ready to be cut down and was thickly starred with wild flowers. Horace of old said that one could not travel rapidly along the Appian Way, on account of the number and variety of its objects of interest; and the same remark holds good at the present day. It would take months to go over in detail all its wonderful relics of the past. At every step you are arrested by something that opens up a fascinating vista into the old family life of the imperial city. At every step you "set your foot upon some reverend history." From morning to sunset I lingered on this haunted path, and tried to enter into sympathy with old-world sorrows that have left behind no chronicles save these silent stones. It is indeed a path sacred to meditation! One has there an overpowering sense of waste—a depressing feeling of vanity. On every side are innumerable tokens of a vast expenditure of human toil, and love, and sorrow; and it seems as if it had been all thrown away. For two miles and a half from the tomb of Cæcilia Metella I counted fifty-three tombs on the right and forty-eight on the left. The margin of the road on either side is strewn with fragments of hewn marble, travertine, and peperino. Broken tablets, retaining a few letters of the epitaphs of the dead; mutilated statues and alto-relievos; drums and capitals of pillars; a hand or a foot, or a fold of marble drapery,—every form and variety of sculpture, the mere crumbs that had fallen from a profuse feast of artistic beauty, which nobody considers it worth while to pick up, lie mouldering among the grass. At frequent intervals, facing the road, you see with mournful interest the exposed interiors of tombs, showing that beautiful and curious opus reticulatum, or reticulated arrangement of bricks or tufa blocks, which is so characteristic of the imperial period, and rows upon rows of neat pigeon-holes in the brickwork, which contained the cinerary urns, all robbed of their treasures, their tear-bottles, and even their bones. Ruthless popes and princes have done their best during all the intervening ages to destroy the monuments by taking away for their own uses the marble and hewn stone which encased them, leaving behind only the inner core of brick and small stones imbedded in mortar which was never meant to be seen. Pitying hands have lately endeavoured to atone for this desecration by lifting here and there out of the rubbish heap on which they were thrown some affecting group of family portraits, some choice specimens of delicate architecture, some mutilated panel on which the stern hard features of a Roman senator look out upon you, and placing them in a prominent position to attract attention. But though they have endeavoured to build up the fragments of the tombs into some semblance of their former appearance, the resuscitation is even more melancholy than was the former ruin. Their efforts at restoration are only the very graves of graves. In some places a side path leading off the main road to a tomb has been uncovered, paved with the original lava-blocks as fresh as when the last mourner retired from it, casting "a lingering look behind;" but it leads now only to a shapeless heap of brick, or to the empty site of a monument that has been razed to the very foundations.

One piece of marble sculpture especially arrests the eye, and awakens a chord of feeling in the most callous heart. It represents one of those Imagines Clipeatæ which the ancient Romans were so fond of sculpturing in their temples or upon their tombs; a clam shell or shield with the bust of a man and a woman carved in relief within it, the hand of the one fondly embracing the neck of the other. Below is a long Latin inscription, telling that this is the tomb of a brother and sister who were devotedly attached to each other. Who this soror and frater were, there is no record to tell. All subsidiary details of their lives have been allowed to pass away with the other decorations of the tomb, leaving behind this beautiful expression of household affection in full and lasting relief. I felt drawn more closely to the distant ages by this little carving than by anything else. The huge monuments around weighed down my spirit to the earth. The very effort to secure immortality by the massiveness of these tombs defeated its own object. They spoke only of dust to dust and ashes to ashes; but that little glimpse into the simple love of simple hearts in the far-off past lifted me above all the decays of the sepulchre. It assured me that our deepest heart-affections are the helpers of our highest hopes, and the instinctive guarantees of a life to come. Love creates its own immortality; for "love is love for evermore."

Along this avenue of death nothing can be more striking than the profusion of life. It seems as if all the vitality of the many buried generations had there passed into the fuller life of nature. You can trace the street of tombs into the far distance, not only by the ruins that line it on both sides, but also by its borders of grass of a darker green and greater luxuriance than the pale, short, sickly verdure of the Campagna; just as you can trace the course of a moorland stream along the heather by the brighter vegetation which its own waters have created. Myriads of flowers gleam in their own atmosphere of living light, like jewels among the rich herbage, so that the feet can hardly be set down without crushing scores of them: the Orchis rubra with its splendid spike of crimson blossoms, the bee and spider orchises in great variety, whose flowers mimic the insects after whom they are named, sweet-scented alyssum, golden buttercups and hawkweeds, Roman daisies, larger and taller than the English ones, with the bold wide-eyed gaze you see in the Roman peasant-girls, scarlet poppies glowing in a sunshine of their own, like flames in the heart of a furnace, vetches bright azure and pale yellow, dark blue hyacinths, pink geraniums, and "moonlit spires of asphodel," suggestive of the flowery fields of the immortals. My footsteps along the dusty road continually disturbed serpents that wriggled away in long ripples of motion among the tall spears of the grass; while green and golden lizards, sunning themselves on the hot stones, disappeared into their holes with a quick rustling sound at my approach. The air was musical with a perfect chorus of larks, whose jubilant song soared above all sorrow and death to heaven's own gate; and now and then a tawny hawk sailed swiftly across the horizon. Huge plants of gray mullein towered here and there above the sward, whose flannel-like leaves afforded a snug shelter to great quantities of wasps just recovering from their winter torpor. On the very tombs themselves there was a lavish adornment of vegetable life: snow-white drifts of hawthorn and honeysuckle wreaths waved on the summits of those on which a sufficient depth of soil had lodged; the wild dog-rose spread its thorny bushes and passionate-coloured crimson blooms as a fence around others; and even on the barest of them nothing could exceed the wealth of orange lichens that redeemed their poverty and gilded their nakedness with frescoes of fadeless beauty. On some of the rugged masses of masonry grew large hoary tufts of the strange roccella or orchil-weed, which yields the famous purple dye—with which, in all likelihood, the robes of the Cæsars were coloured—and which gave wealth, rank, and name to one princely Italian family, the Rucellai. Over the desolate tombs of those who wore the imperial purple, this humble lichen, that yielded the splendid hue, spread its gray hoar-frost of vegetation.

I have already spoken of the solitude of the Campagna; but this part of the Appian Way, leading through it, is exceptionally lonely. It might as well have led over an American prairie or Asiatic steppe on which the foot of man had never intruded. You see along the white reaches of the road at a little distance what looks like a cluster of houses overshadowed by some tall umbrella pine, with all the signs of human life apparently about them; but, as you come near, the sight resolves itself into a mere mass of ruins. The mirage of life turns out to be a tomb—nay, the ruin of a tomb! A carriage full of visitors may, perhaps, be seen at long intervals, their spirits sobered by the melancholy that broods over the scene; or a lumbering cart, laden with wine-casks from Ariccia or Albano, drawn by the soft-eyed mouse-coloured oxen of the Campagna, startles the echoes, and betrays its course by the clouds of dust which it raises. There are no sights or sounds of rural toil in the fields on either side of the way. Only a solitary shepherd, with his picturesque cloak, accompanied by two or three vicious-looking dogs, meets you; or, perhaps, you come unexpectedly upon an artist seated on a tomb and busy sketching the landscape. For hours you may have the scene all to yourself. Even Rome, from this distance, looks like a city of dreams! Its walls and domes have disappeared behind the misty green veil of the horizon; and only the colossal statues of the apostles on the top of the church of S. John Lateran stand out in a halo of golden light, and seem to stretch forth their hands to welcome the approaching pilgrim.

It is well known to historians that the villa of Seneca, in which he put himself to death by command of Nero, stood near the fourth milestone on the Appian Way. The circumstances of his death are exceedingly sad. Wishing to get rid of his former tutor, who had become obnoxious to him, the bloodthirsty emperor first attempted to poison him; and when this failed, he accused him, along with his nephew the poet Lucan and several others, of being concerned in a conspiracy against his life. This accusation was false; but it served the purpose of bringing Seneca within reach of his vengeance, under a colour of justice. A tribune with a cohort of soldiers was sent to intimate his fate to the philosopher; allowing him to execute the sentence of death upon himself by whatever means he preferred. Seneca was at supper with his wife Paulina and two friends when the fatal message came. Without any sign of alarm he rose and opened the veins of his arms and legs, having bade farewell to his friends and embraced his wife; and while the blood, impoverished by old age, ebbed slowly from him, he continued to comfort his friends and exhort them to a life of integrity. The last words of one so justly renowned were taken down, and in the time of Tacitus the record was still extant. We should value much these interesting memorials; but they are now irrecoverably lost. His wife, refusing to live without him, also endeavoured to bleed herself to death; but she was recovered by order of Nero almost at the last moment. She remained pale and emaciated ever after from having followed her husband more than half-way on the road to death.

No trace of the villa where this pathetic tragedy took place can now be seen; but near the spot where it must have stood, close beside the road, is a marble bas-relief of the death of Atys, the son of Croesus, killed in the chase by Adrastus, placed upon a modern pedestal; and this is supposed to have formed part of the tomb of Seneca. There is no inscription; probably none would be allowed during the lifetime of Nero; and we know that his body was burned privately without any of the usual ceremonies. But if this fragment of sculpture be genuine, the well-known classic story which it tells was an appropriate memorial of one who perished in the midst of the greatest prosperity. No one who is familiar with the history of this "seeker after God," this philosopher who was a pagan John the Baptist in the severity and purity of his mode of life, and in the position which he occupied on the border-line between paganism and Christianity, and who left behind him some of the noblest utterances of antiquity, can gaze upon this interesting bas-relief without being deeply moved. It speaks eloquently of the little dependence to be placed upon the favour of princes; and it points a powerful moral that has been repeatedly enforced in sacred as well as profane history, that he who becomes the accomplice of another in crime, strikes, by that complicity, the death-blow of friendship, and makes himself more hated than even the victim of the crime had been. When Seneca sanctioned, and then defended on political grounds, the matricide of Nero, from that moment his own doom was sealed. Over the former "guide, philosopher, and friend," the shadow of this guilty secret rested, and it deepened and darkened until the pupil embrued his hands in the blood of his teacher. This touching fragment of sculpture is all that now remains of the earthly pomp of one who at one time stood on the very highest summit of human wisdom. There is no likelihood that he ever met the Apostle Paul during his residence in the imperial city, or learned from him any of those precepts that are so wonderfully Christian in their spirit and even words; although an early Christian forger thought it worth while to fabricate a supposititious correspondence between them. The only link of connection between them was the problematical one that St. Paul, with his wide sympathies, may have gazed with interest upon Seneca's villa, as it was pointed out to him on his journey to Rome; and that he was on one occasion dragged as a prisoner into the presence of Seneca's elder brother, that Gallio who dismissed the charge and the accusers with contempt.

Passing two massive fragments of a wall, which are supposed to have formed part of a small temple of Jupiter, beside which numerous Christians suffered martyrdom, we come, at the fifth milestone, to a spot associated with one of those poetical legends which occur in the early annals of all nations, and whose hold upon the minds of men is itself an historic truth. Here was the boundary between the territory of Rome and that of Alba. Here was situated the entrenchment called the Cluilian Dyke, where Hannibal encamped, and where previously the Roman and Alban armies were drawn up in battle array, when it was agreed that the quarrel between them should be settled by three champions chosen from each side. Every one knows the story of the Horatii and the Curiatii: how these hapless brothers and cousins fought in sight of both armies with a bravery worthy of the stake; and how, at length, when two of the Roman heroes were slain, and all the Albans were wounded, the third Roman, who was unhurt, feigned to fly, and thus separating his enemies, who followed him as well as their failing strength would permit, easily despatched them one after the other, and thus gained the victory for the Roman cause. This terrible tragedy, which terminated the independent existence of the Alban power, took place in the fields around here; and on the right-hand side of the road are three huge circular mounds, overgrown with long rich grass, planted with tall cypress and ilex trees, and surrounded at the foot with a wall of huge peperino blocks, which antiquarians have determined to be the tombs of the five slaughtered combatants—the farther mound being that of the two Horatii, the second that of one of the Curiatii, and the third that of the other two Curiatii. These tombs are situated exactly where we should have expected to find them from the description of Livy; and they are evidently of far older date than any of the neighbouring tombs of the imperial period. Their form and construction carry us back in imagination to the earliest days of Rome, when Etruscan architecture was universally adopted as a model. For more than twenty-five centuries the huge tent-like mounds have stood, so strikingly different in character from all the other sepulchral monuments of the Appian Way; preserved by the reverential care of successive generations. The modern Romans have not been behind the ancient in the pride with which they have regarded these monuments. They have planted them with the splendid cypress-trees which now add so much to their picturesqueness, and annually repair the ravages of time. I climbed up the steep sides through the long slippery grass to the summits of two of the mounds, and had a grand view of the whole scene of the tragic story, bathed in the dim misty light which always broods over the melancholy Campagna like the spectral presence of the past. The sunshine strove in vain to gild the dark shadows which the cypresses threw over the mound at my feet, and the lonely wind wailed wildly through their closely-huddled shivering branches around me.

On the opposite side of the road, beyond the earthen mounds of the Horatii and Curiatii, a large mass of picturesque ruins covers the Campagna for a considerable distance. The peasants persist in calling this spot Roma Vecchia, under the idea that ancient Rome stood there, and that these ruins are the remains of the city. Antiquarians, however, are agreed that the ruins belong to the large suburban villa of the Quintilii, one of the noblest and most virtuous families of ancient Rome. One member, the celebrated rhetorician Quintilian, was the first who enjoyed the regular salary allotted by Vespasian to those who provided a solid education for the upper classes. In the time of the Emperor Commodus the villa was owned by two brothers of the Quintilian family, Maximus and Condianus, whose fraternal love is as well known almost as the friendship of Damon and Pythias. They were inseparable in all their pursuits and pleasures; they shared this villa and the surrounding property together; they composed a treatise in common, some fragments of which still survive. They were raised together to the consular dignity by Marcus Aurelius, who greatly valued their virtue and their mutual attachment, and were entrusted together with the civil government of Greece. They were both falsely accused of taking part in a plot against the emperor's life; and Commodus, who coveted their property, had them both put to death together. The tyrant then took possession of their villa, which became as notorious for the evil deeds done in it as it was famous before for the virtuous life of its owners. Here Commodus, the base son of a heroic father, practised those lusts and brutalities which have branded his name as that of one of the most unmitigated monsters that ever stained the pages of history. It was here that the people — exasperated by their sufferings through fire and famine, by the open sale of justice and all public offices, and by the blood shed in the streets by the prætorian cavalry—surrounded the villa, and demanded the head of Cleander, a Phrygian slave whom Commodus had placed at the helm of state because he pandered to his master's vices, and gratified him with rich presents obtained by the vilest means. At the entreaties of his sister and his favourite concubine, the emperor sacrificed his minister, who was with him at the time, sharing in his guilty pleasures; and threw out, from one of the windows of the villa, the bloody head among the crowd, who gratified their vengeance by tossing it about like a football. Here, too, the wretched emperor himself was first poisoned by a cup of wine given to him by his favourite mistress Marcia, on his return weary and thirsty from the Colosseum; and then, as the poison operated too slowly, was strangled in his heavy drugged sleep by his favourite gladiator Narcissus. One could not look upon the bare masses of ruins around without thinking of the terrible orgies that took place there, and of the shout of enthusiastic joy when the news reached Rome that the detested tyrant was no more, and the empire was free to breathe again. The fate of Ahab, who coveted the vineyard of Naboth, overtook him; and but for the interference of his successor, the maddened populace would have dragged his corpse through the streets and flung it into the Tiber.

A very extraordinary tomb arrests the attention near the ruins of this villa. It looks like an inverted pyramid, or a huge architectural mushroom. This appearance has been given to the monument by the removal of the large blocks of stone which formed the basement, leaving the massive superincumbent weight to be supported on a very narrow stalk of conglomerate masonry. It is a striking proof of the extraordinary solidity and tenacity of Roman architecture, defying the laws of gravitation. It is called the sepulchre of the Metelli, the family of Cæcilia Metella; but this is a mere guess, as there is no record or inscription to identify it. Next to this singular monument are the remains of a tomb which must be exceedingly interesting to every classical scholar. The inscription indicates that it is the tomb of Quintus Cæcilius, whose nephew and adopted son, Titus Pomponius Atticus, as Cornelius Nepos tells us, was buried in it. This celebrated Roman knight was descended in a direct line from Numa Pompilius. Withdrawing from the civil discords of Rome, he took up his abode in Athens, where he devoted himself to literary and philosophic pursuits and acquired a knowledge of the Greek language so perfect that he could not be distinguished from a native. At the Greek capital, the then university of the world, he secured the devoted friendship of his fellow-student Cicero, whose brother was afterwards married to his sister; and to this intimacy we owe the largest portion of Cicero's unrivalled letters, in which he describes his inmost feelings, as well as the events going on around him. The uncle of Atticus, the brother of his mother, whose family tomb we are now examining, left him at his death an enormous fortune, which he had amassed by usury. Atticus added greatly to it by acting as a kind of publisher to the authors of the day—that is, by employing his numerous slaves in copying and multiplying their manuscripts. He kept himself free from all the political factions of the times, and thus managed to preserve the mutual regard of parties who were hostile to each other,—such as Cæsar and Pompey, Brutus and Antony. He reached the age of seventy-seven years without having had a day's illness; and when at last stricken with an incurable disease, in the spirit of the Epicurean philosophy, since he could enjoy life no longer he starved himself to death, and was interred in his uncle's tomb on the Appian Way. Almost side by side with this ruin is the sepulchre of the family of Cicero's wife, the Terentii, who were related to Pomponius Atticus by the mother's side. In all likelihood Terentia herself, Cicero's brave and devoted but ill-used wife, was interred here with her own friends, for her husband had divorced her in order to marry a beautiful and rich young heiress, whose guardian he had been.

Passing on the same side of the road two or three tombs of obscure persons whose names alone are known, we come at the sixth milestone to one of the most extraordinary sepulchral monuments of the Appian Way, called the Casale Rotondo. This monument marks the limit to which most visitors extend their explorations. It is circular, like the tomb of Cæcilia Metella; but it is of far larger dimensions, being nearly three hundred and fifty feet in diameter. In the fifteenth century this colossal ruin was converted into a fortress by the Orsini family; and of the remains of this fortification a farmhouse and other buildings were constructed, and these now stand on the summit, surrounded by a tolerably-sized oliveyard and garden, with a sloping grass-grown stair leading up to them on the outside. Notwithstanding their dislike of death and their horror of dead bodies, the modern Romans have no more repugnance to the proximity of tombs than their ancestors had. Shepherds fold their sheep and goats in the interior of the old tombs, whose walls are blackened with the smoke of the fires, and retain an odour of human and animal occupancy more disagreeable than any which the original tenants could have exhaled; and it is by no means unfrequent to find a wine-shop, with a noisy company of wayfarers regaling themselves, in a sepulchre that happens to be conveniently situated by the wayside. So far as can be ascertained, the original appearance of the Casale Rotondo seems to have been that of an enormous circular tower, cased with large blocks of travertine, covered with a pyramidal roof of the same material carved into the semblance of tiles, and surmounted with appropriate sculpture. It was surrounded with a wall of peperino, supporting at intervals vases and statues; and on the outside were semicircular stone seats for the benefit of weary wayfarers. This wall is now grown over with turf, but it can be distinctly traced all round; and the hollow space between it and the tomb is covered with thick grass, and is sometimes filled with water like a fosse. Numerous altars, pedestals, and fine specimens of sculpture in marble and peperino, have been disinterred in this spot, and they are now arranged to advantage at the foot of the huge pile fronting the road. Some of these bear inscriptions which would indicate that the tomb was erected to Messalla Corvinus, the friend of Horace and Augustus, and himself a distinguished historian and poet as well as one of the most influential senators of Rome, by his son Marcus Aurelius Corvinus Cotta, who was consul some years after his father's death. Corvinus died in the eleventh year of our era, so that the tomb has stood for upwards of eighteen centuries and a half; and it is as likely to stand as many more, for what remains of it is as firm and enduring as a rock. In the farmhouse built on its massive platform several generations have lived and died. They have eaten and drunk, they have married and been given in marriage, they have cultivated their vines and olives and consumed their products. And all the time their home and their field of labour have been on a tomb! I did not see the tenants of this curious dwelling during my visit; but if the skeleton at the Egyptian feast was a useful reminder of human mortality to the revellers, one would suppose that the thought of the peculiar character of their home would be sufficient to impart a soberer hue to their lives. What is our earth itself but, on a vaster scale, a Casale Rotondo—a garden in a sepulchre—where the dust we tread on was once alive; and we reap our daily bread from human mould—

"Earth builds on the earth castles and towers,
Earth says to the earth—All shall be ours."

At a distance of about seven minutes' walk is an enormous circular tomb, with a medieval tower of lava stones erected upon it, called the Torre di Selce; but there is nothing to indicate who was interred in it, though it must have been a person of some celebrity at the time. An inscription upon a tomb beside it naively tells the passer-by to respect the last resting-place of one who had a shop on the Via Sacra, where he sold jewellery and millinery, and was held in much estimation by his customers. Beyond this point there is nothing of any special interest to arrest our attention, till we come to a considerable mass of ruins, consisting of broken Doric columns of peperino, part of a rough mosaic floor and brick pavement, and fragments of walls lined with tufa squares in the opus reticulatum pattern. These remains are supposed to mark the spot on which stood the Temple of Hercules, erected by Domitian, and alluded to in one of the epigrams of the poet Martial. Near this spot are the tomb of the consul Quintus Veranius, who died in Britain in the year 55 of our era; a lofty circular tomb, to some one unknown, with a rude shepherd's hut on the top of it, to which the peasants have given the name of Torraccio; and the tomb of a marble contractor. It may be remarked, in connection with this last mentioned tomb, that a Roman statuary had his workshops for the manufacture of sepulchral monuments and sarcophagi on the Appian Way, which were of great extent, judging from the quantity of sculpture, finished and unfinished, found on the spot. All the sculpture was manifestly copied from Greek originals, for it is hardly conceivable that such groupings and expressions as we see in these bad copies could have been first executed by such inferior artists. In this neighbourhood were the villa and farm of the poet Persius, and portions of the wall are still standing. At the ninth milestone are the tomb and the remains of the villa of the Emperor Gallienus, slain by a conspiracy among his officers at the siege of Milan in the year 268. This emperor has left nothing behind but the memory of his luxury and his vices. When the site of the villa was excavated by an English artist, Gavin Hamilton, at the end of last century, the famous statue of the Discobolus and several other specimens of ancient sculpture were discovered, which are now in the Vatican Gallery. The ground hereabouts produces a whitish efflorescence, and emits a most offensive sulphurous smell. It exhibits the same evidences of recent volcanic activity as the neighbourhood of Lakes Tartarus and Solfatara on the way to Tivoli.

The road after this descends into a valley, through which the stream of the Ponticello flows, passing a most massive circular tomb, reminding one of the mounds of the Horatii and Curiatii; and as it ascends gradually on the opposite side, two huge sepulchres of the Imperial period — one on the right hand and the other on the left — attract notice, and are the last on this part of the route. The railway to Naples passes across the road at the eleventh milestone, and disturbs the solemn silence three or four times a day by its incongruous noise. Beyond this is the osteria and village of Frattocchie, where the old Appian Way merges into the new, and ascends continuously to Albano. This neighbourhood is full of historical associations. It was at Frattocchie that the body of Clodius was left lying on the road after his fatal encounter with Milo. This fray furnished the occasion for one of Cicero's most eloquent speeches, — that in defence of Milo, — which was written, but owing to the disturbances in the Forum at the time was not delivered. On the left of the village, near a railway bridge and several quarries of very old hard lava, is the site of Appiolæ, one of the cities of the Latin League, destroyed by Tarquinius Priscus. All the male population were killed, and the women and children transferred to Rome; and with the spoils the Capitolium was completed. The remains of the old city are very slight, consisting of a wall, a few vestiges of a temple, and some foundations on a cliff surrounded by a stream, which could be dammed up and flooded so as to form a fosse. On the right of Frattocchie are the ruins of Bovillæ, taken and plundered by Coriolanus, and deserted in the time of Cicero. Some arches of the corridor of an amphitheatre, a reservoir for water, tolerably perfect, and a circus, are still visible. There are also the ruins of a forum. The view, looking back from this elevated position upon the long course of the Appian Way, is exceedingly striking. One feels, when gazing on the long perspective of rugged and mouldering sepulchres, the full force of the name Strada del Diavolo which the peasants give to this street of tombs; and can sympathise with the sentiment that made Charles Dickens say, when standing here at sunset, after having walked all the way from Rome, "I almost felt as if the sun would never rise again, but look its last that night upon a ruined world."

We can picture St. Paul's memorable journey from Puteoli to Rome by this route. The thought that the eye of the great apostle must have rested upon the same features of the landscape, and many of the same objects, though now in ruins, that we still behold, invests them with an indescribable charm. From beyond the gates of Albano, near which stood the lofty tomb of Pompey, whose ashes had only recently been brought from the scene of his murder in Egypt, by his devoted wife Cornelia, he would obtain his first glimpse of Rome. And if now it is the most thrilling moment in a man's life to see Rome in its ruin, what must it have been to see it then in its glory! We can imagine that, with the profound emotion of his Master when gazing upon the splendour of Jerusalem from the slope of Olivet, St. Paul would look down from that spot on the capital of the world, and see before him the signs of a magnificence never before or since equalled; but alas! as he knew well, a magnificence that was only the iridescence of social and spiritual corruption, as the pomp of the sepulchres of the Appian Way was but the shroud of death. Doubtless with a sad and pitying heart, he would be led by the cohort of soldiers along the street of tombs, then the most crowded approach to a city of nearly two millions of souls; tombs whose massiveness and solidity were but a vain craving for immortality, and whose epitaphs were the most deeply touching of all epitaphs, on account of the profound despair with which they bade their eternal farewell. Entering into Rome through the Porta Capena; and winding through the valley between the Coelian and Aventine hills, crowded with temples and palaces, he would be brought to the Forum, then a scene of indescribable grandeur; and from thence he would be finally transferred to the charge of Burrus, the prefect of the imperial guards, at the prætorium of Nero's palace, on the Palatine.

And here he disappears from our view. We only know of a certainty that for two whole years "he dwelt in his own hired house, and received all that came in unto him, preaching the kingdom of God, and teaching those things concerning the Lord Jesus Christ, with all confidence, no man forbidding him."

Of all the splendid associations of the Appian Way, along which history may be said to have marched exclusively for nigh six hundred years, the most splendid by far is its connection with this ever-memorable journey of the great Apostle of the Gentiles. We can trace the influence of the scenes and objects along the route in all his subsequent writings. He had a deeper yearning for the Gentiles, because he thus beheld with his own eyes the places associated with the darkest aspects of paganism; the scenes that gave rise to the pagan ideas of heaven and hell; the splendid temples in which the human soul had debased itself to objects beneath the dignity of its own nature, and thus prepared itself for all moral corruption; and the massive sepulchral monuments in which the hopeless despair of heathenism had, as it were, become petrified by the Gorgon gaze of death. That Appian Way should be to us the most interesting of all the roads of the world; for by it came to us our civilisation and Christianity—the divine principles and hopes that redeem the soul, retrieve the vanity of existence, open up the path of life through the dark valley of death, and disclose the glorious vista of immortality beyond the tomb. And as we gaze upon the remains of that road, and feel how much we owe to it as the material channel of God's grace to us who were far off, we can say with deepest gratitude of those apostles and martyrs who once walked on this lava pavement, but are now standing on the sea of glass before the throne, "How beautiful are the feet of them that preach the gospel of peace, and bring glad tidings of good things!"

CHAPTER III - THE CUMÆAN SIBYL

A part of the monotonous coast-line of Palestine extends into the Mediterranean considerably beyond the rest at Carmel. In this bluff promontory the Holy Land reaches out, as it were, towards the Western World; and like a tie-stone that projects from the gable of the first of a row of houses, indicating that other buildings are to be added, it shows that the inheritance of Israel was not meant to be always exclusive, but was destined to comprehend all the countries which its faith should annex. The remarkable geographical position of this long projecting ridge by the sea — itself a symbol and prophecy — and its peculiar physical features, differing from those of the rest of Palestine, and approximating to a European type of scenery, early marked it out as a religious spot. It was held sacred from time immemorial; an altar existed there long before Elijah's discomfiture of the priests of Baal; the people were accustomed to resort to the sanctuary of its "high place" during new moons and Sabbaths; and to its haunted strand came pilgrims from distant regions, to which the fame of its sanctity had spread. One of the great schools of the prophets of Israel, superintended by Elisha, was planted on one of its mountain prominences. The solitary Elijah found a refuge in its bosom, and came and went from it to the haunts of men like one of its own sudden storms; and in its rocky dells and dense thickets of oaks and evergreens were uttered prophecies of a larger history and a grander salvation, which transcended the narrow circle of Jewish ideas as much as the excellency of Carmel transcended the other landscapes of Palestine.

To this instance of striking correspondence between the peculiar nature of a spot and its peculiar religious history in Asia, a parallel may be found in Europe. A part of the long uniform western coast-line of Italy stretches out into the Mediterranean at Cumæ, near the city of Naples. Early colonists from Greece, in search of a new home, found in its bays, islands, and promontories a touching resemblance to the intricate coast scenery of their own country. On a solitary rock overlooking the sea they built their citadel and established their worship. In this rock was the traditional cave of the Cumæan Sibyl, where she gave utterance to the inspirations of pagan prophecy a thousand years before St. John received the visions of the

Apocalypse on the lone heights of the Ægean isle. The promontory of Cumæ, like that of Carmel, typified the onward course of history and religion — a great advance in men's ideas upon those of the past. The western sea-board is the historic side of Italy. All its great cities and renowned sites are on the western side of the Apennines; the other side, looking eastward, with the exception of Venice and Ravenna, containing hardly any place that stands out prominently in the history of the world. And at Cumæ this western tendency of Italy was most pronounced. On this westmost promontory of the beautiful land — the farthest point reached by the oldest civilisation of Egypt and Greece — the Sibyl stood on her watch-tower, and gazed with prophetic eye upon the distant horizon, seeing beyond the light of the setting sun and "the baths of all the western stars" the dawn of a more wonderful future, and dreamt of a —

"Vast brotherhood of hearts and hands,
Choir of a world in perfect tune."

Cumæ is only five miles distant from Puteoli, and about thirteen west of Naples. But it lies so much out of the way that it is difficult to combine it with the other famous localities in this classic neighbourhood in one day's excursion, and hence it is very often omitted. It amply, however, repays a special visit, not so much by what it reveals as by what it suggests. There are two ways by which it can be approached, either by the Via Cumana, which gradually ascends from Puteoli along the ridge of the low volcanic hills on the western side of Lake Avernus, and passes under the Arco Felice, a huge brick arch, evidently a fragment of an ancient Roman aqueduct, spanning a ravine at a great height; or directly from the western shore of Lake Avernus, by an ancient road paved with blocks of lava, and leading through an enormous tunnel, called the Grotta de Pietro Pace, about three-quarters of a mile long, lighted at intervals by shafts from above, said to have been excavated by Agrippa. Both ways are deeply interesting; but the latter is perhaps preferable because of the saving of time and trouble which it effects.

The first glimpse of Cumæ, though very impressive to the imagination, is not equally so to the eye. Crossing some cultivated fields, a bold eminence of trachytic tufa, covered with scanty grass and tufts of brushwood, rises between you and the sea, forming part of a range of low hills, which evidently mark the ancient coast-line. On this elevated plateau, commanding a most splendid view of the blue, sunlit Mediterranean as far as Gaeta and the Ponza Islands, stood the almost mythical city; and crowning its highest point, where a rocky escarpment, broken down on every side except on the south, by which it can be ascended, the massive foundations of the walls of the Acropolis may still be traced throughout their whole extent. Very few relics of the original Greek colony survive; and these have to be sought chiefly underneath the remains of Roman-Gothic and medieval dynasties, which successively occupied the place, and partially obliterated each other, like the different layers of writing in a palimpsest. Time and the passions of man have dealt more ruthlessly with this than with almost any other of the renowned spots of Italy. Some fragments of the ancient fortifications, a confused and scattered heap of ruins within the line of the city walls, and a portion of a fluted column, and a single Doric capital of the grand old style, supposed to belong to the temple of Apollo, on the summit of the Acropolis, are all that meet the eye to remind us of this home of ancient faith and prophecy. In the plain at the foot of the rock is the Necropolis of Cumæ, the most ancient burial-place in Italy, from whose rifled Greek graves a most valuable collection of archaic vases and personal ornaments were obtained and transferred to the museums of Naples, Paris, and St. Petersburg; but the tombs themselves have now been destroyed, and only a few marble fragments of Roman sepulchral decoration scattered around indicate the spot. And not far off, partially concealed by earth and underwood, may be seen the ruins of the amphitheatre, with its twenty-one tiers of seats leading down to the arena.

You look in vain for any trace of the sanctuary of the most celebrated of the Sibyls. Her tomb is pointed out as a vague ruin a short distance from the Necropolis, among the tombs which line the Via Domitiana; and Justin Martyr and Pausanias both describe a round cinerary urn found in this spot which was said to have contained her ashes. The tufa rock of the Acropolis is pierced with numerous dark caverns and labyrinthine passages, the work of prehistoric inhabitants, which have only been partially explored on account of the difficulty and danger, and any one of which might have been the abode of the prophetess. A larger excavation in the side of the hill facing the sea, with a flight of steps leading up from it into another smaller recess, and numerous lateral openings and subterranean passages, supposed to penetrate into the very heart of the mountain, and even to communicate with Lake Fusaro, is pointed out by the local guides as the Sibyl's Cave, which, as Virgil tells us, had a hundred entrances and issues, from whence as many resounding voices echoed forth the oracles of the inspired priestess. But we are confused in our efforts at identification; for another cavern bore this name in former ages, which was destroyed by the explosion of the combustible materials with which Narses filled it in undermining the citadel. This, we have reason to believe, was the cave which Justin Martyr visited more than seventeen hundred years ago, and of which he has left behind a most interesting account. "We saw," he says, "when we were in Cumæ, a place where a sanctuary is hollowed in the

rock—a thing really wonderful and wort⌐
delivered her oracles, we were told ⌐
their ancestors, and who kept them e
middle of the sanctuary, they showed ⌐
rock, and in which, they being filled wit⌐
and when she resumed her garments, she ⌐
sanctuary, likewise cut in the same rock, and
place in the centre, she prophesied." But after
your attention upon any particular spot, for you
overshadowed by the presence of this mysterious
and bush are invested with an air of solemn majest⌐
of an ancient sanctity.

Nature has taken back the ruins of Cumæ so co
bosom, that it is difficult to believe that on this desol⌐
one of the most powerful cities of antiquity, which colon⌐
Southern Italy. A sad, lonely, fateful place it is, haunted for
of old, the dreams of men. A silence, almost painful in its i⌐
over its deserted fields; hardly a living thing disturbs the sol⌐
traces of man's occupancy are few and faint. The air seems he⌐
breath of the malaria; and no one would care to run the risk ⌐
lingering on the spot to watch the sunset gilding the gloom of the ⌐
with a halo of kindred radiance. Every breeze that stirs the tall gra⌐
the leaves of the brushwood of the dismantled citadel has a wail in
long-drawn murmur of the peaceful sea at the foot of the hill come
with a melancholy cadence to the ear; and even on the beautiful cyclam⌐
and veronicas that strive to enliven the ruins of the temples of Apollo a⌐
Serapis, emblems of the immortal youth and signs of the renewing powe⌐
of Nature as they are, has fallen the gray shadow of the past. Each pathetic
bit of ruin has about it the consciousness of an almost fabulous antiquity,
and by its very vagueness appeals more powerfully to the imagination than
any historical associations. "Time here seems to have folded its wings." In
the immemorial calm that is in the air a thousand years seem as one day.
Through all the dim ages no feature of its rugged face has changed; and all
the potent spell of summer noons can only win from it a languid smile of
faintest verdure. The sight of the scanty walls and scattered bits of Greek
sculpture here take you back to the speechless ages that have left no other
memorials of their activity. What is fact and what is fable it were difficult
to tell in this far-away borderland where they seem to blend. And I do not
envy the man who is not deeply moved at the thought of the simple, old-
world piety that placed a holy presence in this solitary spot, and of the
tender awe with which the mysterious divinity of Cumæ was worshipped

of like passions and sorrows with ourselves — whose very
he shadow of this romantic hill had vanished long ages before
d begun.

choolboy is familiar with the picturesque Roman legend of
is variously told in connection with the elder and the later
two Etruscan kings of Rome; and the scene of it is laid by some
where Tarquinius Superbus spent the last years of his life in
by others in Rome. But the majority of writers associate it with
ng of the great temple of Jupiter on the Capitoline Hill. Several
, significant of the future fate of Rome and of the reigning dynasty,
when the foundations of this temple were dug and the walls of it
fresh human head, dripping gore, was found deep down beneath the
which implied that this spot was destined to become the head of the
world; and hence the old name of the "Saturnine Hill" was changed
"Capitoline." All the gods who had been worshipped from time
emorial on this hill, when consulted by auguries, gave permission for
removal of their shrines and altars in order that room might be provided
the gigantic temple of the great Ruler of the gods, save Terminus and
uth, who refused to abandon the sacred spot, and whose obstinacy was
erefore regarded as a sign that the boundaries of the city should never
e removed, and that her youth would be perpetually renewed. But a still
more wonderful sign of the future of Rome was given on this occasion. A
mysterious woman, endowed with preternatural longevity — believed to be
no other than Deiphobe, the Cumæan Sibyl herself, the daughter of Circe
and Gnostus, who had been the guide of Æneas into the world of the dead —
appeared before Tarquin and offered him for a certain price nine books,
which contained her prophecies in mystic rhyme. Tarquin, ignorant of the
value of the books, refused to buy them. The Sibyl departed, and burned
three of them. Coming back immediately, she offered the remaining six
at the same price that she had asked for the nine. Tarquin again refused;
whereupon the Sibyl burned three more volumes, and returning the third
time, made the same demand for the reduced remnant. Struck with the
singularity of the proceeding, the king consulted the augurs; and learning
from them the inestimable preciousness of the books, he bought them, and
the Sibyl forthwith vanished as mysteriously as she had appeared. This
legend reads like a moral apothegm on the increasing value of life as it
passes away.

Whatever credence we may attach to this account of their origin — or
rather, whatever sediment of historical truth may have been precipitated in
the fable — there can be no doubt that the so-called Sibylline books of Rome
did actually exist, and that for a very long period they were held in the

highest veneration. They were concealed in a stone chest, buried under the ground, in the temple of Jupiter, on the Capitol. Two officers of the highest rank were appointed to guard them, whose punishment, if found unfaithful to their trust, was to be sewed up alive in a sack and thrown into the sea. The number of guardians was afterwards increased, at first to ten and then to fifteen, whose priesthood was for life, and who in consequence were exempted from the obligation of serving in the army and from other public offices in the city. Being regarded as the priests of Apollo, they had each in front of his house a brazen tripod, similar to that on which the priestess of Delphi sat.

The contents of the Sibylline books, being supposed to contain the fate of the Roman Empire, were kept a profound secret, and only on occasions of public danger or calamity, and by special order of the senate, were they allowed to be consulted. When the Capitol was burned in the Marsic war, eighty-two years before Christ, they perished in the flames: but so seriously was the loss regarded that ambassadors were sent to Greece, Asia Minor, and Cumæ, wherever Sibylline inspiration was supposed to exist, to collect the prophetic oracles, and thus make up as far as possible for what had been lost. In Cumæ nothing was discovered; but at Erythræa and Samos a large number of mystic verses, said to have been composed by the Sibyl, were found. Some of them were collected into a volume, after having been purged from all spurious or suspected elements; and the volume was brought to Rome, and deposited in two gilt cases at the base of the statue of Apollo, in the temple of that god on the Palatine.

More than two thousand prophetic books, pretending to be Sibylline oracles, were found by Augustus in the possession of private persons; and these were condemned to be burned, and in future no private person was allowed to keep any writings of the kind. But in spite of every attempt to authenticate the books that were publicly accepted, the new collection was never regarded with the same veneration as the original volumes of Tarquin which it replaced. A certain suspicion of spuriousness continued to cling to it, and greatly diminished its authority. It was seldom consulted. The Roman emperors after Tiberius—who still further sifted it—utterly neglected the received collection; and not till shortly before the fatal battle of the Milvian Bridge, which overthrew paganism, was it again brought out, by Maxentius, for the purpose of indicating the fate of the enterprise. Julian the Apostate, in his attempt to galvanise the dead pagan religion into the semblance of life, sought to revive an interest in the Sibylline oracles, which were so closely identified with the political and religious fortunes of Rome. But his effort was vain: they fell into greater oblivion than before; and at last they were publicly burned by Stilicho, the father-in-law of the Emperor

Honorius—called the Defender of Italy—whose own execution as a traitor at Ravenna shortly afterwards was considered by the pagan zealots as the just vengeance of the gods on his dreadful sacrilege.

Unlike the Jewish and Indian faiths, the Greek and Roman religions had no authoritative writings, and were not embodied in a system of elaborate dogmas. The Sibylline oracles may therefore be said to have formed their sacred scriptures, and to have served the purpose of a common religious creed in securing national unity. The original books of the Cumæan Sibyl were written in Greek, which was the language of the whole of the south of Italy at that time. The oracles were inscribed upon palm leaves; to which circumstance Virgil alludes in his description of the sayings of the Cumæan Sibyl being written upon the leaves of the forest. They were in the form of acrostic verses; the letters of the first verse of each oracle containing in regular sequence the initial letters of all the subsequent verses. They were full of enigmas and mysterious analogies, founded upon the numerical value of the initial letters of certain names. It is supposed that they contained not so much predictions of future events, as directions regarding the means by which the wrath of the gods, as revealed by prodigies and calamities, might be appeased. They seemed to have been consulted in the same way as Eastern nations consult the Koran and Hafiz. There was no attempt made to find a passage suitable to the occasion, but one of the palm leaves after being shuffled was selected at random. To this custom of drawing fateful leaves from the Sibylline books—called in consequence sortes sibyllinæ— there is frequent allusion by classic authors. We know that the writings of Homer and Virgil were thus treated. The elevation of Septimius Severus to the throne of the Roman Empire was supposed to have been foretold by the circumstance that he opened by chance the writings of Lampridius at the verse, "Remember, Roman, with imperial sway to rule the people." The Bible itself was used by the early Christians for such purposes of divination. St. Augustine, though he condemned the practice as an abuse of the Divine Word, yet preferred that men should have recourse to the Gospels rather than to heathen works. Heraclius is reported by Cedrenus to have asked counsel of the New Testament, and to have been thereby persuaded to winter in Albania. Nicephorus Gregoras frequently opened his Psalter at random in order that there he might find support in the trial under which he laboured. And even in these enlightened days, it is by no means rare to find superstitious men and women using the sacred Scriptures as the old Greeks and Romans used the Sibylline oracles—dipping into them by chance for indications of the Divine Will.

The Cumæan Sibyl was not the only prophetess of the kind. There were no less than ten females, endowed with the gift of prevision, and held in high repute, to whom the name of Sibyl was given. We read of the Persian Sibyl, the Libyan, the Delphic, the Erythræan, the Hellespontine, the Phrygian, and the Tiburtine. With the name of the last-mentioned Sibyl tourists make acquaintance at Tivoli. Two ancient temples in tolerable preservation are still standing on the very edge of the deep rocky ravine through which the Anio pours its foaming flood. The one is a small circular building, with ten pillars surrounding the broken-down cella, whose familiar appearance is often represented in plaster models and bronze and marble ornamental articles, taken home as souvenirs by travellers; and the other stands close by, and has been transformed into the present church of St. Giorgio. This latter temple is supposed, from a bas-relief found in it, representing the Sibyl sitting in the act of delivering an oracle, to be the ancient shrine of the Sibyl Albunea mentioned by Horace, Tibullus, and Lactantius. The earliest bronze statues at Rome were those of the three Sibyls, placed near the Rostra, in the middle of the Forum. No specimens of the literature of Rome precede the Sibylline books, except the rude hymn known as the Litany of the Arval Brothers, dating from the time of Romulus himself, which is simply an address to Mars, the Lares, and the Semones, praying for fair weather and for protection to the flocks. And it is thus most interesting to notice that the two compositions which lay at the foundation of all the splendid Latin literature of later ages were of an eminently religious character.

One of the most remarkable things connected with the pagan Sibyls were the apocryphal Jewish and Christian prophecies to which they gave rise. When the sacred oak of Dodona perished down to the ground, out of its roots sprang up a fresh growth of fictitious prophetic literature. This literature emanated from different nationalities and different schools of thought. It combined classical story and Scripture tradition. Most of it was the product of pre-Christian Judaism, and seemed to have been composed in times of great national excitement. The misery of the present, the prospect still more gloomy beyond, impelled its authors to anxious inquiries into the future. The books were written, like the genuine Sibylline books, in the metrical form, which the old Greek tradition had consecrated to religious use; and their style so closely resembled that of the Apocalypse and the Old Testament prophecies, that some pagan writers who accepted them as genuine did not hesitate to say that the writers of the Bible had plagiarised parts of their prophecies from the oracles of the Sibyls.

Few fragments of the genuine Sibylline books remain to us, and these are to be found chiefly in the writings of Ovid and Virgil, whose "Golden Age" and well-known "Fourth Eclogue" were greatly indebted for their materials to them. But we possess a large collection of the Judæo-Christian oracles, which were probably gathered together by some unknown editor in the seventh century. Originally there were fourteen books of unequal antiquity and value, but some of them have been lost. Cardinal Angelo Mai discovered in the Ambrosian Library at Milan a manuscript which contained the eleventh book entire, besides a portion of the sixth and eighth books; and a few years later, among the secret stores of the Vatican Library, he found two other manuscripts which contained entire the last four books of the collection. These were published in Rome in 1828. The best edition of all the extant books is that which M. Alexandre issued in Paris, under the name of Oracula Sibyllina. This editor exaggerates the extent of the Christian element in the Sibylline prophecies; but his dissertation on the origin and value of the several portions of the books is exceedingly interesting. The oldest book is undoubtedly the third, part of which is preserved in the writings of Theophilus of Antioch, and originally consisted of one thousand verses, most of which we possess. It was probably composed at the beginning of the Maccabean period, about 146 B.C., when Ptolemy VII. (Physcon) had become king of Egypt, and the bitter enemy of the Jews in Alexandria, and when the Jewish nation in Palestine had been rejoicing in their independence, through the overthrow of the empire of the Seleucidæ by the usurper Tryphon. The fourth book was written soon after the eruption of Vesuvius in the year of our era 79, and is a most interesting record of Jewish Essenism. It contains the first anticipation of the return of Nero, but in a Jewish form, without Nero's death and resuscitation. The last of the Sibylline books seems to have been written about the beginning of the seventh century, and was directed against the new creed of Islam, which had suddenly sprung up, and in its fierce fanaticism was carrying everything before it. In this apocalyptic literature—the last growth of Judaism—the voice of paganism itself was employed to witness for the supremacy of the Jewish religion. It embraces all history in one great theocratic view, and completes the picture of the Jewish triumph by the prophecy of a great Deliverer, who shall establish the Jewish law as the rule of the whole earth, and shall destroy with a fiery flood all that is corrupt and perishable. In these respects the Jewish Sibylline oracles have an interesting connection with other apocryphal Jewish writings, such as the Fourth Book of Esdras, the Apocalypse of Henoch, and the Book of Jubilees; and they may all be regarded as attempts to carry down the spirit of prophecy beyond the canonical Scriptures, and to furnish a supplement to them.

So highly prized was this group of apocryphal Jewish oracles by the primitive Christians, that several new ones were added to them by Christian hands which have not come down to us in their original state. They were regarded as genuine productions, possessing an independent authority which, if not divine, was certainly supernatural; and some did not hesitate even to place them by the side of the Old Testament prophecies. In the very earliest controversies between Christians and the advocates of paganism, they were appealed to frequently as authorities which both recognised. Christian apologists of the second century, such as Tatian, Athenagoras, and very specially Justin Martyr, implicitly relied upon them as indisputable. Even the oracles of the pagan Sibyl were regarded by Christian writers with an awe and reverence little short of that which they inspired in the minds of the heathen themselves. Clement of Alexandria does not scruple to call the Cumæan Sibyl a true prophetess, and her oracles saving canticles. And St. Augustine includes her among the number of those who belong to the "City of God." And this idea of the Sibyl's sacredness continued to a late age in the Christian Church. She had a place in the prophetic order beside the patriarchs and prophets of old, and joined in the great procession of the witnesses for the faith from Seth and Enoch down to the last Christian saint and martyr. In one of the grandest hymns of the Roman Catholic Church, composed by Tommaso di Celano at the beginning of the fourteenth century, there is an allusion to her, taken from the well-known acrostic in the last judgment scene in the eighth book of the Oracula Sibyllina —

"Dies iræ, dies illa,
Solvet sæclum in favilla,
Teste Dàvid cum Sibylla."

The strange Italian mystic of the fifteenth century, Pico della Mirandola, who sought to reconcile the Christian sentiment with the imagery and legends of pagan religion, rehabilitated the Sibyl, and consecrated her as the servant of the Lord Jesus. And he was but a specimen of the many humanists of that age who believed that no oracle that had once spoken to living men and women could ever wholly lose its vitality. Like the Delphic Pythia, old, but clothed as a maiden, the ancient Sibyl appeared to them in the garments of immortal youth, with the charm of her early prime.

The dim old church of Ara Coeli in Rome, which occupies the site of the celebrated temple of Jupiter on the Capitol, and in which Gibbon conceived the idea of his great work on the Decline and Fall of the Roman Empire, is said to have derived its name from an altar bearing the inscription, "Ara Primogeniti Dei," erected in this place by Augustus, to commemorate the Sibylline prophecy of the coming of our Saviour. She was a favourite subject of Christian art in the middle ages, and was introduced by almost every celebrated painter, along with the prophets and apostles, into the cyclical decorations of the Church. Every visitor to Rome knows the fine picture of the Sibyls by Pinturicchio, on the tribune behind the high altar of the Church of St. Onofrio, where Tasso was buried; and also the still grander head of the Cumæan Sibyl, with its flowing turban by Domenichino, in the great picture gallery of the Borghese Palace. But the highest honour ever conferred upon the Sibyls was that which Michael Angelo bestowed when he painted them on the spandrils of the wonderful roof of the Sistine Chapel. These mysterious beings formed most congenial subjects for the mystic pencil of the great Florentine, and therefore they are more characteristic of his genius than almost any other of his works. He has painted them along with the greater prophets, Isaiah, Jeremiah, Ezekiel, Daniel, Jonah, in throne-like niches surrounding the different incidents of the creation. They look like presiding deities, remote from all human weaknesses, and wearing on their faces an air of profound mystery. They are invested, not with the calm, superficial, unconscious beauty of pagan art, but with the solemn earnestness and travail of soul characteristic of the Christian creed, wrinkled and saddened with thought and worn out with vigils; and are striking examples of the truth, that while each human being can bear his own burden, the burden of the world's mystery and pain crushes us to the earth. The Persian Sibyl, the oldest of the weird sisterhood, to whom the sunset of life had given mystical lore, holds a book close to her eyes, as if from dimness of vision; the Libyan Sibyl lifts a massive volume above her head on to her knees; the Cumæan Sibyl intently reads her book at a distance from her dilated eyes; the Erythræan Sibyl, bareheaded, is about to turn over the page of her book; while the Delphic Sibyl, like Cassandra the youngest and most human-looking of them all, holds a scroll in her hand, and gazes with a dreamy mournfulness into the far futurity. These splendid creations would abundantly reward the minute study of many days. They show how thoroughly the great painter had entered into the history and spirit of these mysterious prophetesses, who, while they bore the sins and sorrows of a corrupt world, had power to look for consolation into the secrets of the future.

Very beautiful was this reverence paid to the Sibyl amid all the idolatries of paganism and the corruptions of later Judaism. We may regard it as a relic of the early piety of the world. One who could pass over the interests and distractions of her own time, and fix her gaze upon the distant future, must have seemed far removed from the common order of mankind, who live exclusively in the present, and can imagine no other or higher state of things than they see around them. Standing as the heirs of all the ages on this elevated vantage-ground and looking back upon the long course of the centuries—upon the eventful future of the Sibyl, which is the past to us—it seems a matter of course that the world should have spun down the ringing grooves of change as it has done; and we fancy that this must have been obvious to the world's gray fathers. But though the age of the Sibyl seemed the very threshold of time, there was nothing to indicate this to her, nothing to show that she lived in the youth of the world, and that it was destined to ripen and expand with the process of the suns. The same horizon that bounds us in these last days, bound her view in these early days; and things seemed as fully developed and stereotyped then as now, and to-morrow promised to be only a repetition of to-day. To realise, therefore, that the world had a future, and to take the trouble of thinking what would happen a thousand years off, indicated no common habit of mind.

And we are the more impressed by it when we consider the spots bewitched by the spell of Circe where it was exercised. That persons dwelling in lonely, northern isles, where the long wash of the waves upon the shore, and the wild wail of the wind in mountain corries stimulated the imagination, and seemed like voices from another world, should see visions and dream dreams, does not surprise us. The power of second sight may seem natural to spots where nature is mysterious and solemn, and full of change and sudden transitions from storm to calm and from sunshine to gloom. But at Cumæ there is a perpetual peace, an unchanging monotony. The same cloudless sky overarches the earth day after day, and dyes to celestial blue the same placid sea that sleeps beside its shore. The fields are drowsy at noon with the same stagnant sunshine; and the same purple glory lies at sunset on the entranced hills; and the olive and the myrtle bloom through the even months with no fading or brightening tint on leaf or stem; and each day is the twin of that which has gone before. Nature in such a region is transparent. No mist, or cloud, or shadow hides her secrets. There is no subtle joy of despair and hope, of decay and growth, connected with the passing of the seasons. In this Arcadian clime we should expect Nature to lull the soul into the sleep of contentment on her lap; and in its perpetual summer happy shepherds might sing eclogues for ever, and, satisfied with the present, have no hope or wish for the future. How wonderful, then, that in such a charmed lotus-land we should meet with the mysterious unrest of soul, and the fixed onward look of the Sibyl to times widely different from her own.

And not only is this forward-looking gaze of the Sibyl contrary to what we should have expected in such a changeless land of beauty and ease; it is also contrary to what we should have expected from the paganism of the people. It is characteristic of the Greek religion, as indeed of all heathen religions, that its golden age should be in the past. It instinctively clings to the memory of a former happier time, and shrinks from the unknown future. Its piety ever looks backward, and aspires to present safety or enjoyment by a faithful imitation of an imaginary past. It is always "returning on the old well-worn path to the paradise of its childhood," and contrasting the gloom that overhangs the present with the radiance that shone on the morning lands. In every crisis of terror or disaster it turns with unutterable yearnings to the tradition of the happy age. Or, if it does look forward to the future, it always pictures "the restoration of the old Saturnian reign"; it has no standard of future excellence or future blessedness to attain to, and no yearnings for consummation and perfection hereafter. The very name given to the south of Italy was Hesperia, the "Land of the Evening Star," as if in token of its exhausted history; and it was regarded as the scene of the fabled golden age from which Saturn and the ancient deities had been expelled by Jupiter. But contrary to this pagan instinct, the Cumæan Sibyl stretched forward to a distant heaven of her aspirations and hopes—to a nobler future of the world, not sentimental and idyllic, but epic and heroic. She pictured the blessing or restoration of this earth itself as distinct from an invisible world of happiness. And in this respect she is more in sympathy with the Jewish and Christian religions than with her own. The golden age of the Hebrews was in the future, and was connected with the coming of the Messiah, who should restore the kingdom again unto Israel. And the characteristic of the Christian religion is hope, the expectation of the times of the restitution of all things, and the realisation of the "one far-off divine event to which the whole creation moves." It is this hopeful element pervading them that gives to the lively oracles of Holy Scripture the triumphant tone which distinguishes them so markedly from the desponding spirit of all false religions, ancient and modern.

The subject of the Sibyl brings us to the vexed question of the connection between pagan and Hebrew prophecy. How are we to regard the vaticinations of the heathen oracle? That the great mass of the Sibylline books is spurious is glaringly obvious. But there is a primitive residuum which seems to remind us that the spirit of early prophecy still retained its hold over human nature amid all the corruptions of heathendom, and secured for the Sibyl a sacred rank and authority. We have seen with what reverence the greatest fathers of the Christian Church regarded her. While there was undoubtedly much delusion and deception, conscious or unconscious, mixed up with it, we are constrained at the same time to acknowledge that there was some reality in this prophetic element of paganism, which cannot be explained away as the result of mere political or intellectual foresight or accidental coincidence. It was not all imposture. As a ray of light is contained in all that shines, so a ray of God's truth was reflected in what was best in this pagan prophecy. The fulfilment of many of the ancient oracles cannot be denied without a perversion of all history. There was no doubt an immense difference between the Hebrew prophets and the pagan Sibyl. The predictions of the Sibyl were accompanied by strange fantastic circumstances, and wore the appearance of a blind caprice or arbitrary fate; whereas the announcements of the Hebrew prophets, founded upon the denunciation of moral evil and the reign of sacred and peremptory principles of righteousness in the world, were calm, dignified, and self-consistent. But we cannot, notwithstanding, deny to pagan prophecy some share in the higher influence which inspired and moulded Hebrew prophecy. The apostle of the Gentiles took this view when he called Epimenides the Cretan a prophet. The Bible recognises the existence of true prophets outside the pale of the Jewish Church. Balaam, the son of Beor, was a heathen living in the mountains beyond the Euphrates; and yet the form as well as the substance of his prophecy was cast into the same mould as that of the Hebrew prophets. He is called in the Book of Numbers "the man whose eyes are open;" and God used this power as His organ of intercourse with and influence upon the world. The grand record of his vision is the first example of prophetic utterance respecting the destinies of the world at large; and we see how the base and grovelling nature of the man was overpowered by the irresistible force of the prophetic impulse within him, so that he was constrained to bless the enemies he was hired to curse. And in this respect he represents the purest of the ancient heathen oracles; and his answer to Balak breathes the very essence of prophetic inspiration, and is far in advance of the spirit and thought of the time, reminding us of the noble rebuke of the Cumæan Sibyl to Aristodicus, and of the oracle of Delphi to Glaucus.

God did not leave the Gentile nations without some glimpses of the truth which He had revealed so fully and brightly to His own chosen people. While He was the glory of His people Israel, we must not forget that He was a light to lighten the Gentiles. He gave to them oracles and sibyls, who had the "open eye," and saw the vision of the years, and witnessed to a light shining in the darkness, and brought God nearer to a faithless world. Beneath the gross external polytheism of the multitude there were deep, primitive springs of godliness, pure and undefiled, working out their manifestation in noble lives; and those who have ears to hear can listen to the sound of these ancient streams as they flow into the river of life that makes glad the city of our God. We gain immensely by considering the prophetical spirit of Israel as a typical endowment, and the training of the Jews in the household of God, and under His own immediate eye, as the key to the right apprehension of the training of Greece and Rome. The unconscious prophecies of heathendom pointed in their own way, as well as the articulate divine prophecies of Israel, to the coming of Him who is the Desire of all nations, and the true Light that lighteth every man that cometh into the world. The wise men of Greece saw the sign of the Son of Man in some such way as the Magi saw the star in the East. They were, according to Hegel's beautiful comparison, "Memnons waiting for the day." And not without deep significance did the female soothsayer from the oracle of Dionysius, the prophet-god of the Macedonians, whom Paul and Silas met when they first landed on European soil, greet them with the words, "These men are the servants of the most high God, which show unto us the way of salvation." In that wonderful confession we recognise the last utterance of the oracle of Delphi and the Sibyl of Cumæ, as they were cast out by a higher and truer faith. Their mission was accomplished and their shrine deserted when God's way was known upon the earth, and His saving health among all nations.

> "And now another Canaan yields
> To thine all-conquering ark;
> Fly from the 'old poetic fields,'
> Ye Paynim shadows dark!
> Immortal Greece, dear land of glorious lays,
> Lo! here the unknown God of thine unconscious praise.

> "The olive wreath, the ivied wand,
> 'The sword in myrtles drest,'
> Each legend of the shadowy strand
> Now wakes a vision blest;
> As little children lisp, and tell of heaven,
> So thoughts beyond their thoughts to
> those high bards were given."

CHAPTER IV - FOOTPRINTS IN ROME

In the fork where a cross-road called the Via Ardeatina branches off from the Appian Way, is a little homely church with the strange name of "Domine quo Vadis." It is associated with one of the most beautiful legends of the early Christian Church touchingly told by St. Ambrose. The Apostle Peter, fleeing from the persecution under Nero that arose after the burning of Rome, came to this spot; and there he saw a vision of the Saviour bearing His cross with His face steadfastly set to go to the city. Filled with wonder and awe, the Apostle exclaimed, "Domine quo Vadis," Lord, whither goest thou? To which the Saviour replied, turning upon Peter the old look of mournful pity when he denied Him in the High Priest's palace at Jerusalem, "Venio Roman iterum crucifigi," I go to Rome to be crucified a second time—and then disappeared. Peter regarding this vision as an indication of his Lord's mind, that he ought not to separate himself from the fortunes of his fellow-Christians, immediately turned back to the city, and met with unflinching courage the martyr's death on the yellow sands of Montorio; being crucified with his head downwards, for he said he was not worthy to die in the same way as his Master. This legend has been made the subject of artistic treatment by Michael Angelo, whose famous statue of our Lord as He appeared in the incident to St. Peter is in the church of Santa Maria sopra Minerva, and was for many years a favourite object of worship, until superseded by the predominant worship of Mary. A cast of this statue stands on the floor in front of the altar in the church of Domine quo Vadis. It represents our Lord in the character of a pilgrim, with a long cross in His hand, and an eager onward look in His face and attitude. It is very simple and impressive, and tells the story very effectually. Besides this plaster statue of the Saviour, a circular stone is placed about the centre of the building, surrounded by a low wooden railing, containing the prints of two feet side by side, impressed upon its surface, as if a person had stopped short on a journey. These are said to be the miraculous prints of the Saviour's feet on the pavement of the road when He appeared to Peter; but like the copy of Michael Angelo's statue, this slab is a facsimile, the original stone being preserved among the relics of the neighbouring basilica of St. Sebastian. Unwilling as one is to disturb a legend so beautiful, and with so touching a moral, there can be no doubt that it was an after-thought to account for the footprints; for the material on which they are impressed being white marble, proves conclusively that the slab could never have formed part of the pavement of the Appian Way, which it is well known was composed of an unusually hard lava, found in a quarry near the tomb of Cæcilia Metella; and the distinct marks of the chisel which the impressions bear—for I examined the original footprints very carefully some years ago—indicate a very earthly origin indeed. The traditional relic in all probability belonged to the early subterranean cemetery—leading by a door out of the left aisle of the church of St. Sebastian, to which the name of Catacomb was originally applied.

Slabs with footprints carved upon them are by no means rare in Rome. In the Kircherian Museum, in the room devoted to early Christian antiquities, there is a square slab of white marble with two pairs of footprints elegantly incised upon it, pointed in opposite directions, as if produced by a person going and returning, or by two persons crossing each other. There is no record from what catacomb this sepulchral slab was taken. We have descriptions of other relics of the same kind from the Roman Catacombs,—such as a marble slab bearing upon it the mark of the sole of a foot, with the words "In Deo" incised upon it at the one end, and at the other an inscription in Greek meaning "Januaria in God"; and a slab with a pair of footprints carved on it covered with sandals, well executed, which was placed by a devoted husband over the loculus or tomb of his wife. Impressions of feet shod with shoes or sandals are much rarer than those of bare feet; and a pair of feet is a more customary representation than a single foot, which, when carved, is usually in profile. In a dark, half-subterranean chapel, green with damp, belonging to the church of St. Christina in the town of Bolsena, on the great Volscian Mere of Macaulay, there is a stone let into the front of the altar, and protected by an iron grating, on which is rudely impressed a pair of misshapen feet very like those in the church of St. Sebastian at Rome. In the lower church at Assisi there is a duplicate of these footprints. The legend connected with them says that they were produced by the feet of a Christian lady named Christina, living in the neighbourhood in pagan times, who was thrown into the adjoining lake by her persecutors, with a large flat stone attached to her body. Instead of sinking her, the stone formed a raft which floated her in a standing attitude safely to the opposite shore, where she landed—leaving the prints of her feet upon the stone as an incontestable proof of the reality of the miracle. The altar with which the slab is engrafted—with a stone baldacchino over it—I may mention, was the scene of the famous miracle of Bolsena, when a Bohemian priest, officiating here in 1263, was cured of his sceptical doubts regarding the reality of transubstantiation by the sudden appearance of drops of blood on the Host which he had just consecrated—an incident which formed the subject of Raphael's well-known picture in the Vatican, and in connection with which Pope Urban IV. instituted the festival of Corpus Christi. On the Lucanian coast, near the little fishing town of Agrapoli, not far from Pæstum, there is shown on the limestone rock the print of a foot which is said by the inhabitants to have been made by the Apostle Paul, who lingered here on his way to Rome. In the famous church of Radegonde at Poitiers, dedicated to the queen of Clothaire I.—who afterwards took the veil, and was distinguished for her piety—there is shown on a white marble slab a well-defined footmark, which is called "Le pas de Dieu," and is said to indicate the spot where the Saviour appeared to the tutelary saint of the place. Near the altar of the church of St. Genaro de Poveri in Naples, Mary's foot is shown suspended in a glazed frame. In the middle of the footprint there is an oval figure with the old initials of mother, water, matter. The footprint of Mary is very common in churches in Italy and Spain, where it is highly venerated.

The significance of these footmarks has been the subject of much controversy. Some have regarded them as symbols of possession—the word "possession" being supposed to be etymologically derived from the Latin words pedis positio, and meaning literally the position of the foot. The adage of the ancient jurists was, "Quicquid pes tuus calcaverit tuum erit." The symbol of a foot was carved on the marble slab that closed the loculus or tomb, to indicate that it was the purchased property of the person who reposed in it. This view, however, has not been generally received with favour by the most competent authorities. A more plausible theory is that which regards the sepulchral footmarks in the Catacombs as votive offerings of gratitude, ordered by Christians to be made in commemoration of the completion of their earthly pilgrimage. It was a common pagan custom for persons who had recovered from disease or injury, to hang up as thankofferings in the shrines of the gods who were supposed to have healed them, images or representations, moulded in metal, clay, or wood, of the part that had been affected. In Italy, votive tablets were dedicated to Iris and Hygiea on which footmarks were engraved; and Hygiea received on one occasion tributes of this kind which recorded the gratitude of some Roman soldiers who escaped the amputation which was inflicted upon their comrades by Hannibal. This custom survived in the early Christian Church, and is still kept up, as any one who visits a modern shrine of pilgrimage in Roman Catholic countries can testify. Among such votive offerings, models and carved and painted representations of feet in stone, or wood, or metal, are frequently suspended before the image of the Madonna, in gratitude for recovery from some disease of the feet. We may suppose that as the ancient

Romans, when they returned safely from some long and dangerous or difficult journey undertaken for business or health, dedicated in gratitude a representation of their feet to their favourite god—so the early Christians, who in their original condition were pagans, and still cherished many of their old customs, ordered these peculiar footmarks to be made upon their graves, in token of thankfulness that for them the pilgrimage of life was over, and the endless rest begun. There can be little doubt that the slab with the so-called footprints of St. Christina on it at Bolsena, already alluded to, was a pagan ex-votive offering; for the altar on which it is engrafted occupies the site of one anciently dedicated to Apollo, and the legend of St. Christina gradually crystallised around it. And the footprint in the church of Radegonde at Poitiers was more likely pagan than Christian, for Poitiers had a Roman origin, and numerous Roman remains have been found in the town and neighbourhood.

A long and curious list might be made of the miraculous impressions said to have been left by our Saviour's feet on the places where He stood. In the centre of the platform at Jerusalem on which the Temple of Solomon stood, covered by the dome of the Sakrah Mosque, a portion of the rough natural limestone rock rises several feet above the marble pavement, and is the principal object of veneration in the place. It has an excavated chamber in one corner, with an aperture through the rocky roof, which has given to the rock the name of "lapis pertusus," or perforated stone. On this rock there are natural or artificial marks, which the successors of the Caliph Omar believed to be the prints of the angel Gabriel's fingers, and the mark of Mohammed's foot, and that of his camel, which performed the whole journey from Mecca to Jerusalem in four bounds. The stone, it is said, originally fell from heaven, and was used as a seat by the venerable prophets of Jerusalem. So long as they enjoyed the gift of prophecy, the stone remained steady under them; but when the gift was withdrawn, and the persecuted seers were compelled to flee for safety to other lands, the stone rose to accompany them: whereupon the angel Gabriel interposed, and prevented the departure of the prophetical chair, leaving on it indelibly the marks of his fingers. It was then supernaturally nailed to its rocky bed by seven brass nails. When any great crisis in the world's fortunes happens, the head of one of these nails disappears; and when they are all gone, the day of judgment will come. There are now only three left, and therefore the Mohammedans believe that the end of all things is not far off. When the Crusaders took possession of the sacred city, they altered the Mohammedan legend, and attributed the mysterious footprint to our Lord when He went out of the Temple to escape the fury of the Jews. There can be no doubt that the marks on the rock are prehistoric, and belong to the primitive worship of Mount Moriah, long before the august associations of Biblical history gathered around it. To this spot the Jews used to come in the fourth century and wail over the rock, and anoint it with oil, as if carrying out some dim tradition of former primitive libations.

In the Octagon Chapel of the Church of the Ascension on the top of the Mount of Olives, so well known for the magnificent view which it commands of Jerusalem and the Dead Sea, is shown the native rock which forms the summit of the hill from which our Lord ascended into heaven. On this rock, it is said by tradition, He left the mark of His footsteps. Arculf, who visited Palestine about the year 700, says: "On the ground in the midst of the church are to be seen the last prints in the dust of our Lord's feet, and the roof appears above where He ascended; and although the earth is daily carried away by believers, yet still it remains as before, and retains the same impression of the feet." Jerome mentions that in his time the same custom was observed, followed by the same singular result. Later writers, however, asserted that the impressions were made, not in the ground, or in the dust, but on the solid rock; and that originally there were two, one of them having been stolen long ago by the Mohammedans, who broke off the fragment of stone on which it was stamped. Sir John Mandeville describes the appearance of the surviving footmark as it looked in his day, 1322: "From that mount our Lord Jesus Christ ascended to heaven on Ascension Day, and yet there appears the impress of His left foot in the stone." What is now seen in the place is a simple rude cavity in the natural rock, which bears but the slightest resemblance to the human foot. It may have been artificially sculptured, or it may be only one of those curious hollows into which limestone rocks are frequently weathered. In either case it naturally lent itself to the sacred legend that has gathered around it.

In the Kaaba, the most ancient and remarkable building of the great Mosque at Mecca, is preserved a miraculous stone with the print of Abraham's feet impressed upon it. It is said, by Mohammedan tradition, to be the identical stone which served the patriarch as a scaffold when he helped Ishmael to rebuild the Kaaba, which had been originally constructed by Seth, and was afterwards destroyed by the Deluge. While Abraham stood upon this stone, it rose and sank with him as he built the walls of the sacred edifice. The relic is said to be a fragment of the same gray Mecca stone of which the whole building is constructed, — in this respect differing from the famous black stone brought to Abraham and Ishmael by the angel Gabriel, and built into the north-east corner of the exterior wall of the Kaaba, which is said by scientific men to be either a meteorite or fragment of volcanic basalt. It is popularly supposed to have been originally a jacinth of dazzling whiteness, but to have been made black as ink by the touch of sinful man, and that it can only recover its original purity and brilliancy at the day of judgment. The millions of kisses and touches impressed by the faithful have worn the surface considerably; but in addition to this, traces of cup-shaped hollows have been observed on it. There can be no doubt that both these relics associated with Abraham are of high antiquity, and may have belonged to the prehistoric worship which marked Mecca as a sacred site, long before the followers of the Prophet had set up their shrine there. In the sacred Mosque of Hebron, built over the cave of Machpelah, is pointed out a footprint of the ordinary size on a slab of stone, variously called that of Adam or of Mohammed. It is said to have been brought from Mecca some six hundred years ago, and is enclosed in a recess at the back of the shrine of Abraham, where it is placed on a sort of shelf about three feet above the floor. On the margin of the tank, in the court of the ruined mosque at Baalbec, there are shown four giant footmarks, which are supposed to have been impressed by some patriarch or prophet, but are more likely to have been connected with the ancient religion of Canaan, which lingered here to the latest days of Roman paganism. In the great Druse shrine of Neby Schaib near Hattin there is a square block of limestone in the centre of which is a piece of alabaster containing the imprint of a human foot of natural size, with the toes very clearly defined. The Druses reverently kiss this impression, asserting that the rock exudes moisture, and that it is never dry. There is a split in the rock across the centre of the footprint, which they account for by saying that when the prophet stepped here he split the rock with his tread. In Damascus there was at one time a sacred building called the Mosque of the Holy Foot, in which there was a stone having upon it the print of the feet of Moses. Ibn Batuta saw this curious relic early in the fourteenth century; but both the mosque and the stone have since disappeared. On the eastern side of the Jordan a Bedouin tribe, called the Adwân, worship the print left on a stone by the roadside by a prophetess while mounting her camel, in order to proceed on a pilgrimage to Mecca. The Kadriyeh dervishes of Egypt adore a gigantic shoe, as an emblem of the sacred foot of the founder of their sect; and near Madura, a large leather shoe is offered in worship to a deity that, like Diana, presides over the chase.

To the student of comparative religion the Phrabat, or Sacred Foot of Buddha, opens up a most interesting field of investigation. In the East, impressions of the feet of this wonderful person are as common as those of Christ and the Virgin Mary in the West. Buddhists are continually increasing the number by copies of the originals; and native painters of Siam who are ambitious of distinction often present these sacred objects to the king, adorned with the highest skill of their art, as the most acceptable gift they can offer. The sacred footprint enters into the very essence of the

Buddhist religion; it claims from the Indo-Chinese nations a degree of veneration scarcely yielding to that which they pay to Buddha himself. It is very ancient, and was framed to embody in one grand symbol a complete system of theology and theogony, which has been gradually forgotten or perverted by succeeding ages to the purposes of a ridiculous superstition. It is elaborately carved and painted with numerous symbols, each of which has a profound significance. The liturgy of the Siamese connected with it consists of fifty measured lines of eight syllables each, and contains the names of a hundred and eight distinct symbolical objects, — such as the lion, the elephant, the sun and moon in their cars drawn by oxen, the horse, the serpents, the spiral building, the tree, the six spheres, the five lakes, and the altar—all of which are represented on the foot. This list of symbolical allusions is recited by the priests, and forms an essential part of the ritual of worship. The Siamese priests say that any mortal about to arrive at the threshold of Nivána has his feet emblazoned spontaneously with all the symbols to be seen on the Phrabat.

The Siamese acknowledge only five genuine Phrabats made by the actual feet of Buddha. They are called the Five Impressions of the Divine Foot. The first is on a rock on the coast of the peninsula of Malacca, where, beside the mark of Buddha's foot, there is also one of a dog's foot, which is much venerated by the natives. The second Phrabat is on the Golden Mountain, the hill with the holy footstep of Buddha, in Siam, which Buddha visited on one occasion. The impression is that of the right foot, and is covered with a maradop, a pyramidal canopy supported by gilded pilasters. The hollow of the footstep is generally filled with water, which the devotee sprinkles over his body to wash away the stain of his sin. The third Phrabat is on a hill on the banks of the Jumna, in the midst of an extensive and deep forest, which spreads over broken ranges of hills. The Phrabat is on a raised terrace, like that on which most of the Buddhist temples are built. The pyramidal structure which shelters it is of hewn stone ninety feet high, and is like the baldacchino of a Roman Catholic church. There are four impressions on different terraces, each rising above the other, corresponding to the four descents of the deity. The fourth Phrabat is also on the banks of the Jumna. But the fifth and most celebrated of all is the print of the sacred foot on the top of the Amala Sri Pada, or Adam's Peak, in Ceylon. On the highest point of this hill there is a pagoda-like building, supported on slender pillars, and open on every side to the winds. Underneath this canopy, in the centre of a huge mass of gneiss and hornblende, forming the living rock, there is the rude outline of a gigantic foot about five feet long, and of proportionate breadth.

Sir Emerson Tennent, who has given a full and interesting account of this last Phrabat in his work on Ceylon, supposes that it was originally a natural hollow in the rock, afterwards artificially enlarged and shaped into its present appearance; but whatever may have been its origin at first, its present shape is undoubtedly of great, perhaps prehistoric, antiquity. In the sacred books of the Buddhists it is referred to, upwards of three hundred years before Christ, as the impression left of Buddha's foot when he visited the earth after the Deluge, with gifts and blessings for his worshippers; and in the first century of the Christian era it is recorded that a king of Cashmere went on a pilgrimage to Ceylon for the express purpose of adoring this Sri-pada, or Sacred Footprint. The Gnostics of the first Christian centuries attributed it to Ieu, the first man; and in one of the oldest manuscripts in existence, now in the British Museum—the Coptic version of the "Faithful Wisdom," said to have been written by the great Gnostic philosopher Valentinus in the fourth century—there is mention made of this venerable relic, the Saviour being said to inform the Virgin Mary that He has appointed the Spirit Kalapataraoth as guardian over it. From the Gnostics the Mohammedans received the tradition; for they believe that when Adam was expelled from Paradise he lived many years on this mountain alone, before he was reunited to Eve on Mount Arafath, which overhangs Mecca. The early Portuguese settlers in the island attributed the sacred footprint to St. Thomas, who is said by tradition to have preached the Gospel, after the ascension of Christ, in Persia and India, and to have suffered martyrdom at Malabar, where he founded the Christian Church, which still goes by the name of the Christians of St. Thomas; and they believed that all the trees on the mountain, and for half a league round about its base, bent their crowns in the direction of this sacred object—a mark of respect which they affirmed could only be offered to the footstep of an apostle. The Brahmins have appropriated the sacred mark as the footprint of their goddess Siva. At the present day the Buddhists are the guardians of the shrine; but the worshippers of other creeds are not prevented from paying their homage at it, and they meet in peace and goodwill around the object of their common adoration. By this circumstance the Christian visitor is reminded of the sacred footprint, already alluded to, on the rock of the Church of the Ascension on the Mount of Olives, which is part of a mosque, and has five altars for the Greek, Latin, Armenian, Syrian, and Coptic Churches, all of whom climb the hill on Ascension Day to celebrate the festival; the Mohammedans, too, coming in and offering their prayers at the same shrine. The worship paid on the mountain of the sacred foot in Ceylon consists of offerings of the crimson flowers of the rhododendron, which grow freely among the crags around, accompanied by various genuflections and shoutings, and concluding with the striking of an ancient bell, and a draught from the sacred well which springs up a little below the summit. These ceremonies point to a very primitive mode of worship; and it is probable that, as Adam's Peak was venerated from a remote antiquity by the aborigines of Ceylon, being connected by them with the worship of the sun, the sacred footprint may belong to this prehistoric cult. Models of the footprint are shown in various temples in Ceylon.

Besides these five great Phrabats, there are others of inferior celebrity in the East. In the P'hra Pathom of the Siamese, Buddha is said to have left impressions of his feet at Lauca and Chakravan. At Ava there is a Phrabat near Prome which is supposed to be a type of the creation. Another is seen in the same country on a large rock lying amidst the hills a day's journey west of Meinbu. Dr. Leyden says that it is in the country of the Lan that all the celebrated founders of the religion of Buddha are reported to have left their most remarkable vestiges. The traces of the sacred foot are sparingly scattered over Pegu, Ava, and Arracan. But among the Lan they are concentrated; and thither devotees repair to worship at the sacred steps of Pra Kukuson, Pra Konnakan, Pra Puttakatsop, and Pra Samutacadam.

The footsteps of Vishnu are also frequent in India. Sir William Jones tells us that in the Puranas mention is made of a white mountain on which King Sravana sat meditating on the divine foot of Vishnu at the station Trevirana. When the Hindoos entered into possession of Gayá—one of the four most sacred places of Buddhism—they found the popular feeling in favour of the sacred footprint there so strong that they were obliged to incorporate the relic into their own religious system, and to attribute it to Vishnu. Thousands of Hindoo pilgrims from all parts of India now visit the shrine every year. Indeed to the worshippers of Vishnu the Temple of Vishnupad at Gayá is one of the most holy in all India; and as we are informed in the great work of Dr. Mitra, the later religious books earnestly enjoin that no one should fail, at least once in his lifetime, to visit the spot. They commend the wish for numerous offspring on the ground that, out of the many, one son might visit Gayá, and by performing the rites prescribed in connection with the holy footstep, rescue his father from eternal destruction. The stone is a large hemispherical block of granite, with an uneven top, bearing the carvings of two human feet. The frequent washings which it daily undergoes have worn out the peculiar sectorial marks which the feet contain, and even the outlines of the feet themselves are but dimly perceptible. English architects are now engaged in preserving the ruins of the splendid temple associated with this footprint, where the ministry of India's great teacher—the "Light of Asia"—began. In the Indian Museum at Calcutta there is a large slab of white marble bearing the figure of a human foot surrounded by two dragons. It was brought from a temple in Burmah, where it used to be worshipped as a representation of Buddha's foot. It is seven inches long and three inches broad, and is divided into a hundred and eight compartments, each of which contains a different mystical mark.

At Gangautri, on the banks of the Ganges, is a wooden temple containing a footprint of Ganga on a black stone. In a strange subterranean temple, inside the great fort at Allahabad, there are two footprints of Vishnu, along with footprints of Rama, and of his wife Sita. In India the "kaddam rassul," or supposed impression of Mohammed's foot in clay, which is kept moist, and enclosed in a sort of cage, is not unfrequently placed at the head of the gravestones of the followers of Islam. On the summit of a mountain one hundred and thirty-six miles south of Bhagalpur is one of the principal places of Jain worship in India. On the table-land are twenty small Jain temples on different craggy heights, which resemble an extinguisher in shape. In each of them is to be found the Vasu Padukas—a sacred foot similar to that which is seen in the Jain temple at Champanagar. The sect of the Jain in South Bihar has two places of pilgrimage. One is a tank choked with weeds and lotus-flowers, which has a small island in the centre containing a temple, with two stones in the interior, on one of which is an inscription and the impression of the two feet of Gautama—the most common object of worship of the Jains in this district. The other is the place in the same part of the country where the body of Mahavira, one of the twenty-four lawgivers, was burnt about six centuries before Christ. It resembles the other temple, and is situated in an island in a tank. The island is terraced round, and in the cavity of the beehive-like top there is the representation of Mahavira's feet, to which crowds of pilgrims are continually flocking. In the centre of the Jain temple at Puri, where this remarkable man died, there are also three representations of his feet, and one impression of the feet of each of his eleven disciples.

But the subject of footprints carries us farther back than the ages of the great historic founders of religion. In almost every part of the earth footprints have been found, cut in the solid rock or impressed upon boulders and other stones. These artificial tracks, like the strange human footprint which Robinson Crusoe discovered on the beach of his lonely island, excite the imagination by their mystery, and open up a vista into a hitherto unexplored world of infinite suggestion. They seem the natural successors of those tracks of birds and reptiles on sandstone and other slabs which form one of the most interesting features in every geological museum; the material on which they are impressed having allowed the substantial forms of the creatures themselves to disappear, while it has carefully preserved the more shadowy and incidental memorials of their life. The naturalist can tell us from the ephemeral impressions on the soft primeval mud, not only what was the true nature of the obscure creatures that produced them untold ages ago, but also the direction in which they were moving along the shore, and the state of the tide and the weather, and the appearance of the country at the time. But regarding those literal human "footprints on the sands of time," which have been left behind by our prehistoric ancestors, we can make no such accurate scientific inductions. They have given rise to much speculation, being considered by many persons to be real impressions of human feet, dating from a time when the material on which they were stamped was still in a state of softness. Superstition has invested them with a sacred veneration, and legends of a wild and mystical character have gathered around them. The slightest acquaintance with the results of geological research has sufficed to dispel this delusion, and to show that these mysterious marks could not have been produced by human beings while the rocks were in a state of fusion; and consequently no intelligent observer now holds this theory of their origin. But superstition dies hard; and there are persons who, though confronted with the clearest evidences of science, still refuse to abandon their old obscurantist ideas. They prefer a supernatural theory that allows free scope to their fancy and religious instinct, to one that offers a more prosaic explanation. There is a charm in the mystery connected with these dim imaginings which they would not wish dispelled by the clear daylight of scientific knowledge. In our own country, footmarks on rocks and stones are by no means of unfrequent occurrence. Some of them, indeed, although associated with myths and fairy tales, have doubtless been produced by natural causes, being the mere chance effects of weathering, without any meaning except to a geologist. But there are others that have been unmistakably produced by artificial means, and have a human history and significance.

In Scotland Tanist stones — so called from the Gaelic word tanaiste, a chief, or the next heir to an estate — have been frequently found. These stones were used in connection with the coronation of a king or the inauguration of a chief. The custom dates from the remotest antiquity. We see traces of it in the Bible, — as when it is mentioned that "Abimelech was made king by the oak of the pillar that was in Shechem"; and "Adonijah slew sheep and oxen and fat cattle by the stone of Zoheleth, which is by En-rogel, and called all his brethren the king's sons, and all the men of Judah the king's servants"; and that when Joash was anointed king by Jehoiada, "the king stood by a pillar, as the manner was"; and again, King Josiah "stood by a pillar" to make a covenant, "and all the people stood to the covenant." The stone connected with the ceremony was regarded as the most sacred attestation of the engagement entered into between the newly-elected king or chief and his people. It was placed in some conspicuous position, upon the top of a "moot-hill," or the open-air place of assembly. Upon it was usually carved an impression of a human foot; and into this impression, during the ceremony of inauguration, the king or chief placed his own right foot, in token that he was installed by right into the possessions of his predecessors, and that he would walk in their footsteps. It may be said literally, that in this way the king or chief came to an understanding with his people; and perhaps the common saying of "stepping into a dead man's shoes" may have originated from this primitive custom.

The most famous of the Tanist stones is the Coronation-stone in Westminster Abbey—the Lia Fail, or Stone of Destiny—on which the ancient kings of Scotland sat or stood when crowned, and which forms a singular link of connection between the primitive rites that entered into the election of a king by the people, and the gorgeous ceremonies by which the hereditary sovereigns of England are installed into their high office. There is no footmark, however, on this stone. It may be mentioned that before the arrival of the Scottish stone there had been for ages a similar stone at Westminster Hall, which gave the name to and was the original place of sitting for the Court of King's Bench. It was no doubt a relic of the primitive Folkmoot of Westminster, which has developed into the Parliament of England. In the neighbourhood of Upsala is the Mora stone, celebrated in Swedish history as the spot where the kings were publicly elected and received the homage of their subjects.

A more characteristic specimen of a Tanist stone may be seen on the top of Dun Add, a rocky isolated hill about two hundred feet high, in Argyleshire, not far from Ardrishaig. On a smooth flat piece of rock which protrudes above the surface there is carved the mark of a right foot, covered with the old cuaran or thick stocking, eleven inches long and four inches and a half broad at the widest part, the heel being an inch less. It is sunk about half an inch in the rock, and is very little weather-worn—the reason being, perhaps, that it has been protected for ages by the turf that has grown over it, and has only recently been exposed. Quite close to it is a smooth polished basin, eleven inches in diameter and eight deep, also scooped out of the rock. With these two curious sculptures is associated a local myth. Ossian, who lived for a time in the neighbourhood, was one day hunting on the mountain above Loch Fyne. A stag which his dogs had brought to bay charged him, and he fled precipitately. Coming to the hill above Kilmichael, he strode in one step across the valley to the top of Rudal Hill, from whence he took a gigantic leap to the summit of Dun Add. But when he alighted he was somewhat exhausted by his great effort, and fell on his knee, and stretched out his hands to prevent him from falling backwards. He thereupon left on the rocky top of Dun Add the enduring impression of his feet and knee which we see at the present day. This myth is of comparatively recent date, and is interesting as showing that all recollection of the original use of the footmark and basin had died away for many ages in the district. There can be no doubt that the footmark indicates the spot to have been at one time the scene of the inauguration of the kings or chiefs of the region; and the basin was in all probability one of those primitive mortars which were in use for grinding corn long before the invention of the quern. Dun Add is one of the oldest sites in Scotland. It has the hoary ruins of a nameless fort, and a well which is traditionally said to ebb and flow with the tide. It was here that the Dalriadic Scots first settled; and Captain Thomas, who is an authority on this subject, supposes that the remarkable relic on Dun Add was made for the inauguration of Fergus More Mac Erca, the first king of Dalriada, who died in Scotland at the beginning of the sixth century, and to have been the exact measure of his foot.

King in his Munimenta Antiqua mentions that in the island of Islay there was on a mound or hill where the high court of judicature sat, a large stone fixed, about seven feet square, in which there was a cavity or deep impression made to receive the feet of Macdonald, who was crowned King of the Isles standing on this stone, and swore that he would continue his vassals in the possession of their lands, and do impartial justice to all his subjects. His father's sword was then put into his hand, and the Bishop of Argyle and seven priests anointed him king in presence of all the heads of the tribes in the Isles and mainland, and at the same time an orator rehearsed a catalogue of his ancestors. In the year 1831, when a mound locally known as the "Fairy Knowe," in the parish of Carmylie, Forfarshire, was levelled in the course of some agricultural improvements in the place, there was found, besides stone cists and a bronze ring, a rude boulder almost two tons in weight, on the under side of which was sculptured the mark of a human foot. The mound or tumulus was in all likelihood a moot-hill, where justice was dispensed and the chieftains of the district were elected. In the same county, in the wild recesses of Glenesk, near Lord Dalhousie's shooting-lodge of Milldam, there is a rough granite boulder, on the upper surface of which a small human foot is scooped out with considerable accuracy, showing traces even of the toes. It is known in the glen as the "Fairy's Footmark." There can be no doubt that this stone was once used in connection with the ceremonial of inaugurating a chief.

A similar stone, carved with a representation of two feet, on which the primitive chiefs stood when publicly invested with the insignia of office, is still, or was lately, in existence in Ladykirk, at Burwick, South Ronaldshay, Orkney. A local tradition, that originated long after the Pictish chiefs passed away, and a new Norse race, ignorant of the customs of their predecessors, came in, says that the stone in question was used by St. Magnus as a boat to ferry him over the Pentland Firth; while an earlier tradition looked upon it as a miraculous whale which opportunely appeared at the prayer of the saint when about to be overwhelmed by a storm, and carried him on its back safely to the shore, where it was converted into a stone, as a perpetual memorial of the marvellous occurrence. In North Yell, Shetland, there is a rude stone lying on the hillside, on which is sculptured with considerable skill the mark of a human foot. It is known in the district as the "Giant's Step"; another of the same kind, it is said, being over in Unst. It is undoubtedly the stone on which, in Celtic times, the native kings of this part were crowned. About a mile from Keill, near Campbeltown, a very old site, closely connected with the early ecclesiastical history of Scotland, may be seen on a rock what is locally called the "Footprint of St. Columba," which he made when he landed on this shore on one occasion from Iona. It is very rude and much effaced; but it carries the imagination much farther back than the days of St. Columba, — when a pagan chief or king was inaugurated here to rule over the district.

In England and Wales there are several interesting examples of footprints on boulders and rocks. A remarkable Tanist stone — which, however, has no carving upon it, I believe — stands, among a number of other and smaller boulders, on the top of a hill near the village of Long Compton, in Cumberland. It is called "The King"; and the popular rhyme of the country people —

"If Long Compton thou canst see,
Then king of England thou shalt be" —

points to the fact that the stone must have been once used as a coronation-stone. Not far from the top of a hill near Barmouth in Wales, in the middle of a rough path, may be seen a flat stone, in which there is a footmark about the natural size, locally known as "Llan Maria," or Mary's step, because the Virgin Mary once, it is supposed, put her foot on this rock, and then walked down the hill to a lower height covered with roots of oak-trees. This impression on the stone is associated with several stone circles and cromlechs — one of which bears upon it the reputed marks of Arthur's fingers, and is called Arthur's Quoit — and with a spring of water and a grove, as the path leading to the hill is still known by a Welsh name which means Grove Lane; and these associations undoubtedly indicate that the spot was once a moot-hill or prehistoric sanctuary, where religious and inauguration rites were performed. At Smithhill's Hall, near Bolton-le-Moors, there is still to be seen an object of curiosity to a large number of visitors — the print of a man's foot in the flagstone. It is said to have been produced by George Marsh, who suffered martyrdom during the persecutions of Queen Mary in

1555. When on one occasion the truth of his words was called in question by his enemies, he stamped his foot upon the stone on which he stood, which ever after bore the ineffaceable impression as a miraculous testimony to his veracity. This story must have been an after-thought, to account for what we may suppose to have been a prehistoric Tanist stone.

In Ireland footmarks are very numerous, and are attributed by the peasantry to different saints. Mr. and Mrs. S.C. Hall, in their account of Ireland, refer to several curious examples which are regarded by the people with superstitious reverence, and are the occasions of religious pilgrimage. Near the chapel of Glenfinlough, in King's County, there is a ridge with a boulder on it called the Fairy's Stone or the Horseman's Stone, which presents on its flat surface, besides cup-like hollows, crosses, and other markings, rudely-carved representations of the human foot. On a stone near Parsonstown, called Fin's Seat, there are similar impressions — also associated with crosses and cup-shaped hollows which are traditionally said to be the marks of Fin Mac Coul's thumb and fingers. On an exposed and smooth surface of rock on the northern slope of the Clare Hills, in the townland of Dromandoora, there is the engraved impression of a foot clothed with a sandal; and near it is sculptured on the rock a figure resembling the caduceus of Mercury, while there are two cromlechs in the immediate vicinity. The inauguration-stone of the Macmahons still exists on the hill of Lech — formerly called Mullach Leaght, or "hill of the stone" — three miles south of Meaghan; but the impression of the foot was unfortunately effaced by the owner of the farm about the year 1809. In the garden of Belmont on the Greencastle road, about a mile from Londonderry, there is the famous stone of St. Columba, held in great veneration as the inauguration-stone of the ancient kings of Aileach, and which St. Patrick is said to have consecrated with his blessing. On this remarkable stone, which is about seven feet square, composed of a hard gneiss, and quite undressed by the chisel, are sculptured two feet, right and left, about ten inches long each. Boullaye le Gouze mentions that in 1644 the print of St. Fin Bar's foot might be seen on a stone in the cemetery of the Cathedral of Cork; it has long since disappeared.

In the Killarney region is the promontory of Coleman's Eye — so called after a legendary person who leapt across the stream, and left his footprints impressed in the solid rock on the other side. These impressions are considered Druidic, and are pointed out as such to the curious stranger by the guides. Near an old church situated on the southern slope of Knockpatrick, in the parish of Graney in Leinster, there is a large flat granite rock with the impression of two feet clearly defined on its surface. Local tradition assigns these footprints to St. Patrick, who addressed the people on this spot, and left behind these enduring signs of his presence. Allusion is made to them in St. Fiaca's Hymn to St. Patrick—"He pressed his foot on the stone; its traces remain, it wears not." Footprints in connection with St. Patrick are to be found in many localities in Ireland, as, for instance, on the seashore south of Skerries, County Dublin, where the apostle landed; and at Skerries, County Antrim, there are marks which are believed to be the footprints of the angel who appeared to St. Patrick. In Ossory two localities are noted as possessing St. Patrick's footprints.

So common are the curious sculptures under consideration in Norway and Sweden, that they are known by the distinct name of Fotsulor, or Footsoles. They are marks of either naked feet, or of feet shod with primitive sandals. On a rock at Brygdæa in Westerbotten, in Norway, there are no less than thirty footmarks carved on a rock at an equal distance from each other. In other parts of Norway these footprints are mixed up with rude outlines of ships, wheels, and other hällristningar, or rock-sculptures. Holmberg has figured many of them in his interesting work entitled Scandinaviens Hällristningar. At Lökeberg Bohnslau, Sweden, there is a group of ten pairs of footmarks, associated with cup-shaped hollows and ship-carvings; and at Backa, in the same district, several pairs of feet, or rather shoe-marks, are engraved upon a rock. In Denmark not a few examples of artificial foot-tracks have been observed and described by Dr. Petersen. One was found on a slab belonging to the covering of a gallery in the inside of a tomb in the island of Seeland, and another on one of the blocks of stone surrounding a tumulus in the island of Laaland. In both cases the soles of the feet are represented as being covered; and in all probability they belong to the late stone or earlier bronze age. With these sepulchral marks are associated curious Danish legends, which refer them to real impressions of human feet. The islands of Denmark were supposed to have been made by enchanters, who wished for greater facilities for going to and fro, and dropped them in the sea as stations or stepping-stones on their way; and hence, in a region where the popular imagination poetises the commonest material objects, and is saturated with stories of elves and giants, with magic swords, and treasures guarded by dragons, it was not difficult to conclude that these mysterious foot-sculptures were made by the tread of supernatural beings. Near the station of Sens, in France, there is a curious dolmen, on one of whose upright stones or props are carved two human feet. And farther north, in Brittany, upon a block of stone in the barrow or tumulus of Petit Mont at Arzon, may be seen carved an outline of the soles of two human feet, right and left, with the impressions of the toes very distinctly cut, like the marks left by a person walking on the soft sandy shore of the sea. They are surrounded by a number of waving circular and serpentine lines exceedingly curious. On Calais pier may be seen a footprint where Louis XVIII. landed in 1814; and on the rocks of Magdesprung, a village in the Hartz Mountains, a couple of hundred feet apart, are two immense footprints, which tradition ascribes to a leap made by a huge giantess from the clouds for the purpose of rescuing one of her maidens from the violence of an ancient baron.

In not a few places in our own country and on the Continent, rough misshapen marks on rocks and stones, bearing a fanciful resemblance to the outline of the human foot, have been supposed by popular superstition to have been made by Satan. Every classical student is familiar with the account which Herodotus gives of the print of Hercules shown by the Scythians in his day upon a rock near the river Tyras, the modern Dnieper. It was said to resemble the footstep of a man, only that it was two cubits long. He will also recall the description given by the same gossipy writer of the Temple of Perseus in the Thebaic district of Egypt, in which a sandal worn by the god, two cubits in length, occasionally made its appearance as a token of the visit of Perseus to the earth, and a sign of prosperity to the land. Pythagoras measured similar footprints at Olympia, and calculated "ex pede Herculem"! Still more famous was the mark on the volcanic rock on the shore of Lake Regillus—the scene of the memorable battle in which the Romans, under the dictator Posthumius, defeated the powerful confederation of the Latin tribes under the Tarquins. According to tradition, the Roman forces were assisted by Castor and Pollux, who helped them to achieve their signal victory. The mark was supposed to have been left by the horse of one of the great twins "who fought so well for Rome," as Macaulay says in his spirited ballad. On the way to the famous convent of Monte Casino, very near the door, there is a cross in the middle of the road. In front of it a grating covers the mark of a knee, which is said to have been left in the rock by St. Benedict, when he knelt there to ask a blessing from heaven before laying the foundation-stone of his convent. As the site of the monastery was previously occupied by a temple of Apollo, and a grove sacred to Venus, where the inhabitants of the surrounding locality worshipped as late as the sixth century,—to which circumstance Dante alludes,—it is probable that the sacred mark on the rock may have belonged to the old pagan idolatry, and have been a cup-marked stone connected with sacrificial libations.

On many rocks of the United States of America may be seen human footprints, either isolated or connected with other designs belonging to the pictorial system of the Aborigines, and commemorating incidents which they thought worthy of being preserved. In the collection of the Smithsonian Museum are three large stone slabs having impressions of the human foot. On two slabs of sandstone, carefully cut from rocks on the banks of the Missouri, may be seen respectively two impressions of feet, carved apparently with moccasins, such as are worn at the present day by the Sioux and other Indians. The other specimen is a flat boulder of white quartz, obtained in Gasconade County, Missouri, which bears on one of its sides the mark of a naked foot, each toe being distinctly scooped out and indicated. The footmark is surrounded by a number of cup-shaped depressions. In many parts of Dacotah, where the route is difficult to find, rocks occur with human footprints carved upon them which were probably meant to serve as geographical landmarks—as they invariably indicate the best route to some Indian encampment or to the shallow parts of some deep river. Among other places these footprints have been met with on the Blue Mountains between Georgia and North Carolina, and also on the Kenawha River. Some stir was made two years ago by the reported discovery of the prints of human feet in a stone quarry on the coast of Lake Managua in Nicaragua. The footprints are remarkably sharp and distinct; one seems that of a little child. The stone in which they are impressed is a spongy volcanic tuff, and the layer superimposed upon them in the quarry was of similar material. These prehistoric footprints were doubtless accidentally impressed upon the volcanic stone, and would seem to throw back the age of man on the earth to a most remote antiquity. In Equatorial Africa footprints have also been found, and are associated with the folklore of the country. Stanley, in his Dark Continent, tells us that in the legendary history of Uganda, Kimera, the third in descent from Ham, was so large and heavy that he made marks in the rocks wherever he trod. The impression of one of his feet is shown at Uganda on a rock near the capital, Ulagolla. It was made by one of his feet slipping while he was in the act of hurling his spear at an elephant. In the South Sea Islands department of the British Museum is an impression of a gigantic footstep five feet in length.

The connection of prehistoric footprints with sacred sites and places of sepulture would indicate that they had a religious significance—an idea still further strengthened by the fact of their being frequently associated with holy wells and groves, and with cup-shaped marks on cromlechs or sacrificial altars, which are supposed to have been used for the purpose of receiving libations; while their universal distribution points to a hoary antiquity, when a primitive natural cultus spread over the whole earth, traces of which are found in every land, behind the more elaborate and systematic faith which afterwards took its place. They are probably among the oldest stone-carvings that have been left to us, and were executed by rude races with rude implements either in the later stone or early bronze age. Their subsequent dedication to holy persons in Christian times was in all likelihood only a survival of their original sacred use long ages after the memory of the particular rites and ceremonies connected with them passed away. A considerable proportion of the sacred marks are said to be impressions of the female foot, attributed to the Virgin Mary; and in this circumstance we may perhaps trace a connection with the worship of the receptive element in nature, which was also a distinctive feature of primitive religion.

It is strange how traces of this primitive worship of footprints survive, not merely in the mythical stories and superstitious practices connected with the objects themselves, but also in curious rites and customs that at first sight might seem to have had no connection with them. The throwing of the shoe after a newly-married couple is said to refer to the primitive mode of marriage by capture; but there is equal plausibility in referring it to the prehistoric worship of the footprint as a symbol of the powers of nature. To the same original source we may perhaps attribute the custom connected with the Levirate law in the Bible, when the woman took off the shoe of the kinsman who refused to marry her, whose name should be afterwards called in Israel "the house of him that hath his shoe loosed."

In regard to the general subject, it may be said that we can discern in the primitive adoration of footprints a somewhat advanced stage in the religious thoughts of man. He has got beyond total unconsciousness of God, and beyond totemism or the mere worship of natural objects—trees, streams, stones, animals, etc. He has reached the conception of a deity who is of a different nature from the objects around him, and whose place of abode is elsewhere. He worships the impression of the foot for the sake of the being who left it; and the impression helps him to realise the presence and to form a picture of his deity. That deity is not a part of nature, because he can make nature plastic to his tread, and leave his footmark on the hard rock as if it were soft mud. He thinks of him as the author and controller of nature, and for the first time rises to the conception of a supernatural being.

CHAPTER V - THE ROMAN FORUM

No spot on earth has a grander name or a more imposing history than the Roman Forum. Its origin takes us far back to geological ages—to a period modern indeed in the inarticulate annals of the earth, but compared with which even those great periods which mark the rise and fall of empires are but as the running of the sands in an hour-glass. It opens up a wonderful chapter in the earth's stony book. Everywhere on the site and in the neighbourhood of Rome striking indications of ancient volcanoes abound. The whole region is as certainly of igneous origin, and was the centre of as violent fiery action, as the vicinity of Naples. The volcanic energy of Italy seems to have begun first in this district, and when exhausted there, to have passed gradually to the south, where Vesuvius, Etna, and Stromboli witness to the great furnace that is still burning fiercely under the beautiful land. No spectacle could have been more sublime than that which the Roman Campagna presented at this period, when no less than ten volcanoes were in full or intermittent action, and poured their clouds of smoke and flame into the lurid sky all around the horizon. Up to the foot of the mountains the sea covered the vast plain; and the action of these waves of fire and steaming floods forms a natural epic of the grandest order. Prodigious quantities of ashes and cinders were discharged from the craters; and these, deposited and hardened by long pressure under water, formed the reddish-brown earthy rock called tufa, of which the seven hills of Rome are composed.

When the sea retired, or rather when the land rose suddenly or gradually, and the volcanoes became extinct, the streams which descended from the mountains and watered the recovered land spread themselves out in numerous fresh-water lakes, which stood an hundred and fifty feet higher than the present bed of the Tiber. In these lakes were formed two kinds of fresh-water strata—the first composed of sand and marl; and the second, where mineral springs gushed forth through the volcanic rock, of travertine—a peculiar reddish-brown or yellow calcareous rock, of which St. Peter's and many of the buildings of modern Rome are composed. We find lacustrine marls on the sides of the Esquiline Hill where it slopes down into the Forum, and fresh-water bivalve and univalve shells in the ground under the equestrian statue of Marcus Aurelius on the Capitol; while on the face of the Aventine Hill, overhanging the Tiber at a height of ninety feet, is a cliff of travertine, which is half a mile long. The lakes which formed these deposits must have covered their sites for many ages. At last, by some new change of level, the lakes retired, and the Tiber scooped out for itself its present channel to the sea.

When man came upon the scene we have no definite information; but numerous flints and stone-weapons have been found among the black pumice breccias of the Campagna mixed with remains of the primitive bison, the elephant, and the rhinoceros. Human eyes must therefore have gazed upon the volcanoes of the Roman plain. Human beings, occupying the outposts of the Sabine Hills, must have seen that plain broken up by the sea into a complicated archipelago, and beheld in the very act of formation that wonderful region destined long ages afterwards to be the scene of some of the greatest events in human history. The Alban Hills, whose present quiet beauty, adorned with white gem-like towns, and softened with the purple hues of heaven, strikes every visitor with admiration, were active volcanoes pouring streams of lava down into the plain even after the foundation of the Eternal City. Livy mentions that under the third king of Rome, a shower of stones, accompanied by a loud noise, was thrown up from the Alban Mount—a prodigy which gave rise to a nine days' festival annually celebrated long after by the people of Latium. The remarkable funereal urns found buried under a bed of volcanic matter between Marino and Castel Gandolfo on the Alban Hills are an incontrovertible proof that showers of volcanic ashes must have been ejected from the neighbouring volcano when the country was inhabited by human beings; nay, when the inhabitants were far advanced in civilisation, for among the objects contained in the funereal urns were implements of writing. At the close of the skirmish between the Romans and Etruscans, near Albano, in which Aruns, the son of Lars Porsenna, was slain, whose tomb may still be seen on the spot, a noise like that which Livy mentions was heard among the surrounding hills.

But the most extraordinary of all the volcanic phenomena within the historical period was the sudden rising on two memorable occasions of the waters of the Alban Lake, which now lie deep down within the basin of an extinct crater. The first swallowed up the royal palace of Alba, and was so sudden and violent that neither the king nor any of his household had time to escape. The other occurred during the romantic siege of the Etruscan city of Veii, near Rome, by Camillus, four hundred years before Christ. The waters on that occasion rose two hundred and forty feet in the crater almost to the very edge, and threatened to overflow and inundate the surrounding country, when they were withdrawn by a subterranean canal cut in the rock, and poured into the Tiber by a connecting stream. This emissary, which may still be seen, was constructed owing to a hint given by an Etruscan soothsayer, that the city of Veii would not be captured till the Alban Lake was emptied into the sea. The deep winding cavern on the face of the Aventine Hill, said to have been inhabited by the monstrous giant Cacus, the son of Vulcan, who vomited fire, and was the terror of the surrounding inhabitants, was evidently of volcanic origin; and the local tradition from which Virgil concocted his fable was undoubtedly derived from a vivid recollection of the active operations of a volcano. When Evander, as described in the eighth Æneid, conducted his distinguished guest to the top of the Tarpeian Rock, in after ages so famous as the place of public execution, and composed of very hard lava, he assured him that an awful terror possessed the place, and that some unknown god had his abode there. The shepherds said it was Jupiter, and that they had often seen him kindling his lightnings and hurling his thunderbolts from thence. Evander then pointed to the ruined cities of Saturnia and Janiculum, on either side of the Tiber, whose destruction had been caused by the wrath of the god. There can be no doubt that this fable clothed with supernatural colouring some volcanic phenomena which had taken place on this spot during the human period. Even as late as three hundred and ninety years after the foundation of Rome, a chasm opened in the Forum, and emitted flames and pestilential vapours. An oracle declared that this chasm would not close until what constituted the glory of Rome should be cast into it. Marcus Curtius asked if anything in Rome was more precious than arms and valour; and arraying himself in his armour, and mounting on a horse splendidly equipped, he leapt in the presence of the Roman people into the abyss, when it instantly closed for ever. We thus see that the geology of the Roman plain throws no inconsiderable light upon the early history and traditions of the Eternal City, and brings within the cycle of natural phenomena what were long supposed to be purely fabulous incidents, the inventions of a poetic imagination. I have dwelt upon these geological incidents so fully, because nowhere does one realise the striking contrast between the shortness of man's existence on earth, as in places like the Roman plain, where the traces of cosmical energy have been greatest and most enduring.

The volcanic origin of the Roman Forum suggests the curious idea of the intimate connection of some of the greatest events of history with volcanic centres. Where the strife of nature has been fiercest, there by a strange coincidence the storm of human passion has been greatest. The geological history of a region is most frequently typical of its human history. We can predicate of a scene where the cosmical disturbance has been great, — where fire and flood have contended for the mastery, leaving the effects of their strife in deepening valleys and ascending hills, — that there man has had a strangely varied and eventful career. The strongholds and citadels of the earth, where the great battles of freedom and civilisation have been fought, were all untold ages previously the centres of violent plutonic disturbances. Edinburgh Castle, enthroned on its trap-rock, once the centre of a volcano, is associated with the most stirring and important events in the history of Scotland; Stirling Castle rises on its trap-rock erupted by volcanic action above a vast plain, across which a hundred battles have swept; Dumbarton Castle, crowning its trappean promontory, has represented in its civil history the protracted periods of earthquake and eruption concerned in the formation of its site; while standing in solitude amid the stormy waters of the Firth of Forth, the Bass Rock, once a scene of fiery confusion, of roaring waves and heaving earthquakes, has formed alternately the prison where religious liberty has been strangled, and the fortress where patriotism has taken its last stand against the forces of the invader. Palestine, Greece, Italy, Switzerland, and Scotland, the countries that have had the most remarkable history, and have done most to advance the human race, are distinguished above other countries for their geological convulsions and revolutions. The Roman Forum is thus but one specimen among numerous others of a law of Providence which has associated the strife of nature with the strife of man, and caused the ravages of the most terrible elements to prepare the way for the highest development of the human race.

Between the Roman Forum and the valley beneath Edinburgh Castle we can trace a striking resemblance, not only in their volcanic origin and the connection between their geological history and their analogous civil history, but also in the fact that they were both filled with small lakes. Between the ridges of the old and new town of Edinburgh, where the railway runs through Princes Street Gardens, there was in the memory of many now living a considerable collection of water called the North Loch. In like manner, in the hollow of the Roman Forum there was originally a small lake, a relic of the numerous lakes of the Campagna, which remained after the last elevation of the land, and which existed pretty far on into the human period. It was fed by three streams flowing from the Palatine, the Capitoline, and the Esquiline Hills, which now run underground and meet at this point.

Let us picture to ourselves the appearance of this lake embosomed in the hollow of its hills in the far-off pastoral times, when the mountains and the high table-lands of Italy were the chosen territory of those tribes whose property consisted chiefly in their flocks. The hills of Rome, whose elevation was far more conspicuous in ancient times than it is now, presented a precipitous front of dark volcanic rock to the lake. Their slopes were covered with grass and with natural copse-wood, intermixed with tall ilex trees, or umbrella pines; while on their summits were little villages surrounded with Cyclopean walls perched there not only for security, but also for the healthier air, just as we see at the present day all over Italy. On the summit of the Capitoline and Esquiline Hills were Sabine settlements, whose origin is lost in the mists of antiquity. To the green wooded slopes of the Palatine, according to a beautiful tradition, sixty years before the destruction of Troy, came Evander and his Arcadians from Greece, and settled there with their flocks and herds, and led a quiet idyllic life. According to another tradition, Æneas, after the destruction of Troy, came to this spot, and marrying the daughter of a neighbouring king, became the ancestor of the twins Romulus and Remus, the popular founders of Rome, whose romantic exposure and nourishment by a she-wolf are known to every schoolboy. Romulus, after slaying his brother, built a stronghold on the Palatine, which he opened as an asylum for outlaws and runaway slaves, who supported themselves chiefly by plunder. The community of this robber-city consisting almost entirely of males, they provided themselves with wives by the famous stratagem known as the "Rape of the Sabine women." Seizing the daughters of their neighbours, the Sabines of the Capitoline and Esquiline Hills, on a festive occasion, they carried them away with them to their fortress. A number of sanguinary fights took place in consequence of this rape around the swampy margin of the lake. In the last of these engagements the combatants were separated by the Sabine women suddenly rushing in with their children between their fathers and brothers and the men who had become their husbands. A mutual reconciliation then ensued, and the two communities contracted a firm and close alliance. The Palatine, Capitoline, and Esquiline villages became henceforth one city, to which from time to time by conquest new accessions were made, until at last all the different settlements on the seven hills of Rome were brought under one rule, and surrounded by a common wall of defence. Mommsen, Niebuhr, Sir George Cornewall Lewis, and other critics, have made sad havoc with these romantic stories of the origin of Rome. But although much of the fabulous undoubtedly mingles with them—for the early history of Rome was not written till it had become a powerful state, and then the historian had no records of days long past save what were embodied in popular tradition and poetry—there has recently been a reaction in favour of them, and they must ever be interesting on account of their own intrinsic charm, the element of truth which they contain, and the indelible associations of schoolboy life.

When a joint city was thus compacted and called Rome—possibly its old Pelasgic appellation—the first effort of the confederated settlements was to drain the geological lake in the centre of the city into the Tiber, a quarter of a mile distant. This they did by means of the celebrated Cloaca Maxima, a part of which may be seen open at the present day under the pavement of the Roman Forum, near the Temple of Castor and Pollux. This common sewer of Rome is one of its oldest and greatest relics. It was built by the first Tarquin, the fifth king of Rome, a century and a half after the foundation of the city; and although two thousand five hundred years have passed away since the architect formed without cement its massive archway of huge volcanic stones found on the spot, and during all the time it has been subjected to the shock of numerous earthquakes, inundations of the Tiber, and the crash of falling ruins, it still serves its original purpose as effectually as ever, and promises to stand for as many ages in the future as it has stood in the past. It is commonly said that we owe the invention of the arch to the Romans; and this work of undoubted Etruscan architecture is usually considered as among the very first applications of the principle. But the arched drains and doorways discovered by Layard at Nineveh prove that the Assyrians employed the arch centuries before Rome was founded. It had however only a subordinate place and a very limited application in the ancient architecture of the East; and it was left to the Romans to give it due prominence in crossing wide spaces, to make it "the bow of promise," the bridge over which they passed to the dominion of the world. The Cloaca Maxima is a tunnel roofed with two concentric rings of enormous stones, the innermost having an interior diameter of nearly fourteen feet, the height being about twelve feet. So capacious was it that Strabo mentions that a waggon loaded with hay might find room in it; and it is recorded that the Consul Agrippa passed through it in a boat. The mouth of the Cloaca opens into the Tiber, near the little round temple of Hercules in the Forum Boarium; but it is often invisible owing to the flooding of the river; and even when the Tiber is low, so much has its bed been silted up that only about three feet below the keystone of the sewer can be seen. Subsequently all the sewers of Rome were connected with it; and at the present day the nose gives infallible proof that it carries off a very large portion of the pollution of the modern city.

By the Cloaca Maxima, the valley between the Capitoline and Palatine Hills was for the first time made dry land; all indeed, except a small swamp which remained in one corner of it to a later age, and which the great sewer was not deep enough to drain entirely. Reeds grew around its margin, and boats were employed to cross it, as Ovid tells us. The name Velabrum—from an Etruscan root, signifying water, occurring in some other Italian names such as Velletri, Velino—still given to this locality, where a church stood in the middle ages called S. Silvestro in Lacu, commemorates the existence of the primeval lake; while the legend of the casting ashore of Romulus and Remus on the slope of the Palatine points to the gradual desiccation of the spot. On the level ground, recovered in this way from the waters, was formed the Roman Forum; the word Forum meaning simply an open space, surrounded by buildings and porticoes, which served the purpose of a market-place, a court of justice, or an exchange; for the Romans transacted more of their public and private business out of doors than the severe climate of our northern latitudes will permit us to do. On this common ground representatives of the separate communities located on the different hills of Rome, and comprehended and confederated within the walls of Servius Tullius, met together for the settlement of affairs that concerned them all. As Rome grew in importance, so did this central representative part of it grow with it, until at last, in the time of the Cæsars, it became the heart of the mighty empire, where its pulse beat loudest. There the fate of the world was discussed. There Cicero spoke, and Cæsar ruled, and Horace meditated. If the Temple of Jerusalem was the shrine of religion, the Forum of Rome was the shrine of law; and from thence has emanated that unrivalled system of jurisprudence which has formed the model of every nation since. Being thus the centre of the political power of the empire, the Roman Forum became also the focus of its architectural and civic splendour. It was crowded with marble temples, state buildings, and courts of law to such an extent that we wonder how there was room for them all within such a narrow area. Monuments of great men, statues of Greek sculpture, colonnades, and porticoes, rich with the spoils of subject kingdoms, adorned its sides. The whole region was resplendent with all the pomp and luxury of paganism in its proudest hour; the word "ambition," which came ultimately to signify all strivings for eminence, resolving itself into the elementary meaning of a walk round the Roman Forum, canvassing for votes at municipal elections.

Thus the Forum continued until the decay of the empire, when hordes of invaders buried its magnificence in ruins. At the beginning of the seventh century it must have been open and comparatively free from débris, as is proved by the fact that the column of Phocas, erected, at that time, stood on the original pavement. Virgil says, in his account of the romantic interview of Evander with Æneas on the spot which was to be afterwards Rome — then a quiet pastoral scene, green with grass, and covered with bushes — that they saw herds of cattle wandering over the Forum, and browsing on the rich pasture around the shores of its blue lake. Strange, the law of circularity, after the lapse of two thousand years, brought round the same state of things in that storied spot. During the middle ages the Roman Forum was known only as the Campo Vaccino, the field of cattle. It was a forlorn waste, with a few ruins scattered over it, and two formal rows of poplar-trees running down the middle of it, and wild-eyed buffaloes and mouse-coloured oxen from the Campagna wandering over the solitude, and cropping the grass and green weeds that grew in the very heart of old Rome. When Gibbon conceived the idea of the Decline and Fall of the Roman Empire, listening to the vespers of the Franciscan friars in the dim church of Ara Coeli in the neighbourhood, the Forum was an unsightly piece of ground, covered with rubbish-heaps, with only a pillar or two emerging from the general filth. When Byron stood beside the "nameless column with the buried base," commemorated in Childe Harold, he little dreamt what a rich collection of the relics of imperial times lay under his feet, as completely buried by the wrecks of ages as Pompeii and Herculaneum under the ashes and lava of Vesuvius. From fifteen to twenty feet of soil had accumulated over them.

The work of excavation was begun seventy-five years ago by the Duchess of Devonshire, who spent the last years of her life in Rome, and formed the centre of its brilliant society. Napoleon III., the late Emperor of the French, carried on the task thus auspiciously commenced, for the purpose of shedding light upon the parts of Roman history connected with Julius Cæsar, the hero of his book. In spite of much opposition from the Papal Government, the work of exhumation was continued in fits and starts after the French emperor had given it up; and ever since the Italian Government have taken the matter in hand, gangs of labourers under the directorship of the accomplished Signor Rosa have been more or less continually employed, with the result that almost the whole area has been laid bare from the Capitol to the Arch of Titus. The British Archæological Society of Rome has given valuable aid according to the funds in its possession, and the contributions sent from this country for the purpose. When first commenced, the changes caused by these excavations were regarded with no favourable eye by either the artists or the people of Rome. The trees were cut down, the mantle of verdure that for centuries had covered the spot—Nature's appropriate pall for the decay of art—was ruthlessly torn up, and great unsightly holes and heaps of débris utterly destroyed the picturesque beauty of the scene. But the loss to romance was a gain to knowledge; and now that the greatest part of the Forum has been cleared down to the ancient pavement, we are able to form a much more vivid and accurate conception of what the place must have been in the days of the empire, and are in a position to identify buildings which previously had been a theme for endless and violent disputes. It is a very interesting and suggestive coincidence that the Forum of Rome should have been thus disentombed at the very time that Italy rose from its grave of ages, and under a free and enlightened government, having its centre once more in the Eternal City, proved that it had inherited no small share of the spirit of the heroic past.

Let us go over in brief detail the various objects of interest that may now be seen in the centre of Roman greatness. Numerous sources of information exist which enable us to identify these monuments, and to form some idea of what they were in their prime. Among these may be mentioned coins and medals of the emperors, with representations upon them of buildings and sculptures in the Forum; a marble stone found at Ancyra, now Angouri in Phrygia, on which is a long inscription regarding the acts and achievements of Augustus, which is of the greatest value in determining the topography of the city; the bas-reliefs on the Arch of Constantine, and on the marble screens of Trajan, recently excavated in the Forum itself, giving a view of its north-western and south-eastern ends; and the remains of the antique marble plan of Rome, now preserved in the Capitoline Museum, originally affixed to the wall of the superb Temple of Rome, and discovered in fragments in 1867 in the garden of the monastery of SS. Cosma e Damiano. We also get most valuable help in the work of identification from the Itineraries of the middle ages—especially from that of the celebrated pilgrim from Einsiedlen, Zwingli's town in Switzerland—who visited Rome in the eighth century, and left his manuscript to his own abbey, where it may still be seen. A vast apparatus of learning has been accumulated from the works of ancient classic authors by the great scholars who have written on the historical localities and buildings of the Forum, from Donati to Becker. Nibby, Canina, Ampère, Bunsen, Plattner, and Uhrlich, in their magnificent works have supplied a mine of wealth from which most subsequent writers on the Forum have enriched their descriptions.

The direction of the Forum is nearly from north to south, trending a little from north-east to south-west. It is surprisingly small to have contained such a large number of buildings, and to have bulked so prominently in the eye of the world; its greatest length being only six hundred and seventy-one feet, and its greatest breadth about two hundred and two feet. Beginning at the north end, we see before us the vast mass of the ancient Capitol, the proudest symbol of the majesty of Rome, crowned with the great staring medieval structures of the Roman municipality, rising up into the campanile of Michael Angelo. Until of late years, this renowned building was completely buried beneath a huge mound of rubbish. Now that it has been removed, the venerable fabric stands out distinctly to view, and we behold the massive walls of the Treasury, the Record Office, and the Senate House. The lowest part, constructed of huge blocks of volcanic stones, was the Ærarium or Public Treasury, and is supposed to have been formed out of the original wall of the city of the Sabines, which surrounded the hill of Saturn, as the Capitoline Mount was originally called, long before Romulus laid the foundation of Rome. As the Roman army was paid in coppers, spacious cellars were required for storing the coin, and these were provided in the underground vaults of the Treasury, partially cut out of the volcanic rock of the Capitol, on which the building rests. Above the Treasury, on the second floor, we see the remains of the Doric portico of the Tabularium or Public Record Office, where the records of Rome, engraved upon bronze tablets, were kept. The place is now converted into an architectural museum, where all the most interesting sculptured fragments found in the Forum are preserved, and are exhibited by gaslight owing to the darkness. These buildings, it must be remembered, form the back of the Capitol fronting the Forum. Strictly speaking, they do not belong to the Forum, which should be traced only from their verge.

The view on the other side of the Capitol, where a gently-inclined staircase leads up from the streets to the piazza at the top, surrounded by the modern municipal buildings, raised upon the ancient substructures above described, is quite different. But the present aspect of the Capitol is quite disappointing to one who comes to it seeking for evidences of its former grandeur. There is no trace of the Temple of Jupiter Capitolinus, to which the triumphal processions of the Roman armies led up, gorgeous with all the attractions of marble architecture, and the richest spoils of the world, the most splendid monument of human pride which the world then contained. Probably its remains were used up in the construction of the gloomy old church of the Ara Coeli, which is supposed by most archæologists to stand upon its site. The Capitol, it may be remarked, was precisely similar to the moot-hill, or open-air court, which existed in our own country in primitive times, and where justice was administered at regular intervals. The tradition of this original use of it still clings to the place as a shadow from the past. The hill has always been appropriated for political purposes. It has continued from the earliest days to be a centre of secular as opposed to ecclesiastical authority. The Popes ceded it to the magistracy, whose municipal buildings now cover it, and placed the church of Ara Coeli—the only one ever built on the Capitoline Hill—under their protection. The place of execution was chosen conveniently near to this moot-hill, or seat of justice; and the criminal, when condemned, was speedily executed, by being hurled over the rock, just outside of the eastern rampart, which surrounded the settlement. We can thus easily understand the association of the Tarpeian Rock with the Capitoline Hill. They were as closely correlated as the moot-hill and the Gallow hill in our own country. The primitive method of execution derived a sanctity from its antiquity, and was continued far on into the most civilised times of the empire.

So densely crowded were the historical buildings and remarkable sites in that part of the Forum which lay immediately behind the Capitol, that it is almost impossible now to identify their position or remains. This spot forms the great battle-ground of the antiquaries, whose conclusions in many instances are mere guess-work. Below the medieval tower of the Capitol is a wide space paved with fragments of coloured marbles, and with indications of the ground-plan of a building. This is supposed to mark the site of the Temple of Concord, erected by the great general Camillus, after the expulsion of the Gauls, to perpetuate the concord between the plebeians and patricians on the vexed question of the election of consuls. It was placed beside the old meeting-place of the privileged families. From the charred state of some of its sculptures discovered on the spot, it is supposed to have been destroyed by fire. It was restored and enlarged a hundred and twenty years before Christ by the Consul Opimius immediately after the murder of Caius Gracchus. To the classical student it is specially interesting as the place where Cicero convoked the senate after the discovery of the Catiline conspiracy, for the purpose of fixing the punishment due to one of the greatest of crimes. Among the senators present on that memorable occasion were men of the highest political and philosophical renown, including Cæsar, Cato, and Cicero. They came to the conclusion that there was no such thing as retribution beyond the grave, no future state of consciousness, no immortality of the soul; consequently death was considered too mild a punishment for the impious treason of the conspirators; and a penalty, which should keep alive instead of extinguishing suffering, was advocated. We learn from this extraordinary argument, as Merivale well says, how utter was the religious scepticism among the brightest intellects of Rome only thirty-seven years before the coming of Christ. The very name of the temple itself, dedicated not to a divine being as in a more pious age, but to a mere political abstraction, a mere symbol of a compact effected between two discordant parties in the state, indicated how greatly the Romans had declined from their primitive faith.

But the most conspicuous of the ancient remains in this quarter, and the first to attract the notice of every visitor, is the Ionic portico of eight columns, called at first the Temple of Jupiter, and then of Vespasian, but now definitely determined to be the Temple of Saturn, for it is closely connected with the Ærarium, and the Ærarium is said by several ancient authors to have led into the podium of the temple by a doorway in its wall still visible. This temple is supposed to be of very early origin, and to have marked the site of an ancient Sabine altar to the oldest of the gods of Italy long before the arrival of the Romans. It was nearly entire so late as the fifteenth century; but its cella was ruthlessly destroyed shortly afterwards, and its marble ornaments used for making lime. The present group of pillars was so clumsily restored by the French at the beginning of this century that they are seen to differ from each other in diameter, and the frieze is composed of fragments that do not harmonise.

But the most remarkable monument of antiquity in this part is the marble triumphal Arch of Septimius Severus, which stands in front of the ruins of the Temple of Concord. It invaded the site of the republican Græcostasis, where foreign ambassadors waited for an audience of the senate, and occupied part of the area of the Comitium, whose original character was thereby destroyed; for it was erected at a time when men ceased to care for the venerable associations connected with the early history of their city. One gazes upon this monument of Roman power and pride with deep respect, for it has stood nearly seventeen centuries; and though rusty and sorely battered, and its sculptures much mutilated, it is still one of the most solid and perfect relics of imperial times. It was raised to commemorate the wars of Septimius Severus in Parthia and Arabia, and represents among its carvings the goddess Rome receiving the homage of the Eastern nations. It exhibits on its panels many scenes connected with his campaigns, the memory of which no humane man would have liked to perpetuate. On the upper part of the Arch is a large inscription in honour of the emperor and his two sons, Caracalla and Geta. The name of Geta, however, was afterwards erased by his brother when he had murdered him, and other words substituted. Marks of the erasure may still be seen perfectly distinct after all these centuries, and vividly recall the terrible associations of the incident. The dislike which Caracalla and Geta had for each other was so virulent that their father took them both with him to Britain, in order that they might forget their mutual animosity while engaged in active warfare. Septimius Severus died during this campaign at York, and his sons returned to Rome to work out soon after the domestic tragedy of which this Arch reminds us. On the top of the Arch there was originally a bronze group of a chariot and four horses, with the emperor and his sons driving it. But this was removed at an early date; and in the middle ages the summit of the Arch supported the campanile of the church of St. Sergius and Bacchus that was built up against its sides. A little to the left, the road passing under the Arch joins the Clivus Capitolinus which wound through the Forum, and led up to the great Temple of Jupiter on the Capitol. The pavement of this ancient road, which still exists, is formed of broad hexagonal slabs of lava, and is as smooth and as finely jointed at this day as when the triumphal processions of the victorious Roman generals used to pass over it.

At the western corner of the Arch of Severus are the scanty remains of a tall conical pyramid, about fifteen feet in diameter, which is identified as the Umbilicus Romæ, placed in the exact centre of old Rome. Not far from it stood the Milliarium Aureum, or Golden Milestone, on which were inscribed all the distances of roads without the walls. The Roman roads throughout the empire terminated at this point. With this central milestone was connected that admirable system of roads which the Romans constructed in our distant island; and it is a remarkable circumstance that the principal railway lines in England are identical with the general direction of the old Roman roads. The Antonine Way is now the Great Western Railway, and the Roman Watling Street, which ran diagonally across the country from Chester in the northwest to Dover in the south-east, is now replaced by the Dover, London, Birmingham, Grand Junction, Chester, and Crewe Railways. The reason of this union of ancient and modern lines of communication is obvious. The Romans formed their roads for the purpose of transporting their armies from place to place, and at certain distances along the roads a series of military stations were established. In course of time these stations became villages, towns, and cities such as Chester, Leicester, Lancaster, Manchester. Thus, strange as it may appear, the Milliarium Aureum of the Roman Forum has had much to do with the origin of our most ancient and important towns, and with the formation of the great lines of railway that now carry on the enormous traffic between them.

The exposed vaults immediately behind the Arch of Severus, bounding the Forum in this direction, are richly draped with the long, delicate fronds of the maidenhair fern. Shaded from the sun, it grows here in the crevices of the old walls in greater luxuriance and profusion than elsewhere in the city. There is something almost pathetic in this association of the frailest of Nature's productions with the ruins of the most enduring of man's works. Strength that is crumbling to dust and ashes, and tender beauty that ever clings to the skirts of time, as she steps over the sepulchres of power, have here in their combination a deep significance. The growth of the soft fern on the mouldering old stones seems like the sad, sweet smile of Nature over a decay with which she sympathises, but which she cannot share. The same feeling took possession of me when, wandering over the ruins of the Palaces of the Cæsars on a sunny February afternoon, I saw above the hoary masses of stone the rose-tinted bloom of almond-trees. Out of the gray relics of man's highest hour of pride, the leafless almond-rod blossomed as of old in the holy place of the Hebrew Tabernacle; and its miracle of colour and tenderness was like the crimson glow that lingers at sunset upon Alpine heights, telling of a glory that had long vanished from the spot.

Beneath these fern-draped vaults is the oldest prison in the world. The celebrated Mamertine Prison takes us back to the very foundation of the city. It was regarded in the time of the Cæsars as one of the most ancient relics of Rome, and was invested with peculiar interest because of its venerable associations. It consists of a series of vaults excavated out of the solid tufa rock, where it slopes down from the Capitoline Hill into the Forum, each lined with massive blocks of red volcanic stone. For a long time these vaults have been used as cellars under a row of tall squalid-looking houses built over them between the Via di Marforio and the Vicolo del Ghettarello; and the sense of smell gives convincing proof that where prisoners of state used to be confined, provisions of wine, cheese, and oil have been stored. The prison has recently passed into the possession of the British and American Archæological Society of Rome, which pays a certain rent to the Italian Government for its use. By this society it is illuminated and shown every Monday afternoon during the season. One of the members conducts the party through the upper and lower prisons, and explains everything of interest connected with them. Dr. Parker, whose labours have done so much to elucidate this part of ancient Rome, was the guide on the occasion of my visit; and as the party was unusually small, we had a better opportunity of seeing what was to be seen, and hearing the guide's observations.

The uppermost vault is still below the level of the surrounding soil, and the entrance to it is by the church of San Giuseppe di Falegnami, the patron of the Roman joiners, built over it. Beneath is a subterranean chapel, forming a sort of crypt to the upper church, called San Pietro in Carcere, containing a curious ancient crucifix, an object of great veneration, and hung round with blazing lamps and rusty daggers, pistols, and other deadly instruments, the votive offerings of bandits and assassins who sought at this shrine of the chief of the apostles to make their peace with heaven. Descending from the chapel by a flight of steps we come through a modern door, opened through the wall for the convenience of the pilgrims who annually visit the sacred spot in crowds, to the ancient vestibule, or grand chamber of the prison, commonly called the Prison of St. Peter from the church tradition which asserts that the great apostle was confined here by order of Nero before his martyrdom. The pillar to which he was bound is still pointed out in the cell; and Dr. Parker, lifting up its cover, showed us a well in the pavement of the floor, which is said to have sprung up miraculously to furnish water for the baptism of the jailors Processus and Martinianus whom he had converted, though, unfortunately for this tradition, the fountain is described by Plutarch as existing in the time of Jugurtha's imprisonment. Indeed there is every reason to believe that this chamber was originally a well-house or a subterranean cistern for collecting water at the foot of the Capitol, from which circumstance it derived its name of Tullianum, from tullius, the old Etruscan word for spring, and not from Servius Tullius, who was erroneously supposed to have built it. The whole chamber in primitive times was filled with water, and the hole in the roof was used for drawing it out. Dr. Parker gave us a little of the water in a goblet, but, notwithstanding its sacred reputation, it tasted very much like ordinary water, being very cool and fresh, with a slight medicinal taste. He also pointed our attention to a rugged hollow in the wall of the staircase, and told us that this was the print of St. Peter's head in the hard stone, said to have been produced as he stumbled and fell against it, coming down the stair a chained prisoner. It requires no small amount of devotional credulity to recognise the likeness or to believe the story.

But there is no need for having recourse to such ecclesiastical legends in order to produce a solemn impression in this chamber. Its classical associations are sufficient of themselves to powerfully affect the imagination. There is no reason to doubt the common belief that this is the identical cell in which the famous Jugurtha was starved to death. The romantic history of this African king is familiar to all readers of Sallust, who gives a masterly account of the Jugurthine war. When finally defeated, after having long defied the Roman army, his person was. taken possession of by treachery and carried in chains to Rome, where he adorned the triumphal procession of his conqueror Marius, and was finally cast into this cell, perishing there of cold and hunger. What a terrible ending to the career of a fierce, free soldier, who had spent his life on horseback in the boundless sultry deserts of Western Africa! The temperature of the place is exceedingly damp and chill. Jugurtha himself, when stripped of his clothes by the executioners, and let down into it from the hole in the roof, exclaimed with grim humour, "By Hercules, how cold your bath is!" A more hideous and heart-breaking dungeon it is impossible to imagine. Not a ray of light can penetrate the profound darkness of this living tomb. Sallust spoke of the appearance of it in his day, from the filth, the gloom, and the smell, as simply terrific. The height of the vault is about sixteen feet, its length thirty feet, and its breadth twenty-two feet. It is cased with huge masses of volcanic stone, arranged in courses, converging towards the roof, not on the principle of the arch, but extending horizontally to a centre, as we see in some of the Etruscan tombs. This peculiar style of construction proves the very high antiquity of the chamber.

This cell played the same part in Roman history which the Tower of London has done in our own. Here, by the orders of Cicero, were strangled Lentulus, Cethegus, and one or two more of the accomplices of Catiline, in his famous conspiracy. Here was murdered, under circumstances of great baseness, Vercingetorix, the young and gallant chief of the Gauls, whose bravery called forth the highest qualities of Julius Cæsar's military genius, and who, when success abandoned his arms, boldly gave himself up as an offering to appease the anger of the Romans. Here perished Sejanus, the minister and son-in-law of Tiberius, who was detected in a conspiracy against the emperor, and richly deserved his fate on account of his cruelty and treachery. Here also was put to death Simon Bar-Gioras, the governor of the revolted Jews during the last dreadful siege of Jerusalem, who was taken prisoner, and after gracing the triumph of the emperor Titus at Rome, shared the fate which usually happened to captives after such an exhibition.

From the Tullianum or Prison of St. Peter, we were led through a tortuous subterranean passage of Etruscan character, a hundred yards long, cut out of the rock. It was so low that we had to stoop all the way, and in some places almost to creep, and so narrow that a very stout person would have some difficulty in forcing himself through. The floor was here and there wet with the overflowing of neighbouring drains, which exhaled a noisome smell; and we had to pick our steps carefully through thick greasy mud, which on the slopes was very slippery and disagreeable. We followed each other in Indian file, stooping low, each with a wax taper burning dimly in the damp atmosphere, and presenting a most picturesque appearance. This passage was discovered only a few years ago. Numerous passages of a similar nature are said to penetrate the volcanic rock on which the Capitol stands, in every direction, like the galleries of an ant's nest. Some of these have been exposed, and others walled up. They connect the Prison with the Cloaca, and doubtless furnished means by which the bodies of criminals who had been executed might be secretly disposed of. The passage in question brought us to four other chambers, each darker and more dismal than the other, and partially filled with heaps of rubbish and masses of stone that had fallen from their roofs and sides. At the top of each vault there was a man-hole for letting a prisoner down with cords into it. A visit to these six vaults of the Mamertine Prison gives one an idea that can never be forgotten of the cruelty and tyranny which underlay all the gorgeous despotism of Rome, alike in the kingly, republican, and imperial periods. Some of the remains may still be seen of the Scalæ Gemoniæ, the "steps of sighs," down which the bodies of those who were executed were thrown, to be exposed to the insults of the populace. The only circumstance that relieves the intolerable gloom of the associations of the Prison is, that Nævius is said to have written two of his plays while he was confined in it for his attacks on the aristocracy; a circumstance which links it to the Tower of London, which has also its literary reminiscences. After having been immured so long in such disagreeable physical darkness — appropriate emblem of the deeds of horror committed in it — we were truly glad to catch at last a faint glimmer of daylight shimmering into the uppermost passage, and to emerge into the open sunshine, from beneath a house at the farther end of the Vicolo del Ghettarello.

A modern carriage-road used to pass along this way, leading up to the Piazza del Campidoglio in front of the Capitol, and cutting the Forum into two parts, concealing a considerable portion of it. This obstruction has now been swept away, and the Forum is fully exposed from end to end. Below this old road we observe the "nameless column" of Childe Harold, which long stood with its base buried, and was taken for the ruins of a temple. When excavated in 1813 it was found to stand on an isolated pedestal, with an inscription recording that it was erected by the exarch Smaragdus to the emperor Phocas; and the mode in which the offering was made was worthy of the infamous subject and the venal dedicator. Nothing can be clearer from the style of the monument than that it was stolen from the Temple of Vespasian adjoining; for it is an exact fellow of the three graceful Corinthian pillars still standing in front of the Ærarium. It was near this pillar, a few years after it was raised, that Gregory the Great, before he became Pope, saw the young Saxon captives exposed to be sold as slaves, and was so struck with their innocent looks and hopeless fate that he asked about their nationality and religion. Being told that they were Angli, he said, "Non Angli, sed Angeli." The impression made upon him led to a mission for converting the natives of Britain, which set out from Rome under St. Augustine in 596. Thus does the column of the infamous usurper Phocas link itself on the historic page with the conversion of Britain to Christianity.

Beside the Pillar of Phocas are two large marble screens or parapets, with magnificent bas-reliefs sculptured on both sides. They were discovered about sixteen years ago in situ, and are among the most interesting and important objects that have been brought to light by the recent excavations in the Forum. Their peculiar form has given rise to much controversy; some antiquarians regarding them as an avenue along which voters went up to the poll at the popular elections of consuls, designed either to preserve the voters from the pressure of the mob, or to prevent any but properly qualified persons from getting admission; while others believe that the passage between the double screen led to an altar. This latter opinion seems the more plausible one, for the sculptures on one side represent the suovetaurilia—a bull, a ram, and a boar, adorned with ribbons and vittæ, walking in file, which were usually sacrificed for the purification of Rome at the Lustrum, as the census taken every five years was called. The other sculptures on the marble screens consist of a number of human figures in greater or less relief; one of them being supposed to commemorate the provision made by Trajan for the children of poor or deceased citizens in the orphanage which he was the first to found in Rome; and the other, the burning of the deeds which contained the evidence of the public debt of the Roman citizens, which the emperor generously cancelled. But the chief significance of the sculptures lies in their background of architectural and other objects indicating the locality of the scenes represented. They place before us a view of the Forum as it appeared in the time of Trajan, and enable us to identify the various objects which then crowded it, and to fix their relative position. The topographical importance of these reliefs has been well discussed by Signor Brizio and Professor Henzen in the Proceedings of the Roman Archæological Institute; and also in a paper read by Mr. Nichols before the Society of Antiquaries in London in 1875. By translating into perspective their somewhat conventional representations of temples, basilicas, and arches, Mr. Nichols has given us in his monograph on the subject two very effective pictorial restorations of the Forum as it was in the days of Trajan. Both the screens exhibit, very distinctly sculptured, a fig-tree and a statue on a pedestal, which are interesting from their classical associations. The tree is not the famous Ruminal fig-tree originally of the Palatine and then of the Comitium, but, as Pliny tells us, a self-sown tree which grew in the mid Forum on the site of the Lake of Curtius, which in Ovid's time, as we learn from himself, was a dry space of natural ground marked off by a low fence, and including an altar. This fig-tree, along with a vine and an olive, which grew associated with it, was much prized on account of the shade which it afforded. The figure under the fig-tree, carrying a vine stem on its left shoulder, and uplifting its right arm, has been recognised as that of Marsyas, whose statue was often put in market-places as an emblem of plenty and indulgence. Martial, Horace, Seneca, and Pliny all alluded to this statue in the Forum, which stood near the edge of the Lake of Curtius, and was crowned with garlands by Julia, the daughter of Augustus, during her disgraceful assignations beside it with her lovers at night.

On the east side of the Forum the excavations have been stopped in the meantime, as the modern level of the ground is occupied by valuable houses, and two very interesting old churches, Santa Martina and Sta. Adriano. Under the part not yet exhumed lie the remains of the earliest of all the Basilicas, the Basilica of Porcia, built by the elder Cato in the immediate vicinity of the Curia, and also those of the famous Basilica Æmilia, which probably extended along the greater part of the east side of the Forum. Some of the most important monuments of ancient Rome, known to us only by the writings of classic authors, doubtless lie buried in this locality. Under the church of Sta. Adriano, the famous Curia Hostilia or Senate House, attributed to Tullus Hostilius, stood. The original building was destroyed by fire at the funeral of Clodius, through the carelessness of the populace, who insisted upon burning his body within it; but it was replaced by the Curia Julia, which was rebuilt by Augustus, who added to it an important structure, called in the Ancyran inscription Chalcidicum, for the convenience of the senators. Around it stood the statues of men who had rendered important services to the state; and not far off was an altar and statue of Victory, which formed the last rallying-ground of expiring paganism against the dominating Christianity of the empire. In the year 382 the Christian party had removed this altar and statue; and when their restoration was demanded by Symmachus, the request was refused by Ambrose, as opposed to the conscience of the Christian senators; and this decision being ratified by the votes of the assembly, the doom of paganism, as the national religion, was in consequence sealed. The Curia Julia ceased to serve its original purpose at the death of Caligula, when the consuls convoked the senate in the Capitol instead, to mark their aversion to the rule of the Cæsars; and the building was probably burnt down and finally rebuilt in the time of Diocletian. One of the most curious uses to which it was put, was to mark the Suprema tempestas, which closed the hours of legal business, by means of its shadow projected on the pavement; a primitive mode of reckoning time which existed before the first Punic war, and was afterwards superseded by a sun-dial and a clepsydra or water-clock erected in the Forum.

Near the Curia under the present roadway must lie the site of the Comitium, or meeting-place of the Roman burgesses. This was far the most important spot in the Forum in the days of the Republic. It was not a covered building, but a templum or a consecrated space open to the air. In its area grew a fig-tree, in commemoration of the sacred tree which sheltered Romulus and Remus in their infancy; and we read of drops of blood and milk falling upon it as omens from the sky. One of the stones on its pavement, from its extraordinary blackness, was called the tombstone of Romulus, and a number of statues adorned its sides, including the three Sibyls, which gave the name of "In Tria Fata" down to medieval times to this part of the Forum. From its rostra, or stone platform, addresses were delivered by political agitators to open-air assemblies of the people. The Comitium reminds us very strikingly of the municipal origin of the Roman empire. In primitive times that mode of government was admirably adapted to the necessities of the city; but when Rome became mistress of the world it was found unfitted to discharge imperial functions. The establishment of the monarchical form of Government overthrew the Comitium, and with it the very life of the Roman city.

In front of the church of S. Adriano—said to be no other than the actual Curia of Diocletian, though greatly altered and partly rebuilt by Pope Honorius I. in the year 630—are some fragments of the Basilica Æmilia. This court was erected on the site of the Basilica Fulvia, and superseded by a more splendid building called the Basilica Pauli, which was the Bourse or

Exchange of ancient Rome. The building of this last Basilica was interrupted for a long time by the disorders consequent on the assassination of Cæsar. When finished, it was considered to be one of the most magnificent buildings in the world; and was especially admired on account of its beautiful columns of Phrygian marble. These were afterwards removed to decorate the church of St. Paul outside the gate, where some of them that survived the burning of the old edifice may be seen behind the high altar of the new. Between the Curia and the Basilica Æmilia is supposed to have stood the celebrated Temple of Janus, built according to Livy by Numa Pompilius, the closing or opening of which was the signal of peace or war. It was probably at first one of the ancient gates in a line of fortifications uniting the Capitol with the Palatine; and afterwards comprised, besides a passage-way through which a great part of the traffic of Rome passed, a diminutive bronze temple containing a bronze statue of the venerable deity of the Sabines, whose one face looked to the east, and the other to the west. The bronze gates of the temple were closed by Augustus for the third time after the battle of Actium, and finally shut when Christianity became the religion of the empire. Procopius saw the temple still standing in the sixth century; and he tells us that, during the siege of the city by the Goths, when it was defended by Belisarius, some of the adherents of the old pagan superstition made a secret attempt to open the shrine and set the god at liberty.

One gazes at the wall of earth and rubbish, fifteen feet deep, marking the present limit of the excavations in this direction, with a profound longing that the obstruction could be removed at once, and the rich antiquarian treasures lying hid underneath brought to light. Few things in Rome appealed more powerfully to my curiosity than this huge bank of débris, behind and beneath which imagination was free to picture all kinds of possibilities. On the part that has been uncovered, we see a row of brick bases on which had stood monuments of gilt bronze to some of the distinguished men of Rome; the remains of a line of shops of the third century demolished during the excavations; the pedestal of what is said by some to have been Domitian's and by others Constantine's gigantic equestrian statue; and farther down, rude heaps of masonry, belonging to the substructures of the Rostra and Temple of Julius Cæsar. Part of the curved wall of the Rostra may still be seen built of large blocks of travertine; and in front is a fixed platform, where a large number of people could stand and listen to the speaker. This Rostra is specially interesting because it was constructed in the year of Cæsar's death, and was intended to mark the design of the great triumvir to destroy the memory of the old oligarchy by separating the rostra or "hustings" from their former connection with the senate and comitia, and make them entirely popular institutions. The front of it was afterwards adorned by Augustus with the beaks of ships taken at Actium. The small Heroön or Temple of Cæsar behind the Rostra was erected on the spot where the body of Cæsar was burned before the house which he had so long inhabited, and in a part of the Forum especially associated with his greatest political triumphs. It superseded an altar and lofty column of Numidian marble, at which the people had previously offered sacrifices to the memory of their idol, the first mortal in Rome raised to the rank of the gods; an honour justified, they imagined, not only by his great deeds, but also by his alleged descent from Venus Anadyomene.

Running down the middle of the Forum is a rough, ancient causeway, with its blocks of lava still in their original position, but so disjointed that it is no easy task walking over them. On the other side is the raised platform of the Basilica Julia of Augustus, extending from north to south, the whole length of the Forum, with steps leading up to it from the paved street. This stupendous law court, the grandest in Rome where Trajan sat to administer justice, and from whose roof Caligula day after day lavishly threw down money to the people, has, by its own identity being established beyond dispute, more than any other discovery helped to determine the topography of the Roman Forum. It was begun by Julius Cæsar on the site of the older Basilica Sempronia, which had previously partially replaced the Veteres Tabernæ or shops of early times required for the trades carried on in a market-place, and also the schools for children where Appius Claudius had first seen Virginia reading. Having been partially destroyed by fire, Augustus afterwards completed and greatly enlarged the building. It was used as the place of meeting of the Centumviri, a court which we learn from the younger Pliny, who himself practised before it, had a hundred and eight judges sitting in four separate tribunals, within sight and hearing of one another, like the old courts in Westminster Hall. The Basilica is not yet entirely excavated, a large part of its breadth being still under modern buildings. It consisted of a series of plain, massive arches built of travertine. The pavement is wonderfully perfect, being composed of a mosaic pattern of valuable marbles, doubtless saved from destruction or removal to build some church or palace by the fortunate circumstance that the ruins of the Basilica covered and concealed them at an early period. On this pavement and on the steps leading up to it are incised numerous squares and circles which are supposed to have been tabulæ lusoriæ, or gaming-tables. A few have inscriptions near them alluding to their use. Cicero mentions the dice-players of the Forum with reprobation; and the fact that such sports should have intruded into the courts of justice shows that the Romans had lost at this time their early veneration for the law. The rows of brick arches seen on the platform are mere modern restorations, placed there by Cavaliere Rosa to indicate the supposed original plan of the building. At the south end of it an opening in the pavement shows a part of the Cloaca Maxima, with the sewerage passing through it underneath.

The ancient street between the Basilica Julia and the Temple of Castor and Pollux, is undoubtedly the famous Vicus Tuscus, so called after the Etruscan soldiers who belonged to the army of Porsenna, and, being defeated at Ariccia, took refuge in this part of Rome. This street, so often mentioned by classic writers, led to the Circus Maximus, and is now identified with the Via dei Fienili; the point of departure from the Forum being marked by a statue of Vertumnus, the Etruscan god, the ruined pedestal of which, in all likelihood, is that which has lately been unveiled on the steps at the north-east corner of the Basilica Julia. It was considered almost as sacred as the Via Sacra itself, being the route taken by the great procession of the Circensian games, in which the statues of the gods were carried in cars from the Capitol through the Forum to the circus. In front of the Basilica Julia, and on the opposite side of the way, so numerous were the statues which Julius Cæsar contrived to crowd together, that the Emperor Constantine, during his famous visit to Rome, is said to have been almost stupefied with amazement. Some such feeling is produced in our own minds when we reflect that the bewildering array of sculptures in the Roman galleries, admired by a concourse of pilgrims from every country, are but chance discoveries, unnoticed by history, and of no account in their own time. What must have been the feast of splendour of which these are but the crumbs!

Perhaps the most beautiful of the ruins of the Forum are the three marble columns of the Temple of Castor and Pollux near the Basilica Julia. They are the only prominent objects on the south-west side of the Forum, and at once arrest the eye by their matchless symmetry and grace. Time has dealt very hardly with them, battering their shapely columns and rich Corinthian capitals, and discolouring their pure white Pentelic marble. But it has not succeeded in destroying their wonderful beauty; and the russet hues with which they have been stained by the long lapse of the ages have rather added to them the charm of antique picturesqueness. They rest upon a huge mound of broken masonry, in the interstices of which Nature has sown her seeds of minute life, which spread over it a tender pall of bright vegetation. The three columns are bound together by iron rods, and still further kept in position by the fragments of architrave and cornice supported by them. They are forty-eight feet in height and nearly five feet in diameter, while their flutings are nine inches across. Around the basement a large quantity of broken columns, capitals, and pedestals has been disinterred, some of which have acquired an historic renown on account of the purposes which they have served in the fine arts. Michael Angelo converted one huge fragment into the pedestal of the celebrated bronze equestrian statue of Marcus Aurelius, which he transferred from its original site in front of the Arch of Septimius Severus, where it had stood for thirteen or fourteen centuries, to the front of the Capitol; while out of another fragment Raphael carved the well-known statue of Jonah sitting on a whale, to be seen in the Chigi Chapel of Sta. Maria del Popolo, the only piece of sculpture executed by the immortal painter. The Italian Government has entirely excavated the ruins, and thus set at rest the numerous controversies among antiquaries regarding its true name.

The temple of Castor and Pollux probably dates as far back as the year 487 before Christ, when the dictator Postumius vowed to build a monument in commemoration of his victory at the great battle of Lake Regillus, with which the mythical history of Rome closes. It recalls the well-known romantic legend of the mysterious interference of the Dioscuri in that memorable struggle which Macaulay has woven into one of the most spirited of his Lays. The temple is supposed to have been erected on the spot where the divine Twins announced the victory to the people in the Forum at the close of the day. About twenty feet from the eastern corner of the temple are slight remains of a shallow oval basin, which has been identified as the lake or fountain of Juturna, the wife of Janus, the Sabine war-god, where the Dioscuri washed their armour and horses from the blood and dust of the fray. It was probably at first a natural spring gushing out of the tufa rock of the Palatine Hill, but being dried up, it became in later times a lacus or basin artificially supplied with water. For long ages afterwards the anniversary of the great battle was celebrated every year on the fifteenth of July by a splendid pageant worthy of the greatness of the empire. The Roman knights, clothed in purple robes, and crowned with olive wreaths, and bearing their trophies, first offered sacrifice in the shrine of Castor and Pollux, and then formed a procession, in which five thousand persons sometimes took part, which filed in front of the temple and marched through the city.

The original building having stood for nearly five hundred years, it began to exhibit signs of decay, and accordingly it was rebuilt upon the old foundations by Augustus, and dedicated by Tiberius. The podium or mass of rubble masonry therefore which we see beneath the three columns at the present day belongs to the time of the kings, while the columns themselves belong to the imperial period. Caligula used the temple as a vestibule to his palace on the Palatine Hill immediately behind. On the brow of that hill, separated only by the pavement of the modern street, projects a labyrinth of vaults, arches, and broken walls, a mighty maze of desolation without a plan, so interspersed with verdure and foliage that "it looks as much a landscape as a ruin." This is supposed to be the palace of Caligula; and its remains abundantly attest the extraordinary magnificence of this imperial domain, which contained all that was rich and rare from the golden East, from beyond the snowy Alps, and from Greece, the home of art. The substructions of this mighty ruin are truly astonishing; they are so vast, so massive, so enduring, that they seem as if built by giants. Concealed by modern houses built up against the foot of the palace, some of the remains of the famous bridge which Caligula threw obliquely over the Forum can be made out; two of the tall brick piers are visible above the houses, and in the gable of the outer house the spring of one of the arches can be distinctly seen. The bridge was constructed by Caligula for the purpose of connecting his palace with the Capitol, on the summit of which stood the magnificent Temple of Jupiter, so that, as he said himself, he might be able to converse conveniently with his colleague, the greatest of the gods! It is probable that it served more than one purpose; that it was used both as an aqueduct and a road for horses and chariots from the Palatine to the Capitol. Be this as it may, it must have been a stupendous structure, nearly a quarter of a mile long, and about a hundred feet high, striding over the whole diagonal of the Forum, with a double or triple tier of arches, like the remains of the Claudian aqueduct that spans the Campagna.

The immediate vicinity of the Temple of Castor and Pollux is full of interest to the classical student. To the right of it are the remains of the Regia or Royal Palace, the official residence of the early kings of Rome, and afterwards, during the whole period of the Republic, of the Pontifex Maximus, as the real head of the State as well as the Church. Numa Pompilius resided here in the hope that, by occupying neutral ground, he might conciliate the Latins of the Palatine and the Sabines of the Capitoline Hills. It was also the home of Julius Cæsar during the greater part of his life, where Calpurnia, his wife, dreamed that the pediment of the house had fallen down, and the sacred weapons in the Sacrarium were stirred by a supernatural power; an omen that was but too truly fulfilled when Cæsar went forth to the Forum on the fatal Ides of March, and was carried back a bloody corpse from the Curia of Pompey. It ceased to become the residence of the Pontifex when Augustus bought the house of Hortensius on the Palatine, and elected to dwell there instead; and was therefore given over to the Vestal Virgins to increase their scanty accommodation. The Atrium Vestæ, or convent of the Vestal Virgins, adjoined the Regia, and behind it, along the lower slope of the Palatine, stretched the sacred grove of Vesta, which seems to have been used as a place of privileged interment for the sisterhood, as a number of gravestones with the names of vestal virgins upon them were found in digging the foundations of the church of Sta. Maria Liberatrice in the seventeenth century. The residence of the Pontifex

Maximus and of the Vestal Virgins, who were regarded as the highest and holiest personages in the State, gave an air of great respectability to this neighbourhood, and it became in consequence the fashionable quarter of Rome. Close beside the house of the Vestal Virgins was the far-famed Temple of Vesta, in which they ministered, whose podium or basement, which is a mere circular mound of rough masonry, may be seen on the spot.

The worship of Vesta, the goddess of the household fire, was one of the most primitive forms of religion. It doubtless arose from the great difficulty in prehistoric times of producing fire by rubbing two sticks against one another. Such a flame once procured would be carefully guarded against extinction in some central spot by the unmarried women of the household, who had nothing else to do. And from this central fire all the household fires of the settlement would be obtained. A relic of this prehistoric custom existed in the rule that if the sacred vestal fire was ever allowed to go out it could only be kindled anew by the primitive process of friction. The worship of Vesta survived an old world of exhausted craters and extinct volcanoes, with which was buried a world of lost nations. The Pelasgians brought to Italy the stone of the domestic hearth, the foundation of the family, and the tombstone, the boundary of the fields divided after the death of the head of the family, the foundation of property; and upon this double base arose the great distinctive edifice of the Roman Law, the special gift of Rome to the civilisation of the world. Rhea Sylvia, mother of Romulus, was a Vestal Virgin of Alba, which shows that the worship of Vesta existed in this region long before the foundation of Rome. The origin of the first temple and of the institutions of Vestal Virgins for its service was attributed to Numa Pompilius. The first building, as Ovid tells us, was constructed with wattled walls and a thatched roof like the primitive huts of the inhabitants. It was little more than a covered fireplace. It was the public hearth of the new city, round which were gathered all the private ones. On it burned continually the sacred fire, the symbol of the life of the state, which was believed to have been brought from Troy, and the continuance of which was connected by superstition with the fortunes of Rome. In the secret penetralia of the temple, where no man was allowed to enter, was kept with scrupulous care, for its preservation was equally bound up with the safety of the empire, the Palladium, or image of Pallas, saved from the destruction of Troy, and which was supposed to have originally fallen from heaven. The circular form and the domed roof of the temple were survivals of the prehistoric huts of the Aborigines, which were invariably round, as the traces of their foundations show. With the exception of the Palladium, which remained invisible during all the ages to ordinary mortal eyes until the destructive fire in the Forum, in the reign of Commodus, compelled the Vestal Virgins to expose it in removing it for safety to the imperial court, there was in primitive times no statue or material representation of the goddess except the sacred fire in the mysterious shrine of the temple. Indeed the Romans, as Plutarch tells us, raised no statue to the gods until the year of Rome 170. In this respect the religion of the Romans, whose divinities had no participation in the life and passions of men, and had nothing to do with the human form, differed widely from the religion of the Greeks, which, inspired by the sentiment of the beautiful in man and nature, gave birth to art.

The Temple of Vesta, as might have been expected, shared in all the wonderful changes of Roman history. It was abandoned when the Gauls entered Rome, and the Vestal Virgins took the sacred fire and the Palladium to Cære in Etruria for safety. It was destroyed two hundred and forty-one years before Christ, when L. Metellus, the Pontifex Maximus at the time, saved the Palladium with the loss of his eyesight, and consequently of his priesthood, for which a statue was erected to him in the Capitol. It was consumed in the great fire of Nero, and rebuilt by Vespasian, on some of whose coins it is represented. It was finally burnt down in the fire of Commodus, which destroyed at the same time many important buildings in the Forum. The worship of Vesta was prohibited by Gratianus in the year 382 of our era, and the public maintenance of the Vestal Virgins abandoned, in spite of the protestations of Symmachus and the forlorn hope of the pagan party. Great as was the reverence paid to the shrine of Vesta, not being a temple in the proper sense of the term, as it was not consecrated by augury, it had not the right of sanctuary. Mucius Scævola, the unfortunate Pontifex Maximus, was murdered beside the altar by order of Marius, and his blood sprinkled the image of the goddess; and Piso Licinianus, the adopted son of Galba, after the assassination of that emperor beside the Curtian Lake in the Forum, was dragged out from the innermost shrine of the temple, to which he had fled for refuge, and barbarously massacred at the door. But it is impossible to dwell upon all the remarkable events with which this haunted shrine of Rome's earliest and most beautiful worship is associated. Certainly no greater object of interest has been exhumed among all the antiquities of the Eternal City than the little round mass of shapeless masonry which has been identified beyond all reasonable doubt as the basement of the world-renowned temple, the household hearth of old Rome.

Opposite the Temple of Vesta, at the north-east corner of the Forum, where it ends, is the magnificent façade of the Temple of Antoninus Pius and Faustina, the most perfect of all the Roman temples. There are six splendid Corinthian columns in front and two at the sides, each composed of a single block of green ripple-marked Cipollino marble, about forty-six feet in height and five feet in diameter, with bases and capitals of marble, originally white, but now rusty and discoloured by age; all beautifully proportioned and carved in the finest style of ancient art. These columns were buried to half their height in medieval times; and houses were built up against and between them, the marks of whose roofs are still visible in indentations near their summits. These houses were removed, and the ground excavated down to the bases of the columns in the sixteenth century by Palladio, revealing a grand flight of marble steps, twenty-one in number, leading up to the temple from the street. The excavations at that time were made for the purpose of finding marbles and building materials for the Church of St. Peter's. Two sides of the cella of the temple still remain, formed by large massive blocks of peperino, probably taken from the second wall of Rome, which must have passed very near to the east end of this temple; for the ancient Roman architects were as unscrupulous in appropriating the relics of former ages as their successors. The roughness of these walls was hidden by an outer casing of marble, ornamented with pilasters, of which only the small capitals now remain. Both the cella and the portico still retain a large portion of their magnificent marble entablature; and the frieze and cornice are richly covered with carvings of vases and candelabra, guarded by griffins, exquisite in design and execution. The marble slabs that covered the whole outside of the temple had been burnt for lime in a kiln that stood in front of the portico in the sixteenth century, and in this lime-kiln were found fragments of statues, bas-reliefs, and inscriptions, which were about to be destroyed in that barbarous fashion.

The temple was originally begun by Antoninus Pius to the memory of his unworthy wife Faustina in the year 142 of our era, but being unfinished at his death, it was dedicated by the senate to both their names. We see it represented in all its magnificence on some of the coins of this emperor. In the year 1430 Pope Martin V. built over its remains a church called S. Lorenzo in Miranda, whose singular ugliness was in striking contrast to the grandeur of the venerable ruin which embraced it. The floor of this church was ten feet above the original level of the temple, and its roof was carried twenty feet above its cornice. It contained several tombs of the Roman apothecaries, to whose Corporation it belonged. No one will regret that it has been removed; the excavations in front of it having reduced the level of the ground far below its doorway, and thus cut off the approach. It is strange to think of the two different kinds of worship carried on at such widely separated intervals within this remarkable building, first a pagan temple and then a Christian church—worship so different in name and yet so like in reality; for the divine honours paid to a mortal emperor and his wife were transferred in after ages to frail mortals such as Saint Laurence and the Virgin Mary. We are reminded by the inscription above the portico of the temple, "Divo Antonino et Divæ Faustina," that the government of the Cæsars had become an earthly omnipotence in the estimation of the Romans and the subject nations. They looked alone to Cæsar for all their good, and from him they feared their chiefest evil. He had become to them their providence or their fate. The adoration offered to him was not a mere act of homage or sign of fealty, but was most truly and in the highest sense a worship as to a divine being.

The view in this part of the Forum, looking down from the Antonine Temple, is most striking and suggestive. It reveals some of the grandest objects of ancient Rome. Immediately beyond is the hoary old church of SS. Cosma e Damiano, with mosaics of the sixth century on its tribune, built out of three ancient temples, as Dr. Parker has clearly proved — the round Temple of Romulus Maxentius, the Temple of Venus, and the Temple of Rome. The south wall of this last-mentioned temple, built of huge square blocks of tufa, to which the marble plan of Rome was fastened by metal hooks, may still be seen in the church; and it is interesting as being the last pagan temple which remained in use in Rome. Here was the last struggle of paganism with the unbelief which itself inspired. The gods of the Pantheon had lost all significance. The worship of abstract qualities, such as Concord and Victory, or of the personification of a local providence in the city of Rome itself, could not satisfy the longing of the human soul. As religion decayed the worship of the gods was superseded by the worship of the emperor. Their statues were decapitated and the head of the emperor was placed upon them. On the statue of Olympic Jove appeared the bust of the contemptible Caligula; and this incongruous adaptation represented the change of the popular faith from its former heavenly idealisations to the most grovelling fetish worship of the time. This deification of the emperors avenged its terrible blasphemy by the sublime wickedness of those who were so raised above humanity. Here, in this last pagan temple of Rome, converted into one of the earliest Christian churches, we see the darkness and despair of the heathen world preparing for that joyful morning light of Christianity which has transferred the faith of mankind to foundations which can never more be shaken. Immediately beyond in the background are the huge gloomy arches of the Basilica of Constantine, fretted with coffers, suspended in mid-air for upwards of sixteen centuries, in defiance of the laws of gravity and the ravages of time and of human destroyers, taken as a model for churches by Roman architects, though built originally for a law court. In front is the Arch of Titus, with its well-known sculptures of the spoils from the Temple of Jerusalem, spanning the highest point of the Via Sacra. And closing up the view is the grandest ruin in the world, the stupendous broken circle of the Colosseum, rising tier above tier into the blue sky, burnt deep brown by the suns of ages, holding the spectator breathless with wonder, and thrilling the mind with the awful associations connected with it.

The Forum lies like an open sepulchre in the heart of old Rome. All is death there; the death of nature and the death of a race whose long history has done more to shape the destiny of the world than any other. The soil beneath our feet is formed by the ashes of an extinct fire, and by the dust of a vanished empire. Everywhere the ruins of time and of man are mingled with the relics of an older creation; and the sculptured marbles of the temples and law courts, where Cæsar worshipped and Cicero pled, lie scattered amid the tufa-blocks, the cinders of the long quiescent volcanoes of the Campagna. Nature and man have both accomplished their work in this spot; and the relics they have left behind are only the exuviæ of the chrysalis out of which the butterfly has emerged, or the empty wave-worn shells left high and dry upon an ancient coast-line. It is a remarkable circumstance that the way in which the Forum originated was the very way in which it was destroyed. The cradle of Roman greatness became its tomb. The Forum originated in the volcanic fires of earth; it passed away in the incendiary fires of man. In the month of May 1084 the Norman leader, Robert Guiscard, came with his troops to rescue Gregory VII. from the German army which besieged Rome. Then broke out—whether by accident or design is not known—the terrible conflagration which extended from the Capitol to the Coelian Hill, but raged with the greatest intensity in the Forum. In that catastrophe classical Rome passed away, and from the ashes of the fire arose the Phoenix of modern Rome. The greatest of physical empires was wrecked on this spot, and out of the wreck was constructed the greatest spiritual empire the world has ever known. For the Roman Pontificate, to use the famous saying of Hobbes, was but the ghost of the deceased Roman Empire sitting crowned upon the grave thereof.

CHAPTER VI - THE EGYPTIAN OBELISKS

Among the first objects that arrest the attention and powerfully excite the curiosity of the visitor in Rome are the Egyptian obelisks. They remind him impressively that the oldest things in this city of ages are but as of yesterday in comparison with these imperishable relics of the earliest civilisation. At one time it is said that there were no less than forty-eight obelisks erected in Rome, — six of the largest size and forty-two of the smaller, — all conveyed at enormous cost and with almost incredible labour from the banks of the Nile to the banks of the Tiber. Upwards of thirty of them have perished without leaving any trace behind. They are doubtless buried deep under the ruins of ancient Rome, but the chance of their disinterment is very problematical. One obelisk, indeed, was exposed a hundred and forty years ago in the square of the principal church of the Jesuits, near the Pantheon; but being found to be broken, and also to underlie a corner of the church and the greater part of an adjoining palace, so that it could not be extracted without seriously injuring these buildings, it was covered up again, and was thus lost to the world. As it is, we find in Rome the largest collection of obelisks that exists at the present day in the world, and the best field for studying them.

Obelisks were dedicated to the sun, which was the central object of worship, and occupied the most conspicuous position in the religious system of the oldest nations. Sun-worship, that which waited upon some hill-top to catch the first beams of the morning that created a new day, is the oldest and the most natural of all kinds of worship. He was adored as the source of all the life and motion and force in the world by the most primitive people; and we find numerous traces of this ancient sun-worship in the rude stone monuments, with their cup-shaped symbols, that have survived on our moors, in many of the old customs which still linger in our Christianity, and in the name by which the most sacred day of the week is commonly known among us. All the benefits conferred upon our world by the sun must have been strikingly apparent to the ancient Egyptians, dwelling in a land exposed to the sun's vertical rays, and clothed with almost tropical beauty and luxuriance. When they watched the ebbing of the overflowing waters of the Nile, and saw the moist earth on which the sun's rays fell, quickened at once into a marvellous profusion of plant and animal life, they naturally regarded the sun as the Creator, and so deified him in that capacity. The origin of all life, vegetable and animal, to those who stood, as it were, by its cradle, when the world was young and haunted by heaven, seemed a greater mystery and wonder than it is to us in these later faithless ages. Long familiarity with it in its full-grown proportions has made it commonplace to us.

Both the obelisk and the pyramid were solar symbols, the obelisk being the symbol of the rising sun, and the pyramid of the setting. The fundamental idea of the obelisk was that of creation by light; that of the pyramid, death through the extinction of light. And this symbolical difference between the two objects was practically expressed by the different situations in which they were placed; the obelisks being all located on the eastern side of the Nile, that being the region of the rising sun, and of the dawn of life; while the pyramids are all found on the western bank of the river, the region of the sunset, with its awfully sterile hills and silent untravelled desert of sand from which no tidings had ever come to living man, where the dead were buried under the shades of night, in their rock-cut cemeteries. It might thus seem, that by placing obelisks in our churchyards in association with the dead, we were violating their original significance, and guilty of adding another to the many incongruities which have arisen from adopting pagan symbols in Christian burying-places. But in reality we find a deeper reason for the association. In some of the oldest sculptures in Egypt, an obelisk is represented as standing on the top of a pyramid; and by this combination it was meant to signify the power of life triumphing over death. And hence the obelisk is the most suitable of all forms to indicate in our cemeteries the glorious truth of the resurrection, life rising victorious out of the transitory condition of death.

And how admirably did the obelisk lend itself to its symbolical purposes! There was a most wonderful harmony between the idea and the object which expressed it. Being composed of the most durable of all materials, the hard indestructible granite, the eternal sun was thus fittingly represented by an object that lifts its stern finger in unchangeable defiance of the vicissitudes of the seasons and the ages. Its highly polished surface and rich rosy red colour, its sharply defined lines and narrow proportions, combined with its immense height, suggested the brilliancy and hue and form of a pencil of light. Its tall red column flashing in the strong morning radiance, like a tongue of flame mounting up to its source in the solar fire, or like a ray of the halo that rises up on the low horizon of the Libyan desert, when the dawn has crimsoned all the eastern heavens, might thus well be selected as the most suitable object to bring the invisible sun-god within the ken of human vision and the range of human worship. The poetical imagination may detect a significance even in the difference between the material used in the construction of the obelisk, and that used in the construction of the pyramid, though this may not have been designed by the makers. The obelisks are all formed of granite, the foundation-stone of the globe, belonging to the oldest azoic formation, which laid down the first basis for the appearing of life. The pyramids were nearly all made of nummulitic limestone composed of the remains of organic life; a material which belonged to the latest geologic ages, when whole generations and different platforms of life had come and gone. Thus significantly does the obelisk of granite suggest by its material as by its form the origin of life, as the pyramid suggests by its material and form the extinction of life.

But not only was the obelisk raised in connection with the worship of the sun,—it was also intended to honour the reigning monarch who erected it, and whose name and titles were engraved upon it along with the name of the sun. For it was a fundamental idea of the Egyptian religion that the king was not only the son of the solar god, but also the visible human representative of his glory. This was a favourite conception of the ancients. The Incas of Peru regarded themselves as direct descendants of the sun; and the monarchs of the burning Asiatic lands, where the sun rules and dominates everything, assume the name and title of his sons, and clothe themselves with his splendour. The obelisks were thus the symbols of the two great correlative conceptions of the sun in the heavens, and his satellite and representative on the earth—god and the king. This Egyptian faith, as attested by the obelisks, the oldest of all the creeds, antecedent to the theologies of India, Greece, and Rome, ceased not to be venerated till the advent of Christianity swept all material worship away. It awed, as Mr. Cooper has well observed, the mixed multitude in Alexandria under the Cæsars, as it had done the primitive Egyptians under the oldest Pharaohs. It extended over a space of more than three thousand years. During all that long period the obelisk was "the emblem at once of the vivifying power of the sun and of the divine nature of the king, a witness for the divine claim of the sun to be worshipped, and of the right divine of the king to rule." Where is there in all the world, in its most ancient cities, in its loneliest deserts, any class of objects which has been held continuously sacred for so long a time? The description of the sun itself by Ossian applies almost equally well to his worship as thus represented.

Obelisks as symbols of the sun and of the creative power of nature, were not confined to Egypt. They belonged to the mythology of all ancient nations. There are modifications of them in India, in prehistoric America, and among the archæological remains of our own country. They were common objects in connection with the Assyrian, Persian and Phoenician religions. And it has been conjectured with much plausibility that the image of gold, whose height was threescore cubits, and the breadth six, the usual proportions of an obelisk, which Nebuchadnezzar set up in the plain of Dura, in the province of Babylon, and commanded Shadrach, Meshach, and Abednego to adore, was in reality an obelisk after the Egyptian pattern. Such an obelisk was often gilded, and was associated with the worship of the king as its material purpose, and with the creation and origin of life as its symbolic meaning. And if this was the case, there was an unusual aggravation in this idolatry; for the Egyptian obelisks themselves were never worshipped, but were always regarded as the signs of the higher powers whose glory they expressed.

The question is naturally asked, Where were the obelisks originally placed? At the present day we find those of them that remain in Egypt, solitary objects without anything near them, and those that have been carried to other lands have been set up in great open squares, or on river embankments in the heart of the largest cities. Fortunately, there is no doubt at all on this point. They stood in pairs at the doors of the great temples, one on each side, where they served the same purpose which the campanile of the Italian church or the spire of a cathedral serves at the present day. Indeed, architects are of opinion that church towers and steeples are mere survivals of the old Egyptian obelisks, which furnished the original conception. The tower corresponded to the shaft of the obelisk, and the steeple to the sharp pyramidal part in which the summit of the obelisk terminated. And though there is usually only one spire or tower now in connection with our churches, there used to be two, as many old examples still extant testify, one standing on each side of the principal entrance after the manner of the Egyptian obelisks. The slender round towers of Brechin and Abernethy, and of Devenish and other places in Ireland, capped by a conical stone roof terminating in a single stone, which were for a long time a puzzle to the antiquary, are now ascertained to be simply steeples connected with Christian churches of the tenth and eleventh centuries. And just as these towers are now left isolated and solitary without a trace of the buildings with which they were associated, so the Egyptian temples have passed away, and the obelisks are left alone in the desert. But we can reconstruct in imagination the massive and lofty buildings in front of which they stood, and where they showed to the greatest advantage. Instead of being dwarfed by the enormous masses of the propylons, their height gained by the near comparison. The obelisks in our squares and vast open spaces have their effect destroyed by the buildings being at a distance from them. There is no scale near at hand to assist the eye in estimating the height; consequently they seem much smaller than they really are. But when seen in the narrow precincts of a temple court, from whose floor they shot up into the blue sky overhead, surrounded by great columns and lofty gates, breaking the monotony of the heavy masses of masonry of which the Egyptian temples were composed, and acting the part which campanili and spires perform in modern churches, a standard of comparison was thus furnished which greatly enhanced their magnitude.

Nothing could be grander than the objects associated with the obelisks where they stood. The temple was approached by an avenue of huge sphinxes, in some cases a mile and a half long. Drawing nearer, the worshipper saw two lofty obelisks towering up a hundred feet in height, on the right and left. Behind these he would observe with awe four or six gigantic statues seated with their hands on their knees. And at the back of the statues he would gaze with astonishment upon two massive towers or pylons, broader at the base than at the summit, two hundred feet wide and a hundred and twenty feet high, crowned by a gigantic cornice, with their whole surface covered with coloured sculptures, representing one of the great dramas in the reign of a victorious monarch. Above them would rise the tall masts of coloured cedar-wood, inserted in sinkings chased into the wall, surmounted by the expanded banners of the king, or the heraldic bearings of the temple floating in the breeze. Between the huge propylons opened up the great gateway of the temple, sixty feet high, which led into a vast court, surrounded by columns and open to the sky. Beyond were walls whose roofs were supported by a forest of enormous pillars, which seemed to have been raised by giants. Each hall diminished in size, but increased in sacredness, until the inmost sanctuary was reached; small, dark, and awful in its obscurity. Here was the holy shrine in the shape of a boat or ark, having in it a kind of chest partially veiled, in which was hid the mystic symbol of the god. Like the tabernacle of Israel, the common people were not allowed to go farther than the outer court beyond the obelisks; only kings and priests being permitted to penetrate into the interior recesses, there to observe the ritual ceremonies of the mysterious Egyptian worship. On the plan of the Egyptian temple were modelled the sacred buildings of the Jews; and the famous pillars of burnished brass, wonderful for their workmanship and their costly material, which Solomon erected in the court of his temple, called Jachin and Boaz, had their prototypes in the obelisks of the Nile.

The obelisk belongs essentially to a level country; and there is no habitable region in the world so uniformly flat and unbroken by any elevations or depressions of surface as the valley of the Nile. There it produces its greatest effect; its size is not dwarfed by surrounding heights, and comes out by contrast with the small objects that diversify the plain. It forms a conspicuous landmark, a salient point on which the eye may rest with relief as it takes in the wide featureless horizon. In an artificial landscape, where there is no wild unmixed nature, where every inch of ground is cultivated, it is the appropriate culmination of that triumph of human art which is visible everywhere. It was a sense of this harmony of relation that induced the builders of the great cathedrals and temples of the world to place them, not amid varied and rugged scenery, where they might be brought into comparison with nature's work, but uniformly on level expanses of land. There they form the crowning symbol of man's loving care and painstaking endeavour, and give to the artificial landscape, which man has entirely subdued for his own uses, the finishing touch of power.

Obelisks are the most enduring monuments of antiquity, and yet no class of objects has undergone such extraordinary vicissitudes. The history of the changes to which they have been subjected reads like a romance. At a remote age, not long after they were erected, most of them were cast down during some political catastrophe, which shook the whole country to its foundations. Under a subsequent dynasty the obelisks seem to have been lifted up to their former places, and regarded with the old veneration. After the lapse of nearly a thousand years, the land was again convulsed by a terrible revolution, the nature of which is still wrapped up in almost impenetrable mystery. A warlike migratory race came from the north-east, and subdued the whole country. This is known as the Hyksos invasion, or the invasion of the Shepherd Kings, and produced the same effects in Egypt as the Norman invasion produced in England. Previous to this period the horse seemed to have been altogether unknown; but after this date it uniformly appears in Egyptian paintings and sculptures. The Hyksos must therefore have been a pastoral race, in all likelihood belonging to the plains of Tartary; and, mounted on horses, they would find little difficulty in overcoming the foot soldiery of Egypt. When they had obtained possession of the country, they burnt down the cities, demolished the temples, and overthrew the obelisks. This disaster, the most dreadful which Egypt had ever known, followed suddenly upon a period of extraordinary prosperity, when new cities were built, and old cities enlarged; works of great public utility were constructed, a mercantile intercourse established with the surrounding nations, and the arts of painting, sculpture, and architecture, favoured by the long peace and the abundant resources of the country, reached their highest excellence. The reversal of all these signs of prosperity was so overwhelming, that the Egyptians of subsequent ages looked back upon this period of subjection under a foreign yoke which lay upon them for five hundred years, with bitter resentment. When the hated dynasty was at an end, the Egyptians obliterated, as far as they could, every sign of its supremacy, chiselled out the names of its kings on their monuments, and destroyed their records, so that few traces of this revolution remain to dispel the strange mystery in which it is involved. They could never bear to hear the detested names of the Shepherd Kings; and this circumstance throws light upon the passage in Genesis which says that the occupation of a shepherd was an abomination to the Egyptians. Under the patronage of the new dynasty the arts which had been destroyed were again restored, the monuments of the suppressed religion were freed from their indignities, and once more reinstated with the old honours, and the whole country was reconstructed. But, while the temples were re-erected, and the old worship established with even greater splendour, there can be no doubt that many of the earlier obelisks, owing to their smaller size, as compared with the other gigantic monuments of Egypt, had been destroyed past all reconstruction; and some of them remain in the land at the present day on the sites where, and in the exact manner in which, they were overturned by the Shepherd Kings.

But greater changes still happened to the Egyptian obelisks after this. Previously they had been devastated and overturned on their own soil. But now they excited the cupidity of the foreign invaders of Egypt, and were carried away to distant lands as trophies of their victories. The first obelisks that were removed in this way were two of the principal ones that adorned one of the temples of Thebes. After the capture of Thebes by Assurbanipal, the Assyrian king, the famous Sardanapalus of the Greeks, they were transported to the conqueror's palace at Nineveh, and were afterwards lost for ever in the destruction of that city, about sixty years later, or about six hundred years before Christ. The transportation of these enormous masses of stone across the country to the seashore, down the Red Sea, over the Indian Ocean, up the Persian Gulf, and the river Tigris, to their destination in the palace of Nineveh, nearly two thousand miles, must have been a feat of engineering skill at that early period of the world's history, far more wonderful in regard to the difficulties overcome, without any precedent to guide, and considering the rudeness of the means of transport, than anything that has ever been attempted since in the same line. The example of the Assyrian tyrant was followed, after a long interval, by the Romans, who sought to magnify and commemorate their conquests in Egypt by spoiling the land of its characteristic monuments. The Cæsars, one after another, for more than a hundred years, took advantage of their victories and the ruin of the unhappy land of Egypt to convey its beautiful obelisks to their own capital to permanently adorn one or other of the various places of public resort. They seem to have set almost the same high value upon these singular monuments which their inventors did. Pliny and Suetonius describe the almost incredible magnitude of the vessels in which these gigantic masses of stone were conveyed to Ostia, the harbour town, and from thence up the Tiber to Rome. The huge triremes were propelled by the force of hundreds of rowers across the waters of the Mediterranean. From the quay at Rome they were dragged and pushed, by the brute force of thousands in the old Egyptian manner, on low carts supported on rollers instead of wheels, to their destination, where they were set upright by a complicated machinery of ropes and huge upright beams.

How many obelisks of Egyptian origin existed at one time in the world we do not know. They were undoubtedly very numerous; but many of them were broken up for building materials. The famous column called Pompey's Pillar stands upon a fragment of an ancient obelisk; and tradition asserts that there are many similar fragments of greater or less antiquity under the ruins of the older houses of Alexandria. At present forty-two obelisks are known to be in existence in different parts of the world. Of these, seventeen remain in Egypt on their original sites, of which no less than eleven are prostrate on the ground, having been overturned by some political or religious revolution, by the force of an earthquake, or by the slow undermining of the infiltrated waters of the Nile. No less than twelve of the oldest and grandest are still to be seen standing erect in Rome, where they constitute by far the most striking and memorable monuments. The others are distributed in various places wide apart. One is in Paris, two are in Constantinople, a fourth, the famous Cleopatra's Needle, is on the Thames Embankment, in the heart of London; a fifth, its old companion in Alexandria, is now in one of the public squares of New York. And there are several diminutive ones, from eight feet in height downwards, in the British Museum, in the Florentine Museum in Florence, in Benevento in Italy, and in the town of Alnwick in Northumberland.

The oldest of all the obelisks is the beautiful one of rosy granite which stands alone among the green fields on the banks of the Nile not far from Cairo. It is the gravestone of a great ancient city which has vanished and left only this relic behind. That city was the Bethshemesh of Scripture, the famous On, which is memorable to all Bible readers as the residence of the priest Potipherah whose daughter Asenath Joseph married. The Greeks called it Heliopolis, the city of the sun, because there the worship of the sun had its chief centre and its most sacred shrines. It was the seat of the most ancient university in the world, to which youthful students came from all parts of the world, to learn the occult wisdom which the priests of On alone could teach. Thales, Solon, Eudoxus, Pythagoras, and Plato, all studied there, perhaps Moses too. It was also the birthplace of the sacred literature of Egypt, where were written on papyrus leaves the original chapters of the oldest book in the world, generally known as the "Book of the Dead," giving a most striking account of the conflicts and triumphs of the life after death; a whole copy or fragment of which every Egyptian, rich or poor, wished to have buried with him in his coffin, and portions of which are found inscribed on every mummy case and on the walls of every tomb. In front of one of the principal temples of the sun, in this magnificent city, stood along with a companion, long since destroyed, the solitary obelisk which we now behold on the spot. It alone, as I have said, has survived the wreck of all the glory of the place, as if to assure us that what is given to God, however ignorantly and superstitiously, endures, while all the other works of man perish. It was constructed by Usirtesen I., who is supposed to have reigned two thousand eight hundred years before Christ, and has outlasted all the dynastic changes of the land, and still stands where it originally stood nearly forty-seven centuries ago. What appears of its shaft above ground is sixty-eight feet in height, but its base is buried in the mud of the Nile; and year after year the inundation of the river deposits its film of soil around its foot, and buries it still deeper in its sacred grave. Down the centre of each of its four faces runs a line of deeply-cut hieroglyphics, in whose cavities the wild mason-bees construct their mud-cells and store their honey. Nothing can exceed the beauty and distinctness of these carvings. The pictures of birds and beasts, chiselled in the hard polished granite, have a purity of form and line, a directness of expression and intention, which is most impressive. Its top is somewhat damaged, having been originally protected, as was the case with many of the obelisks which were not finely finished to a point, with a capping of gilded bronze that remained intact till the thirteen century. The inscription on its sides contains nothing of historic value. It is simply a dedication to Usirtesen, who constructed it, under the title of Horus, or the rising sun, which was borne, as I have said, by the kings of Egypt on account of their supposed origin as an incarnation of the sun.

At Luxor, a single obelisk, the property of the English, still maintains its ancient position. It is very beautiful, formed of red granite, and covered with elegantly carved inscriptions, running up each of the four faces. The hieroglyphics are cut to an unusual depth, and are remarkably clear and well-formed, indicating that the monument was raised in honour of Rameses the Great, the most illustrious of all the Egyptian monarchs, and the most magnificent and prolific architect the world has ever seen. The top of the obelisk was originally left in a rough unfinished state, the roughness having been concealed by a capping of bronze; but this having been removed long ago, the surface has become very much eroded by exposure, which somewhat detracts from the elegance of the shaft. It has also the peculiarity that its two inner faces are sensibly curved—a peculiarity which it is supposed was designed to make the sunlight fall with softer effect, so as to make the shadows less crude, and the angles less sharp. The shaft, which is eighty-two feet high by eight feet in diameter at the base, is elevated upon a pedestal, which is adorned by statues in high relief of dog-headed monkeys standing in an attitude of adoration at the corners worshipping the sun, and also by standing figures of the god of the Nile presenting offerings, incised in the stone like the hieroglyphics of the shaft. The surroundings of this obelisk are far grander than those of any other obelisk in the world. At present the extent and dimensions of the ruins of Thebes produce an overwhelming effect upon the visitor. But it is almost impossible for us to imagine its magnificence when its temples and obelisks were in their full perfection, and the great Rameses was carried on the shoulders of his officers through the ranks of adoring slaves to behold the completion of the works which had been designed to perpetuate his glory. The ancient city, divided in the middle by the Nile, as London is by the Thames or Glasgow by the Clyde, covered the vast plain, with great houses in the outskirts standing in richly cultivated gardens, each temple surrounded by its own little sacred lake, over which the bodies of the dead were carried by the priests before burial, and the beautiful Mokattam Hills bounding the view, wearing the soft lilac hue of distance. Only two or three places on earth can rival the overwhelming interest which the city possesses. But the colossal associated temples of Karnac and Luxor are absolutely unique. There is nothing on earth to equal them. They are man's greatest achievements in religious architecture. Long rows of stupendous pillars, covered from base to top with coloured pictures and hieroglyphics, containing a whole library of actually written and pictured history and religion, look "like a Brobdingnagian forest turned into stone," in the midst of which the visitor feels himself an insignificant insect. A sense of superhuman awfulness, of personal nothingness and irresistible power, is what these stupendous structures inspire in even the most callous spectator. A confused mass of broken columns and heaps of huge sculptured stones present an appearance as if the old giants had been at war on the spot, hurling rocks at each other. Between Luxor and Karnac extended an avenue of sphinxes, two miles long, numbering more than four thousand pieces of sculpture, now represented by mutilated formless blocks of stone. We see in these vast temples, which were raised by a people inspired with the sentiment that they were the greatest of all nations, to be the chief shrines of the religion of the country, the fruits of the plunder and the tribute of Asia and Africa. The funds necessary to build them had been procured by robbing other nations; and most of the work was done by captives taken in war. Many a fair province had been desolated of its inhabitants, many a splendid city spoiled of its riches, in order to construct these awful halls. Unfortunately, the annual overflow of the inundation of the Nile covers the ground to the depth of a foot or two, staining and eating away the bases of the columns, and overthrowing their enormous drums and architraves. The destruction cannot be prevented, for the water infiltrates through the soil; and some day, ere long, the remaining columns will be hurled down, and the pride of Karnac will lie prone in the dust.

Passing westward to Rome, the largest obelisk not only in the Eternal City but in the whole world is that which now adorns the square of St. John Lateran. It is, as usual, of red granite much darkened and corroded by time, and stands with its pedestal and cross one hundred and forty-one feet high; the shaft alone being one hundred and eight feet seven inches in height, with faces about nine feet and a half wide at the base; the whole mass weighing upwards of four hundred and sixty tons. It was found among the ruins of the Circus Maximus broken into three pieces, and was dug up by order of Pope Sixtus V., conveyed to its present site, and re-erected by the celebrated architect Fontana in 1588. The lower end had been so much injured by its fall, that in order to enable it to stand, it was found necessary to cut off about two feet and a half to obtain a level base. On the top of it Fontana added by way of ornament four bronze lions, surmounted by three mountain peaks, out of which sprung the cross, as the armorial bearings of the Popes. Thus crowned with the cross, and consecrated to the honour of Christianity, this noble relic of antiquity acquires an additional interest from its nearness to the great Basilica of the Lateran, which is the representative cathedral of the Papacy and the mother church of Christendom, and to the Lateran Palace, for a thousand years the residence of the Popes of Rome.

The history of the Lateran obelisk is unusually varied. It was originally constructed by Thothmes III., and set up by him before the great temple of Amen at Heliopolis. But being an old man at the time, he left his successor to complete it by adding most of the hieroglyphics. It took thirty-six years to carve these sculptures; the four sides from top to bottom being covered with inscriptions in the purest style of Egyptian art. From one of these inscriptions we learn that the obelisk was thrown down in Egypt probably during the invasion of the Shepherd Kings, and was re-erected by the great Rameses, who did not, contrary to the usual custom, arrogate to himself the honours of his predecessor. These sculptures tell us of monarchs who had reigned, and conquered, and died long before the mythic times, when the "pious Æneas," as Virgil tells us, landed on the Italian shore, and Romulus ploughed his significant furrow round the Palatine Hill. A thousand years before the foundation of Rome, and two thousand years before the Christian era, it had been excavated from the quarries of Syene and worshipped at Heliopolis. It was as old to the Cæsars as the days of the Cæsars are to us. Pliny tells us that the work of quarrying, conveying, and setting it up employed twenty thousand men; and there is a dim tradition that so anxious was the king for its safety, when it was erected, that in order to ensure this he bound his own son to the top of it. A close examination of the hieroglyphics reveals the curious fact that the name of the god Amen wherever it occurs, is more deeply carved than the other figures, in order to obliterate the name of some other deity which had previously occupied its place. It is supposed that this circumstance indicates a theological revolution which happened in the history of Egypt when Amenhotep III., the Memnon of the Greek historian, married an Arabian wife of the name of Taia, who introduced her own religion into her adopted country, as Jezebel, the wife of Ahab, introduced the worship of Baal into Israel. When this dynasty was overthrown, in the course of about fifty years, the old faith was restored, and the names of the old gods substituted for those which had usurped their place on the religious monuments. It is supposed that the Lateran obelisk was the one before which Cambyses, the great Persian conqueror, stood lost in admiration, arrested in his semi-religious course of destroying the popular monuments of Egypt. Augustus intended to have removed it to Rome, but was deterred by the difficulty of the undertaking, and also by superstitious scruples, because it had been specially dedicated to the sun, and fixed immovably in his temple. Constantine the Great had no such scruples, believing, as he said, that "he did no injury to religion if he removed a wonder from one temple, and again consecrated it in Rome, the temple of the whole world." He died, however, before he had completed his design, having succeeded only in transporting the obelisk to Alexandria, from whence his son and successor Constantius transferred it to Rome, and placed it on the Spina of the Great Circus. So clumsily, however, was it erected in this place, that several deep holes had to be drilled in the upper part of it, in order that ropes for hauling it up might be put through them; a defect in engineering skill which has disfigured the obelisk, and contrasts strikingly with the resources of the ancient Egyptians, who were able to raise the stone to its position without such a device. The obelisk is thus an enduring monument of three great rulers—Thothmes, who first constructed it in Heliopolis; Constantine, who removed it to Rome; and Pope Sixtus V., who conveyed it from the Circus Maximus, and re-erected it where it now stands.

Next in point of height to the Lateran obelisk is the one that stands in the great square of St. Peter's, between two beautiful fountains that are continually showering high in the air their radiant sunlit spray. It is meant to serve as the gnomon of a gigantic dial, traced in lines of white marble in the pavement of the square. Its rosy surface glistening in the rays of the sun, and its long shadow cast before it on the ground, make it a very impressive object. Its origin is involved in mystery, for there is no inscription on it to tell who erected it, or where it came from. This absence of hieroglyphics points to its having been an unfinished work—something having prevented its constructor from recording on it the purpose of its erection, as was usually the case. But as the vacant shadow of the dial and the blank empty lines of the spectrum are more suggestive than any sunlit spaces, so the blank unwritten sides of this obelisk give rise to more speculations than if they had been carved from head to foot with hieroglyphics. On account of this peculiarity, some authors have not hesitated to consider it a mere imitation obelisk, constructed by the Romans at a comparatively late period. This idea, however, is refuted by the evidence of Pliny, who regarded it as a genuine Egyptian relic, and tells us that it was cut from the quarry of Syene, and dedicated to the sun by the son of Sesores, in obedience to an oracle, after his recovery from blindness. It is generally believed that it first stood before one of the temples of Heliopolis, was then removed to Alexandria, and finally transported to Rome by Caligula. This emperor constructed a special vessel for the purpose, of greater dimensions than had ever been seen before; and after it had brought the obelisk to the banks of the Tiber, he commanded it to be filled with stones, and sunk as a caisson in the harbour of Ostia, which he was constructing at the time. On arriving at Rome the obelisk was set up on the Spina of the Circus of Nero, which is now occupied by the sacristy of St. Peter's Church. For fifteen centuries the obelisk remained undisturbed on its site, the only one in the city that escaped being overthrown. At last its foundation giving way, so that it leaned dangerously towards the old Basilica of St. Peter's, Sixtus V. formed the design of removing it to where it now stands, a very short distance from the original spot. The record of its re-erection, the first in papal Rome, by Fontana—a work of extreme difficulty and imposing ceremonial magnificence, which was richly rewarded by the grateful Pope—is exceedingly interesting. A curious legend is usually related in connection with it. A papal edict was proclaimed threatening death to any one who should utter a loud word while the operation of lifting and settling the obelisk was going on. As the "huge crystallisation of Egyptian sweat" rose on its basis there was a sudden stoppage, the hempen cables refused to do their work, and the hanging mass of stone threatened to fall and destroy itself. Suddenly from out the breathless crowd rose a loud, clear voice, "Wet the ropes." There was inspiration in the suggestion; the architect acted upon it, and the obelisk at once took its stand on its base, where it has firmly remained ever since. Not only was the sailor Bresca pardoned for transgressing the papal command, but he was rewarded, and the district of Bordighera, from which he came, received the privilege of supplying the palm leaves for the use of Rome on Palm Sunday — a privilege which it still possesses, and which forms the principal trade of the place.

To me the most familiar and interesting of all the Roman obelisks is that which stands in the centre of the Piazza del Popolo, the finest and largest square in Rome. It is about eighty feet high, carved with hieroglyphics, with four marble Egyptian lions, one at each corner of the platform on which it stands, pouring from their mouths copious streams of water into large basins, with a refreshing sound. Lions in Egypt were regarded as symbols of the sun when passing through the zodiacal sign of Leo, the time when the annual inundation of the Nile occurred. They had thus a deep significance in connection with water. The obelisk was originally erected in front of the Temple of the Sun at Heliopolis, by the great Rameses, the Sesostris of the Greeks, whose personal character and wide conquests fill a larger space in the history of ancient Egypt than those of any other monarch. From Heliopolis it was removed to Rome, after the battle of Actium, by Augustus, and placed on the Spina of the Circus Maximus, the sports of which were under the special protection of Apollo, the sun-god, by whose favour it was supposed that the Egyptian victory had been achieved. For four hundred years it acted as a gnomon, regulating by the length and direction of its shadow the hours of the public games of the circus; and then it was overturned during those troublous days in which the empire was rent asunder. Twelve centuries of decay and wreck had buried it from the eyes of men, until it was dug up and placed where it now stands, in 1587, by Pope Sixtus V., to whom modern Rome is indebted for the restoration of many of her ancient monuments, and the construction of many of her public buildings and streets. With the cross planted on its summit, this noble monument was long the first object which met the traveller's eye as he entered Rome from the north by the old Flaminian way. Brought to commemorate the overthrow of the land from whence it came, it has witnessed the overthrow of the conquerors in turn; and now re-erected in the modern capital, it will endure when its glory too has passed away. And out of the ruins of the city of the Popes, as out of the ruins of the city of the Cæsars, some future architect will dig it up to grace the triumph of a brighter and freer resuscitation of the Eternal City than the world has yet seen.

The association of fountains at its base with this obelisk seems at first sight as incongruous as the crowning of its apex with a metal cross, for the Christian emblem can never alter the nature of the pagan monument. There is no natural harmony in the association, for there are no fountains or streams of running water in the desert. The obelisk belongs essentially to the dry and parched east; the fountain is the birth of the happier west, bright with the sparkle and musical with the sound of many waters. The obelisk relieves the monotony of immeasurable plains over which a sky of serene unstained blue arches itself in infinite altitude, the image of eternal purity, and the sun rises day after day with the same unsullied brilliance, and sets with the same unmitigable glory. The fountain, on the other hand, is the child of lands whose mountains kiss the clouds and gleam with the purity of everlasting snows, and where each day brings out new beauties, and each season reveals a fresh and ever-varying charm. But although there is no geographical reason why these two objects should be associated, there is a poetical fitness. The obelisk is the symbol of the perpetual past, holding in its changeless unity, as on its carved sides, the memories of former ages; the fountain is the symbol of the perpetual present, ever changing, ever new. The one speaks to us of a petrified old age; the other of an immortal youth. And thus it is in life, each passing moment flowing on with all its changes beside the stern, hard, enduring monument of the irrevocable past on which what is written is changelessly written. How different too are the bright sparkling fountains that leap with ever-varying beauty at the foot of the Flaminian obelisk now, from the dull, sleepy monotonous river that, like a Lethe flood, flowed past it in the old days at Heliopolis! Are they not both symbolical of the new and the old world, of the Christian faith, with its progressive thought and varied expanding life, and the stagnant pagan creed, which impressed the soul with the sense of human helplessness in the face of an unchangeable iron order alike of nature and of society?

Another of the great obelisks of Rome is that which stands on Monte Citorio, in front of the present Parliament House. It was brought to Rome by Augustus, who dedicated it anew to the sun, and placed it as the gnomon of a meridian in the midst of the Campus Martius. Originally it had been erected at Heliopolis in honour of Psammeticus I., who reigned about seven hundred years before Christ. This monarch lived during a time when the national religion had become corrupted, and the whole land had come under the influence of Greek thought and Greek customs. But the obelisk which he erected is worthy of the best period of Egyptian art. It is universally admired for the remarkable beauty of its hieroglyphics. The anonymous pilgrim of Einsiedlen mentions that this obelisk was still erect when he visited Rome about the beginning of the ninth century. It seems, however, to have fallen and to have been broken in pieces, nearly three hundred years later, during the terrible conflagration caused by the Norman troops of Robert Guiscard. Several fragments of it were dug up, one after another, during the sixteenth century. The principal part of the shaft was discovered in 1748, among the ruins beneath the choir of the Church of San

Lorenzo in Lucina. These portions were damaged in such a way as to show clearly the action of fire, proving that the obelisk had been destroyed in the great fire of 1084. Pope Pius VI. gathered together the fragments, and with the aid of granite pieces taken from the ruined column of Antoninus Pius, which stood in the neighbourhood, he formed of these a whole shaft, which represents, as nearly as possible, the original obelisk. It is seventy-two feet high, and is surmounted by a globe and a small pyramid of bronze, which, along with its pedestal, increases its height to one hundred and thirty-four feet. A portion of the lines of the celebrated sun-dial, whose gnomon it formed, was brought to light under the sacristy of San Lorenzo in Lucina in 1463.

All the other obelisks in Rome belong to comparatively recent periods, to the decadence of Egypt. None of them are of any great significance to the student of archæology. Several of them were executed in Egypt by order of the Roman emperors, and are therefore not genuine but imitation obelisks. Of this kind may be mentioned the Esquiline and Quirinal obelisks, which were brought to Rome by the emperor Claudius, and placed in the old Egyptian manner, one on each side of the entrance to the great mausoleum of Augustus in the Campus Martius. They are both destitute of hieroglyphics and are broken into several pieces. One now stands on Monte Cavallo, in front of the great Quirinal Palace, betwixt the two well-known gigantic groups of men and horses, statues of Greek origin, supposed to be those of Castor and Pollux, executed by Pheidias and Praxiteles; and the other in the large open space in front of the great Basilica of Santa Maria Maggiore. Another of these bastard obelisks occupies a commanding position at the top of the Spanish Stairs, in front of the Church of Trinita dei Monti. It stood originally on the spina of the circus of Sallust, in his gardens, and is covered with hieroglyphics of the rudest workmanship, which sufficiently proclaim their origin, as a Roman forgery probably of the period of the Antonine emperors. In the midst of the public gardens, on the Pincian Hill, there is another Roman obelisk about thirty feet high, excavated from the quarries of Syene, and set up by Hadrian originally at Antinopolis in Egypt in front of a temple dedicated to the deified Antinous, the lamented favourite of the emperor. It was afterwards transferred to the imperial villa at Tivoli, near Rome, and subsequently to the grounds of the Church of Santa Croce in Gerusalemme, from whence it was finally taken to its present site. This obelisk has a special interest because it commemorates one of the most beautiful and touching examples of self-sacrifice which the annals of paganism afford. We are apt to judge of Antinous from the languid beauty of the statue of him in the Roman galleries, as simply the pampered sycophant of a court. But behind his sensual beauty and softness there was an unselfish devotion which the caresses of royalty and the favours of fortune could not spoil. When the oracle declared that the happiness of Hadrian, who was afflicted with a profound melancholy, could only be secured by the sacrifice of what was most dear to him, Antinous went at once and drowned himself in the Nile, and thus gave his life for his imperial friend, who, instead of being made better by the sacrifice, was left altogether inconsolable. The magnificent city founded to perpetuate his memory is now a heap of ruined mounds, and the obelisk that bore his name in Egypt now stands far away in Rome; but time cannot quench the glow of sympathy that kindles in the heart of every one who remembers his story of noble self-sacrificing love.

There are three or four obelisks that mark the introduction of the Egyptian worship of Isis into the imperial city of the later emperors. At one time everything Egyptian was fashionable in Rome, and the goddess of Egypt was domesticated in the Roman Pantheon, and temples in her honour were erected in several parts of the city and throughout the empire. Obelisks, fashioned in Egypt by command of the Romans, were often placed in front of the temples. But these spurious obelisks have little dignity or significance, and suffer wofully when brought into comparison with specimens of the genuine work of old Egypt. The largest and most imposing of these monuments of the new faith of the city is the one that now stands in the Piazza Navona, formerly called the Pamphilian Obelisk, in honour of the family name of Pope Innocent X., who placed it there. It is forty feet high, of red granite, broken into five pieces, and covered with hieroglyphics, the whole style and execution of which are so inferior that Winkelman long ago, although he knew nothing of their import, detected the fact of the obelisk being a mere imitation. It was cut and engraved at Syene by order of the emperor Domitian, who designed it to adorn his villa on the Lake of Albano. From thence it was removed by the usurper Maxentius to the circus on the Appian Way, founded by him, and named after his son Romulus. It is now on the site of the old Circus Agonalis, whose form and boundaries are marked out by the houses of the Piazza Navona. Surmounted by the Pope's device of a dove with an olive branch, a vain substitute of heraldry for sacred symbolism, and standing on an artificial rock-work about forty feet high, composed of figures of Tritons and nymphs, disporting themselves amid plashing fountains and marble foliage, the whole subject is incongruous and utterly opposed to the simplicity and majesty of the ancient monuments.

Near the Pantheon there is a pair of obelisks which were brought from the East, and stood together before the temple of Isis and Serapis, which is supposed to have been situated on the site of the Dominican Church of Santa Maria Sopra Minerva. They were found when digging the foundations of the church in 1667, along with an altar of Isis, now in the Capitoline Museum. One of these obelisks was erected by Clement XI. in 1711, in front of the Pantheon, in the midst of the fountain of the Piazza. Its height is only about seventeen feet, and the hieroglyphics on it indicate that it was constructed by Psammeticus II., the supposed Hophra of Hebrew history. This same monarch also constructed its twin-fellow which now stands in the Piazza Minerva in the near neighbourhood. The celebrated sculptor Bernini, when re-erecting it at the command of Pope Alexander VII. in 1660, had the exceedingly bad taste to balance it on the back of a marble elephant, the work of his pupil Ferrata; on account of which absurd incongruity Bernini received from the satirical Roman populace the nickname of "The Elephant." Only one obelisk in Rome was not restored or re-erected by any Pope, viz. that which stands in the beautiful grounds of the Villa Mattei in the Coelian Hill. It was found near the Capitol on the site of an ancient temple of Isis, and was presented by the magistrates to the owner of the villa, a great collector of antiquities. It is said that when it was raised in 1563, on its red granite pedestal, the mason who superintended the work incautiously rested his hand on the block, when the shaft suddenly slid down and crushed it, the bones of the imprisoned member being still held between the two stones.

The foregoing were the last obelisks erected in Rome by the emperors. After them no more were constructed either in the imperial city or in their native land of Egypt. The language inscribed upon them had come to be superseded by the universal use of the Greek tongue; there was no use therefore in making monuments for the reception of hieroglyphic records which nobody could understand or interpret. The sudden craze for the Egyptian idolatry passed away as suddenly as it sprang up, and Christianity established itself as the religion of the civilised world. The temples in Egypt and Rome were closed, the altars overthrown, and the objects connected with the material symbolism of paganism were destroyed, and objects connected with the spiritual symbolism of Christianity set up in their place. And thus the obelisk, the oldest of all religious symbols, which was constructed at the very dawn of human existence, to mark the worship of the material luminary, fell into disuse and oblivion, when "the Sun of Righteousness" rose above the horizon of the world, with healing in His wings, dispelling all the mists and delusions of error. The art of constructing obelisks followed the usual stages in the history of all human art. Its best period was that which indicated the greatest faith; its worst that which marked the decay of faith. The oldest specimens are invariably the most perfect and beautiful; the most recent exhibit too marked signs of the decrepitude of skill that had come over their makers. Between the oldest specimens and their surroundings there was a harmony and an appropriateness which solemnised the scene and excited feelings of adoration and awe. Between the latest specimens and their surroundings there was an incongruity which proved them to be aliens and strangers on the scene, and was fatal to all reverence; an incongruity which the modern Romans have only intensified by raising them on pedestals of most uncongenial forms, and crowning them with hideous masses of metal, representing the insignia of popes or other objects equally unsuitable. We see in the oldest obelisks a wonderful ease and an exquisite finish of execution, a maturity of thought and skill which none of the later obelisks reached, and which indicate the high-water mark of man's achievement in that line. There is also "a bloom of youth and of the earth's morning" about them which is quite indescribable, and which doubtless came to them because of the power and reality of faith. They were the fresh natural originals in which a deep primitive spontaneous adoration that dominated the whole nature of man expressed itself; while the specimens that were executed afterwards were slavish imitations, expressing a worship and a creed which had become fixed and formal.

One of the most valuable results of the expedition of the great Napoleon to Egypt, ostensibly for scientific and antiquarian purposes, but really for military glory, was the acquisition of the Rosetta stone now in the British Museum—which afforded the key to the decipherment of the Egyptian hieroglyphics—and of the obelisk of Luxor which now adorns the noble Place de la Concord in Paris. The history of the engineering difficulties overcome in bringing this obelisk to France is extremely interesting. Indeed, the story of the transportation of the obelisks from their native home, from time to time, to other lands, is no less romantic and worthy of study than the artistic, religious, or antiquarian phases of the subject. It forms a special literature of its own to which Commander Gorringe of the United States Navy, in his elaborate and magnificent work on Egyptian obelisks, has done the amplest justice. It cost upwards of £100,000 to bring the Luxor Obelisk to Paris, owing to the inexperience of the engineers and the imperfection of their method. But it was worthy of this vast expenditure of toil and money; for standing in an open circus unimpeded by narrow streets, and unspoiled by the tawdry ornaments which disfigure the Roman obelisks, it adds to the magnificent modern city the charm of antique majesty. It stands seventy-six feet and a half in height, with its apex left rough and unfinished, destitute of the gilded cap which formerly completed and protected it. Each of its four sides contains three vertical lines of well-executed hieroglyphics, which show that it was raised in honour of Rameses II., to adorn the stupendous temple of Luxor at Thebes which he constructed. When it lay on its original site, previous to its being transported, it was found to have been cracked at the time of its first erection, and repaired by means of two dove-tailed wedges of wood which had perished long ago. But this defect is not now noticeable. The companion of this obelisk is still standing at Luxor, and has already been described. Both of them show a peculiarity in their lines, which could only be noticed effectually when the pair stood together. This peculiarity is a convexity, or entasis, as it is called, on the inner faces. Even to the untrained eye its sides seem not of equal dimensions; and actual measurement shows the irregularity more clearly. This is said, however, to be exceptional to the general rule, and to be foreign to the design of an obelisk in the best period of the Pharaonic art. Still, several magnificent specimens, such as the Luxor and Flaminian obelisks, exhibit it. And they are an illustration of what was a marked characteristic of all classic architecture, which shows a slight curvature or entasis in its long lines.

It was early found out that mathematical exactness and beauty were not the same. By making its two sides geometrically equal, the living expression of the most beautiful marble statue is destroyed, and it becomes simply a piece of architecture. It is well known that the two sides of the human face are not precisely the same; the irregularity of the one modifies the irregularity of the other, and thus a higher symmetry and harmony is the result. The two sides of the leaf of the begonia are unequal, and if folded together will not correspond. The same is true of the leaf of the elm and the lime. But when the mass of the foliage is seen together, this irregularity gives an added charm to the whole. Every object in nature has some imperfection, which indicates that it has a relation to some other object, and is but a part of a greater whole. The intentional irregularity of the windows in the Doge's Palace at Venice enhances the effect of the marvellous façade. By comparing the Parthenon at Athens, with its curves and inclinations, with the Madeleine at Paris, we see how far short the copy comes of the original in beauty and expressiveness, because of the exact formality of its right angles. The ancient Egyptians understood this well; and in their architecture they sought to rise to a higher symmetry through irregularity; and we can see in their frequent departure from upright and parallel lines in the construction of their temples, an effort to escape from formal exactness, and a longing for the nobler unity which is realised to the full in the rich variety of the Gothic. We may be sure that "every attempt in art that seeks a theoretical completeness, in so doing sinks from the natural into the artificial, from the living and the divine into the mechanical and commonplace." The Egyptian obelisk is thus but a type of a great law of nature. In this simplest and most primitive specimen of architecture we have an illustration of the principle which gives its expressiveness to the human face, beauty to the flowers of the field, and grandeur to the highest triumphs of human art.

The obelisks that remain to be described are the two which to us are the most interesting; the pair of "Cleopatra's Needles" which so long stood side by side at Alexandria, and are now separated by the Atlantic Ocean; one standing on the Thames Embankment in London, and the other in Central Park, New York. They were both set up in front of the great temple of the Sun at Heliopolis, about fifteen centuries before Christ, by Thothmes III., and engraved by Rameses II., the two mightiest of the kings of Egypt. After standing on their original site for fourteen centuries, witnessing the rise and fall of many native dynasties, and the establishment of the Greek dominion under the Ptolemies, they were, when Egypt became a province of Imperial Rome, transferred by Cæsar Augustus to Alexandria. There they adorned the Cæsareum or palace of the Cæsars, which stood by the side of the harbour, was surrounded with a sacred grove, and was the greatest building in the city. What Thebes and Heliopolis were in the time of the Pharaohs, Alexandria became in the time of the Ptolemies. And though, being a parasitical growth, it could not originate works of genius, like its ancient prototypes, it could appropriate those which Heliopolis and Thebes had created. The tragic death of Cleopatra, the last of the dynasty of the Ptolemies, had taken place seven years before the setting up of these obelisks at Alexandria; so that she had in reality nothing to do with them personally. For about fifteen centuries the two obelisks stood in their new position before the Cæsareum. They saw the gradual overthrow, by time's resistless hand, of the magnificent palace which they adorned; and they themselves felt the slow undermining of the sea as it encroached upon the land, until at last one of them fell to the ground about three hundred years ago, and got partially covered over with sand, leaving the other to stand alone.

Then came the French invasion of Egypt, and the victories of Nelson and Abercromby, when Mahomet Ali, the ruler of the land, offered the prostrate obelisk to the British nation as a token of gratitude. The offer, however, was not taken advantage of, for various reasons. At last the patriotism and enterprise of a private individual, the late Sir Erasmus Wilson, came to the rescue, when the stone was about to be broken up into building material by the proprietor of the ground on which it lay. An iron water-tight cylinder was constructed for its transport, in which, with much toil, the obelisk was encased and floated. It was taken in tow by a steam-tug, which encountered a fearful storm in the Bay of Biscay. This led to the abandonment of the pontoon cylinder, which floated about for three days, and was at last picked up by a passing steamer, and towed to the coast of Spain; from whence it was brought to England, and set up where it now stands on the Thames Embankment. Its transport cost altogether about £13,000, and was a work of great anxiety and difficulty. Standing seventy feet high on its present site, it forms one of the noblest and most appropriate monuments of the greatest city in the world; awakening the curiosity of every passer-by regarding the mysteries revealed in its enigmatical sculptures.

The companion obelisk which had been left standing at Alexandria, after having suffered much from neglect, in the midst of its mean and filthy surroundings, was presented to the American Government by the Khedive of Egypt. But that Government acted in the same supine spirit in which our own had acted; and it was left to the ability of Captain Corringe as engineer, and to the liberality of the millionaire Vanderbilt, who paid the expenses incurred, amounting to £20,000, to bring the obelisk in the hold of a chartered steamer across the Atlantic, and set it up in the midst of New York city. And if the one obelisk is a remarkable sight in London, the other is a still more remarkable sight in New York. There, amid the latest inventions of the West, surrounded by the most recent civilisation of the world, rises up serenely, unchanged to heaven, the earliest monument of the East, surrounded by the most ancient civilisation of the world. "Westward the course of empire takes its way;" and as the old obelisk of Heliopolis witnessed the ending of the four first dramas of human history, so shall it close the fifth and last. The sun in the East rose over its birth; the sun in the West shall set over its death.

It is possible that when all the stores of coal and other fuel which form the source of the mechanical power and commercial greatness of northern and western nations shall have been exhausted, a method of directly utilising solar radiation may be discovered. And if so, then the seat of empire will be transferred to parts of the earth that are now burnt up by the intense heat of the sun, but which then will be the most valuable of all possessions. The vast solar radiance now wasted on the furnace-like shores of the Red Sea will be stored up as a source of mechanical power. The commerce of the West will once more return to the East where it began; and the whole region will be repeopled with the life that swarmed there in the best days of old Egypt. But under that new civilisation there will be no return of the old religion of the obelisks; for men will no longer worship the sun as a god, but will use him for the common purposes of life, as a slave.

After having thus passed in review so many noble obelisks, a mere tithe of what once existed, the conviction is deepened in our minds that no nation had ever devoted so much time, treasure, and skill to the service of religion as the Egyptian. While the Jews had only one tabernacle and one temple, every city in Egypt—and no country had so many great cities—had its magnificent temple and its hosts of obelisks. The spoils of the whole world were devoted to their construction; a third of the produce of the whole land of Egypt was spent in their maintenance. The daily life of the people was moulded entirely upon the religion of these temples and obelisks; their art and their literature were inspired by it. It organised their society; it built up their empire; and it was the salt which for more than three thousand years conserved a civilisation which has been the marvel and the mystery of every succeeding age. Surely the Light which lighteth every man that cometh into the world, shone on those who were thus fervently stretching the tendrils of their souls to its dawning in the East, who raised these obelisks as symbols of the glorious and beneficent sunlight of the world.

CHAPTER VII - THE PAINTED TOMB AT VEII

Rome after a season becomes oppressive. Your capacity of enjoyment is exhausted. The atmosphere of excitement in which you live, owing to the number, variety, and transcendent interest of the sights that have to be seen, wears out the nervous system, and you have an ardent desire for a little respite and change of scene. I remember that after the first month I had a deep longing to get away into the heart of an old wood, or into a lonely glen among the mountains, where I should see no trace of man's handiwork, and recover the tone of my spirit amid the wildness of nature. For this inevitable reaction of sight-seeing in the city, a remedy may be found by retiring for a day or two to some one or other of the numerous beautiful scenes in the neighbourhood. There is no city in the world more favourably situated for this purpose than Rome. Some of the most charming excursions may be made from it as a centre, starting in the morning and returning at night. Every tourist who stays but a fortnight in the city makes a point of seeing the idyllic waterfalls of Tivoli, the extensive ruins of Hadrian's Villa, the picturesque olive-clad slopes of Frascati and Tusculum, and the lovely environs of Albano on the edge of its richly-wooded lake. But there are spots that are less known at no greater distance, which yet do not yield in beauty or interest to these familiar resorts. Chief among these is Veii, whose very name has in it a far-off old-world sound. When the Campagna has quickened under the breath of the Italian spring into a tender greenness, and is starred with orchids and sweet-scented narcissuses, I know nothing more pleasant than a visit to this renowned spot.

Veii was the greatest city of the Etruscan confederacy. When Rome was in its infancy it was in the height of its grandeur. After a ten years' siege it was captured by Camillus; and so stately were its buildings, so beautiful was the scenery around it, and so strong its natural defences, that it was seriously proposed to abandon Rome and transfer the population to it, and thus save the rebuilding of the houses and temples that had been destroyed during the invasion of the Gauls. It was only by a small majority that this project was set aside. Veii never recovered from its overthrow. In vain the Romans attempted to make it one of their own cities by colonising it. Many families established themselves there, but they were afterwards recalled by a decree of the senate, which made it an offence punishable with death for any Roman to remain at Veii beyond a prescribed period. By degrees it dwindled away, until in the days of Propertius its site was converted into pastures; and the shepherd roamed over it with his flocks, unconscious that one of the most famous cities of Italy once stood on the spot. So long ago as the reign of the emperor Hadrian its very locality was forgotten, and its former existence regarded by many with incredulity as a myth of early times. It was left to the enlightened antiquarian skill of our own times, so fruitful in similar discoveries and resuscitations, to find out among the fastnesses of the wilderness around Rome its true position. And although all the difficult problems connected with its citadel and the circuit of its walls have not yet been solved, there can be no doubt that the city stood in the very place which modern archæologists have determined. This place is a little village called Isola Farnese, about eleven miles north-west of Rome. The way that leads to it branches off by a side path for about three miles from the old diligence road between Florence and Rome at La Storta—the last post station where horses were changed about eight miles from the city. It is situated amid ground so broken into heights and hollows that you see no indications of it until you come abruptly upon it, hid in a fold of the undulating Campagna. And the loneliness of the district and of all the paths leading to it is hardly relieved by the appearance of the village itself.

I shall not soon forget my visit to this romantic spot, and the delightful day I spent there with a congenial friend. We left Rome in an open one-horse carriage early one morning about the end of April. Passing out at the Porta del Popolo, we quickly traversed the squalid suburb and crossed the Ponte Molle—the famous old Milvian Bridge. We proceeded as far as the Via Cassia on the old Flaminian Way. At the junction of these roads the villa and gardens of Ovid were situated; but their site is now occupied by a humble osteria or wayside tavern. The road passes over an undulating country entirely uncultivated, diversified here and there with copses and thickets of wild figs intermixed with hawthorn, rose-bushes, and broom. A few ilexes and stone-pines arched their evergreen foliage over the road; and the succulent milky stems of the wild fig-trees were covered with the small green fruit, while the downy leaves were just beginning to peep from their sheaths. It was one of those quiet gray days that give a mystic tone to a landscape. The cloudy sky was in harmony with the dim Campagna, that looked under the sunless smoky light unutterably sad and forlorn. Wreaths of mist lingered in the hollows like the shadowy forms of the past; the lark was silent in the sky; and on the desolate bluffs and headlands, where once stood populous cities, were a few hoary tombs whose very names had perished ages ago. But inexpressibly sad as the landscape looked it was relieved by the grand background of the Sabine range capped with snow. The village of La Storta, that flourished in the old posting days, had fallen into decay when the railway diverted the traffic from it; and its inn, with a rude model of St. Peter's carved in wood projecting above its door, was silent and deserted. Passing down a narrow glen, fringed with wood for three miles from this point, we came in sight of the village of Isola. Its situation is romantic, perched on the summit of a steep cliff, with deep richly-wooded ravines around it, and long swelling downs rising beyond. It is surrounded by two streams which unite and fall along with the Formello into the river called La Valca, which has been identified with the fatal Cremera that was dyed red with the blood of the three hundred Fabii.

The rock of Isola is most interesting to the geologist, consisting of large fragments of black pumice cemented together by volcanic ashes deposited under water. It is literally a huge heap of cinders thrown out by the rapidly intermittent action of some neighbouring volcano, probably the crater of Baccano, or that which is now filled with the blue waters of Lake Bracciano. The whole mass is very friable, and in every direction the soft rock is hollowed out into sepulchral caves. By many this isolated rock is considered the arx or citadel of Veii; but the existence of so many sepulchral caves in it is, as Mr. Dennis says, conclusive of the fact that it was the Necropolis of the ancient city, which must therefore, according to Etruscan and Roman usage regarding the interment of the dead, have been outside the walls. The tombs have all been rifled and destroyed, and many of the sepulchral caves have been turned to the basest uses for stalling goats and cattle. An air of profound melancholy breathes around the whole spot. It seems to be more connected with the dead than with the living world. And the hamlet which now occupies the commanding site is of the most wretched description. All its houses, which date from the fifteenth century, are ruinous, and are among the worst in Italy; and the baronial castle which crowns the highest point, — built nearly a thousand years ago, the scene of many a conflict between the Colonnas and the Orsinis, and captured on one occasion after a twelve days' siege by Cæsar Borgia, — has been converted into a barn. The inhabitants of the village do not exceed a hundred in number, and present a haggard and sallow appearance — the effect of the dreadful malaria which haunts the spot. It is strange to contrast this blighted and fever-stricken aspect of the place with the description of Dionysius, who praised its air as in his time exceedingly pure and healthy, and its territory as smiling and fruitful. In the little square of the village are several fragments of marble and other relics of Roman domination; and the church, about four or five hundred years old, dedicated to St. Pancrazio, is in a state of great decay.

The walls are damp and mouldy, and all the pictures and ornaments are of the rudest description, with the exception of a faded fresco of the coronation of the Virgin, which is a fair specimen of the art of the fifteenth century. The service of the church is supplied by some distant priest or friar in orders.

We left our conveyance in the piazza, and took our lunch in one of the houses. We brought our provisions with us from Rome, but we got a coarse but palatable wine from the people, and a rude but clean room in which to enjoy our repast. This inn — if it may be called, so — had at one time a very evil reputation. But nothing could be more simple-hearted than the landlord and his wife, with their group of timid children who clung to their mother's skirts in dread of the strangers. They told us that the poverty of the place was deplorable. Nearly all the people were laid down during the heats of summer with fever; and they were so poor that they could not afford to keep a doctor. Many deaths occurred, and the survivors, emaciated by the disease, were left to drag on a weary existence embittered by numerous privations. At a distance the village on its lofty rock, surrounded by its richly-wooded ravines, looked like a picture of Arcadia; but near at hand the sad reality dispelled the idyllic dream.

Taking with us from Isola a guide, originally a big burly man, but now a sad victim to malaria, we set out to visit the site of the ancient city and the few relics which survive. It takes about four hours to complete the circuit of the walls; but there are four objects of special interest, the Arx, the Columbarium, the Ponte Sodo, and the Painted Tomb, which may be visited in less than three. The extent of the city is surprising to those who have been in the habit of thinking that all the ancient towns in the neighbourhood of Rome were mere villages. Dionysius says that it was equal in size to Athens. Veii was indeed fully larger, and was about the dimensions of the city of Rome, included within the walls of Servius Tullius. It occupied the whole extent of the platform on which it was situated; and as the area was bounded on every side by deep ravines, its size was thus absolutely circumscribed. Built for security and not for the comfort and progress of its inhabitants, its confined and inaccessible situation would have unfitted it to become the capital of a great nation, as was at one time proposed. Passing down a richly-wooded glen by a path overhanging a stream, we came to a molino or polenta mill, most romantically situated. Here a fine cascade, about eighty feet high, plunges over the volcanic rock into a deep gulley overshadowed by bushy ilexes. The scenery is very picturesque, and differs widely from that of the rest of the Campagna. In its profusion of broom and hawthorn bushes, whose golden and snowy blossoms contrasted beautifully with the dark hues of the evergreen oaks, and in the snowy gleam of its falling waters, and the hoary gray of its lichen-clad cliffs, it presented features of resemblance to Scottish scenery. It had indeed a peculiar home look about it which produced a very pleasing impression upon our minds. Crossing the stream above the cascade by stepping-stones, between which the water rushed with a strong current, we entered the wide down upon which Veii stood. No one would have supposed that this was the site of one of the most important ancient cities, which held at bay for ten long years the Roman army, and yielded at last to stratagem and not to force. Not a vestige of a ruin could be seen. In the heart of the city the grass was growing in all the soft green transparency of spring, and a few fields of corn were marked out and showed the tender braird above the soil. The relics of the walls that crowned the cliffs have almost entirely disappeared. No Etruscan site has so few remains; and yet its interest is intensified by the extreme desolation. It is more suggestive to the imagination because of the paucity of its objects to appeal to the eye. Legend and history haunt the spot with nothing to distract the mind or dispel its musing melancholy. All trace of human passion has disappeared, and only the eternal calm of nature broods over the spot; the calm that was before man came upon the scene, and that shall be after all his labour is over.

On a part of these downs overgrown with briars was situated the Roman Municipium, a colony founded after the subjugation of Veii. It did not cover more than a third of the area of the ancient city. Several excavations were made here, which resulted in the discovery, among other interesting relics of the imperial period, of the colossal heads of Augustus and Tiberius and the mutilated statue of Germanicus now in the Vatican Gallery. On this spot were also found the twelve Ionic columns of white marble which now form the portico of the post-office in the Piazza Colonna at Rome, and also a few of the pillars which adorn the magnificent Basilica of St. Paul's on the Ostian Road. No one looking at these grand columns, so stainless in hue and so perfect in form, would have supposed that they had formed part of the Roman Forum of Veii more than two thousand years ago. Those in front of the post-office look newer than the rest of the building, which is not more than sixty years old. They owed their perfect preservation doubtless to the fact that they were buried deep under the dry volcanic soil for most of the intervening period. It seems strange to think of these ancient columns, that looked down upon the legal transactions of Roman Veii, now standing in one of the busiest squares of modern Rome, associated with one of the most characteristic and important of our modern institutions, of which ancient Rome had not even the germ.

Passing through a beautiful copse wood, where cyclamens grew in lavish profusion, forming little rosy clusters about the oak-stools and diffusing a faint spicy smell through the warm air, we came out at one of the gates of the city into open ground. This gate is simply a gap in a shapeless mound, with traces of an ancient roadway passing through it and fragments of walls on either side. Where the stones can be seen projecting through the turf embankment they are smaller than usual in Etruscan cities. Sir William Gell found hereabouts a portion of the wall composed of enormous blocks of tufa—three or four yards long and more than five feet in height—based upon three courses of thin bricks three feet in length, that rested upon the naked rock. Such a mode of wall construction has no resemblance to anything remaining in Rome or in any Etruscan city. It indicates a still higher antiquity; while the brick foundations remind us of the fame which the Etruscans and particularly the people of Veii had acquired on account of their skill in works of terra cotta. The famous Quadriga or brick chariot which adorned the pediment of the great temple of Jupiter on the Capitol at Rome was made at Veii, and was a remarkable proof of the superiority of its people in this species of art. Indeed the name of Veii is supposed to have been derived from its skill in the manufacture of terra cotta chariots. The old gateway through which we passed out of the wood was probably the principal entrance into the city, and the one over which Tolumnius King of Veii appeared, standing on the wall, during the famous siege when he was challenged to mortal combat by Cornelius Cossus, as graphically described by Livy.

Beneath this gate there is a remarkable tunnel called the Ponte Sodo, bored in the volcanic rock for the passage of the river. It is not, however, visible from this point. You require to descend the steep banks of the river to see it; and a very extraordinary excavation it is, two hundred and forty feet long, sixteen feet wide, and twenty feet high. It was doubtless made to prevent the evil effects of winter floods by the inhabitants of Veii, who had considerable skill in such engineering works. The river sometimes fills the tunnel to the very roof, leaving behind trunks and branches of trees firmly wedged in the clefts of the rock in the inside. It was extremely interesting to stand on this spot and see before me this wonderful Etruscan work, and to lave my hands in the waters of the Formello, which, under the classical name of the Cremera, was prominently associated with early Roman history. It would be difficult to find a lovelier dimple in the fair face of mother earth than the valley through which the Formello flows. Precipitous cliffs rose from the bed of the river opposite to me, enriched with all the hues that volcanic rock assumes under the influences of the weather and the garniture of moss and lichen. A perfect tangle of vegetation crowned their tops and fringed their sides; the dark unchanging verdure of the evergreen oak and ivy contrasting beautifully with the tender autumn-like tints in which the varied spring foliage of the brushwood appeared. Bright flowers and gay blossoms grew in every crevice and nook. The shallow river flowed at my feet through ruts of dark volcanic sand, and amid masses of rock fallen from the cliffs, and stones whose artificial appearance showed that they had formed part of the ramparts that once ran round the whole circuit of the heights. The sunshine sparkled on the gray-green waters, and followed them in bright coruscations for a short distance into the mouth of the tunnel, the other end of which, diminished by the distance, opened into the daylight like the eye-piece of an inverted telescope. I found in the bed of the river fragments of marble and porphyry, cut and polished, that had doubtless come from the pavement of some palace or temple, and attested the truth of the report that has come down to us, that the buildings of Veii were stately and magnificent. To me there is something peculiarly impressive in the presence of a stream in a scene of vanished human greatness. Its eternal sameness contrasts with the momentous changes that have taken place; its motion with the death around; its sunny sparkle with the gloom; while its murmur seems the very requiem of the past. In this giant sepulchre, into which, like the Gulf of Curtius in the Forum, all the greatness of Etruscan and Roman Veii had gone down, the abundance of life was most remarkable. The vegetation sprang up with a rank luxuriance unknown in northern latitudes; lizards darted through the long grass; one snake of considerable length and girth uncoiled itself before me and crawled leisurely away; and the air, as bright and warm as it is in July with us, was murmurous with the hum of insects that danced in the April sunshine.

Beyond the Ponte Sodo the precipices disappear and the ground slopes down gently to the edge of the river. Here the valley of the Formello opens up—a quiet green pastoral spot rising on the right hand into bare swelling downs, without a tree, or a bush, or a rock to diversify their surface. On the sloping banks of the river the rock has been cut into a number of basins filled with water, where Sir William Gell supposes that the nymphs of Veii, like those of Troy, "washed their white garments in the days of peace;" but they were in all likelihood only holes caused by the quarrying of the blocks of stone used in the construction of the walls and buildings of the city. The slopes of this valley seem to have formed the principal Necropolis of Veii. Numerous tombs were discovered in it; but after having been rifled of their contents they were filled up again, and all traces of them have disappeared. Only one sepulchre now remains open in the Necropolis, half way up the slope of a mound called the Poggio Reale. It is commonly known as "The Painted Tomb," or La Grotta Campana—after its discoverer, the Marchese Campana of Rome—who got permission forty-five years ago from the Queen of Sardinia, to whom the property then belonged, to dig in this locality for jewels and other relics of antiquity. Instead of closing the tomb, as was done in the other cases, this accomplished antiquarian, with the good taste for which he was distinguished, left it in the exact condition in which he had found it, so that it might be an object of interest to future visitors. Ascending the slope, we entered a long narrow passage about six feet wide and about fourteen feet deep cut through the tufa rock. This was the original entrance to the tomb; and the discoverer had cleared it out by removing the earth that had accumulated in the course of ages. A solitary crouching lion, carved in a species of volcanic stone, guarded the entrance of the passage. Its companion had been removed some distance, and lay neglected on the slope of the hill. The sculpture is exceedingly uncouth and primitive. At the inner end of the passage a couple of similar lions crouch, one on each side of the door of the tomb. They were placed there in all likelihood as symbols of avenging wrath to inspire fear, and thus prevent the desecration of the dead. Originally the tomb was closed by a great slab of volcanic stone: but this having been broken to pieces and carried away to build the first sheepfold or the nearest peasant's hut, it has been replaced by an iron gate. The walls around were damp and covered with moss and weeds, and the bars of the gate were rusty. Our guide applied the key he had brought with him, and the gate opened with a creaking sound. Lighting a candle, he preceded us into the tomb. I cannot describe the strange mixture of feelings which took possession of me, — wonder, curiosity, and awe. This was my first visit to an Etruscan tomb. In Rome I had been familiar with the monuments of a remote past; I had gazed with interest upon objects over which twenty centuries had passed. But here I was to behold one of the mysterious relics of the world's childhood. I had previously read with deep interest the graphic account of this tomb, which Mr. Dennis gives in his Cities and Cemeteries of Etruria, and was therefore prepared in large measure for what I was about to see.

I found myself when I entered in a gloomy chamber hewn out of a brown arenaceous clay. The floor was a loose mud, somewhat slippery; and on it I noticed a number of vases, large and small, and of various forms. They were not like the exquisite painted vases which we are accustomed to associate with the name of Etruscan, but of the simplest and most archaic shapes, formed out of the coarsest clay. Some of them had a curious squat appearance, with rude figures painted on them; while others of them were about three feet high, of dark-brown earthenware, and were ornamented with some simple device in neutral tints or in very low relief. They were empty now; but when found they contained ashes and fragments of calcined bones. Just within the door there were two stone benches, on each of which, when the tomb was opened, was stretched a skeleton, which rapidly crumbled under the pressure of the air into a cloud of dust. That on the left was supposed to have been a female; and her companion on the right had doubtless been a warrior, judging from the bronze helmet and breastplate, both much corroded, that were left lying on the bench. He had evidently come by a violent death, for at the back of the helmet was an ugly hole, whose ragged side was outwards, showing that the fierce thrust of the spear had crashed through the face, and protruded beyond the casque. The combination of cinerary urns containing ashes, and of stone couches on which dead bodies were extended in the same tomb, is curious, showing that both modes of sepulture were practised at this period. The skeletons found entire were evidently those of the master and mistress of the household, persons of consideration; and the ashes in the jars were probably the remains of the servants and dependants. On the benches beside the skeletons were a bronze laver and mirror, a simple candlestick, and a brazier used for burning perfumes. The vases were exceedingly interesting, as the first rude attempts of the Etruscans in an art in which afterwards they attained to such marvellous perfection, and the only relics now remaining of the fictile statuary for which Veil was so celebrated.

But my interest in these objects was speedily transferred to a far more wonderful sight, which the candle of the guide disclosed to me. On the inner wall, which divided the tomb into two chambers, and on the right and left of the door leading from the one to the other, was a most extraordinary fresco. Seen in the dim light of the candle passing over the different parts, it had a singularly weird and grotesque appearance. The colours were as fresh as if they had been laid on yesterday; and the thought at first flashed across my mind that I was gazing not upon a painting which had been sealed up for nearly thirty centuries, but upon the rude attempts at art of some modern shepherd or rustic belonging to the village of Isola, who sought thus to amuse his leisure moments. But such a thought was dismissed at once as absurd. No one after a few moments' inspection could doubt the genuineness of the painting. It is difficult to describe it, for it is altogether unlike anything to be seen elsewhere in Egyptian or Assyrian, in Greek or Roman tombs. On the right side of the door the upper half of the wall was panelled off by a band of colour, and represented one scene or picture. In the centre was a large horse, that reminded me of a child's wooden toy-horse, such as one sees at a country fair. Its legs were unnaturally long and thin; and the slenderness of its barrel was utterly disproportioned to the breadth of its chest. It was coloured in the most curious fashion: the head, hind-quarters, and near-leg being black; the tail and mane and off-legs yellow; and the rest of the body red, with round yellow spots. It was led by a tall groom; a diminutive youth was mounted upon its back; and a proud, dignified-looking personage, having a double-headed axe or hammer on his shoulder, strode in front. These human figures were all naked, and painted of a deep-red colour. In the same picture I noticed two strange-looking nondescript animals, very rudely drawn, and party-coloured like the horse. One probably represented a cat without a tail, like the Manx breed, half-lying upon the back of the horse, and laying its paw on the shoulder of the youth mounted before it; and the other looked like a dog, with open mouth, apparently barking with all his might, running among the feet of the horse. Interspersed with these figures were most uncouth drawings of flowers, growing up from the ground, and forming fantastic wreaths round the picture, all party-coloured in the same way as the animals.

This extraordinary fresco seemed like the scene which presented itself to the apostle, when one of the seals of the Apocalyptic book was opened. I wished that I had beside me some authoritative interpreter who could read for me "this mystic handwriting on the wall." It has been suggested that the silent scene before me represented the passage of a soul to the world of the dead. The lean and starved-looking horse symbolised death; and its red and yellow spots indicated corruption. It may have been the ghost of the horse that was burned with the body of his dead master; for we know that the tribes, from which the Etruscans were supposed to be descended, if not the Etruscans themselves, not only burned their dead, but offered along with them the wives, slaves, horses, and other property of the dead upon their funeral pyre. The horse in this remarkable fresco may therefore have been the death-horse, which is well-known in Eastern and European folklore. The diminutive figure which it carried on its back was the soul of the dead person buried in this tomb; and its small size and the fact of its being on horseback might have been suggested by the thought of the long way it had to go, and its last appearance to the mortal eyes that had anxiously watched it from the extreme verge of this world as it vanished in the dim distance of the world beyond. The groom that led the horse and his rider was the Thanatis or Fate that had inflicted the death-blow; and the figure with the hammer was probably intended for the Mantus — the Etruscan Dispater — who led the way to another state of existence. The deep-red colour of the human figures indicated not only that they belonged to the male sex, but also that they were in a state of glorification. This is further confirmed by the flowers, which looked like those of the lotus, universally regarded amongst the ancients as symbols of immortality. It is difficult to say what part the domestic animals were meant to play in this scene of apotheosis. Painted with the same hues as those of the steed, they were doubtless sacrificed at the death of their master, in order that they might share his fortunes and accompany him into the unseen world; their affection for him, and the reluctance with which they parted from him, being indicated by the cat putting its paw upon his shoulder as if to pull him back, and the dog barking furiously at the heels of the horse. But all this is merely conjectural. And yet I caught such a glimpse of the general significance of the picture, of the spirit that prompted it, as deeply impressed me. It seemed as if my own searching dimly with a candle in the inside of a dark sepulchral cave into the meaning of this fresco of death was emblematical of the groping of the ancient Etruscans, by such feeble light of nature as they possessed, in the midst of the profound, terrible darkness of death, for the great truths of immortality. They had not heard of One who alone with returning footsteps had broken the eternal silence of the tomb, and brought the hope of immortal life to the sleeping dead around. These Etruscan sleepers had been laid to rest in their narrow cell ages before the Son of Man had rolled away the stone from the door of the sepulchre, and carried captivity captive; but He whom they ignorantly worshipped had partially lifted the veil and given them faint glimpses of the things unseen and eternal. And these were doubtless sufficient to redeem their life from its vanity and their death from its fear.

Below the fresco which I have thus minutely described is another about the same size, representing a sphinx, with a nondescript animal, which may be either an ass or a young deer standing below it, and a panther or leopard sitting behind in a rampant attitude, with one paw on the haunch of the sphinx, and the other on the tail, and its face turned towards the spectator. The face of the sphinx is painted red. The figure bears some resemblance to the Egyptian type of that chimera in its straight black hair depending behind, and its oblique eyes; but in other respects it diverges widely. On Egyptian monuments the sphinx never appears standing as in this fresco, but crouching in the attitude of reposeful observation. Its form also was always fuller and more rounded than the long-legged, attenuated spectre before us, and it was invariably wingless; whereas the Etruscan sphinx had short wings with curling points, spotted and barred with stripes of black, red, and yellow. This strange mixture of the human and the brutal might be regarded as a symbol of the religious state of the people. We see in it higher conceptions of religion struggling out of lower. In the recumbent wingless sphinx of Egypt we see anthropomorphic ideas of religion emerging out of the gross animal-worship of more primitive times. In the standing and winged Etruscan Sphinx we see these ideas assuming a more predominant form; while in the Greek mythology the emancipation of the human from the brutal was complete, and the gods appeared wholly in the likeness of men.

On the wall on the opposite side of the door were two other frescoes, somewhat similar in general appearance to those already described. On the upper panel was a horse with a boy on his back, and a panther sitting on the ground behind him; while on the lower panel there was a huge standing panther or leopard, with his long tongue hanging out of his mouth, and a couple of dogs beneath him, one lifting up its paw, and the other trying to catch the protruded tongue of the panther. All the figures in the four frescoes were painted in the same bizarre style of red, yellow, and black characteristic of the first fresco described; and they had all the same Oriental border of lotus flowers. They had evidently all the same symbolic import; for the sphinx guarded the gate of the unseen world, and leopards or panthers were frequently introduced into the paintings of Etruscan tombs as guardians of the dead.

Passing through the doorway I entered an inner and smaller chamber, whose only decoration was six small round discs on the opposite wall, each about fifteen inches in diameter, painted in little segments of various colours,—black, blue, red, yellow, and gray. What they were meant to represent no one has satisfactorily explained. Above them I observed a number of rusty nails fixed in the wall, and traces of others that had fallen out around the doorway. On these nails were originally suspended various articles of household economy or of personal ornament; for the Etruscan sepulchres were always furnished with such things as the tenants took delight in when living. For a proof of this nothing could be more satisfactory than a thorough study of Inghirami's voluminous work. Indeed, all ancient nations buried their dead not only with their weapons and armour, but also with their most precious possessions; and in proportion to the rank and wealth of the deceased were the number and value of the offerings deposited with him in his tomb. We are amazed at the variety and preciousness of the golden ornaments found by Dr. Schliemann in the tombs at Mycenæ; and every Etruscan cemetery that has been opened has yielded an immense number of most precious articles, which the devotion of the survivors sacrificed to the manes of their departed friends. It is to this propensity that we owe all our knowledge of this mysterious race. But the fact, as Mr. Dennis says, that the nails in the interior of this tomb were empty, and that no fragments of the objects suspended were found at the foot of the wall, indicated either that the articles had decayed, being of a perishable nature, or that they had been carried off on account of their superior value. This last is the more probable supposition. The Marchese Campana, who opened the tomb, was late in the field, and had in all likelihood been anticipated by some previous explorer. The work of plundering Etruscan tombs was begun, we have reason to believe, in the time of the early Romans, who were attracted, not merely by the precious metals which they contained, but also by the reputation of their vases, which in the days of the Empire were held in as high esteem as now. Many tombs have doubtless been repeatedly searched. The very architects employed in their construction, as Signor Avolta conjectures, may have preserved the secret of the concealed entrance, and used it for the purpose of spoliation afterwards. Indeed, an unviolated tomb is a very rare exception. No modern excavations were made till about sixty years ago; and yet during that short interval many tombs that were opened and filled up again have been forgotten; and now they are being dug afresh by persons ignorant of this, who spend their labour only to be disappointed. There is little reason, therefore, to believe that the Painted Tomb of Veii was so fortunate as to escape all notice until the Marchese Campana had discovered it. Former visitors had robbed it in all likelihood of any objects of intrinsic value it may have contained, and left only the bronze utensils and armour and the rude archaic vases.

On the roughly-hewn roof of this inner chamber of the tomb were carved in high relief two beams in imitation of the rafters of a house; and round the walls at the foot ran a low ledge formed out of the rock, like a family couch, on which stood three very curious boxes of earthenware, about a foot and a half long and a foot high, covered with a projecting lid on which was moulded a human head. These were sepulchral urns of a most primitive form, intermediate between the so-called hut-urns found under the lava in the Necropolis of Alba Longa, and supposed to represent the tents in which the Etruscans lived at the time of their arrival in Italy, and the round vases of a later period. On the same ledge were several vases painted in bands of red and yellow, with a row of uncouth animals executed in relief upon the rim. The form and contents of this chamber afforded striking proof of the fact that the Etruscan tombs were imitations of the homes of the living. These tombs were constructed upon two types: one rising in the form of a tumulus or conical mound above the ground when the situation was a level table-land, and the other consisting of one or two chambers excavated out of the rock when the tomb was situated on the precipitous face of a hill. Dr. Isaac Taylor, in his admirable Etruscan Researches, says that the former type recalled the tent, and the latter the cave, which were the original habitations of men. The ancestors of the Etruscans are supposed by him to have been a nomadic race, wandering over the steppes of Asia, and to have dwelt either in caves or tents. At the present day the yourts or permanent houses in Siberia and Tartary are modelled on the plan of both kinds of habitation — the upper part being above the ground, representing the tent; and the lower part being subterranean, representing the cave. And so the descendants of this Asiatic horde, having migrated at a remote period to Italy, preserved the burial traditions of their remote ancestors, and formed their tombs after the model of the tent or cave, according as they were constructed on the level plateau or in the rocky brow of a hill. In further illustration of this theory he says that in olden times when a member of the Tartar tribe died, the tent in which he breathed his last, with all its contents intact, was converted into a tomb by simply covering it with a conical mound of earth or stones, in order to preserve it from the ravages of wolves and other beasts of prey. Even the row of stones that surrounded the outside of the tent and kept down the skins that covered it from being blown away by the storms of the steppe, was introduced into the structure of the tomb, and continued to surround the base of the funeral mound. He finds traces of this circle of stones in the podium or low wall of masonry which encircled every Etruscan tumulus or outside tomb, and a remarkable example in the mounds of the Horatii and Curiatii on the Appian Way at Rome.

This theory, however, it is only fair to state, is disputed by other writers, who assert that there was no intentional imitation of tents in Etruscan tombs; for if this had been the design there would have been a correspondence between the conical outside and the conical interior, and no Etruscan tomb has been found with a bell-shaped chamber. The tent-like tumulus, say they, was but the mere rude mound of earth heaped over the dead in an uncultured age; and the mound would be made higher and larger according to the dignity of the deceased; and the podium or row of stones around its foot was simply the retaining wall necessary to give it stability and shape. The tomb at Veii had a narrow entrance-passage; and we find this a marked feature in all Etruscan tombs, which are approached by a vaulted passage of masonry, varying from twelve to a hundred feet in length. This also, according to Dr. Taylor, was but a survival of the low entrance-passage through which the ancient Siberians crept into their subterranean habitations, and which the modern Laplanders and Esquimaux still construct before their snow-huts and underground dwellings, to serve the purpose of a door in keeping out the wind and maintaining the temperature of the interior.

The other, or cave type of Etruscan tomb, is that which we see at Veii, and of which there are hundreds of examples all over Central Italy, wherever there are deep valleys bounded by low cliffs. This, too, was modelled after the pattern of the house. There were usually two chambers, an outer and an inner one. The outer was the place of meeting between the living and the dead; the surviving friends feasted there during their annual visit to the tomb, while the dead were laid in the inner chamber in the midst of familiar objects. Here everything was designed to keep up the delusion that the dead were still living in their own homes. The roof of the chamber was carved in imitation of the roof-tree, the rafters, and even the tiles of the house; the rock around was hewn into couches, with cushions and footstools like those on which they reposed when living; on the floor were the wine-jars, the vases, and utensils, consecrated by long use; on the various projections were suspended the mirrors, arms, and golden ornaments that were most prized; while the walls were painted with gay frescoes, representing scenes of festivity in which eating and drinking, music and dancing, played a prominent part. And as the ordinary habitation contained the family, the grandparents, the parents, and the children, all living under the same roof, so the Etruscan tombs were all family abodes—the dead of a whole generation being deposited in the same inner chamber.

To the outer chamber, as I have said, came the surviving members of the family at least once a year to hold a funeral feast, and pay their devotions to their departed friends. The tombs of this people were thus at the same time also their temples—the sacred places where they came to perform the rites of their religion, which consisted in worshipping the lares and penates of their beloved dead, and making offerings to them. And by this striking link of the cultus of the dead the ancient Etruscans were connected with the present inhabitants of Northern Asia, the Finns, Laplanders, Tartars, Mongols, and Chinese, who have no temples or places of special honour for their idols, but assemble once a year or oftener at the graves of their ancestors to worship the dead. But after all there is no great difference in this respect between the races, ancient and modern; for the churchyard and the church, the burial vaults and monuments within the cathedral and chapel, show how universal is the instinct that associates the dead with the shrine of religion, and makes the tomb the most appropriate place for giving expression to those blessed hopes of immortality upon which all religion is founded. The sanctuary of the Holy Land derived its sacredness, as well as the charter of its inheritance, from the cave of Machpelah. Around that patriarchal tomb clustered all the grand religious hopes of the covenant people. The early Christians adopted and purified the Etruscan custom which they found in Rome, and erected over the tombs of the martyrs and other illustrious persons Cellæ Memoriæ, or memorial chapels, in which on anniversary occasions the friends and brethren assembled to partake of a funeral feast in honour of the dead. The primitive Agapæ, or love-feasts, were often nothing more than such banquets in the memorial cells at the tombs of the faithful. And in our own country, many of our most important churches, towns, and villages took their origin and name from the grave of some saint, who in far-off times hallowed the spot and made it a shrine of worship.

There are numerous indications that this Painted Tomb at Veii is of very great antiquity, and may be considered as probably the oldest tomb in Europe. No inscription of any kind has been found on its walls or any of its contents; and this circumstance, which is almost singular so far as all Etruscan tombs yet discovered are concerned, of itself indicates a very remote date, when the art of letters if known at all was only known to a privileged few, and confined to public and sacred monuments. No clue remains to inform us who the Veientine warrior was who met his death in so tragic a manner, and who lay down with his wife and dependants in this tomb, and took the last long sleep without a thought of posterity or the conclusions they might form regarding him. And the argument of hoary antiquity derived from this speechless silence of the tomb is still further strengthened by architectural evidence. The outer wall as seen from the inside is built of rough uncemented blocks of the earliest polygonal construction, such as we see in a few of the oldest Cyclopean cities of Central Italy; and the doorway is formed by the gradual convergence of stones laid in horizontal courses, instead of being arched by regular wedges of stone held together. Now, as the perfect arch was known and constructed in Etruria at a very early period, this pseudo-vault, which indicates complete ignorance of the principle, must belong to a very remote age indeed — to the period of the Cyclopean gateways of Italy and Greece, whose origin is lost in the mist of a far-off antiquity. There are two limits within which the date of the tomb may probably be placed. While its style and decorations are genuinely national and characteristic of the primitive Etruscan tomb, there can be no doubt that several Egyptian features in it, such as the sphinx and the lotus, and in some respects the colouring and physiognomy of the human figures, indicate some acquaintance with the land of the Nile. Now an inscription has been found at Karnac which records that Egypt was invaded by a confederation of Libyans, Etruscans, and other races, and was only saved after a desperate struggle by the valour of Menephtah I. of the Nineteenth Dynasty. The allied forces occupied the country for a time, and took away with them when they departed large spoils, consisting among other things of bronze knives and armour. This happened in the fourteenth or fifteenth century before Christ. There can be no doubt, therefore, that the civilisation of Egypt must at this period have been spread by commerce or war among the Western nations, and produced a powerful influence upon the Etruscans. The imitation of Egyptian models is not so decided in this tomb as it is in the painted tombs of Tarquinii and other Etruscan cities of later date; and this circumstance would indicate that it was constructed at the very commencement of the intercourse of Etruria with Egypt. If we take this historic fact as the limit in one direction, the tomb cannot be older than three thousand three hundred years. On the other hand, we know that Veii was destroyed about four hundred years before Christ, and remained uninhabited and desolate till the commencement of the Empire; we have, therefore, the surest ground for fixing the date of the tomb prior to that event. Somewhere between the invasion of Egypt by the Etruscan confederacy and the fall of Veii — that is, somewhere between the fourteenth and the fourth century before Christ — this sepulchre was hewn in the rock and its tenants interred in it.

Carlo Avolta of Corneto on one occasion, opening an Etruscan tomb at Tarquinii, saw a most wonderful sight. From an aperture which he had made above the door of the sepulchre he looked in, and for fully five minutes "gazed upon an Etruscan monarch lying on his stone bier, crowned with gold, clothed in armour, with a shield, spear, and arrows by his side." But as he gazed the figure collapsed, and finally disappeared; and by the time an entrance was made all that remained was the golden crown, some fragments of armour, and a handful of gray dust. Like that Etruscan tomb has been the fate of the Etruscan confederacy. This mighty people left traces of their civilisation "inferior in grandeur perhaps to the monuments of Egypt, in beauty to those of Greece, but with these exceptions surpassing in both the relics of any other nation of remote antiquity." At the period of their highest power they lived in close neighbourhood and connection with a people who got its laws, its rulers, its arts, its religion from them — and might therefore if only in gratitude have preserved their history. But their fate was that of the similar civilisation of Mexico and Peru, which its selfish Spanish conquerors instead of preserving sought studiously to obliterate. The comprehensive history of Etruria written in twenty volumes by the emperor Claudius — who, though very feeble in other things, was yet a scholar, and could have given us much interesting information — perished. Their language, which survived their absorption by Rome, almost as late as the time of the Cæsars, finally disappeared; and though thousands of inscriptions in tombs and on works of art remain — which we are able to read from the close resemblance of the alphabet to the Greek — the key to the interpretation of the language is gone beyond recall. In an age that has unravelled the Egyptian hieroglyphics, and the cuneiform characters of Assyria, and the runic inscriptions of Northern Europe, the Etruscan language presents almost the only philological problem that refuses to be solved. Thus when the air and the light of modern investigation penetrated into the mystery which surrounded this strange people, all that was most important had vanished; and only the few ornaments of the tomb remained to tell us of a lost world of art, literature, and human life which had perished not by internal exhaustion, but had fallen before the arms of Rome in the full maturity of its civilisation.

CHAPTER VIII - HOLED STONES AND MARTYR WEIGHTS

In the porch of the interesting old church of Sta. Maria in Cosmedin near the Tiber is preserved a huge circular stone like a millstone. It is composed of white marble, upwards of five feet in diameter, and is finished after the model of the dramatic mask used in the ancient theatres. In the centre is a round hole perforating the mass right through, forming the mouth of the mask. It is called the Bocca della Verita, and has given its name to the irregular piazza in which the church is situated. It is so called from the use to which it has been put from time immemorial, as an ordeal for testing the guilt or innocence of an accused person. If the suspected individual on making an affirmation thrust his hand through the hole and was able to draw it back again, he was pronounced innocent; but if, on the contrary, the hand remained fixed in the marble jaws, the person was declared to have sworn falsely and was pronounced guilty. The marble mouth was supposed by the superstitious to contract or expand itself according to the moral character of the arraigned person. No reason has been given why this singular marble mask should have been placed in this church, nor is anything known of its previous history. Some have conjectured that it served as an impluvium or mouth of a drain in the centre of a court to let the water run off; and others regard it as having been an ornament for a fountain, like the colossal mask of marble out of the mouth of which a jet of water falls into a fountain in the Via de Mascherone, called after it, near the Farnese Palace, and the marble mask which belongs to a small fountain on the opposite side of the river near the Palazzo Salviati. But the question arises, Why should the Bocca della Verita, if such was its origin, have been used for the superstitious purpose connected with it? Our answer to this question must lead us back to the Temple of Ceres and Proserpine which originally stood on the site of the church of Sta. Maria in Cosmedin, and of the materials of which the Christian edifice was largely built.

In primitive times the worship of clefts in rocks, holes in the earth, or stones having a natural or artificial perforation, appears to have been almost universal. We find traces of it in almost every country, and amongst almost every people. These sacred chasms or holes were regarded as emblems of the celestial mother, and persons went into them and came out again, so as to be born anew, or squeezed themselves through the holes in order to obtain the remission of their sins. In ancient Palestine this form of idolatry was known as the worship of Baal-perazim, or Baal of the clefts or breaches. David obtained a signal victory over the Philistines at one of the shrines of this god, and burnt there the images peculiar to this mode of worship which the enemy had left behind in its flight. About two miles from Bombay there is a rock on the promontory of the Malabar Hill, which has a natural crevice, communicating with a cavity below, and opening upon the sea. This crevice is too narrow for corpulent persons to squeeze through, but it is constantly resorted to for purposes of moral purification. Through natural or artificial caverns in India pilgrims enter at the south side, and make their exit at the northern, as was anciently the custom in the Mithraic mysteries. Those who pass through such caves are considered to receive by this action a new birth of the soul. According to the same idea the rulers of Travancore, who are Nairs by caste, are made into Brahmins when they ascend the throne by passing through a hole in a large golden image of a cow or lotus flower, which then becomes the property of the Brahmin priests. It is possible that there may be an allusion to this primitive custom in the rule of the Jewish Temple, mentioned by Ezekiel, — "He that entereth in by the way of the north gate to worship shall go out by the way of the south gate; and he that entereth by the way of the south gate shall go forth by the way of the north gate: he shall not return by the way of the gate whereby he came in, but shall go forth over against it." This arrangement may have been made not as a mere matter of convenience, but as a survival of the old practice of "passing through" a sacred cave or crevice for the forgiveness of sins; — a survival purified and ennobled in the service of God.

The oldest of all religious monuments of which we have any existing trace are cromlechs, found mostly in waste, uncultivated places. These are of various forms, but they are mostly tripods, consisting of a copestone poised upon three other stones, two at the head and one at the foot. The supports are rough boulders, the largest masses of stone that could be found or moved; and the copestone is an enormous flat square block, often with cup-shaped hollows carved upon its surface. Under this copestone there was a vacant space, varying in size from a foot or two to the height of a man on horseback. Through this vacant space persons used to pass; and the narrower the space, the more difficult the feat of crawling through, the more meritorious was the act. In our own country there are numerous relics of this primitive custom. In Cornwall there are two holed stones, one called Tolven, situated near St. Buryan, and the other called Men-an-tol, near Madron, which have been used within living memory for curing infirm children by passing them through the aperture. In the parish of Minchin Hampton, Gloucestershire, is a stone called Long Stone, seven or eight feet in height, having near the bottom of it a large perforation, through which, not many years since, children brought from a considerable distance were passed for the cure of measles and whooping-cough. On the west side of the Island of Tyree in Scotland is a rock with a crevice in it through which children were put when suffering from various infantile diseases. In connection with the ancient ruined church of St. Molaisse on the Island of Devenish in Loch Erne in Ireland, there is an artificially perforated stone, through which persons still pass, when the opening will admit, in order to be regenerated. If the hole be too small, they put the hand or the foot through it, and the effect is thus limited. Examples of such holed stones are to be found in some of the old churches of Ireland, such as Castledermot, County Kildare; Kilmalkedar, County Kerry; Kilbarry, near Tarmon Barry, on the Shannon. In Madras, diseased children are passed under the lintels of doorways; and in rural parts of England they used to be passed through a cleft ash tree. At Maryhill, in the neighbourhood of Glasgow, about a year ago, when an epidemic of measles and whooping-cough was prevalent, two mothers took advantage, for the carrying out of this superstition, of the presence in the village of an ass which drew the cart of a travelling rag-gatherer. They stood one on each side of the animal. One woman then took one of the children and passed it face downward through below the ass's belly to the other woman, who in turn handed it back with its face this time turned towards the sky. The process having been repeated three times, the child was taken away to the house, and then the second child was similarly treated. The mothers were thoroughly satisfied that their children were the better of the magic process.

A mysterious virtue was supposed to be connected with passing under the ancient gate of Mycenæ by the primitive race who constructed it. Jacob's words at Bethel, "This is the gate of heaven," may have an allusion to the prehistoric custom of the place; for we have reason to believe that a dolmen existed there, consecrated to solar worship, the original name of Bethel being Beth-on, the house of the sun. The hollow space beneath the dolmen was considered the altar-gate leading to paradise, so that whosoever passed through it was certain to obtain new life or immortality. It was an old superstition that the dead required to be brought out of the house not by the ordinary door of the living, but by a breach made specially in the wall, in order that they might thus pass through a species of purgatory. We find an exceedingly interesting example of this primitive superstition in the punishment that was imposed upon the survivor in the famous combat between the Horatii and Curiatii, when he murdered his sister, on account of her unpatriotic devotion to her slain lover. The father of Horatius, after making a piacular sacrifice, erected a beam across the street leading from the Vicus Cyprius to the Carinæ, with an altar on each side — the one dedicated to Juno Sororia and the other to Janus Curiatius — and under this yoke he made his son pass with his head veiled. This beam long survived under the name of Tigillum Sororium or Sister's Beam, and was constantly repaired at the public expense.

In modern times there are two most remarkable survivals of the same kind. One of them is in the corridor of the mosque of Aksa at Jerusalem. In this place are two pillars, standing close together, and like those in the mosque of Omar at Cairo, they are used as a test of character. It is said that whosoever can squeeze himself between them is certain of paradise, and must be a good Moslem. The pillars have been worn thin by the friction of countless devotees. An iron bar has now, however, been placed between the pillars by the present enlightened Pasha of Jerusalem to prevent the practice in future. The other instance is what is popularly known as "threading the needle" in the Cathedral of Ripon. Beneath the central tower of this minster there is a small crypt or vaulted cell entered from the nave by a narrow passage. At the north side of this crypt there is an opening thirteen inches by eighteen, called St. Wilfred's needle. This passage was formerly used as a test of character; for only an honest man, one new-born, could pass through it. "They pricked their credits who could not thread the needle," was the quaint remark of old Fuller in reference to the original use of the opening. It may be remarked that the well-known boys' game of "Through the needle's e'e, boys," had its origin in all likelihood in the old superstition. Thus we can trace the use made of the Bocca della Verita in Rome to the primitive idolatry associated perhaps with the Temple of Ceres that formerly stood on the spot.

Some other superstitious practices of a closely allied nature may be traced to the same source. In the Orkney Islands, not far from the famous Standing Stones of Stennis, there is a single monolith with a large hole through it, which has become celebrated, owing to the allusion to it of Sir Walter Scott in his novel of the Pirate. It is called Odin's Stone; and till a very recent period it was the local custom to take an oath by joining hands through the hole in it; and this oath was considered even by the regular courts of Orkney as peculiarly solemn and binding; the person who violated it being accounted infamous and excluded from society. In the old churchyard of the ruined monastery of Saints Island in the Shannon, there is an ancient black marble flagstone called the "Cremave" or "swearing stone." The saints are said to have made it a revealer of truth. Any one suspected of falsehood is brought here, and if the accused swears falsely the stone has the power to set a mark upon him and his family for several generations. But if no mark appears he is known to be innocent. Many other equally interesting instances might be quoted all akin to the superstition in Rome. It is not too fanciful to suppose that even the Jewish mode of making a covenant had something to do with this primitive custom. The animal offered in sacrifice was divided into two pieces, and so arranged that a space was left between them. Through this space, between the parts, the contracting persons passed in order to ratify the covenant. We have a striking account of this ceremony in the case of Abraham; and it is in allusion to it that the author of the Epistle to the Hebrews says that we have boldness to enter into the holiest "by a new and living way, which he hath consecrated for us, through the veil, that is to say, his flesh."

The superstitious practices connected with clefts and holed stones were denounced by councils of the Christian Church, which subjected transgressors to various penalties. Consequently this mode of worship came into evil repute; and what was formerly considered a meritorious action, securing the cure of disease or future happiness, became a deed of evil, to be followed by some calamity. For this reason the primitive symbolism was reversed in many cases, such as "passing under a ladder," which is now considered unlucky; or in Eastern lands going between a wall and a pole, between two women or two dogs, which the Talmud forbids as an omen of evil.

Passing from the subject of holed stones I proceed to consider another class of interesting prehistoric objects that survive in the more primitive churches of Rome. In the same church of Sta. Maria in Cosmedin—where the Bocca della Verita which I have described occurs—there is a curious crypt called the chapel of St. Cyril, who undertook a mission about the year eight hundred and sixty to convert the Slavs in Bulgaria to Christianity, and suffered martyrdom in the attempt. Beside an ancient altar of primitive construction on one side is preserved a large slab of granite on which St. Cyril is said to have knelt when he was put to death; and half-sunk in the wall opposite are two large, smooth, dark-coloured stones, in shape not unlike curling stones—or an orange from which a portion has been sliced off horizontally. They cannot fail to be seen when attention is directed to them.

Such stones, often made level at the top and bottom, and with a ring inserted in the upper surface, are not uncommon in the older churches of Rome, although they are very seldom noticed, as their significance is only known to a few experts. One is placed in the centre of the middle nave of Santa Sabina, on the Aventine, on the top of a short spirally-fluted column of white marble, which marks the spot where St. Dominic, the founder of the order of the Dominicans, used to kneel down and pray. It has received the name of Pietra di Paragone, or the Touchstone. Another may be seen at the entrance of the church of Santa Pudenziana, on the Esquiline, supposed to have been built on the site of the house of the Roman senator Pudens, whose daughter, Pudentiana, St. Peter is said to have converted to Christianity. A third exists among the extensive collection of relics belonging to the ten thousand three hundred martyrs whose remains, according to tradition, were deposited in the church of S. Prassede, at the beginning of the ninth century, by Paschal I. Two stones may be observed upon the gable wall immediately above the basins of holy water in the interior of the church of S. Nicolo in Carcere, near the Ghetto. Two others are inserted in the wall of the Baptistery of St. John Lateran, between the vestibule and the octagonal area containing the so-called gigantic font in which Constantine was baptized. A very interesting stone hangs suspended from the gilded iron grating which protects the crypt or confessional of St. Laurence, immediately underneath the high altar of the great Basilica of San Lorenzo beyond the Gate. A stone still more remarkable, guarded by a strong iron grating, projects half its bulk from the wall on the right-hand side of the arch which divides the transept from the middle nave in the venerable church of Santa Maria in Trastevere. Two other stones may be seen in the quaint old church of SS. Cosma e Damiano at the south-eastern angle of the Roman Forum, composed of portions of three pagan temples. They are inserted in the plain whitewashed walls on both sides of the circular arch through which you pass from the round vestibule into the interior of the church. I have noticed similar stones in no less than twenty places besides those I have mentioned; and I am assured that they may be seen in many more churches.

It is very difficult to obtain any accurate or satisfactory information regarding these curious stones. They go by the name of Lapides Martyrum, or Martyr-stones. During the persecutions of the early Christians in Rome they are said to have been hung round the necks of those who were condemned to be drowned in the Tiber. In the reign of the emperor Diocletian many martyrs perished in this way, and the stones by which they were sunk beneath the fatal waters, according to the popular idea, were afterwards found, and carefully preserved as holy relics in the churches in which they are now to be seen. Beyond doubt they are genuine remains of antiquity, and some of them at least may have been used for the purpose alleged; although we cannot be sure, in any case, that the story connected with particular stones is authentic. St. Sabine desired that the stone which was to be tied to him when thrown in the river should be buried with his body, and this might have been done in the case of other martyrs. The stones in the church of SS. Cosma e Damiano are supposed to have been the very ones that were fastened to the necks of these devoted Christians when they were thrown into the Tiber in the reign of Maximian. But as the place and manner of their martyrdom are involved in hopeless obscurity, the various accounts given of both being contradictory, the ecclesiastical legend has no weight. Cosma and Damian were Arabian doctors who were converted to Christianity, and belonged to the class called "silverless martyrs" — that is, physicians who took no fee from those whom they cured, but only stipulated that they should believe in Christ the Great Physician. They occupied in Christian hagiology the same place as the ancient myth of Esculapius occupied in pagan mythology.

Around the stone in the church of Santa Sabina a curious legend has gathered. The sacristan, a Dominican friar of the neighbouring convent, is in the habit of telling the visitors that the devil one day, while St. Dominic was kneeling on the pavement as usual, hurled the huge stone in question, with his utmost force, against the head of the saint; but, strange to say, it either missed him altogether or failed to do him any injury, the saint going calmly on with his devotions as if nothing had happened. On the stone in the church of Santa Maria in Trastevere there is an inscription in Latin, informing us that it was fastened round the neck of St. Calixtus, the Bishop of Rome, who, after having been scourged during an outbreak of pagan hostility, was thrown out of a window in his house in the Trastevere, and flung into a well. The stone in the Basilica of S. Lorenzo is connected with the sufferings and death either of St. Justinian or of St. Stephen, the proto-martyr, who was stoned to death in Palestine, and whose remains, miraculously recovered, are supposed to rest in the crypt below, along with those of St. Laurence. All these relics are devoutly worshipped, and they are believed to cure diseases, and to protect against evil those who touch them.

Examining the martyr-stones more closely, we find abundant evidence to confirm the account which is usually given of their origin, viz. that they were first used as Roman measures of weight. Several of them have inscribed upon their upper surface the names of the quæstors or prefects who issued them, as well as the number of pounds and ounces which they represented; the pounds being distinguished by figures, and the ounces expressed by dots or small circles. Numbers of such ancient Roman weights of stone, similarly inscribed, may be seen in the Kircherian Museum in the Collegio Romano. One specimen bears an inscription which signifies that, by the authority of Augustus, the weight was preserved in the temple of the goddess Ops, the wife of Saturn, and one of the most ancient deities of Italy, where the public money was deposited. Montfaucon, in the third volume of his learned and elaborate work on Antiquity, has a plate illustrating a number of characteristic specimens of these weights from the cabinet of St.

Germain's. This previous use would lead us to suspect that all the stones in the Roman churches did not figure in scenes of martyrdom. Some of them, indeed, were found in the loculi or graves of the Catacombs; but this circumstance of itself does not prove that the body interred therein had been that of a martyr, and that the stone had been employed in his execution. We know that the early Christians were in the habit of depositing in the graves of their friends the articles that were most valued by them during life. And hence, in the Catacombs, a singular variety of objects have been found. Stone weights, therefore, may have been put into the graves of Christians, not as instruments of suffering but as objects typical of the occupation of the departed in this life, in accordance with the habit of their pagan forefathers, which the Roman Christians had adopted. Some, however, of the stones, as I have said, may have been used according to the popular legend for the drowning of martyrs; and these weights were conveniently at hand in places of public resort, and lent themselves readily, by the rings inserted in many of them, to the persecutor's purpose.

The material of which they are composed is in nearly all cases the same. It is a stone of extreme hardness and of various shades of colour, from a light green to a dark olive, with a degree of transparency equal to that of wax and susceptible of a fine polish. By some writers it is called a black stone; but this colour may have been given to it by frequent handling when in use, and by the grime of age since. It was called by the Romans, from the use made of it in fabricating measures of weight, lapis æquipondus, and from its supposed efficacy in the cure of diseases of the kidneys lapis nephriticus. Fabreti says that it got the name of lapis Lydius from the locality from which it was believed to have come. It is a kind of nephrite or jade, a mineral which usually occurs in talcose or magnesian rocks. At one time it was supposed to exist only on the river Kara-Kash, in the Kuen Luen mountains north of Cashmere, and for thousands of years the mines of that locality were the only known worked ones of pure jade. It has since, however, been found in New Zealand and in India; while the discoverers of South America obtained specimens of it in its natural state from the natives of Peru, who used it for making axes and arrow-heads, and gave it the name of piedra de yjada, from which comes our common word jade, on account of its use as a supposed cure for the iliac passion. It may be mentioned that there is a mineral closely allied to jade called "Saussurite," discovered by the great geologist whose name it bears near Monte Rosa, and since found on the borders of the Lake of Geneva, near Genoa, and in Corsica. It is possible that the martyr-stones may be made of this mineral, for they have not been analysed. But if they are, as it is supposed, made of true jade, the fact opens up many important questions.

No stone has a more remarkable history. It is an object of interest alike to the geologist and the antiquarian; and in spite of the most patient inquiry its antecedents are surrounded with a mystery which cannot be satisfactorily solved. Its antiquity is beyond doubt. In the most ancient books of China it is noticed as one of the articles of tribute paid to the emperor. Dr. Schliemann found it among the ruins of Troy. But its history stretches into the misty past far anterior in time to all ordinary records, to Cyclopean constructions, or to pictured and sculptured stones. One of the most curious things brought to light in connection with the prehistoric annals of our race is the wide diffusion of this mineral in regions as far apart as China and Britain. Owing to its extreme hardness and susceptibility to polish, it was highly prized by the neolithic races for the manufacture of stone axes and hammers. In nearly every European country implements of jade belonging to the primitive inhabitants have been discovered. Some of the most beautiful belonged to one of the latest settlements of the stone age at Gerlafingen, in the Lake of Bienne, and were mixed with bronze celts of primitive type, indicating that the people of these lake-dwellings lived during the transition period between stone and bronze.

The presence of such celts made of jade obviously points to a connection at a very early period with the East, from whence the stone must have been brought, for it has never been found in a natural state west of the Caspian. An interesting controversy upon this subject was created about eight years ago by the finding in the bed of the Rhone of a jade strigil, an instrument curved and hollowed like a spoon used to scrape the skin while bathing. Various conjectures were formed as to how this isolated object could have found its way from its distant quarry in the East to this obscure spot among the Alps. Professor Max Müller, and those who along with him advocate the Oriental origin of the first settlers in Europe, are of opinion that this strigil and the various jade implements found in the Swiss lake-dwellings, are relics of this Western migration from the primitive cradle of the Aryan race on the plateaus of Central Asia. The implements could only have come from the East, for the other sources of jade supply in New Zealand and America—since discovered—were altogether unknown in those primitive times. And this conclusion is supported by an imposing array of concurrent philological evidence, based upon the resemblances between the Aryan languages of Europe, so strangely akin to each other, and the ancient dialects of India and Persia. But plausible as this argument looks, the more probable explanation is that the inhabitants of Europe obtained the material which they laboriously fashioned into tools from the East, according to a system of barter similar to that which still exists amongst tribes more rude and savage than the Swiss lake-dwellers. Numerous facts of a like tendency are on record, such as the finding in the mounds of the Mississippi valley, side by side, obsidian from Mexico and mica from the Alleghanies, and in the mounds around the great northern lakes large tropical shells two thousand miles from their native habitat. The ancient inhabitants of China and India found at a very early period that they possessed in their jade rocks a very valuable material, in exchange for which they could get what they wanted from the Western races; while these Western races had at least one article which they could barter for the much-prized jade implements, viz. linen cloth, the weaving of which was practised in the oldest settlements, hanks of unspun flax and thread, nets and cloth of the same material having been found not unfrequently in the lake dwellings.

What an interesting glimpse into the far-off past does this link of connection between the East and the West give us! It indicates a degree of civilisation which we are not accustomed to associate with these primeval times. Archæologists are of opinion that the race who inhabited Central Europe during the earlier part of the stone age were akin to the modern Laplanders. The people of the lake dwellings, however, and especially those who used jade implements, who replaced them, were a superior and more civilised race. The evidence of the articles which they used, with the exception of jade itself, points not to an Asiatic origin, but rather to a connection with the shores on both sides of the Mediterranean. When they migrated northwards they brought with them the flax and the cereals of Egypt, and introduced with them the southern weeds which grew among these cultivated plants. The seeds of the catch-fly of Crete, which does not grow in Switzerland or Germany, have been found among the relics of the earliest of the lake dwellings; while the familiar corn blue-bottle of our autumn fields was first brought from its native Sicily by this lacustrine people in whose cultivated fields it grew as a weed, and by them spread over all Western and Northern Europe. Such are the interesting associations and profound problems connected with the material of the martyr weights. And it is unique in this respect, that it meets us as far back as the first traces of neolithic man in Central Europe—nay, farther back still, in the palæolithic flints found in the caves near Mentone; and that it is still used in the countries where it is found for a great variety of useful and ornamental purposes, idols being carved out of it, and altars adorned with its semi-transparent olive-green slabs. The inhabitants of the South Sea Islands until recently used it for their stone implements in the same way that the ancient lake dwellers did; and the Mogul emperors of Delhi set such a high value upon it on account of its superstitious virtues that they had it cut, jewelled, and enamelled into the most exquisite forms.

In Rome the martyr weights, as relics of the stone age, afford a curious example of a very primitive epoch projecting far into a highly-civilised one. Stone weights continued in use long after bronze and iron implements were constructed, on account of the sacred associations connected with them. Weights and measures were regarded by the Romans as invested with a peculiar religious significance; the stone of which the weights were composed was called from that circumstance, or because of the occult qualities attributed to it, lapis divinus; and therefore there was a deep-seated prejudice, which reached down to the days of the highest splendour of the Empire, against the introduction of a new substance. This was the case with all articles used in religious ceremonies. As late as the period of St. Paul's residence in Rome, and at the time of the first persecution of the Christians, ancient pagan rites were celebrated in the Forum, in which the use of metal was forbidden; and only stone hatchets could be employed in slaughtering animals, and only earthen vessels used in carrying the significant parts of the sacrifices into the temples. Treaties were also ratified by striking the victim offered on the occasion with a flint hatchet. The ancient Egyptians, although using iron and bronze for other objects, invariably used stone knives in preparing bodies for the process of embalming. The sacrifices which the Mexicans offered to their idols at the time of the Spanish conquest were cut up by means of knives of obsidian, which they obtained from the lavas of their volcanoes. In the Bible we have several traces of the same universal custom. The Jews seem to have performed the rite of circumcision with flint implements, for we read in Exodus that Zipporah, the wife of Moses, took a sharp stone for that purpose; and the phrase translated "sharp knives" in Joshua v. 2 — "At that time the Lord said unto Joshua, Make thee sharp knives, and circumcise again the children of Israel the second time" — should be translated, as in the marginal reference, knives of flint. To the same ancient widespread habit may doubtless be referred the prohibition, mentioned in Exodus and Deuteronomy, against making an altar in any special place where God recorded His name, of hewn stone, or polluting it by lifting up any iron tool upon it. So strong is the conservative instinct in religion that to this very day the enlightened Brahmin of India will not use ordinary fire for sacred purposes, will not procure a fresh spark even from flint and steel, but reverts to, or rather continues the primitive way of obtaining it by friction with a wooden drill. Everywhere innovations in religious worship are resisted with more or less reason or prejudice. The instinct is universal, and has its good and its evil side.

CHAPTER IX - ST. ONOFRIO AND TASSO

One of the most romantic shrines of pilgrimage in Rome is the church of St. Onofrio. It is situated in the Trastevere, that portion of the city beyond the Tiber whose inhabitants boast of their pure descent from the ancient Romans. A steep ascent on the slope of the Janiculum, through a somewhat squalid but picturesque street, and terminating in a series of broad steps, leads up to it from the Porta di San Spirito, not far from the Vatican. The ground here is open and stretches away, free from buildings, to the walls of the city. The church has a simple old-fashioned appearance; its roof, walls, and small campanile are painted with the rusty gold of lichens that have sprung from the kisses of four centuries of rain and sun. It was erected in the reign of Pope Eugenius IV. by Nicolo da Forca Palena, an ancestor of that Conte di Palena who was a great friend of Torquato Tasso at Naples. It was dedicated to the Egyptian hermit Honuphrius, who for sixty years lived in a cave in the desert of Thebes, without seeing a human being or speaking a word, consorting with birds and beasts, and living upon roots and wild herbs. A subtle harmony is felt between the history of the hermit and the character of this building raised in his honour. A spot more drowsy and secluded, more steeped in the dreams of the older ages, is not to be found in the whole city. In front of the church there is a long, narrow portico, supported by eight antique columns of the simplest construction, in all likelihood borrowed from some old pagan temple. Under this portico is a beautiful fresco of the Madonna and Child by Domenichino. To the right are three lunettes, which contain paintings by the same great master, representing the Baptism, Temptation, and Flagellation of St. Jerome. On the left of the arcade are portraits of the most prominent saints of the Hieronomyte order. Exposed to the weather at first, these invaluable frescoes had faded into mere spectres of pictures; but they are now protected from further injury by glass.

Usually the church is closed, except in the early morning, and visitors are admitted by the custode on ringing a door bell under the portico. The interior is dark and solemn, with much less gilding and meretricious ornament than is usual in Roman churches. It contains, in the side chapels, many objects of interest; frescoes and altar-pieces by Annibale Caracci,

Pinturicchio, and Peruzzi; and splendid sepulchral monuments. Of the last the most conspicuous are the marble tomb of Alessandro Guidi, the Italian lyric poet, who died in 1712; and the simple cenotaph in the last chapel on the left of one of the titular cardinals of the church, who died in 1849, the celebrated linguist Mezzofante. But the tomb upon which the visitor will gaze with deepest interest is that of Torquato Tasso, who died in the adjacent monastery in 1595. The chapel of St. Jerome, in which it is situated, the first on the left as you enter, was restored by public subscription in 1857, in a manner which does not reflect much credit upon the artistic taste of modern Rome. Previous to this the remains of the poet reposed for two hundred years in an obscure part of the church close to the door, indicated by a tablet. Above this spot there is a portrait of the time, which from an artistic point of view is very poor, but is said to be a good likeness. Removed on the anniversary of his death, about thirty years ago, to the chapel of St. Jerome, the poet's remains are now covered by a huge marble monument in the cinque-cento style, adorned by a bas-relief of his funeral and a statue of him by Fabris. Whatever may be said regarding the artistic merits of this monument, no one who has read the poet's immortal epic, and is conversant with the sad incidents of his life, can stand on the spot without being deeply moved.

Connected with the church is a monastery dedicated to St. Jerome. In one of the upper corridors is a beautiful arched fresco of the Madonna and Child, by Leonardo da Vinci, with the donor of the picture in profile kneeling before her. The picture is surrounded by a frame of fruit and flowers on an enamelled ground. The soft, tender features of the infant Jesus, and the quiet dignity and grace of the smiling Madonna, are so characteristic of the style of Leonardo da Vinci that the picture would be at once referred to him by one who did not know its origin. The chamber where Tasso spent the last days of his life is on the upper floor, and is the most conveniently situated in the whole building. It is left very much in the same state as when he lived in it. The walls and ceiling are bare and whitewashed, without any decoration. Here and there are several pale marks, indicating the places of objects that had been removed. In one part is painted on the plaster a false door partially open, behind which is seen the figure of Tasso about to enter; but every person of good taste must condemn the melodramatic exhibition, and wish that he could obliterate it with a daub of whitewash. The custode directed my attention to it with an air of great admiration, and could not understand the scowl with which I turned away my face. There are several most interesting relics of Tasso preserved in this chamber—his table, with an inkstand of wood; his great chair covered with Cordova leather, very aged and worn-looking; the belt which he wore; a small German cabinet;

a large China bowl, evidently an heirloom; a metal crucifix of singular workmanship, given to him by Pope Clement VIII., which soothed his dying moments; several of his letters, and an autograph copy of verses. In one corner is the leaden coffin, much corroded, in which his remains were originally deposited. On the table is a mask in reddish wax moulded from the dead face of the poet, and placed upon a plaster bust—a most fantastic combination. From this mask, which is an undoubted original, numerous copies have been taken, which are scattered throughout Europe. It is in consequence somewhat effaced, but it still shows the characteristic features of the poet—the purity of the profile, the fineness of the mouth, and the spiritual beauty and fascinating expression of the whole face. But the incoherence of the adaptation makes it painful to think that this is the best representation of the poet we possess.

The extensive garden behind the convent combines a considerable variety of natural features. The monks grow large quantities of lettuce and fennochio; and interspersed among the beds of vegetables are orange and other fruit trees, and little trellises of cane, wreathed with vines. A large tank is supplied with water from a spring whose murmur gives a feeling of animation to the spot. The garden rises at the end into broken elevated ground showing the native rock through its grassy sides. A row of tall old cypresses crowns the ridge—their fluted trunks gray with lichen-stains, and their deep green spires of foliage forming harp-strings on which the evening winds discourse solemn music, as if the spirit of the poet haunted them still. On one side are the picturesque ruins of a shrine overarching a fountain, now dry and choked up with weeds, and fringed with ferns. Cyclamens—called by the Italians viola pazze, "mad violets" — grow on its margin in glowing masses; sweet-scented violets in profusion perfume all the air; and a few Judas-trees, loaded with crimson blossoms, without a single leaf to relieve the gorgeous colour, serve as an admirable background, almost blending with the clouds on the low horizon. On the other side the hill slopes down in a series of terraces to the crowded streets of the Trastevere, forming a spacious out-door amphitheatre, in which the Arcadian Academy of Rome used to hold its meetings during the summer months, and where St. Filippo Neri was wont to give those half-dramatic musical entertainments which, originating in the oratory of the religious community established by him, are now known throughout the world as oratorios. Between these two objects still stands the large torso of a tree which bears the name of "Tasso's oak," because the poet's favourite seat was under its shadow. It suffered much from the violence of a thunderstorm in 1842, but numerous branches have since sprouted from the old trunk, and it now affords a capacious shade from the noonday heat. It is a variety of the

Valonia oak, with delicate, downy, pale-green leaves, much serrated, and contrasts beautifully with the dark green spires of the cypresses behind. The leaves at the time of my visit had but recently unfolded, and exhibited all the delicacy of tint and perfection of outline so characteristic of young foliage. The garden was in the first fresh flush of spring—that idyllic season which, in Italy more than in any other land, realises the glowing descriptions of the poets. Plucking a leafy twig from the branches and a gray lichen from the trunk as mementoes of the place, I sat down on the mossy hole, and tried to bring back in imagination the haunted past. Nature was renewing her old life; the same flowers still covered the earth with their divine frescoes; but where was he whose spirit informed all the beauty and translated its mystic language into human words? The permanency of nature and the vanity of human life seemed here to acquire new significance.

The spot on which I sat commands one of the finest views of Rome and the surrounding country. Down below to the left is the enormous group of buildings connected with St Peter's and the Vatican, whose yellow travertine glows in the afternoon sun like dead gold. Beyond rise the steep green slopes of Monte Mario, with vineyards and olive-groves nestling in its warm folds, crowned with the Villa Mellini beside the "Turner pine," a familiar object in many of the great artist's pictures. Stretching away in the direction of the old diligence road from Florence is a succession of gentle ridges and bluffs of volcanic rock covered with brushwood, among which you can trace the bold headland of the citadel of Fidenæ, and the green lonely site of Antemnæ, and the plateau on which are the scanty remains of the almost mythical Etruscan city of Veii, the Troy of Italy. The view in this direction is bounded by the advanced guard of the Sabine range, the blue peak of Soracte looking, as Lord Byron graphically says, like the crest of a billow about to break. In front, at your feet, is the city, broken up into the most picturesque masses by the irregularity of the ground; here and there a brighter light glistening on some stately campanile or cupola, and flashing back from the graceful columns of Trajan and Antonine. The Tiber flows between you and that wilderness of reddish-brown roofs cleaving the city in twain. For a brief space you see it on both sides of the Bridge of Hadrian, overlooked by the gloomy mass of the Castle of St. Angelo, and then it hides itself under the shadow of the Aventine Hill, and at last emerges beyond the walls, to pursue its desolate way to the sea through one of the saddest tracts of country in all the world. Away to the right, where the mass of modern buildings ceases, the great shattered circle of the Colosseum stands up against the sky, indicating by its presence where lie, unseen from this point of view, the ruins of the palaces of the Cæsars and the Forum. Beyond the city stretches away the undulating bosom of the Campagna, bathed in a misty azure light; bridged over by the weird, endless arches of the Claudian aqueduct, throwing long shadows before them in the westering sun. Worthy framework for such a picture, the noble semicircle of the Sabine Hills rises on the horizon to the left, terminating in the grand rugged peak of Monte Gennaro, whose every cliff and scar are distinctly visible, and concealing in its bosom the romantic waterfalls of Tivoli and the lone ancestral farm of Horace. On the right the crested Alban heights form the boundary, crowned on the summit with the white convent of Monte Cavo—the ancient temple of Jupiter Latialis, up to which the Roman consuls came to triumph when the Latin States were merged in the Roman Commonwealth—and bearing on their shoulders the sparkling, gem-like towns of Frascati and Albano, with their thrilling memories of Cicero and Pompey; the whole range melting away into the blue vault of heaven in delicate gradations of pale pink and purple. In the wide gap between these ranges of hills—beyond the stone pines and ilex groves of Præneste—the far perspective is closed by a glorious vision of the snow-crowned mountains of the Abruzzi, giving an air of alpine grandeur to the view. And all this vast and varied landscape, comprehending all glories of nature and art, all zones and climates, from the tropical aloes and palms of the Pincian Hill to the arctic snows of the Apennines, is seen through air that acts upon the spirits like wine, and gives the ideal beauty of a picture to the meanest things.

Italian poets share in the wonderful charm that belongs to everything connected with their lovely land. They are seen, like the early Tuscan paintings, against a golden background of romance. Petrarch, Dante, Ariosto, invested with this magic light, are themselves more attractive even than their poetic creations. But Torquato Tasso, perhaps, more than them all, appeals to our deepest feelings. No sadder or more romantic life than his can be found in the annals of literature. He was one of those "infanti perduti" to whom life was one long avenue of darkened days. In his temperament, in the character of his genius, and in the story of his life, we can discern striking features of resemblance between him and the wayward, sorrowful Rousseau. Hercules, according to the old fable, "was afflicted with madness as a punishment for his being so near the gods;" and the imaginativeness of a brain which had in it a fibre of insanity, near which genius often perilously lies, may be supposed to account for much that is strange and sad in his career. The place of his birth was a fit cradle for a poet. On the edge of a bold cliff, overlooking the sea at Sorrento, is the Hotel Tasso, known to every traveller in that region. Here, according to the voice of tradition, the immortal poet was born on the 11th of March 1544, eleven years after the death of Ariosto. It is said that the identical chamber in which the event took place has since disappeared, owing to the portion of rock on which it stood having been undermined by the sea; and, as if to give countenance to this, some of the existing apartments are perilously propped up on the very edge of the cliff by buttresses, which, giving way, would hurl the superstructure into the abyss. The original building stood on the site of an ancient temple; and it is probable that, with the exception of one of the bedrooms, which is said to have been Tasso's cabinet, the edifice retains none of the features which it possessed in the days of the poet.

But whatever changes may have taken place in the human habitation, the scenes of Nature around, from which he drew the inspirations of his youthful genius, remain unchanged. Every feature of landscape loveliness is focussed in that matchless panorama. Behind is a range of wild mountains, whose many-shaped peaks and crags, clad with pine and olive, assume, as the day wears on, the golden and purple hues of the sky — sloping down into the midst of vineyards and groves of orange, myrtle, and all the luxuriant verdure which the warm sun of the South calls forth, out of which gleam at frequent intervals picturesque villages and farms, which seem more the creation of Nature than of Art. In front is a glorious view of the Bay of Naples, with the enchanted isles of Capri and Ischia sleeping on its bosom, and the reflected images of domes and palaces all along its curving shores "charming its blue waters;" while dominating the whole horizon are the snowy mountains of Campania, broken by the dark purple mass of Vesuvius, rising up with gradual slope to its rounded cone, over which rests continually a column of flame or smoke, "stimulating the imagination by its mystery and terror." Apart from its associations, that landscape would have been one to gaze on entranced, and to dream of for years afterwards. But with its countless memories of all that is greatest and saddest in human history clinging to almost every object, it is indeed one of the most impressive in the world. The land is the land of Magna Græcia. The sea is the sea of Homer and Pindar. Near at hand are the Isles of the Sirens, who allured Ulysses with their magic song; away in the dim distance are the wonderful Doric temples of Pæstum, which go back to the mythical times of Jason and the Argonauts. On the opposite shore is the tomb of Virgil, on the threshold of the scenes which he loved to describe, — the Holy Land of Paganism, the Phlegræan Fields, with the terrible Avernus and the Cave of the Sibyl, and all the spots associated with the Pagan heaven and hell; and in the near neighbourhood Baiæ, with its awful memories of Roman luxury and cruelty, and Puteoli, with its inspiring associations of the Apostle Paul's visit, and the introduction of Christianity into Italy. Meet nurse for any poetic child, the place of his birth was peculiarly so for such a child as Tasso; and we can detect in the subjects of his Muse in after years, the very themes which such a region would naturally have suggested and inspired.

The age in which he was born was also eminently favourable for the development of the poetic faculty. By the wonderful discoveries of the starry Galileo, man's intellectual vision was infinitely extended, and the great fundamental idea of modern astronomy—infinite space peopled with worlds like our own—was for the first time realised. It was an era of maritime enterprise; the world was circumnavigated, and new ideas streamed in from each newly-visited region. It was pre-eminently the period of art. Leonardo da Vinci and Raphael had just passed away, but Michael Angelo, Titian, Tintoretto, and Paul Veronese were still living, freeing men's spirits by the productions of their pencil from formal fancies and conventional fetters, and sending them back to the fresh teaching of Nature. The art of printing was giving a new birth to letters, and the reformation of religion a new growth to human thought. A new power had descended into the stagnant waters of European life, and imparted to them a wonderful energy. Along with the revival of classical learning and the general quickening of men's minds, there was blended in the South of Europe a lingering love of romance and chivalry, and a strong religious feeling, which had arisen out of the vigorous reaction of Roman Catholicism. Italy was at this time the acknowledged parent both of the poetry and the general literature of Europe; and the immortal works of Dante, Petrarch, and Ariosto had formed an almost perfect vernacular language in which the creations of genius could find fittest expression.

But Tasso was not only born in a poetic region and in a poetic age: he was also the son of a poet. He inherited the divine faculty; he was cradled in poetry. His father, Bernardo, though he has been put into the shade by his more gifted son, has claims of his own to be remembered by posterity. He occupies a high place in the well-defined group of the chivalric poets of Italy. His principal poem, the Amadigi, which was composed about the time of his son's birth, though not published for sixteen years afterwards, treats in a hundred cantos the romantic history of Amadis of Gaul, and deals in giants, enchanted swords, prodigious wounds, and miraculous cures. Various estimates of this long poem have been formed by critics from the favourable analysis of Ginguéné to the severe censure of Sismondi. But in spite of its lack of dramatic power, and the monotony of its imagery, the heat of his genius crystallising only a part of the substance of his work, there can be no question that the poem is distinguished by a certain gravity and elevation of sentiment, which places it high above the romances of the older school, and brings it near to the dignity of epic poetry. In this respect the Amadigi may be said to form an interesting transition from the irregular romance of Ariosto to the symmetrical epic of his own son. The son's poetic path was thus prepared, and the mould in which his immortal work was cast was formed by his father. The fortunes of the two poets read remarkably alike. They are marked by the same extraordinary vicissitudes, and the same general sadness and gloom.

The family of Tasso belonged to Bergamo, in the north of Italy, a region which has given birth to several eminent men, among others to Tiraboschi, the historian of Italian literature. It was originally noble, and had large territorial possessions. One ancestor, Omodeo, who lived in the year 1290, is worthy of special mention as the inventor of the system of postal communication, to which the world owes so much; and hence the family arms of a courier's horn and a badger's skin — tasso being the Italian for badger — which the post-horses, down to within fifty years ago, wore upon their harness. In the time of Bernardo, however, the fortunes of the family had decayed, and the early days of the poet were passed in poverty. Adopted after the death of his parents by his father's brother, the Bishop of Recanati, he was placed at school, where he soon acquired a wonderful familiarity with the Greek and Latin authors, then newly restored to Europe. Highly cultivated, refined, and possessed of great personal beauty, while manifesting at the same time a peculiar talent for diplomacy, Bernardo speedily won his way to distinction. His first work, which was a collection principally of love-poems, celebrating his passion for the beautiful Genevra Malatesta, who belonged to the same family as the ill-fated Parasina of Byron, attracted the attention of the reigning Prince of Salerno, Ferrante Sanseverino, one of the chief patrons of literature in Italy, who thereupon engaged him as his private secretary. At the court of this prince he met Porzia de' Rossi, a lady of noble birth, who was beautiful and accomplished, and possessed what was considered in those days a large fortune. After his marriage with this lady Bernardo and his bride retired to a villa which he had purchased at Sorrento, where he enjoyed for several years an exceptional share of domestic felicity, his wife having proved a most devoted helpmeet to him.

In these propitious circumstances the infant that was destined afterwards to confer the greatest lustre upon the family name was born. His father was absent at the time with the Prince of Salerno, who had joined the Spanish army in the new war that had arisen between Charles V. and Francis I.; a war whose chivalrous and inspiring acts the Marquis d'Azeglio made use of in 1866 in his romance of history, Fieramosca, to rouse again a spirit of independence in his countrymen. A friend of his father, therefore, held the child at the baptismal font, in the cathedral of Sorrento, where he received the name of Torquato — a name which his elder brother, who lived only a few days, had previously borne. The treaty of Crepi, which concluded the war between Charles V. and Francis I., in which the former was victorious, allowed Bernardo Tasso to return home with his patron ten months after the birth of his son. By this treaty the French king, who had previously assumed the title of King of Naples, resigned all claims upon that State, and the inhabitants were henceforth subjected entirely to the dominion of the Spanish sovereigns of the house of Austria. The emperor, Charles V., appointed the Marquis de Villafranca, better known as Don Pedro de Toledo, to be Viceroy of Naples, who, like his despotic master, carried out his so-called reforms with a high hand, and interfered with the personal and domestic affairs of the inhabitants, so that he speedily roused their resentment. Against the establishment of the Inquisition, which he set about under the mask of zeal for religion, but in reality for the intimidation of the nobles, the whole city rose up in violent opposition. After having exhausted itself in a vain struggle with the viceroy, it resolved to petition the emperor, and commissioned the Prince of Salerno to plead its cause at the Court of Nuremberg. But in consequence of being forestalled by the cunning Don Pedro, the prince, when he arrived, found the case prejudged, and all his arguments and pleadings were of no avail. Disgusted with the failure of his errand, with the coldness of his reception, and with other indignities which he received at the hands of the emperor and his viceroy, he determined to abandon altogether the cause of Austria. Repairing to Venice, he publicly gave effect to his decision; whereupon Don Pedro, too glad to have an opportunity of oppressing his personal enemy, declared the prince a rebel, confiscated his estates, and seized all his personal property. In the misfortunes of his patron Bernardo Tasso shared. He too was proscribed as a rebel; his property at Salerno was seized, and his wife and children were transferred by the viceroy's orders to Naples, where her family resided, and where, under their cruel treatment, instigated by the viceroy, she was deprived of her fortune, and virtually held a prisoner to the day of her death.

Such were the dark clouds that, after a brief gleam of the brightest prosperity, hung over the early years of Torquato Tasso. Deprived of the care of a father who followed from court to court the varied fortunes of his benefactor, and in the company of a mother worse than widowed, dependent upon the cold and niggardly charity of friends who were either too timid or superstitious to oppose the patron of the Inquisition, the child grew up in melancholy solitude, like an etiolated plant that has been deprived of the sunshine. The original sadness and sensitiveness of his disposition was much increased by the family misfortunes. In his seventh year he was sent to a school in the neighbourhood, opened by the Jesuits, who were at this time beginning to exert a powerful influence upon society, principally on account of their zeal in the cause of education. At this school he remained for three years, acquiring a wonderful knowledge of Latin and Greek, and manifesting such enthusiasm in his studies that he rose long before daybreak, and was so impatient to get to school that his mother was often obliged to send him away in the dark with a lantern. Here he showed the first symptoms of his genius for poetry and rhetoric, and gave public testimony to the deep religious feeling which he inherited from his parents, and which had been so carefully cultivated by his ecclesiastical masters, by joining the communion of the Church. In his tenth year his father left the court of Henry III. of France, and settled in Rome, where he had apartments assigned him in the immense palace of Cardinal Hippolito of the house of Ferrara. These apartments were furnished as handsomely as his impoverished resources allowed, in the hope that he might have his wife and children to live with him. But in spite of all his efforts and entreaties his wife was not allowed by her brothers to rejoin him; while his own position as an outlaw made it impossible for him to enter the kingdom of Naples to rescue her. The only concession he could get from the authorities was permission for her to enter with her daughter Cornelia as pensioners among the nuns in the convent of San Festo; and no sooner was this step taken than her friends openly seized her dowry, on the plea that it would otherwise belong to the convent, as her husband's outlawry cancelled his claims to it. Her boy, of course, could not enter the convent with her; he was therefore sent to his father in Rome. The separation between mother and son, we are told, was most affecting. To her it was the climax of her trials; and, bowed down beneath the weight of her accumulated sufferings, she fell an easy victim to an attack of fever, which, in the short space of twenty-four hours, ended her wretched life. Upon Tasso the parting from a mother whom he was never to see again, and whose personal qualities and grievous trials had greatly endeared her to him, produced an impression which even the great troubles of his after life could never efface.

With a mind richly stored, notwithstanding his youthful age, with classic lore, and quickened and made sensitive by a varied and sorrowful career, Torquato Tasso came to Rome. The first occasion of seeing the imperial city must have been exciting and awakening in a high degree to such a boy. He was leaving behind the passive simplicity of the child, and had already a keen interest in the things ennobled by history and cared for by grown-up men. This dawn of a higher consciousness found a congenial sphere in the city of the soul. With what absorbing eagerness his young mind would be drawn to the study of the immortal deeds, which were the inheritance of his race, on the very spot where they were done. He would behold with his eyes the glorious things of which he had heard. There would be much that would shock and disappoint him when he came to be familiar with it. Many of the ancient monuments had been destroyed; and many of the ancient sites, especially the Forum and the Palatine, were deserted wastes which had not yet yielded up their buried treasures of art to the pick and spade of the antiquarian. The ravages inflicted by the ferocious hordes of the Constable Bourbon in 1527 had not yet been obliterated by the restorations and repairs undertaken by Pope Paul III. The city had lost much of its ancient glory, and had not yet exchanged its gloomy medieval aspect for that of modern civilisation. But, in spite of every drawback, he could not sufficiently admire the buildings and the sites which bore witness of all that was grandest in human history. Along with a young relative, Christopher Tasso, he pursued his classical studies in the midst of all these stimulating associations under the tutorship of Maurizio Cattaneo, the most learned master in Italy. The companionship of a youth of his own age did him a great deal of good. It satisfied his affections, it saved him from the loneliness to which his father's ill-health at the time would otherwise have consigned him, and it spurred him on to a healthful exercise of his mental powers. For a short time he led a comparatively happy life in Rome. His father's prospects had somewhat improved. Cardinal Caraffa, who was a personal friend of his, ascended the pontifical throne under the name of Paul IV.; and as they were on the same political side, he hoped that his fortunes would now be retrieved. But this gleam of prosperity speedily vanished. The imperial enmity, which had been the cause of all his previous misfortunes, continued to pursue him like a relentless fate. Philip II. of Spain and the Pope having quarrelled, the formidable Duke of Alba, the new Viceroy of Naples, invaded the Papal States, took Ostia and Tivoli, and threatened Rome itself. With extreme difficulty Bernardo Tasso managed to make his escape to Ravenna, with nothing left him but the manuscript of his Amadigi. In the meantime his son was taken to his relatives at Bergamo. In this city, under the shadow of the Alps, Torquato remained for a year in the home of his Roman schoolfellow. The inhabitants have ever since cherished with pride the connection of the Tassos with their town, and have erected a splendid monument to Torquato in the market-place. The exquisite scenery in the neighbourhood had a wonderful effect upon the mind of the youthful poet. It put the finishing touch to his varied education. The snows of the North and the fires of the South, the wild grandeur of the mountains and the soft beauty of the sea, the solitudes of Nature where only the effects of storm and sunshine are chronicled, and the crowded scenes of the most inspiring events in human history, had their share in moulding his temperament and colouring his poetry.

From Bergamo Torquato was summoned to Pesaro, since known as the birthplace of Rossini, hence called the "Swan of Pesaro." His father had found a home with the Duke of Urbino, who treated him with the utmost kindness. In the Villa Barachetto, on the shores of the Adriatic, surrounded by the most beautiful scenery and by the finest treasures of art, which have long since been transferred to Paris and Rome, Bernardo Tasso at last completed his Amadigi; while, captivated by his grace and intelligence, the duke made Torquato the companion of his son, Francesco Maria, in all his studies and amusements. For two years father and son enjoyed in this place a grateful repose from the buffetings of fortune. But, fired by ambition, Bernardo left Pesaro for Venice, in order to see his poem through the press of Aldus Manutius; and being not only welcomed with open arms by his literary friends in that city, but also appointed secretary of the great Venetian Academy "Della Fama," with a handsome salary, he sent for his son, took a house in a good situation, and resolved to settle down in the place. There was much to captivate the imagination of the youthful Torquato in this wonderful city of the sea, then in the zenith of its fame, surpassing all the capitals of transalpine Europe in the extent of its commerce, in refinement of manners, and in the cultivation of learning and the arts. Its romantic situation, its weird history, its splendid palaces, its silent water-ways, its stirring commerce, its inspiring arts, must have kindled all the enthusiasm of his nature. But he did not yield himself up to the siren attractions of the place, and muse in idleness upon its varied charms. On the contrary, the time that he spent in Venice was the busiest of his life. He was absorbed in the study of Dante and Petrarch; and the results of his devotion may still be seen in the numerous annotations in his handwriting in the copies of these poets which belonged to him, now preserved in the Vatican Library in Rome and the Laurentian Library in Florence. He was also employed by his father in transcribing for the press considerable portions of his poetical works; and these studies and exercises were of much use to him in enabling him to form a graphic and elegant literary style. His own compositions, both in prose and verse, were by this time pretty numerous, though nothing of his had found its way into print as yet.

His father saw with much concern the development of his son's genius. Anxious to save him from the trials which he himself had experienced in his literary career, he sent him to the University of Padua to study law, which he thought would be a surer provision for his future life than a devotion to the Muses. One great branch of law, that which relates to ecclesiastical jurisprudence, has always been much esteemed in Italy, and the study of it, in many instances, has paved the way to high honours. Almost all the eminent poets of Italy, Petrarch, Ariosto, Marino, Metastasio, spent their earlier years in this pursuit; but, like Ovid and our own Milton, their nature rebelled against the bondage. They took greater pleasure in the study of the laws for rhyme than in the study of the Pandects of Justinian or the Decretals of Isidore. It was so with Tasso. He attended faithfully the lectures of Guido

Panciroli, although these were not compulsory, and waited patiently at the University during the three years of residence which is required for a law degree. But all the time his mind was occupied with other thoughts than those connected with his law studies. Still, uncongenial as they must have been to him, he could not have attended for three years to such studies without unconsciously deriving much benefit from them. They must have impressed upon him those ideas of order and logical arrangement which he afterwards carried out in his writings, and which separate them so markedly from the confused, inconsistent license of the older literature of Italy; and he could not have resided in the birthplace of Livy, in constant association with the highest minds of the time, as a member of a University then the most famous in Europe, numbering no less than ten thousand students from all parts of the world, without his intellectual life being greatly quickened.

During ten months of enthusiastic work he produced his first great poem, which, considering his age—for he was then only in his eighteenth year—and the short time occupied in its composition, is one of the most remarkable efforts of genius. He called his poem Rinaldo, after the name of the knight whose romantic adventures it celebrates—not the Rinaldo of the Gerusalemme Liberata, but the Paladin of whom so much is said in the poems of Boiardo and Ariosto,—and dedicated it to Cardinal Lewis of Este, then one of the most distinguished patrons of literature in Italy. It contains a beautiful allusion to his father's genius as the source of his own inspiration. It abounds in the supernatural incidents and personified abstractions characteristic of the romantic school of poetry; and though Galileo said of it that it reminded him of a picture formed of inlaid work, rather than of a painting in oil, it has nevertheless a unity of plot, a sustained interest, and a uniform elevation of style, which distinguishes it from all the poetry of the period. Our own Spenser has imbibed the spirit of some of its most beautiful passages; and several striking coincidences between his Faerie Queen and the Rinaldo can be traced, particularly in the account of the lion tamed by Clarillo, and the well-known incident of Una and the lion in Spenser. The poem of Rinaldo will always be read with interest, as it strikes the keynote of Tasso's great epic, the Gerusalemme Liberata, many of the finest fictions of which were adopted with very little modification from the earlier work. His letter asking his father's permission to publish it came at a very inopportune moment. Bernardo was smarting just then under the disappointments connected with the reception of his own poem, the Amadigi. It produced little impression upon the general public; the copies which he distributed among the Italian nobles procured him nothing but conventional thanks and polite praise; while the magnificent edition which he prepared specially for presentation to Philip II. of Spain, in the hope that he might thereby be induced to interest himself in the restoration of his wife's property at Naples, was not even acknowledged. Wounded thus in his deepest sensibilities, and bewailing the misfortunes of his literary career, we need not wonder that he should have sent a reply peremptorily commanding his son to give up poetry and stick to the law. The young poet in his distress sought the intervention of some of his father's literary friends, and through their mediation the destiny of Torquato Tasso and of Italian poetry was accomplished, and the poem of Rinaldo was given to the world through the renowned press of the Franceschi of Venice. No sooner was it published than it achieved an extraordinary success, for Cervantes had not yet made this class of fiction for ever ridiculous.

Notwithstanding that the public were surfeited with romantic poetry, the merits of this new work, constructed upon different principles and carried out in an original style, were such that the literary schools were carried by storm, and the young Tasso, or Tassino, as he was now called to distinguish him from his father, at once leapt into fame. So great was his reputation, that the newly-restored University of Bologna invited him to reside there, so that it might share in the distinction conferred by his name. In this magnificent seat of learning he remained, enjoying the advantage of literary intercourse with the great scholars who then occupied the chairs of the University, until the publication of some anonymous pasquinades, reflecting severely upon the leading inhabitants, of which he was falsely supposed to be the author. In his absence the Government officials visited his rooms and seized his papers. The sensitive poet regarded this suspicion as a stain upon his honour, and the outrage he never forgave. Shaking the dust from his shoes, he departed from Bologna, and for some time led an unsettled life, enjoying the generous hospitality of the nobles whose names he had celebrated in his Rinaldo. Returning at length to Padua, where he engaged in the study of Aristotle and Plato, and delivered three discourses on Heroic Poetry in the Academia degli Eterei, or the Ethereals—in which he developed the whole theory of his poetical design—which were afterwards published, the office of Laureate at the court of Ferrara was offered to him by Cardinal Lewis of Este, to whom, as I have said, he had dedicated his Rinaldo.

Torquato Tasso was now in the full bloom of opening manhood. He was distinguished, like his father, for his personal beauty and grace, with a high, noble forehead, deep gray melancholy eyes, regular well-cut features, and hair of a light brown. He had the advantage of all the culture of his time. His manners were refined by familiar intercourse with the highest nobles of the land, and his mind richly furnished, not only with the stores of classic literature, but also with the literary treasures of his own country; while a residence, more or less prolonged, in the most famous towns, and among the most romantic scenes of Italy, had widened his mental horizon and expanded his sympathies. He had already mounted almost to the highest step of the literary ladder. Nothing could exceed the tokens of respect with which he was everywhere received. But, in spite of all these advantages, Tasso was now beginning to realise the shadows that accompany even the most splendid literary career. His own experience was now confirming to him the truth of what his father had often sought to impress upon his mind, — that the favour of princes was capricious, and that a life of dependence at a court was of all others the most unsatisfactory. Constitutionally disposed to melancholy, irritable and sensitive to the last degree, he brooded over the fancied wrongs and slights which he had received; and at first he was disposed to accept the advice of his father's friend, the well-known Sperone, who strongly dissuaded him from going to the court of Ferrara, painting the nature of the life he would lead there in the most forbidding colours. It would have been well had he listened to this wise counsel, strengthened as it was by his own better judgment; for in that case he might have been spared the mortifications which made the whole of his after life one continued martyrdom. But recovering from a protracted illness, into which the agitation of his spirits threw him, when on a visit to his father at the court of the Duke of Mantua, he passed from the depths of despondency to the opposite extreme of eagerness, and, fired by ambition, he resolved to enter upon the path to distinction which now opened before him. And here we come to the crisis of his life.

In the fifteenth and sixteenth centuries a state of things existed in Italy somewhat similar to that which existed in the Highlands of Scotland in earlier times. Each Highland chief maintained an independent court, and among his personal retainers a bard who should celebrate his deeds was considered indispensable. So was it with the princes of Italy. In their train was always found a man of letters whose poetic Muse was dedicated to laureate duties, and was valued in proportion as it recorded the triumphs of the protecting court. For this patronage of art and letters no court was more distinguished than that of Ferrara.

"Whoe'er in Italy is known to fame,

This lordly home as frequent guest can claim."

The family of Este was the most ancient and illustrious in Italy. The house of Brunswick, from which our own royal family is descended, was a shoot from this parent stock. It intermarried with the principal reigning families of Europe. Leibnitz, Muratori, and our own great historian, Gibbon, have traced the lineage and chronicled the family incidents of this ducal house. Lucrezia Borgia and the Parasina of Byron were members of it. For several generations the men and women were remarkable for the curious contrasts of a violent character and the pursuits of the arts of peace which they displayed. Poisonings, assassinations, adulteries, imprisonments for life, conspiracies, were by no means uncommon incidents in their tragical history. And yet under their government Ferrara became the first really modern city in Europe, with well-built streets, a large population, and flourishing trade, attracting wealthy settlers from all parts of Italy. Nearly all the members of the reigning house were distinguished for their personal attractions and their mental capacities. They were also notorious for their love of display. We have books, such as the Antiquities of the House of Este by Muratori, the Chivalries of Ferrara, the Borseid, and the Hecatommiti of Giraldi, which were written almost to order for the purpose of gratifying this vanity. Borso, the first duke, caused his portrait to be painted in a series of historical representations in one of his principal palaces; Hercules I. kept the anniversary of his accession to the throne by a splendid procession, which was compared to the festival of Corpus Christi; an Order, which had nothing in common with medieval chivalry, called the Order of the Golden Spur, was instituted by his court, and conferred upon those who reflected lustre by their deeds or their literary gifts upon the house of Este; while, to crown all, we read at this day on the tower of the cathedral of Ferrara the dedicatory inscription beginning with "To the god Hercules II.," which the complaisant inhabitants had put there, — an apotheosis which reminds us of the worst slavery of imperial Rome under Caligula and Domitian. Some of the greatest names of Italy, such as Petrarch, Boiardo, Ariosto, the wonderful prodigy Olympia Morata, and the celebrated poetess Vittoria Colonna—the friend of Michael Angelo—were connected with this brilliant court. The well-known French poet Clement Marot fled to it to escape persecution in his native country. Calvin found a refuge there for some months under the assumed name of Charles d'Heppeville, during which he converted the duchess to the reformed faith. The father of Tasso visited it when it was at the height of its splendour and renown. Hercules II., the then reigning prince, son of Lucrezia Borgia, had earned a great reputation for his literary works and patronage of the fine arts; and his wife, the friend of Calvin, the youngest daughter of Louis XII. of France, was even more remarkable for her talents, being equally skilled in the Latin and Greek languages. This renowned couple drew around them a circle of the most accomplished men and women in Europe, in whose congenial society Bernardo Tasso spent a few months of great enjoyment, delighting all by his wit and social qualities.

But notwithstanding all this magnificence and love of learning, the house of Este, among its other contradictory qualities, was distinguished for capriciousness and meanness. Even Muratori, their ardent panegyrist, does not attempt to conceal this blemish. We must deduct a good deal from the high-sounding praise which the courtly writers of Italy bestowed upon this house for its splendid patronage of literature, when we remember that Ariosto, who passed his life in its service, was treated with niggardliness and contempt. He had a place assigned him among the musicians and jugglers, and was regarded as one of the common domestics of the establishment. Guarini, the well-known author of the Pastor Fido, contemporary with Tasso, met with much indignity in the service of Alphonso II.; while Panigarola and several other distinguished men were compelled to leave the service of the ducal family by persecution. Benvenuto Cellini, who resided at the court of Ferrara twenty-five years before Tasso, gives a very unfavourable account of the avarice and rapacity which characterised it; and Serassi, the biographer of Tasso, remarks that the court seems to have been extremely dangerous, especially to literary men. It was not therefore, we may suppose, without other reasons than his being merely a Guelph, that Dante in his Inferno placed one of the scions of the house in hell, and uniformly regarded the family with dislike. Tasso himself was destined to experience both the favour and the hostility, the generosity and the neglect, of this capricious house.

Ferrara is now a dull sleepy city of less than thirty thousand inhabitants. It is a place that continues to exist not because of its vitality, but by the mere force of habit. Its broad deserted streets and decaying palaces lie silent and sad in the drowsy noon sunshine, like the aisles of a September forest. But in the days of Tasso it was one of the gayest cities of Italy, which looked upon itself as the centre of the world, and all beyond as mere margin. It was always festa, always carnival, in Ferrara; and when the poet came to it in his twentieth year, on the last day of October 1565, he found it one brilliant theatre. The reigning duke, Alphonso II., had just been married to the daughter of Ferdinand I., Emperor of Austria; and this splendid alliance was celebrated by tournaments, balls, feasts, and other pageantry, which transcended everything of the kind that had previously been seen in Italy, with the exception, perhaps, of the fêtes connected with the marriage of Lucrezia Borgia to his grandfather. The ardent mind of the poet, it need hardly be said, was completely fascinated. He saw himself surrounded daily with all the splendours of chivalry, and lived in the midst of scenes such as haunt the dreams of poets and inspire the pages of romance. Goethe, in his Torquato Tasso, an exquisite poem, it may be said, but wanting in dramatic action, gives a vivid picture of the poet's life at the court of Ferrara, which bore some resemblance to his own at the court of Weimar.

Two sisters of the reigning prince lived in the palace, and by their beauty and accomplishments imparted to the court an air of great refinement. The younger, the famous Leonora of Este, was about thirty years of age at this time, and therefore considerably older than Tasso. A severe and protracted illness had shut her out from the festivities connected with her brother's marriage, and communicated to her mind a touch of sadness, and to her features a spiritual delicacy which greatly increased her attractiveness. The numerous writers by whom she is mentioned talk with rapture, not only of her beauty and genius, but also of her saintly goodness, which was so great that a single prayer of hers on one occasion was said to have rescued Ferrara from the wrath of Heaven evinced in the inundation of the Po. In the society of these ladies Tasso spent a great deal of his time; and perhaps his intercourse with them, unconstrained by court conventionalities, was not altogether free from those tender feelings which the charms of a lovely and accomplished woman, whatever her rank, might readily excite in a poetic temperament. The author of the Sorrows of Werther did not, therefore, perhaps draw exclusively upon his imagination in picturing the rise and struggle of an unhappy passion for Leonora d'Este in the bosom of the young poet. Whatever may be said regarding this passion, however, there can be no doubt that his heart was at this time enslaved by younger and humbler beauties. He had much of the temperament of his father, who, although exemplary in his single and married life, was distinguished for his Platonic gallantry, and cherished a poetic attachment, according to the fashion of the day, for various ladies throughout his career, such as Genevra Malatesta, the beautiful Tullia of Arragon, and Marguerite de Valois, sister of Henry III. These follies were but the froth of his genius, however; and in this respect his son followed his example. Lucrezia Bendidio, a young lady at court gifted with singular beauty and musical talent, reigned for a while supreme over his affections. But she had other suitors, including the author of the Pastor Fido, and the poet Pigna, who was the secretary and favourite of the reigning duke. The Princess Leonora tried to cure Tasso of this passion by persuading him to illustrate the verses of his rival Pigna. Nothing came of this first love, therefore, and the object of it soon after married into the house of Machiavelli.

In the congenial atmosphere of the court of Ferrara, surrounded by the flower of beauty and chivalry, stimulated by the associations of his master Ariosto, which every object around recalled, and encouraged by the praises of the sweetest lips in the palace, Tasso set himself diligently to the composition of the great work of his life, the Gerusalemme Liberata, the plan of which he had formed before he left the University of Padua. Among the treasures of the Vatican Library I have seen a sketch in the poet's own handwriting of the first three cantos. This sketch he now modified and enlarged, and in the space of a few months completed five entire cantos. He read the poem as it proceeded to the fair sisters of his patron, and received the benefit of their criticisms. This work, which is "the great epic poem in the strict sense of modern times," occupied altogether eighteen years of the author's life. It was begun in extreme youth, and finished in middle age, and is a most remarkable example of a young man's devotion to one absorbing object. The opening chapters were written amid the bright dreams of youth, and in the happiest circumstances; the closing ones were composed amid the dark clouds of a morbid melancholy, and during an imprisonment tyrannical in all its features. Placed side by side with Homer and Virgil, it may be said with Voltaire that Tasso was more fortunate than either of these immortals in the choice of his subject. It was based, not upon tradition, but upon true history. It appealed not merely to the passions of love and ambition, but to the deepest feelings of the soul, to faith in the unseen and eternal. To humanity at large the wars of the Cross must be more interesting than the wrath of Achilles, and the recovery of the Holy Sepulchre than the siege of Troy. No theme could be more susceptible of poetic treatment than the Crusades. They were full of stirring incident, of continually changing objects and images. The strife took place amid scenes from which the most familiar stories of our childhood have come, and around which have gathered the most sacred associations of the heart. And Tasso's mind was one that was peculiarly adapted to reflect all the special characteristics of the theme. It was deeply religious in its tone, and therefore could enter into the struggle with all the sympathy of real conviction. His luxuriant imagination was chastened by his classical culture; while the pervading melancholy of his temperament gave to the scenes which he described an effect such as a thin veil of mist that comes and goes gives to a mountain landscape. The gorgeous Oriental world of the palm tree and the camel, seen through this sad poetic haze, has all the shadows of the deep northern forests and the tender gloom of the western hills. The rigid outlines of history fade in it to the indefiniteness of fable, and fact becomes as flexible as fancy.

The circumstances of the times were also peculiarly favourable for the composition of such a poem. He was at the proper focal distance to appreciate the full interest of the Crusades, not too near to be absorbed in observation and engrossed in the immediate results; not too far off to lose the sympathy for the religious chivalry which inspired the Holy War. Earlier, in the intensely prosaic period that immediately succeeded, the romance of the Crusades was gone; later, Europe was girding itself for the sterner task of reformation. Before the time of Tasso, Peter the Hermit would have been deemed a foolish enthusiast; later, he would have been sent to a lunatic asylum. But just at the time when Tasso wrote there was much, especially in Italy, of that spirit which roused and quickened Europe in the eleventh century, much that appealed to the natural poetry in the human heart. The recent victory of the Christian forces at the famous battle of Lepanto checked the spread of Mohammedanism in Eastern Europe, and turned men's thoughts back into the old channel of the Crusades; so that Gregory XIII., who ascended the pontifical throne about the time that Tasso had resumed the writing of his Gerusalemme, had actually planned an expedition to the Holy Land, like that which his predecessor, Urban II., had sent out. And one of the principal events which the poet witnessed after his arrival at Ferrara, when the marriage rejoicings were over, was the departure of the reigning duke with a company of three hundred gentlemen of his court, arrayed in all the pomp and splendour of the famous Paladins of the first Crusade, to assist the Emperor of Austria in repelling an invasion of the Turks into Hungary. Many of the noble houses of Europe at this time were extremely anxious to trace their origin to the Crusades; and the vanity of the house of Este required that Tasso should make the great hero of his epic—the brave and chivalrous Rinaldo—an ancestor of their family. The scenes and associations, too, in the midst of which his daily life was spent, helped him to realise vividly the pageantry connected with the heroes of his epic.

Thus happy in the choice of a subject, and favoured by the spirit of the time and the circumstances in which he was placed, Tasso gave himself up to the composition of his poem with a most absorbing devotion. Like Virgil, he first sketched out his work in prose, and on this groundwork elaborated the charms of colouring and harmony which distinguish the poem. So carefully did he study the military art of his day that all his battles and contests are scientifically described, and are in entire accordance with the most rigorous rules of war; and so thoroughly did he make himself acquainted with the topography of the Holy Land by the aid of books, that Chateaubriand, who read the Gerusalemme under the walls of Jerusalem, was struck with the fidelity of the local descriptions. Tasso occasionally sought relief from his great task by the composition of sonnets and lyrics, which were published in the Rime of the Paduan Academy, and contributed to make him still more popular all over Italy. He also took part in those literary disputations in public which were characteristic of the age; and for three days in the Academy of Ferrara, in the presence of the court, defended against both sexes fifty "Amorous Conclusions" which he had drawn up—a form of controversy which seems to have been a relic of the courts or parliaments of love, very popular in the twelfth and thirteenth centuries. One of the ladies of the court impugned with success his twenty-first conclusion "that man loves more intensely and with more stability than woman;" but whether this success was the result of the goodness of her cause, and not rather of her own ability or of Tasso's gallantry, may be left an open question. He afterwards published the whole series of the "Amorous Conclusions," and dedicated them to Genevra Malatesta, who now, as an old married woman, was greatly touched by receiving such a compliment from the son of her former lover.

Tasso's father was now dying at Ostiglia, a small place on the Po, of which the Duke of Mantua had made him governor. With talents unimpaired, at the age of seventy-six, and while preparing a new poem upon the episode of Floridante in the Amadigi, he was seized with his last illness. His son, full of filial anxiety, hastened to see him, and found the house in wretched disorder; the servants having taken advantage of the helplessness of their master to neglect their duties and steal any valuable property they could lay their hands upon, so that Tasso had not only to take charge of the household affairs, but also to defray out of his own scanty resources the domestic expenditure. After a month's severe struggle his father died in his arms, to the regret of all Italy, and his remains were interred with great pomp by the Duke of Mantua in a marble cenotaph in the principal church of his capital, and were afterwards transferred by Tasso to the church of St. Paul in Ferrara, where they now lie. Thus passed away one of the most conspicuous and unfortunate persons of his age, of whom it has been said that he was "a politician, unlucky in the choice of his party; a client, unlucky in the choice of his patrons; and a poet, unlucky in the choice of his theme."

The fatigue and sorrow connected with this bereavement brought on a severe illness, from which Torquato recovered with a sense of loneliness and depression which only deepened as the years went on. From this melancholy he enjoyed, however, a temporary respite by a visit to Paris. The house of Este by frequent intermarriages was connected with the French court, in consequence of which they had a right to use the golden lilies of France in their armorial bearings; and many of the ecclesiastics of the family held rich benefices in that country as well as in their own. Cardinal Lewis, the brother of the reigning duke, resolved to inspect the abbeys that belonged to him in France, and to strengthen the Roman Catholic cause, which had received a severe blow from the Reformation; and among the gentlemen of his train he took with him Tasso, in order to introduce him to his cousin Charles IX., who himself dabbled in poetry and had a fine literary taste. From the French monarch the poet obtained a gracious reception; and by the whole court he was warmly welcomed as one who had worthily commemorated the gallant deeds of the Paladins of France at the siege of Jerusalem. For nearly a year he resided in different parts of France, and notwithstanding the numerous distractions of such a novel mode of life, he added many admirable stanzas to his great epic, inspired by the very scenes among which his hero, Godfrey, and his knights had lived. He left just in time to escape the dreadful massacre of St. Bartholomew; but he may be said to have suffered indirectly on account of it. Though treated with distinction by the French court, his personal wants were left unsupplied, and his patron, Cardinal Lewis, did not make up for this meanness. Voltaire, therefore, had reason to indulge in a cynical sneer at the glowing accounts of his visit given by Italian writers; and Balzac's statement that Tasso left France in the same suit of clothes that he brought with him, after having worn it for a year, is not without foundation. This shabby treatment, however, was part of a wider State policy. The year of Tasso's residence in France was one of preparation for the massacre of St. Bartholomew; but in order to avert the suspicions of the intended victims, the Huguenots were treated with such extraordinary favour by the authorities that the Pope himself was incensed, and remonstrated with the King. Tasso, ignorant of the dreadful secret, spoke candidly and vehemently against the reformed doctrines and those who professed them. His patron therefore simulated deep indignation on account of this imprudence; and as the step fell in both with his personal avarice and his State policy, he broke off the cordial relations that formerly existed between them.

On the return of Tasso to Ferrara he occupied himself for about two months with the composition of a pastoral drama called the Aminta. This species of poem, which originated with Theocritus, who represented the shepherds of Sicily nearly as they were, and was imitated by Virgil, who idealised the shepherd life, was revived at the court of Ferrara; and some years before a local poet wrote a pastoral describing a romantic Arcadia, which was acted at the palace, and seems to have inspired Tasso with the idea of writing one too. But all previous pastorals—the Sacrifizio of Beccari, the Aretusa of Lollio, the Sfortunato of Argenti—were rough and incongruous medleys compared with the finished production of Tasso, which may be said to mark an era in the history of dramatic poetry. Although Tasso himself did not think much of it, and did not take any steps to publish it, the judgment of his contemporaries and of posterity has placed it next in point of merit to the Gerusalemme; and by Italians it is especially admired for its graceful elegance of diction. Leigh Hunt executed a very good translation of it, which he dedicated to Keats. Its choruses, which are so many "lyrical voices floating in the air," are very beautiful. It was designed for the theatre, and was acted with great splendour at the court of Ferrara, and a few years later at Mantua, when the well-known artist and architect Buontalenti painted the scenery. This fact, however, shows how primitive was the state of the theatre at this time; and how the spectators, little accustomed to histrionic representations, were content to witness dramas that had no plot or action, and to follow the progress of a beautiful poem rather than a dramatic development. The Aminta long retained its popularity as an acted poem in Italy. It was often represented in open-air theatres, like the ancient Greek plays, in gardens or in woods, where Nature supplied the scenery, and the scalinata or stage was only some rising piece of ground. Traces of one of these sylvan theatres may still be seen in the grounds of the Villa Madama, on the eastern slopes of Monte Mario near Rome; and one cannot help thinking that a poem so redolent of the open air, so full of Nature and still natural life, which Tasso himself called Favola Boschereccia, or a Sylvan Fable, was better adapted for such a stage than for the heated air and artificial surroundings of the Italian theatres. Such a pastoral was in entire keeping with the manners of the Italian peasants; and the scenes of Arcadia which it represented might be seen almost everywhere in the beautiful valleys and chestnut-covered hills of their native land. The exquisite loveliness of the climate, and the simplicity and indolence of the people, lent themselves naturally to such ideal dreams. And Tasso in his Aminta only gave expression to the same happy thoughts which the same scenery and the same people had ages before inspired in the mind of Virgil when he wrote his Eclogues.

After a few months' quiet sojourn with Lucrezia d'Este, now Duchess of Urbino, at that court, he was appointed secretary to the Duke of Ferrara, in room of his rival Pigna, who for this reason became his mortal enemy, and stirred up against him the persecution which embittered his whole subsequent life. But standing high, as he did, in the favour of the duke, he enjoyed for a while a season of calm repose, during which he finished the great epic poem, which was eagerly looked for throughout Italy. Anxious to make this cherished work of his genius as perfect as possible, he unfortunately was imprudent enough to submit portions of his work to all his learned friends for their opinion. Besides in this way getting the most contradictory advices, sacrificing his own independent judgment, and imposing an unworthy yoke upon his genius, the result was that the fragments of the poem passed from hand to hand, and so got into the possession of the printers, who, eager to profit by the public curiosity, pieced them together, and clandestinely printed them. Even in this fragmentary form, the cantos that appeared in various cities of Italy were received with unbounded applause. The author, as may be imagined, was intensely annoyed at this wrong that had been done to him, and wrote to the Pope, to the Republic of Genoa, and to all the Italian princes who had any authority in the case, to put a stop to the publication of a work which had been circulated without his sanction, but in vain. Even the first complete edition, which was issued in 1581, seems to have been without his consent; for the author complains that he was compelled, by the surreptitious publication of parts of his poem, to finish the work in haste, and he wished for more time to elaborate the plot and polish the style. In the later editions, no less than seven of which appeared the same year, Tasso seems to have been to some extent consulted; but it may be said that the great epic was given to the world in the form in which we now have it, without the author's imprimatur, and without the benefit of his finishing touches. But in spite of this disadvantage it took the whole country at once by storm. Two thousand copies were sold in two days. Throughout literary circles nothing else was spoken of. The exquisite stanzas, full of the true chivalric spirit, touched a responsive chord in every Italian bosom. Not only in the academies of the learned was the poem discussed, not only was it recited before princes amid the splendours of courts, but priests mused over it in the solitude of the cloister, and peasants chanted its sonorous strains as they worked in the fields. Quotations from it, we are told, might be heard from the gondolier on the Grand Canal of Venice, as he greeted his neighbour in passing by, and from the brigand on the far heights of the Abruzzi, as he lay in wait for the unsuspecting traveller; and "a portion of the Crusader's Litany was a favourite chant of the galley-slaves of Leghorn, as, chained together, they dragged their weary steps along the shore."

There is no book which it is easier to find fault with than the Gerusalemme when estimated by the satiated critical spirit of modern times, which insists upon brevity, and demands in each line a certain poetic excellence; especially if the poem is known only through the medium of a translation, which, however faithful, is but the turning of the wrong side of a piece of tapestry. We may object to the want of originality in the leading characters, to the occasional inflated style, and the conceits and plays upon words now and then introduced, to the apparently disproportionate influence of love upon the action of the poem, as Hallam has remarked, giving it an effeminate tone, and, above all, to the introduction of so much supernatural machinery in the form of magic and demons; for such supernaturalism is out of keeping altogether with our vaster knowledge of the universe, and our more solemn ideas of Him who pervades it. But it is not by an analysis of particular parts, or a criticism of special peculiarities, that the Gerusalemme should be judged. It is by its effect as a whole, as a highly finished work of art. A single campaign of the first crusade—that of 1099—embraces the whole action of the poem; but the numerous episodes form each a perfect picture, that, like a flower floating on a stream, and illumined by a special gleam of sunlight, does not interrupt the continuous flow of the narrative. In a state of society characterised by much corruption, the sentiments are uniformly pure; and in an artificial age, when Nature was regarded as only the background of human action, the descriptions of the objects of Nature are wonderfully accurate; and the mind of the poet towards the flowers and trees, the woods and hills and streams, was in a childlike state, and had all the freshness and joyousness of childhood. The student is not to be envied who can read without emotion the enthusiastic description of the Crusader's first sight of Jerusalem, the touching pathos of Clorinda's death, and the sublime account of the ruins of Carthage. It would indeed refresh many a mind, surfeited by the vast mass of our modern literature, to go back to the green pastures and still waters of this grand old poem.

Every visitor to Florence knows the venerable monastery of San Marco, with its hallowed relics of Savonarola, and its beautiful frescoes of Fra Angelico. In a large apartment of this monastery, which was formerly the library of the monks, are now held the meetings of the famous Della Cruscan Academy, instituted in 1582 for the purpose of purifying the national language. At that time every town of the least importance in Italy had its academy with some strange fantastic name, which was an important element in the intellectual life of the people, and exercised a critical control over the literature of the day. Up to the year 1814 the Della Cruscans assembled in the Palazzo Riccardi, the ancient palace of the Medici; but that stately building being required for Government purposes, the members have since been accommodated in San Marco, where they have sunk into obscurity, many of the inhabitants of Florence being altogether ignorant of the existence of such an institution in their city. I had considerable difficulty in finding out the locality. The furniture of the apartment is exceedingly curious, and is meant to indicate the object of the Academy, which—as its name literally translated, of the bran or chaff, signifies—is to sift the fine flour of the language from the corrupt bran that has gathered around it. The chairs are made in imitation of a baker's basket, turned bottom upwards and painted red. On the wall behind each chair is suspended a shovel, with the name of its owner painted upon it, along with a group of flowers in allusion to the famous motto of the Academy, "Il più bel fior ne coglie," "It plucks the fairest flower." On the table, during my visit, there was a model of a flour-dressing machine and some meal sacks; while several printed sheets of a new edition of the Italian Dictionary, which the members were engaged in publishing at the time, with manuscript corrections, were scattered about. At present the Academy, besides doing this important work, occasionally holds public sessions; but it is an effete institution, that has little more than an archæological interest. It was very different, however, in the sixteenth century. Then, in point of numbers and reputation, it was the outstanding literary academy of Italy, and occupied the commanding position from which the all-powerful humanists of the previous age had been driven by the counter reformation. It is chiefly, however, by its attacks upon Tasso that it is now known to fame.

No sooner was the Gerusalemme published than comparisons began to be instituted between it and the Orlando Furioso of Ariosto. This latter poem was then in the zenith of its reputation; it was regarded as the supreme standard of literary excellence, and it was slavishly imitated by all the inferior poets of Italy. It was inevitable, therefore, that the two works should be compared together. But as well might the Æneid of Virgil be compared with the Metamorphoses of Ovid. The Orlando Furioso is a romantic poem in the manner of Ovid, whereas the Gerusalemme Liberata is an epic poem in the manner of Homer and Virgil. No Italian poet previous to Tasso had written an epic; and Tasso himself distinctly avowed that he had chosen that form of poetry deliberately; not only as being more congenial to his own mind, but also that he might avoid following in the steps of Ariosto, whose work he regarded as, in its own department, incapable of being excelled, or even equalled. In reply to the generous letter of Ariosto's nephew, who wrote him a letter of congratulation, he said, "The crown you would honour me with already adorns the head of the poet to whom you are related, from whence it would be as easy to snatch it as to wrest the club from the hand of Hercules. I would no more receive it from your hand than I would snatch it myself."

But in spite of the altogether different nature of the two poems, and in spite of the distinct disavowals of Tasso, the critics persisted in accusing him of the presumption of entering the lists with Ariosto. And in this idea they were strengthened by the injudicious praises of Camillo Pellegrini, who in a dialogue entitled Caraffa or Epic Poetry, likened the Orlando Furioso to a palace, the plan of which is defective, but which contains superb rooms splendidly adorned, and is therefore very captivating to the simple and ignorant; while the Gerusalemme Liberata resembles a smaller palace, whose architecture is perfect, and whose rooms are suitable and elegant without being gaudy, delighting the true masters of art. This squib was published in Florence, and at once aroused the hostility of the Della Cruscans. They were already prejudiced against Tasso on account of his connection with the court of Ferrara, between which and the court of Florence there was a bitter rivalry; and that offence was intensified by the unguarded way in which he spoke of the Florentines as being under the yoke of the Medici, whom he denounced as tyrants. The Academy, which at the time enjoyed the patronage of the Grand Duke of Tuscany, was therefore too glad to seize upon Pellegrini's squib as a pretext for a vehement attack upon Tasso's epic. Ariosto was dead, had passed among the immortals, and was therefore beyond all envy; but here was a living poet, who belonged to a court which had cruelly treated the daughter of their ruler, Lucrezia de Medici, the first wife of Alfonso of Ferrara, and was a mere youth, who was guilty of the sacrilege of seeking to dethrone their favourite. Ariosto had greatly admired Florence, and celebrated its beauties in one of his finest poems; and was it to be borne that this young upstart, who had presumed to speak disparagingly of their city, should be preferred to him? It would be a useless waste of time to go over in detail the absurd criticisms by which they attempted to throw ridicule upon the Gerusalemme Liberata. They would have passed into utter oblivion had not Tasso himself, by condescending to reply to them, given to them an immortality of shame. Not contented with abusing his poem and himself, they also attacked his father, asserting that his Amadigi was a most miserable work, and was pillaged wholesale from the writings of others, and thus wounded the poet in the most tender part.

By this combination of critical cavils against him, Tasso was thrown back from the land of poetical vision into a dreary mental wilderness. The effect upon one of his most sensitive nature, predisposed by temperament and the vicissitudes of his life to profound melancholy, was most disastrous. We can trace to this cause the commencement of those mental disorders which, if they never reached actual insanity, bordered upon it, and darkened the rest of his life. His overwrought mind gave way to all kinds of morbid fancies. His body became enfeebled by the agitation of his mind; and the powerful medicines which he was prevailed upon to take to cure his troubles only increased them. Like Rousseau during his sad visit to England, he became suspicious of every one, and lost faith even in himself. Religious doubts commenced to agitate his mind. Distracted by this worst of all evils, he put himself into the hands of the Holy Fraternity at Bologna; and though the inquisitors had sense enough to see that what he considered atheistical doubts were only the illusions of hypochondria, and tried to reassure him as to their belief in the soundness of his faith, he was not satisfied with the absolution which they had given to him.

The court of Ferrara was full of unscrupulous intriguers. Tasso's wonderful success could not be forgiven by some of the petty aspirants after literary fame who haunted the ducal precincts. Pigna, whose place as secretary he had usurped, stirred up the jealousy of the other courtiers into open persecution. Leonardo Salvinati, the leader of the Della Cruscan Academy, wishing to ingratiate himself with the court, joined in the hostility. Tasso's papers were stolen, and his letters intercepted and read, and a false construction was put upon everything he did. At first the duke refused to hear the various accusations that were brought against him, and continued to show him every mark of esteem. He had the privilege, in that ceremonious age a very high one, of dining daily with the prince at his own private table. He accompanied the princesses to their country retreats at Urbino, Belriguarda, or Consandoli, where in healthy country pursuits he forgot for a time his troubles. At Urbino he wrote the unfinished canzone to the river Metauro, one of the most touching of his compositions, in which he laments the wounds which fortune had inflicted upon him through the whole of his hapless life.

But the tenure of princely favour at Italian courts, amid so many ambitious patrons and anxious suitors, was very precarious. It was uncommonly so at Ferrara. After a while a sudden change passed over the mind of the duke towards Tasso. Whether tired of the poet's incessant complaints, irritated at his incautious conduct—going the length on two occasions of drawing his sword, when provoked, upon members of the ducal household,—or whether his suspicions were aroused regarding the relations between him and his sister Leonora, is not known, but from this time he began to treat Tasso as if he were a madman. He was placed under the charge of the ducal physicians and servants, who reported to their employer every careless word. Removed from Belriguarda, he was ordered to be confined in the Ferrarese convent of San Francisco; and two friars were appointed to watch over him continually. Such a life was unendurable to the proud poet, who disliked the nauseous medicines of the convent as much as its restraint; and taking advantage of a festa, when his keepers were unusually negligent, he made his escape by a window. In the disguise of a shepherd he travelled on foot over the mountains of the Abruzzi, getting a morsel of bread and a lodging from the peasants by the way, to his sister's house at Sorrento, now the Vigna Sersale. There he remained during the whole summer, soothed by his sister's affectionate kindness. The monotony of the life, however, began to pall upon him, and he longed to get back to his old scenes of excitement. Undeterred by an evasive reply which the duke sent to an urgent letter of his, he set out for Ferrara; and on his arrival, meeting with a cold reception, he was obliged again to leave the place where he had once been so happy. For a year and a half he wandered over almost the whole of Northern Italy, visiting in turn Venice, Urbino, Mantua, Padua, Rome, and Turin. At the last place he arrived without a passport, and in such a miserable condition that the guards at the gates of the city would not have admitted him had he not been recognised by a Venetian printer who happened to be present. His startled looks, his nervous manner, and his perpetual restlessness, confirmed wherever he went the rumour of his madness; and, even if he were not mad, the object of Alfonso of Este's anger might be a dangerous associate. During all this time he was in the greatest poverty, being obliged to sell for bread the splendid ruby and collar of gold which the Duchess of Urbino had presented to him when he recited to her at her own court his pastoral poem of Aminta.

From the Duke of Urbino and Prince Charles Emanuel of Savoy, however, he received generous treatment; but a fatal spell carried him back a third time to Ferrara. His arrival by an unfortunate coincidence happened to be on the very day that Margaret Gonzaga, daughter of the Duke of Mantua, was to come home as the third bride of Alfonso. The duke, preoccupied with the stately ceremonies connected with his nuptials, took no notice of him; and many of the courtiers from whom he expected an affectionate welcome, taking their cue from their master, turned their backs upon him. What a contrast to his first reception at that court fourteen years before, when he stood among the noble spectators of Alfonso's marriage with his first wife, the Archduchess of Austria, as one of the most honoured of the guests! He now gazed upon the splendours of this third marriage ceremony, by far the greatest poet of his age, but a homeless vagrant, a reputed maniac, treated with neglect or contumely on every side! No wonder that his cup of misery, which had previously been filled to the brim, overflowed with this last and crowning insult; and, scarce knowing what he did, he broke forth into the most vehement denunciations of the duke and his whole court, declaring that they were all "a gang of poltroons, ingrates, and scoundrels." These fiery reproaches, which his misery had wrung from the poor poet, were carried by his enemies to the ear of the Duke, and Tasso was immediately seized and imprisoned as a lunatic in the hospital of Santa Anna in Ferrara—in the same year and the same month, it may be mentioned, in which another of the great epic poets of the world, Camoens, the author of the Lusiad, finished as a pauper in an hospital his miserable career.

While madness was alleged as the ostensible reason, the real motives of this step are involved in as deep a mystery as the cause of Ovid's banishment to Tomi, on the Euxine. Muratori, the author of the Antiquities of the House of Este, says that he was confined principally in order that he might be cured; while the Abbate Serassi, who wrote a life of the poet, attributes his imprisonment to his insolence to the duke and his court, and to his desire, repeatedly expressed and acted upon, to leave his patron's service. But both these writers considered the interests of the house of Este more sacred than those of truth. The cause generally accepted is Tasso's supposed attachment to Leonora, the sister of the duke. For a long time he is said to have cherished this passion in secret, concealing it even from the object of it, although evidences of it may be found in some marked form or playful allusion in nearly all his poetical writings; the episode of Olinda and Sophronia in the Gerusalemme, which he was urged in vain by his friends to withdraw on the ground of its irrelevancy, being intended to represent his own ill-fated love. On one occasion, however, in a confiding mood, he told the secret to one of the courtiers of Ferrara, whom he believed to be his devoted friend. But what was thus whispered in the closet was proclaimed upon the house-top; and a duel was the result, in which Tasso, as expert in the use of the sword as of the pen, put to flight the cowardly traitor and his two brothers, whom he had brought with him to attack the poet. This adventure, and the cause of it, reached the ears of the duke, whose resentment was kindled by the audacity of a poor poet and dependant of his court in falling in love with a lady of royal birth. On the strength of this suspicion his papers were seized, and all the sonnets, madrigals, and canzones that were supposed to give countenance to it, confiscated. The manuscript of the Gerusalemme itself was retained, and a deaf ear was turned to the poet's entreaties for its restoration. Gibbon, in his Antiquities of the House of Brunswick, relates that one day at court, when the duke and his sister Leonora were present, Tasso was so struck with the beauty of the princess, that, in a transport of passion, he approached and kissed her before all the assembly; whereupon the duke, gravely turning to his courtiers, expressed his regret that so great a man should have been thus suddenly bereft of reason, and made the circumstance the pretext for shutting him up in the madhouse of St. Anne. An abortive attempt was made to prove the attachment, about fifty years ago, by a certain Count Alberti, who published a manuscript correspondence purporting to be between Tasso and Leonora, which he discovered in the library of the Falconieri Palace at Rome. The alleged discovery excited an immense amount of interest in this country and on the Continent; but ere the edition was completed the author was accused of having forged the manuscripts in question, and was condemned to the galleys.

The story of this hapless love is so romantic in itself, and has been made the theme of so much pathetic poetry, that it would be almost a pity to destroy by proof any foundation upon which it may rest. And yet it is difficult to agree with Professor Rosini, who has ably treated the whole question in a work entitled Amore de Tasso, and has come to the conclusion, after carefully weighing all the evidence, that this was the rock upon which Tasso's life made shipwreck. On this theory several circumstances are altogether inexplicable. We may dismiss at once the famous kiss as certainly a myth. Besides the disparity of age, the ill-health, severe piety, and exalted rank of Leonora were formidable barriers in the way of Tasso's contracting a passion for her; and it is well known that the poet, who could not have forgotten so soon a devoted love, did not offer a single tribute of regret to her memory when she died a few years afterwards. It is also but too certain that Leonora left her supposed lover to languish in a dungeon without any reply to his pathetic complaints. The force of gravitation is a mutual thing; and just as the great sun himself cannot but bend a little in turn to the smallest orb that wheels around him, so the august Princess of Este could not but have regarded with womanly interest a devoted admirer, however humble. The poetical gallantry of the day will account for all Tasso's lyrical effusions in praise of Leonora. They were in most instances simply the tributes that were expected from the laureate of a court, especially a laureate who was accused, with some show of reason, by the courtiers of Ferrara, of an enthusiastic devotion to women, and of wasting his life with the day-dreams of love and chivalry.

Regarding the question of his madness, which was, as I have said, the ostensible cause of his imprisonment, we are left in almost equal uncertainty. His morbid sensibility, irritated by the treatment which he received alike from his friends and foes, his repeated complaints and occasional violences and extravagances of conduct, may have seemed to a selfish prince to border closely upon mental derangement. But his whole conduct during his imprisonment, the nature of the numerous writings which he produced during that dark period, forbid us to suppose that his intellect ever crossed the line which separates reason from insanity. From out the gloom that surrounds the whole case two points stand out clear and indisputable, that no indiscretion of conduct or aberration of mind on the part of Tasso can possibly have merited the sufferings to which he was subjected, and that whatever may have been Alfonso's suspicions, his fiendish vengeance is one of history's darkest crimes, and covers the tyrant with everlasting disgrace.

Three objects attract the steps of the modern pilgrim in desolate grass-grown Ferrara; the house, distinguished by a tablet, in which Ariosto was born; the ancient castle in the centre of the town, in whose courtyard Ugo and Parasina, whom Byron has immortalised, were beheaded; and next door to the chief hotel—the Europa—and beside the post-office, the huge hospital of St. Anne, in which Tasso was confined. This last object is by far the most interesting. The sight of it is not needed to sadden one more than the deserted streets themselves do. The dungeon, indicated by a long inscription over the door, is below the ground-floor of the hospital; it is twelve feet long, nine feet wide, and seven feet high, and the light penetrates through its grated windows from a small yard. By several authors, including Goethe, considerable doubts have been expressed regarding the authenticity of this cell; and certainly the present features of the place are not confirmatory of the tradition. This doubt, however, has not prevented relic-hunters—among whom Shelley may be included—from carrying off in small fragments the whole of the bedstead that once stood there, as well as cutting off large pieces from the door which still survives. Lamartine wrote in pencil some poetical lines upon the wall; and Byron, with his intense realism, caused himself to be locked for an hour in it, that he might be able to form some idea of the sufferings which he recorded in his Lament of Tasso.

Less than sixty years ago the insane were treated with the utmost inhumanity as accursed of God; and the asylums in which they were shut up were dismal prisons, where the unfortunate inmates were left in a state of the utmost filth, or were chained and lashed at the caprice of savage keepers. The madhouse which Hogarth drew will aid us in forming a conception of an Italian asylum in the sixteenth century, which was much worse than anything known in our country. The other inmates of the hospital of St. Anne suffered much doubtless; but they were really mad, and were therefore unconscious of their misery. But that alleviation was wanting in the case of Tasso. He was sane and conscious, and his sanity intensified the horror of his situation, "enabling him to gauge with fearful accuracy the depths of the abyss into which he had fallen." One glimpse of him is given to us by Montaigne, who visited the cell, where it seems the unfortunate inmate was made a show of to all whom curiosity or pity attracted to the hospital. "I had even more indignation than compassion when I saw him at Ferrara in so piteous a state—a living shadow of himself." His jailer was Agostino Mosti, who, although he was himself a man of letters, and therefore should have sympathised with Tasso, on the contrary carried out to the utmost the cruel commands of his prince, and by his harsh language and unceasing vigilance immensely aggravated the sufferings of his victim. This inhuman persecution was caused by Mosti's jealously of Tasso as the rival of his beloved master Ariosto, to whom at his own cost he had erected a monument in the church of the Benedictines at Ferrara.

For a whole year Tasso endured all the horrors of the sordid cell in which he was immured. After a while he was removed to a larger apartment, in which he could walk about; and permission was granted to him sometimes to leave the hospital for part of a day. But whatever alleviations he might thus have occasionally enjoyed, he was for seven long years a prisoner in the asylum, tantalised by continual expectations held out to him of approaching release. One person only—the nephew of his churlish jailer—acted the part of the Good Samaritan towards him, cheered his solitude, wrote for him, and transmitted the letters of complaint or entreaty which he addressed to his friends, and which would otherwise have been suppressed or forwarded to his relentless enemy. His sufferings increased as the slow weary months passed on, so that we need not wonder that the last years of his captivity should sometimes have been overclouded by visions of a tormenting demon, of flames and frightful noises, with an apparition of the Virgin and Child sent to comfort him. That he should have been able to preserve the general balance of his mind at all in circumstances sufficient to unseat the reason of most men, is a convincing proof of the stability of his intellect, and his unshaken trust in the God of the sorrowful. While we think of this protracted cruelty of the author of his imprisonment, it is some consolation to know that he met with what we may well call a merited retribution. Alfonso, as Sir John Hobhouse tells us, in spite of his haughty splendour, led an unhappy life, and was deserted in the hour of death by his courtiers, who suffered his body to be interred without even the ceremonies that were paid to the meanest of his subjects. His last wishes were neglected; his will was cancelled. He was succeeded by the descendant of a natural son of Alfonso I., the husband of Lucrezia Borgia; and he, falling under the displeasure of the Vatican, was excommunicated; and Ferrara, having been claimed by Pope Clement VIII. as a vacant fief, passed away for ever from the house of Este.

"The link
Thou formest in his fortunes bids us think
Of thy poor malice, naming thee with scorn,
Alfonso! How thy ducal pageants shrink
From thee! if in another station born,
Scarce fit to be the slave of him thou mad'st to mourn."

At no period of his life was the mind of Tasso more active than during his imprisonment. In the absence of all nourishment from the bright world of Nature which he loved so passionately, his fancy could grow and keep itself leafy, like the cress-seed, which germinates and produces its anti-scorbutic foliage on a bit of flannel moistened with water, without any contact with soil or sunlight, in the long Arctic night of the ice-bound ship. With the ravings of madmen ringing in his ears, he composed some of the most beautiful of his writings, both in prose and verse. Among the manuscripts of the British Museum are preserved some of these writings, whose withered vellum pages we turn over with profound pity, as we think of the sad circumstances in which they were composed. The most valuable of these is the manuscript of the Torrismondo, in Tasso's own handwriting, and in the original parchment binding. This work was begun before his imprisonment, and it was not finished until the year after his liberation; but the greater part of it was composed in the wretchedness of his cell at Ferrara. The story upon which it is founded is a very harrowing one, a king of the Ostrogoths marrying his own sister, mistaking her for a foreign princess; but it is treated with very inadequate tragic power, and, like the Aminta, displays no real action. Its beauty chiefly consists in its choral odes on the vanity of all earthly things, which are exquisitely sad and touching. We hear in them the wild wail of the poet over his own misfortunes, and the vanishing of the dreams of glory which haloed his life. The chorus with which the tragedy winds up—"Ahi! lagrime; Ahi! dolore"—the words appropriately carved upon his tombstone at St. Onofrio—is unspeakably pathetic. It is his own dirge, the cry of a heart whose strings are about to break. It is as untranslatable as the sigh of the wind in a pine forest. If the words are changed, the spell is lost, and the way to the heart is missed.

At last the solicitations of the most powerful princes of Italy on Tasso's behalf overcame the tenacity of Alfonso's will, and the victim was released; but not till he had become so weak and ill that, if the imprisonment had continued a little longer, death would inevitably have opened the door for him. When the order for his liberation had been obtained, his friends made known to him by slow degrees the glad tidings, lest a too sudden shock should prove fatal. He was now free to go wherever he pleased, and to behold the beauties of Nature, which had been the mirage of his prison dreams; but the elasticity of his spirits was gone for ever; the bow had been too long bent to recover its original spring, and the memory of his sufferings haunted him continually, and cast a dark shadow over everything. He could not altogether shake off the fear that he was still in Alfonso's power, and wherever he went he fancied that an officer was in pursuit of him to drag him back to the foul prison in St. Anne's. A modern Italian poet, Aleardo Aleardi, has graphically described the feelings of the gentle poet-knight, roaming, pale and dishevelled, as a mendicant from door to door. But the sufferings that had thus maimed him bodily and mentally had spiritually ennobled him; and there is not a more touching incident in all history than his entreaty to be allowed to kiss the hand of the cruel tyrant, as a last favour before leaving Ferrara for ever, in token of his gratitude for the benefits conferred upon him in happier days, — a favour which Alfonso, to his eternal disgrace, refused to grant.

At first Tasso took up his abode at the court of the Duke of Mantua, whose son, Vincenzo Gonzaga, had been the principal instrument in his release, on the occasion of his marriage with the sister of Alfonso of Ferrara. This Vincenzo Gonzaga is shown by the light of history in two opposite characters: as the generous friend and patron of Tasso, and as the pupil of the Admirable Crichton, who in a midnight brawl slew his tutor in circumstances of the utmost baseness and treachery. For a while Tasso was treated with great kindness at Mantua, but, the father dying, the son no sooner ascended the ducal throne than, with the capriciousness peculiar to Italian princes, he turned his back upon the poet whom he had formerly befriended. The incident I have mentioned would have prepared us for this dastardly conduct; the evil side of his nature, which was kept in abeyance during his political pupilage, assuming the predominance on his accession to power. Tasso's proud spirit could not endure the neglect of his once ardent friend, and he set out again into the cold inhospitable world, imploring in his great poverty from a former patron the loan of ten scudi, to pay the expenses of his journey to Rome. On the way he turned aside to make a pilgrimage to Loretto, in order to satisfy that earnest religious feeling which had been the inspiration of his genius, but the bane of his life. The searching scrutinies and the solemn acquittals of the inquisitors of Bologna, Ferrara, and the great tribunal of Rome itself, had not satisfied his morbid mind. And he thought that he might get that peace of conscience which nothing else could give by a visit to the Casa Santa—the house of the Virgin Mary at Loretto. Worn out by the long journey, which he made in the old fashion on foot, he knelt in prayer before the magnificent shrine; and thus, admitted as it were within the domestic enclosure of the holy household, he felt that the Blessed Virgin had given him that calmness and repose of heart which he had not known since he had prayed as a boy beside his mother's knee. Strengthened by the successful accomplishment of his vow, he went on to Rome; but the stern Sixtus V., who was now upon the Papal throne, was too much occupied with the architectural reconstruction of Rome, and with the suppression of brigandage in the Papal States, to bestow any attention upon literature; and Tasso had lost whatever energy he once possessed to assert his claims to recognition among the multitude of sycophants at the Vatican.

Sick at heart, he left the imperial city, and directed his steps to Naples, in the hope that on the spot he might succeed in recovering his father's possession and his mother's dowry. But here, too, the same ill-fortune that had hitherto dogged his steps attended him. The lawsuit which he instituted, though it promised well at first, proved a will-o'-the-wisp, which lured him into the bog of absolute penury. His sister was dead; his mother's relatives, formerly hostile, were now, because of the lawsuit, doubly embittered against him. In his distress he sought refuge in the Benedictine monastery of Monte Oliveto, which is now occupied by the offices of the Municipality of Naples, and the monastery garden converted into a market-place. Here, in one of the finest situations in Naples, commanding one of the loveliest views in the world, and in the congenial society of the monks, his shattered health was recruited, and his mind tranquillised by the beauties of Nature and the exercises of religion. He repaid the kindness of his hosts by writing a poem on the origin of their Order, and by addressing to them one of his best sonnets. Among the visitors who sought him out in this retreat was John Battista Manso, Marquis of Villa, who afterwards became his biographer. This accomplished nobleman, "whose name the friendship and Latin hexameters of Milton have rendered at once familiar and musical to English ears," was by far the kindest and most consistent patron that Tasso ever met with. He loaded him with presents, and showed him the most delicate and thoughtful attentions during Tasso's visit at his beautiful villa on the seashore near Naples. He took him with him to his tower of Bisaccio, where he remained all October and November, spending his days, with great advantage to his health, in hunting, and his nights in music and dancing, taking special delight in the marvellous performances of the improvisatori. Milton's acquaintance with Manso may be regarded as one of the most fortunate incidents of his foreign travels, inasmuch as his conversations about Tasso are supposed to have suggested to him the design of writing an epic work like the Gerusalemme; and indeed Milton is supposed to have borrowed some of his ideas for Paradise Lost from the Sette Giornate, or Seven Days of Creation, a fragmentary poem in blank verse, which Tasso began under the roof of his friend at Naples. This work is now very little known, but it is worthy of being read, if only for the lofty dignity of its style, and the beauty of some of its descriptive parts, particularly the creation of light on the first day, and of the firmament on the second, and the episode of the Phoenix on the fifth. Its association with Milton's far grander work, as literary twins laid for a while in the same cradle, will always invest it with deep interest to the student.

Tasso occupied himself at the same time with an altered version of his great poem, which he called the Gerusalemme Conquistata. He was induced to undertake this work in order to triumph over his truculent critics, the Della Cruscans, who had condemned the former version. In the Imperial Library at Vienna is preserved the manuscript of this version, with its numerous alterations and erasures, showing how laborious the task of remodelling must have been. He suppressed the touching incident of Olinda and Sophronia. He changed the name of Rinaldo to Riccardo; and ruthlessly swept his pen through all the flatteries, direct and indirect, which he had originally bestowed upon the house of Este. There is hardly a single stanza that is not changed. But in the process of revision he deprived his poem of all life. Religious mysticism has been substituted for the refined chivalry of the Crusades, and poetry and romance have been sacrificed for classical regularity and religious orthodoxy. To any one familiar with the original, the Conquistata must be regarded as the most melancholy book in any language; a sad monument of a noble genius robbed of its power and depressed by calamity. And it is all the more melancholy that the author himself was utterly unconscious of its defects, and got so enamoured of what he considered his improvements, that he wrote and published a discourse called the Giudizio—a cold pedantic work, in which he explained the principles upon which he made his alterations. In vain, however, did the author thus commit literary suicide. His immortal poem had passed beyond the reach of revision, and stamped itself too deeply upon the minds and hearts of his countrymen to be effaced by any after version. And now the Conquistata has sunk into well-merited oblivion, while the Liberata—"his youthful poetical sin," as he himself called it—is everywhere admired as one of the great classics of the world.

For nine years Tasso lived after his imprisonment. But his free life was only a little less burdensome than his prison one. With impaired health and extinguished hope, and only the wreck of his great intellect, he wandered a homeless pilgrim from court to court, drawn like a moth to the brilliant flame that had wrought his ruin. Well would it have been for him had he settled down to some quiet independent pursuit that would have taken him away from the atmosphere of court life altogether, such as the Professorship of Poetry and Ethics which had been offered to him by the Genoese Academy. But the habits of a whole lifetime could not now be given up. His education and training had fitted him for no other mode of life. Without the patronage of the great, literature in those days had not a chance of success; and a thousand incidents in the life of Tasso serve to show that "genius was considered the property, not of the individual, but of his patron"; and with petty meanness was the reward allotted for this appropriation dealt out. His experience of the favour of princes at this period was only a repetition of his own earlier one, and that of his father. His patrons, one after another, got tired of him; and yet he persisted in soliciting their favour. From the door of his former friend, Cardinal Gonzaga, at Rome, he was turned away; and as a fever-stricken mendicant he sought refuge in the Bergamese Hospital of that city, founded by a relative of his own, who little thought that it would one day afford an asylum to the most illustrious of his name.

But fate had now discharged its last evil arrow, and began to relent during the two remaining years of his life. The sun that was all day obscured, as it struggled with dark clouds, emerged at last, and made the western sky ablaze with splendour. All over the country nothing was to be heard but the echoes of Tasso's praises. From the fountains of the Adige to the Straits of Messina, in the valleys of Savoy, and in the capitals of Spain and France, his immortal epic was read or recited by the highest and the lowest. Fortunes were made by its sale. The famous bandit Sciarra, who with his troop of robbers had terrified the whole of Southern Italy, hearing that Tasso was at Gaeta, on his journey from Naples to Rome, sent to compliment him, and offer him, not only a free passage, but protection by the way. At Florence, whither he went at the invitation of the Grand Duke of Tuscany, the whole literary society of the place, even including many of the Della Cruscans, showered honours upon him. While at Rome Pope Clement VIII. gave him the most flattering reception, assigned to him an apartment in the Vatican, and an annual income of two hundred scudi. From the representatives of his mother's friends at Naples he was also offered an annuity of two hundred ducats, and a considerable sum in hand, on condition of stopping the lawsuit. Thus furnished with what he had vainly looked for all his life, the means of a comfortable subsistence, his closing days promised a happiness to which he had hitherto been a stranger. But the gifts of fortune were brought to him with sad auguries, like the soft sunny smiles of September skies, which gild the fading leaves with a mockery of May. Tasso came to Rome in November. But the state of his health was so deplorable that he could not remain with safety in the room assigned to him in the Vatican. It was thought, therefore, that the elevated position and salubrious air, as well as the quiet life of the monastery of St. Onofrio, not far off on the same side of the Tiber, would be more suitable for his restoration. Accordingly, Cardinal Cynthio Aldobrandini, nephew of Clement VIII., who had befriended him on many occasions, brought him to St. Onofrio in his own carriage. And as his weary steps crossed the threshold, he said to the monks, who received him with pitying looks, "I come to die among you."

Whenever he was able to go out, he spent the last days of his life in the garden of the monastery. There he sat under the shadow of the aged oak that has since become historical; and as he watched the sunset of his life, he would gaze upon the mighty ruins and the glorious view stretching before him with that inspired vision which creates half the beauty it beholds, and with that enhanced appreciation caused by the prospect of the coming darkness which would hide it for ever from his sight. We love to think of the poet in this quiet resting-place, where the noises of the great world reached him only in subdued murmurs. Heaven was above him, and the world beneath. The memory of his wrongs and his ambitions alike vanished in the shadow cast before by his approaching death. Alfonso and Ferrara faded away upon the horizon of eternity; even the fame of his Gerusalemme, the great object for which he had lived, had become utterly indifferent to him. In the monastery of St. Onofrio, a bent, sorrow-stricken man, old before his time, joining with the monks in the duties of religion, Tasso appeals more powerfully to our feelings than when in the full flush of youth and happiness he shone the brightest star in the royal court of Alfonso.

Awakening to the sense of the great loss that Italy was about to sustain in his death, his friends and admirers proposed that the Pope should confer upon him at the Capitol the laurel wreath that had crowned the brow of Petrarch. But the weather during the winter proved singularly unpropitious for such a ceremony. Rain fell almost every day, and constant sirocco winds depressed the spirits of the people and prevented all outdoor enjoyments. And thus the season wore on till April dawned with the promise of brighter skies, and the day was fixed, and all the élite of Rome and of the chief cities of Italy were invited to attend the coronation. Extensive preparations were made; the whole city was in a flutter of excitement, and the people looked forward to a holiday such as Rome had not seen since the days of the Cæsars. But by this time the poet was dying, fever-wasted, in his lonely cell. He could see from his window, as he lay propped up with pillows on his narrow couch, across the river and its broad valley crowded with houses, the slender campanile of Michael Angelo ascending from the Capitoline Hill, marking the spot where at the moment the people were busy preparing for the magnificent ceremony of the morrow. But not for him was the triumph; it came too late. "Tomorrow," he said, "I shall be beyond the reach of all earthly honour." He received the last rites of the Church from the hands of the diocesan, and passed quietly away with the unfinished sentence upon his lips, "Into thy hands, O Lord," while the concluding strains of the vesper hymn were chanted by the monks. And they who came on the morrow, to summon him to his coronation, found him in the sleep of death. The laurel wreath that was meant for his brow was laid upon his coffin, as it was carried on the very day of his intended coronation, with great pomp, cardinals and princes bearing up the pall, and deposited in the neighbouring church of the monastery. Ever since, the anniversary of his death has been religiously kept by the monks of St. Onofrio. They throw open on that day, the 25th of April, the monastery and garden to the general public; ladies are freely admitted, and a festival is observed, during which portions of the poet's writings are read, his relics exhibited, and his tomb wreathed with flowers.

Tasso died, like Virgil his model, in his fifty-first year. Short and chequered and full of trouble as was his life, it is amazing what an immense amount of literary work he accomplished. Since the publication of his Rinaldo, in his seventeenth year, he never ceased writing, even in the most unfavourable circumstances. Of his prose and poetical works no less than twenty-five volumes remain to us. These works are all rich in biographical materials. They show an ideal tenderness of feeling, an intense love for everything beautiful, and a deep piety, not only of sentiment but of duty. They are specially interesting to us as links connecting the ancient world with the modern. We can trace the influence of Tasso's genius in very varied quarters. He not only gave a new impulse to the literature of his own country, but even inspired the artistic productions of the day. The most beautiful passages of Spenser's Faerie Queen were suggested by his pastoral poetry; while his chivalrous epic was to Milton at once the incentive and the model of his own immortal work. It is probable that the New Heloïse of Rousseau, and the tragedy of Zaire by Voltaire, would not have been written had not Tasso invested the subject of romantic love and of the Crusades with such a deep interest to the authors. We of this age may miss in Tasso's poetical works the dramatic force to which we are accustomed in such productions; but we acknowledge the spell which the lyrical element that pervades them all, and towards which Tasso's genius was most strongly bent, casts over us. His own personal history strikingly illustrates the vanity of a life spent in dependence upon princes. But fortunately the lesson is no longer needed; for a wide and intelligent constituency of readers all over the world now afford the patronage to literature which was formerly the special privilege of single individuals favoured by rank or fortune. Both to authors and readers this emancipation has been productive of the happiest results.

CHAPTER X - THE MARBLES
OF ANCIENT ROME

Marble-hunting is one of the regular pursuits of the visitor in Rome. The ground in almost every part of the ancient city is strewn with fragments of historical monuments. The largest and most valuable pieces have long since been removed by builders and sculptors, to fashion some Papal palace, or to adorn some pretentious church; and at the present day, in almost every stone-mason's shed, blocks of marble belonging to ancient edifices may be seen in process of conversion into articles of modern furniture. Many bits of the rarest kinds, however, still remain, which not unfrequently bear traces of the richest carving. For ages such spots have been quarries to visitors from all parts of the world, who wished to bring home some memorial of their sojourn in the Eternal City, and the supply is still far from being exhausted. That so much material should have survived the wholesale conversion, during the middle ages, of columns and statues into lime, in kilns erected where the temples and palaces were most crowded, and the vast exportation of objects of antiquity to other countries, is a striking proof of the prodigious quantity of marble that must have existed in ancient Rome. Now, however, such relics are more carefully preserved; and as the places where they are found in greatest quantity have been taken under the charge of the Government, and soldiers are constantly on the watch, it is not so easy as it used to be to abstract a fragment that has taken one's fancy.

Marble fragments are so eagerly sought after because they make most suitable and convenient souvenirs. Their own beauty and rarity, apart from all historical associations, are a great attraction. Many of them will form, when cut and polished by the lapidary, pretty tazzas and paper-weights, and even the smallest bits can be put together in a mosaic pattern, so as to make extremely beautiful table-tops. Whole rows of lapidary shops in the English quarter of the city, especially in the Via Babuino and the Via Sistina, are maintained by this curious traffic. In the Forum and Colosseum great quantities of marble and alabaster used to be found; but these localities have been so much ransacked that they now afford very scanty gleanings. The Baths of Caracalla and Titus, the recent excavations on the Esquiline, the ruins of the palaces of the Cæsars on the Palatine, and the open space marked out for new squares and streets between Sta. Maria Maggiore and St. John Lateran, are the best situations within the walls of the city. Outside the supply is almost as large as ever. All over the vast Campagna the foot of the wayfarer strikes against some precious or beautiful relic; and along the Appian and Latin Ways broken pieces of different kinds may be found in such profusion that such spots look like the rubbish-heap around a marble quarry. In the vast grounds over which the imposing ruins of Hadrian's Villa spread, heaps of fragments of marble flooring or casing may be seen in almost every neglected corner, from which it is easy to obtain some lovely bit of giallo antico or pavonazzetto or green porphyry. Beside the ancient quay of Rome, leading to the ruins of the Emporium or Custom-house — at a spot called in modern phrase "La Marmorata," because marble vessels still discharge their cargoes there — immense quantities of marble, alabaster, and porphyry are piled up, that were unshipped untold ages ago for Roman use; and a vineyard a short way off, on the slope of the Aventine, is much frequented by collectors on account of the richness of its finds.

But it is not as a mere amusement, or as a means of collecting pretty souvenirs of travel, that such marble-hunting expeditions are to be recommended. They may have a much higher value. The different kinds of marble collected are peculiarly interesting owing to their association with the different epochs of the history of the city and empire; and as the specimens which the geologist obtains throw light upon the formation of the rocky strata of the earth, so the small marble fragments which the student finds in Rome afford a clue to the various stages of its existence. Indeed, a competent knowledge of the marbles of Rome is indispensable to a clear understanding of the age of its ancient monuments. An immense amount of controversy has raged round some remarkable building or statue, which would have been prevented had the nature and origin of the marble of which it was composed been first investigated. The famous statue of the Apollo Belvedere in the Vatican, for instance, was long regarded as an original production either of Pheidias himself or of his school. But the discovery that the marble of which it is wrought is Lunar or Carrara marble — which was unknown until the time of Julius Cæsar, who first introduced it into Rome — is of itself a proof that it is not a genuine work of Greek art of the best period, but a monument of the decadence, or a copy of an original, wrought in imperial times for the adornment of a summer palace in Italy. In numberless other cases, ancient monuments have been identified by the mineral character and history of their marble materials. The first thing, therefore, which the student during his visit to the city ought to do, is to make himself acquainted with the different varieties of marble that have been found within the walls or in the neighbourhood. For this purpose the Museum in the Collegio della Sapienza or University of Rome will afford invaluable aid. In this institution, conveniently arranged in glass cases, are no less than 607 specimens of various marbles and alabasters used by the ancient Romans in the building or decoration of their houses and public monuments. The collection was made by the late Signor Sanginetti, Professor of Mineralogy in the University, and is quite unique. A great deal of instruction may also be obtained from the mineralogical study of the thousands of marble columns still standing in the older churches and palaces of Rome, most of which have been derived from the ruins of ancient temples and basilicas. Several excellent books may also be consulted with advantage—especially Faustino Corsi's Treatise on the Stones of Antiquity, Trattato delle Pietre Antiche, which is the most approved Italian work on the subject, and from which much of the information contained in the following pages has been obtained.

No marble quarries exist in the vicinity of Rome. The Sabine Hills are indeed of limestone formation, and large masses of travertine, a fresh-water limestone of igneous origin, occur here and there, but no mineral approaching marble in texture and appearance is found within a very considerable radius of the city. The nearest source of supply is at Cesi, near the celebrated "Falls of Terni," about forty-five miles from Rome, where "Cotanella," the red marble of the Roman States, is found, of which the great columns supporting the arches of the side aisles of St. Peter's are formed. The hills and rocks of Rome are all volcanic, and only the different varieties of eruptive rock were first employed for building purposes. The oldest monuments of the kingly period, such as the Cloaca Maxima, the Mamertine Prison, the Walls of Servius Tullius, and some of the earliest substructures on the Palatine Hill, were all built of the brown volcanic tufa found on or near their sites. This is the material of which the famous Tarpeian Rock and the lower part of most of the Seven Hills is composed. It is the oldest of the igneous deposits of Rome, and seems to have been formed by a conglomerate of ashes and fragments of pumice ejected from submarine volcanoes whose craters have been completely obliterated. It reposes upon marine tertiary deposits, and over it, near the Church of Sta. Agnese, where it is still quarried for building stone, rests a quaternary deposit, in which numerous remains of primeval elephants have been found. Though the Consular or Republican period was a very stormy one, and the reconstruction of the city, after its partial demolition by the Gauls, seems to have been too hurried to allow much attention to be paid to the materials and designs of architecture, yet there are numerous indications in the existing remains of that period that there was a decided advance in these respects upon the ruder art of a former age. Finer and more ornamental varieties of volcanic stone were introduced from a distance, such as the peperino or grayish-green tufa of the Alban Hills, the Lapis Albanus of the ancients, with its glittering particles of mica interspersed throughout its mass; the hard basaltine lava from a quarry near the tomb of Cæcilia Metella, on the Appian Way, and from the bed of the Lago della Colonna, once the celebrated Lake Regillus, to which the name of Lapis Tusculanus or Selce was given; and the Lapis Gabinus or Sperone, a compact volcanic concrete found in the neighbourhood of the ancient Gabii on the road to Tivoli, extensively used in the construction of the earliest monuments, particularly the Tabularium and the huge Arco de Pantani. Brick was also largely employed in the construction of the foundations and inner walls of public buildings, being arranged at a later date into ornamental patterns, to which the names of opus incertum and opus reticulatum were given; and in the manufacture of this substance, which they were probably at first taught by the Etruscan artificers of Veii in the neighbourhood, the Romans reached a high degree of perfection. The earliest tombs along the Appian Way were constructed of these different varieties of building materials. The sarcophagi of the Scipios were hollowed out of simple blocks of peperino stone; and the sculptor's art and the material in which he wrought were worthy of the severe simplicity of the heroic age.

But towards the close of the Republican period, Rome began to be distinguished for the magnificence of its public monuments. As its area of conquest spread, so did its luxury increase. New divinities were introduced from foreign countries, and domesticated in the Capitol; and these required more sumptuous fanes than those with which the native deities had been contented. The brown tufa of the Tarpeian Rock sufficed for the rude sanctuary of Vesta, the primitive hearth-stone of ancient Rome; but in the reconstruction of the sumptuous temple of Jupiter Capitolinus, which marked the grandest period of Roman history, the most precious stones of Asia and Africa were employed. Statues were imported wholesale from Greece to adorn temples and theatres, constructed after the models of Greek architecture, with pillars, friezes, and floors of precious Pentelic and Sicilian marble. During the last century of the Republic marble became a common building-stone. The tomb of Cæcilia Metella, and the temples of Ceres, Juno Sospita, and Castor and Pollux, indicate the introduction of this precious and beautiful material. But it was reserved for the period of the Empire to complete the architectural glories of the city. Travertine, usually called Lapis Tiburtinus, a straw-coloured volcanic limestone excavated in the plain below Tivoli, which has the useful property of hardening on exposure, was now used as the principal building-stone instead of the former lavas and tufas; and the Colosseum, entirely constructed of travertine, which was treated in the middle ages as a quarry, out of which were built many of the palaces and churches of Rome, attests to this day the beauty and durability of this material. Quarries of crystalline marbles, admirably adapted for the purposes of the sculptor and architect, were opened in the range of the Apennines overlooking the beautiful Bay of Spezia, in the vicinity of Carrara, Massa, and Seravezza, and largely worked in the time of Augustus. This emperor could boast that he had found Rome of brick, and left it of marble. The marbles of each new territory annexed to the Empire were brought at enormous expense into the Imperial City. A quay, to which reference has already been made, was constructed at the broadest part of the Tiber, where the vessels that transported marbles from Africa, and from the most distant parts of Eastern Europe and Western Asia, landed their cargoes. Here numerous blocks of marble were lately found, one of which was identified as that sent to Nero from a quarry in Carinthia; and another, a column of even more colossal dimensions, weighing about thirty-four tons of valuable African marble, was meant to serve as a memorial pillar of the Council of 1870 on the Janiculum, but the intention was never carried out. So abundant was marble during the first two centuries of the Empire, that it was nothing accounted of. Every temple, palace, and public edifice was built of it either in whole or in part. The tombs that lined the Appian Way on either side for fifteen miles had their brick cores covered with marble slabs; and their magnificence must have impressed every visitor who entered the Imperial City through this avenue of architectural glory shrouding the decays of death. It is obvious, then, that by studying the history of the conquests of Rome, the student can ascertain at what period a particular kind of marble was introduced from its native country, and the proximate date of the building in which this marble had been used.

It was a fortunate circumstance for the preservation of the precious marbles of Rome that Christianity laid its cuckoo egg in the nest of the Pagan city. When the capture of Rome by Alaric gave the final blow to heathen worship, by the overthrow of the ruling classes, who alone cherished the proud memories of the ancient faith, the greater number of the temples were still standing without any one to look after the edifices or maintain the religious services. The Christians were therefore free to take possession of the deserted shrines; and they speedily transferred to their own churches the columns and marble decorations that adorned the temples of the gods. Many of the precious stones that once beautified the palaces of emperors and senators were employed to form the altars and the mosaic flooring of the memorial chapels. Almost all the early churches were constructed on or near the sites of the temples, so that the materials of the one might be transported to the other with the least difficulty and expense, just as the settler in the back-woods of America erects his log-house in the immediate vicinity of the trees that are most suitable for his purpose. And the striking contrast between the plain, mean exteriors of the oldest Roman churches—rough, time-stained, and unfinished since their erection—and their gorgeous interiors, with their forests of columns separating the aisles, and the series of richly-sculptured and brilliantly-frescoed chapels, all blazing with gold and marble,—a contrast that reminds us of the surprising difference between the outside of a common clumsy geode lying in the mud, and the sparkling crystals in the drusic cavity at the heart of it,—would lead us to infer that the outer walls were raised in haste to secure the valuable materials on the spot, before they could be otherwise appropriated. Marangoni, a learned Roman archæologist, mentions thirty-five churches in Rome as all raised upon the sites and out of the remains of ancient temples; and no less than six hundred and eighty-eight large columns of marble, granite, porphyry, and other valuable stones, as among the relics of heathen fanes transferred to sacred ground within the city, when the bronze Jupiter was metamorphosed into the Jew Peter,

"And Pan to Moses lent his pagan horn."

Many of these relics can be traced and identified, for it may be generally presumed, for the reason already given, that none are very far removed from their original situation.

I know no more interesting pursuit in Rome than such an investigation; the objects, when their history is ascertained, acquiring a charm from association, over and above their own intrinsic beauty and interest. Most of the materials with which the three hundred and sixty-five churches of modern Rome have been constructed have been derived from the ruins of the ancient city. With the exception of a few comparatively insignificant portions brought from the modern quarries of Carrara, Siena, and Sicily, to complete subordinate details and to give a finish to the work, no marbles, it is said, have been used in ecclesiastical and palatial architecture for the last fifteen hundred years, save those found conveniently on the spot; and hardly a brick has been made or a stone of travertine or tufa hewn out for domestic buildings within the same period. The construction of St. Peter's itself involved more destruction of classical monuments than all the appropriations of previous and subsequent Vandals put together. Much has been lost on account of this extraordinary transmutation and reconsecration, whose loss we can never cease to deplore; but we must not forget at the same time that much has been conserved which would otherwise have wasted away under the slow ravages of time, been consigned to the lime-kiln, or disappeared in obscure and ignoble use. Enough remains to overwhelm us with astonishment, and furnish materials for the study of years.

The white marbles of Greece were the first introduced into Rome. Paros supplied the earliest specimens, and long held a monopoly of the trade. Marmor Parium, or Marmo Greco duro, as it is called by the modern Italians, is the very flower and consummation of the rocks. This material seems to have been created specially for the use of the sculptor—as that in which he can express most clearly and beautifully his ideal conceptions; and the surpassing excellence of ancient Greek sculpture was largely due to the suitability for high art of the marble of the country, which was so stainlessly pure, delicate, and uniform—as Ruskin remarks, so soft as to allow the sculptor to work it without force, and trace on it his finest lines, and yet so hard as never to betray the touch or moulder away beneath the chisel. Parian marble is by far the most beautiful of the Greek marbles. It is a nearly pure carbonate of lime of creamy whiteness, with a finely crystalline granular structure, and is nearly translucent. It may be readily distinguished from all other white marbles by the peculiarly sparkling light that shines from its crystalline facets on being freshly broken; and this peculiarity enables the expert at once to determine the origin of any fragment of Greek or Roman statuary. The ancient quarries in the island of Paros are still wrought, though very little marble from this source is exported to other countries. In the entablature around the tomb of Cæcilia Metella, which is composed of Parian marble, we see the first example in Rome of the use of ornaments in marble upon the outside of a building; an example that was afterwards extensively followed, for all the tombs of a later age on the Appian Way had their exteriors sheathed with a veneer of marble. The beautiful sarcophagus which contained the remains of the noble lady for whom this gigantic pile was erected, and which is now in the Farnese Palace, was also formed of this material. Most beautiful examples of Parian marble may be seen in the three elegant columns of the Temple of Castor and Pollux in the Roman Forum, belonging to the best period of Græco-Roman architecture; and in the nineteen fluted Corinthian pillars which form the little circular temple of Hercules on the banks of the Tiber, long supposed to be the Temple of Vesta. By far the largest mass of this marble in Rome is the colossal fragment in front of the Colosseum that belonged to the Temple of Venus and Rome; and it helps to give one an idea of the extraordinary grandeur and magnificence of this building in its prime, whose fluted columns, six feet in diameter, and the sheathing of whose outside walls of great thickness, were all made of Parian marble.

More extensively employed in Greek and Roman statuary and architecture was the Marmor Pentelicum, or Marmo Greco fino of the modern Italians. The quarries which yielded inexhaustible materials for the public buildings and statues of Greece, and for the great monuments of Rome, were situated on the slopes of Mount Pentelicus, near Athens; and after having been closed for ages, have recently been reopened for the restoration of some of the buildings in the Greek capital. The marble is dazzlingly white and fine-grained, but it sometimes contains little pieces of quartz or flint, which give some trouble to the workmen. The Parthenon, crowning like a perfect capital of human art the summit of Nature's rough workmanship in the Acropolis, was built of this marble; and the immortal sculpture of Pheidias on the metopes, the frieze of the cella, and the tympana of the pediments of the temple, known as the Elgin Marbles, were carved out of a material worthy of their incomparable beauty. Innumerable specimens at one time existed in Rome. The arch of Septimius Severus and the Arch of Titus are built of it, although the rusty and weather-beaten hue of these venerable monuments hides the nature of the material. Domitian, who restored the celebrated Temple of Jupiter on the Capitol, procured columns of Pentelic marble for the purpose from Athens; two of these are now in the nave of the church of Ara Coeli, built upon the site of the temple; and portions of the others, and of the marble decorations, were presented by the magistrates to the Franciscan friars of the neighbouring convent, and by them were wrought in 1348 into the conspicuous staircase leading to the façade of the church, which pious Catholics used to mount on their knees in the manner of the ancient worshippers of Jupiter. Among the statues wrought of this marble may be mentioned the famous group of the Laocoon found in the Baths of Titus; the beautiful Venus de Medici, discovered in the Villa of Hadrian, near Tivoli, and now in the Uffizi Gallery in Florence; and the well-known "Farnese Bull," sculptured out of a single block of huge dimensions, unearthed out of the ruins of the Baths of Caracalla, and now in the Museum of Naples. Massimo d'Azeglio, in his Recollections, gives an interesting instance of the value set upon this marble by modern Roman sculptors. Pacetti having purchased an ancient Greek statue of the best period in Pentelic marble, greatly mutilated, and wishing to repair it, could find nothing among the best products of the Carrara quarries to match the marble in purity and fineness of texture, and was therefore obliged to destroy another Greek statue of inferior merit in order to get materials for the restoration. From this combination he succeeded in producing the sleeping figure known as the Barberini Faun, whose forcible abduction by the Pontifical Government on the eve of its being sold to a German prince, so preyed upon the mind of the cruelly-wronged sculptor, that he took to his bed and died.

Very like Pentelic marble, but easily distinguishable, is the Marmor Porinum, the Marmo Grechetto duro of the Italians. It is intermediate in the quality of its grain between Parian and Pentelic marble, being finer than the former and not so fine as the latter. The column in front of the Church of Santa Maria Maggiore, removed by Paul V. in 1614 from the Basilica of Constantine, is composed of this species; as well as the celebrated Torso Belvedere of the Vatican, found near the site of the Theatre of Pompey, to which Michael Angelo traced much of his inspiration, and which, as we learn from a Greek Inscription at the base, was the work of the Rhodian sculptor Apollonios, who carved the group of the "Farnese Bull."

Not unlike this Porine marble was the Marmor Hymettium of the ancients; but it was never a great favourite in Rome on account of its large grain and dingy white colour, slightly tinged with green and marked by long parallel dark gray veins of unequal breadth. The metamorphic action was not sufficiently energetic to destroy the last traces of organic matter and the original stratification of the rock; and the crystallising force was not sufficiently exercised to allow of the entire rearrangement of the whole of the particles so as to expel the included impurities. This marble was not therefore fitted for sculpture; but it could be used for certain architectural purposes and for ornamentation. It used to be quarried extensively on Hymettus, the well-known mountain of Attica, celebrated for the quantity and excellence of its honey. The rock on which the aromatic flowers grew in such profusion for the bees, did not, however, partake of the same delightful quality. In working it a peculiar fetid odour of sulphuretted hydrogen, somewhat like that of a stale onion, was emitted, which gave rise to its modern Italian name—Marmo Cipolla. This repulsive quality, however, disappeared quickly on exposure. The finest specimens of this marble in Rome are the forty-six columns in the Church of St. Paul's, outside the gate, which belonged originally to the Basilica Æmilia in the Forum, founded about forty-five years before Christ, and were transferred to the new building when the venerable old church, in which they had stood for fifteen hundred years, was destroyed by fire. Nothing too can be finer than the two rows of Ionic columns of Hymettian marble which divide the immense nave of Santa Maria Maggiore from the side aisles. There are eighteen on either side, each upwards of eight feet in circumference, and are supposed to have been taken from the Temple of Juno Lucina, whose site is assigned by antiquaries to the immediate vicinity. Similar rows of fluted Doric columns of the same marble, ten on each side, adorn the Church of St. Pietro in Vincoli. They are ancient, and belonged to some temple or basilica of the Forum. There are also five ancient pillars of Hymettian marble in the upper Church of San Clemente, taken from the same prolific source. The wall which surrounds the unique choir or presbytery of this most interesting old church is also composed of great slabs of Hymettian marble, taken from the original subterranean church and hastily put together. Some of the ancient pillars of Hymettian marble belonging to the peristyle of the temple of Ceres and Proserpine, still as widely spaced as they used to be, adorn the Church of Santa Maria in Cosmedin, built on the foundation of that shrine; while twenty-four remarkably fine fluted Corinthian columns of the same material divide the triple nave of Santa Sabina on the Aventine, and are supposed to have belonged to the ancient Temple of Juno Regina, erected by Camillus after the destruction of the Etruscan city of Veii. Hymettian marble was one of the first—if not actually the first—species introduced into Rome. In the year of Rome 662, Lucius Crassus the orator brought to the city six columns of it, each twelve feet in height, with which he adorned his house on the Palatine Hill, receiving, on account of this circumstance, from Marcus Brutus the nickname of the Palatine Venus. At the present day the marble is used for corner-stones in the ordinary houses of Athens.

Another livid white marble, somewhat resembling the Hymettian, is that which is known to the Italians as Marmo Greco livido. It was called by the ancients Marmor Thasium, from Thasos, now Thapso, an island in the north of the Ægean Sea, off the coast of Thrace. The marble dug from the rocky sides of Mount Ipsario—a romantic hill thickly covered with fir trees, and rising three thousand four hundred and twenty-eight feet above the sea—enjoyed considerable reputation among the ancients. In Rome it must have been very common, if the name of Thasian is to be given to all the fragments of nondescript dusky white marble which are found among the ruins. Seneca says that the fish-ponds in his day were formed of that Thasian marble, with which at one time it was rare to adorn even temples. It was considered the least valuable of the white Greek marbles, and was used for the more ordinary purposes; Statius mentioning, in order to show the surpassing splendour of a particular building, that Thasian marble was not admitted into it. But there are not many well-defined monuments of it remaining in Rome. The chief are the bust of Euripides in the Vatican, and the outside casing of the pyramid of Caius Cestius, near the Protestant cemetery, now so weather-beaten and stained with dusky lichens that it is difficult to identify the material of which it is composed.

From this marble, by a slight tinge of yellow and a little darker shade, the livid white marble of Lesbos, the Marmor Lesbium, or Marmo Greco Giallognolo, may be distinguished. It is not a beautiful material; and yet, strange to say, the statues of some of the most beautiful women of antiquity, such as those of Julia Pia in the Vatican, and of the Capitoline Venus in the Museum of the Capitol, were made of this marble, obtained from the birthplace of Sappho. More beautiful is the kind known as the Marmor Tyrium, or the Greco-Turchinicchio, which has a light bluish tinge. It was shipped by the ancients at the port of Tyre from some unknown quarry in Mount Lebanon, which supplied the marble used without stint in the building and decoration of Solomon's Temple and Palace. In this quarry every block was shaped and polished before it was sent to be inserted in its place in the Temple wall, which therefore, as Heber beautifully says, sprang up like some tall palm in majestic silence. In Rome this marble was very rare. The doors in the great piers which support the dome of St. Peter's are each flanked by a pair of spirally-fluted columns of Tyrian marble, supposed to have been brought to Rome by Titus from the Temple of Jerusalem. They originally decorated the confessional of the old Basilica. The twenty-eight steps of the Scala Santa at the Lateran, said by ecclesiastical tradition to have belonged to Pilate's house in Jerusalem, and to have been the identical ones which our Saviour descended when He left the judgment-hall, are made of this marble; so that, whatever we may think of the tradition itself, there is a feature of verisimilitude in the material.

The chief supply of pure white marble in Rome was derived from the quarries in the mountains at Luna, an old Etruscan town near the Bay of Spezia, which fell to decay under the later Roman emperors. This ancient Marmor Lunense is called by the Italians Marmo di Carrara, because it is identical with the famous modern Carrara marble, and belongs to the same range of strata; the ruins of the ancient Luna being only a few miles from the flourishing town of Carrara, the metropolis of the marble trade. From Parian and Pentelic marble, Lunar marble, as already mentioned, can be easily distinguished by the less brilliant sparkle of its crystal facets, as shown by a fresh surface, and also by its more soapy-white colour. It is simply an ordinary Jurassic limestone altered by subsequent metamorphic action. The mountains which contain the quarries are highly picturesque, rising with serried outline to a height of upwards of five thousand feet, their flanks scarred by deep gorges and torrent-beds, and their lower slopes clothed with olive groves, vineyards, and forest trees. Lunar marble was first brought to Rome in the time of Julius Cæsar; and Mamurra, so bitterly reviled by Catullus, the commander of the artificers in Cæsar's army in Gaul, lined with great slabs of this marble the outside and inside of his house on the Coelian Hill—the first recorded instance of veneering or incrusting walls with marble. The discovery of this method of cutting marble into thin slices, and decorating structures of ordinary materials with them, was stigmatised by Pliny as an unreasonable mode of extending luxury. The use of Lunar marble, on account of its easy accessibility, speedily extended to every kind of building, public and private. So vast were the quantities sent to Rome, that Ovid expressed his fear lest the mountains themselves should disappear through the digging out of this marble; and Pliny anticipated that dreadful consequences would be produced by the removal in this way of the great barriers erected by Nature.

Many fine specimens still survive the ravages of ages, among which may be mentioned the eleven massive Corinthian columns, upwards of forty-two feet high, and four and a half feet in diameter, which form the peristyle of the Temple of Neptune in the Piazza di Pietra, well known as the old Custom-house. These pillars suffered severely from the action of fire, and are much worn and defaced, but there is a grandeur about them still which deeply impresses the spectator; and the blocks of marble which form the inner part of the architrave and entablature, as seen from the inner side of the court, are so stupendous that the ruins "overhang like a beetling rock of marble on a mountain peak." Grander still is the majestic column of Lunar marble dedicated to Marcus Aurelius, in the Piazza Colonna, which rears aloft its shaft one hundred and twenty-two feet in the air, wreathed around with spiral bands of historic reliefs, illustrating the Roman conquests over the German tribes north of the Danube. Very splendid specimens of the same marble may be seen in the three fluted Corinthian columns and a pilaster belonging to the Temple of Mars Ultor erected by Augustus in his Forum after the battle of Actium, which are the largest columns of any kind of marble in Rome, being eighteen feet in circumference, and upwards of fifty-four feet high. The two well-known pillars of the portico of the Temple of Minerva, called Le Colonnacce, belonging to the adjoining Forum of Nerva, are also composed of the same material; as also the three deeply-fluted Corinthian columns that remain of the Temple of Vespasian in the Roman Forum, which still retain some traces of the purple colour with which they appear to have been painted. By far the largest single masses of Lunar marble are the two portions of a gigantic frieze and entablature, highly ornamented with sculpture, one measuring one thousand four hundred and ninety cubic feet, and weighing upwards of one hundred tons, lying in the Colonna gardens on the slope of the Quirinal. These relics are supposed to have belonged to the splendid Temple of the Sun, which Aurelian erected after the conquest of Palmyra, and in which he deposited the rich spoils of that city. They are associated therefore with romantic memories of the famous Queen Zenobia, who spent her last days near Tivoli, after having been led captive in fetters of gold to grace the triumphal procession of her conqueror.

For statuary purposes Lunar marble was extensively used in ancient Rome. It formed the material out of which the sculptor produced some of the noblest creations of his genius. Of these the Apollo Belvedere in the Vatican collection is one of the most remarkable. The evidence of its own material, as already mentioned, has dispelled the old idea that it is one of the masterpieces of the Greek school; and Canova's conjecture, based upon some peculiarities of its drapery, is in all likelihood true, viz. that it was a copy of a bronze original, made, probably at the order of Nero, for one of the baths of the imperial villa at Antium, in whose ruins it was found in the fifteenth century. From the time of the Romans, the white marble of the Montes Lunenses has been used for decorative purposes in many of the churches and public buildings of Italy. It formed the material out of which Michael Angelo, Canova, and Thorwaldsen chiselled their immortal works. Its quality and composition, however, vary very considerably, and small crystals of perfectly limpid quartz, called Carrara diamonds, and iron pyrites, occasionally occur, to the annoyance of the sculptor. It becomes soon discoloured when exposed even to the pure air of Italy, but it is capable of resisting decay for very long periods. The opinion current in Paris, that the marbles of Carrara are unable to withstand the effects of the climate of that city, is due to the frequent use of inferior qualities, which are known to artists as Saloni and Ravaccioni, and whose particles have but a feeble cohesion, and consequently slight durability.

All the white marbles which I have thus described were used in Rome principally for external architecture; and beautiful as a city largely built of them may have looked, it must have had, nevertheless, a garishness and artificiality which would offend the artistic eye. When newly constructed, the Roman temples in the time of the emperors must have been oppressive, reflecting the hot sunshine from their snowy cellæ and pillared porticoes with an insufferable glare. Marble—unlike sandstones, clay-slates, and basalts, which are kindred to the earth and the elements, and find themselves at home in any situation, all things making friends with them, mosses, lichens, ivies—is a dead, cold material, and does not harmonise with surrounding circumstances. Like the snow, which hides the familiar brown soil from us, with its unearthly and uncongenial whiteness, its perpetual snow chills and repels human sympathies. Nature, for a similar reason, introduces white flowers very sparingly into the landscape; and their dazzling whiteness is toned down by the greenery around them, and the balancing of coloured objects near at hand, so that they do not in reality attract more notice than other flowers. The ancient Greeks themselves, keenly sensitive as they were to all external influences, had a fine instinct for this want of harmony between white marble and the tones of nature and the feelings of man; and therefore, in many instances, they coloured not only the marble buildings exposed to view outside, but even the marble statues carefully secluded in the niches within. The Parthenon was thus tinted with vermilion, blue, and gold, which seems to us, who now see only the golden hue with which the suns of ages have dyed its pure Pentelic marble, a barbarous superfluity, but which, to the people of the time, was necessary on account of the dazzling brightness of its material, concealing the exquisite beauty of the workmanship, and the finished grace of its proportions. Colour was used with perfect taste to relieve the sculptured details of the exterior, to articulate and ornament mouldings, and to harmonise the pure white temple with the dark blue sky of Greece and the rich warm tones of her landscape. The magnificent sarcophagi of white marble recently discovered at Sidon, belonging to the best type of Greek art, are most effectively adorned with different tints and gradations of red and purple, gold being sparingly applied. We see many traces of bright colouring on the columns and other parts of the buildings in the Roman Forum. The bas-reliefs on the Lumachella marble of Trajan's Column were originally picked out with profuse gilding and vivid colours; the egg and arrow moulding of the capital being tinted green, red and yellow, the abacus blue and red, the spirals yellow, the prominent figures gilt against backgrounds of different hues, and the water of the various rivers blue. Statues of the deities in Rome were nearly all coloured; and they received a fresh coat of vermilion—which, although it was the hue of divinity, was extremely fugacious—on anniversary occasions or in times of great national rejoicing.

All this pleads powerfully in behalf of Gibson's colour-creed, which has had so much prejudice to overcome. The beauty and expression of ancient sculpture, whether for outside or inside decoration, were greatly heightened by this tinting. In cases where it was not employed, Nature herself became the artist, and has burnt into the marble statue or the marble pillar the warm hue of life; and the rusty, withered look of the ruins, over which ages of change have passed, touches us more than the pure white marble structure could have done in the pride of its splendour, and appeals to the tenderest sympathies of beings who see in themselves, and in all around them, the tokens of death and decay. The graceful Corinthian pillars of the Temple of Castor and Pollux in the Forum, the three surviving witnesses of its former grandeur, are all the more suggestive to us by reason of the russet hues with which time has stained the snowy purity of their Parian marble; and it is difficult to say, as some one has shrewdly remarked, how much of the touching effect which the drooping figure of the Dying Gladiator of the Capitol produces upon us may be attributed to its discoloration, and to the absence of the dainty spotlessness of the original Greek marble. That grime of ages "lends a sort of warmth, and suggests flesh and blood," so that the suffering is not a cold and frosty incrustation, with which we have nothing to do, but a real tragedy going on before our eyes, by which our sympathies are most deeply moved. In a dry, hot climate, like that of Rome, there are no tender tones of vegetable colouring, no moss or lichen touches of gold or gray or green to relieve the bare cold surface, and the rigid formal outlines of the marble; but out of the sky itself the marble gathers the soft shadows and the rich brown hues that reconcile its strange, unnatural whiteness with the homely ways of the familiar earth. That wonderful violet sky of Rome would glorify the meanest object. The common red brick glows in its translucent atmosphere like a ruby; and the russet defaced column, as it comes out against its vivid light, becomes luminous like a pillar of gold. Brick and marble are of equal æsthetic value in this magic city, in which the uncomely parts and materials have a more abundant comeliness by reason of the medium through which they are seen. Over all things lingers permanently the transfiguring glow that comes to northern lands only in the afternoon. In that land it is always afternoon; the ruins bathe as it were in a perpetual sunset. The air is constantly flooded with a radiance which seems to transfuse itself through every part of the city, making all its ruinous and hoary age bright and living, forming pictures and harmonies indescribable of the humblest objects.

The white marbles hitherto described were principally for exterior use. But as Roman wealth and luxury increased coloured marbles were employed for internal decoration; and the effects which the Greeks obtained by the application of pigments, the Romans obtained by the rich hues of precious marbles incrusting their buildings, and durable as these buildings themselves. At first these rare materials were used with a degree of moderation, chiefly in the form of mosaics of small discs or cubes for the pavements of halls and courts. But at length massive pillars were constructed of them, and the vast inside brick surfaces of imperial baths and palaces were crusted over and concealed by slabs of rare and splendid marbles, the lines of which had no necessary connection with the mass behind or beneath. Carthage from the spoils of its temples supplied Rome with many of its rarest columns; and it is probable that not a few of these survive in the Christian basilicas that occupy the sites and were built out of the materials of the old Pagan structures. With the decay of the Roman Empire the use of coloured marbles in art increased, so that even busts and statues had their faces and necks cut in white and the drapery in coloured marble. It attained its fullest development in the Byzantine style, of which, as it appeals to the senses more by colour than by form, it is a predominant characteristic, necessary to its vitality and expression. The early Christian builders contemplated this mode of decoration for their interiors only. Very rarely had they the means to apply it to the outside surface, as in St. Mark's in Venice, which is the great type of the Byzantine church, coloured within and without with the rich hues of marbles and mosaics. Our great Gothic cathedrals, as an eminent architect has said, were the creation of one thought, and hence they were complete when the workmen of the architects left them, and their whole effect is dominated by one idea or one set of ideas; but the early Roman churches were the results of a general co-operation of associated art, and the large and plain surfaces of the interiors were regarded by the sculptor as a framework for the exhibition of his decorative art. Colour was lavished in veneers of rare marbles, and costly mosaics and frescoes covering the walls. There was thus "less unity of purely architectural design, but a greater amount of general artistic wealth."

Intermediate between the white marbles used for external architecture and the coloured marbles used for internal decoration, and forming the link between them, is the variety called by the Italians cipollino, or onion-stone. Its classical name is Marmor Carystium, from Carystos, a town of Euboea, mentioned by Homer, situated on the south coast of the island at the foot of Mount Oche. This town was chiefly celebrated for its marble, which was in great request at Rome, and also for its large quantities of valuable asbestos, which received the name of Carystian stone, and was manufactured by the Romans into incombustible cloth for the preservation of the ashes of the dead in the process of cremation. The asbestos occurs in the same quarries with this marble, just as this mineral is usually associated with talc schist, in which chlorite and mica are often present. Strabo places the quarries of cipollino at Marmorium, a place upon the coast near Carystos; but Mr. Hawkins mentions in Walpole's Travels that he found the ancient works upon Mount Oche at a distance of three miles from the sea, the place being indicated by some old half-worked columns, lying apparently on the spot where they had been quarried. This marble is very peculiar, and is at once recognised by its gray-green ground colour and the streaks of darker green running through the calcareous substance like the coats of an onion, hence its name. These streaks belong to a different mineral formation. They are micaceous strata; and thus the true cipollino is a mixture of talcose schist with white saccharoidal marble, and may be said to form a transition link between marble and common stone. It belongs to the Dolomitic group of rocks, which forms so large a part of the romantic scenery of South-Eastern Europe, and yields all over the world some of the best and most ornamental building-stones. In this group calc-spar or dolomite wholly replaces the quartz and films of argillaceous matter, of which, especially in Scotland, micaceous schist is usually composed. There are many varieties of cipollino, the most common being the typical marble, a gray-green stone, sometimes more or less white, with veins of a darker green, forming waves rippling over it like those of the sea. It occurs so often among the ruins that it must have been perhaps more frequently used in Rome than any other marble. It was also one of the first introduced, for Mamurra lined the walls of his house on the Coelian with it, as well as with Lunar marble, in the time of Julius Cæsar; but Statius mentions that it was not very highly esteemed, especially in later times, when more valuable marbles came into use.

One remarkably fine variety called Cipollino marino is distinguished by its minute curling veins of light green on a ground of clear white. Four very large columns in the Braccio Nuova of the Vatican, which may have belonged originally, like the two large columns of giallo antico in the same apartment, to some sumptuous tomb on the Appian Way, are formed of this variety, and are unique among all the other pillars of cipollino marble to be seen in Rome for the brightness of their colour and the exquisite beauty of their venation. Nothing can be more striking and beautiful than the rich wavelike ripples of green on the cipollino marbles that encase the Baptistery of St. Mark's in Venice, as if the breakers on the Lido shore had been frost-bound before they fell, and the sea-nymphs had sculptured them into the walls of this "ecclesiastical sea-cave." Indeed all the outside and inside walls of the glorious old church are cased with this marble—in the interior up to the height of the capitals of the columns; while above that, every part of the vaults and domes is incrusted with a truly Byzantine profusion of gold mosaics—fit image, as Ruskin beautifully says, of the sea on which, like a halcyon's nest, Venice rests, and of the glowing golden sky that shines above it. Line after line of pleasant undulation ripples on the smooth polished marble as the sea ebbs and flows through the narrow streets of the city. In the churches and palaces of Rome specimens of all the varieties of cipollino may be found, taken from the old ruins, for the marble is not now worked in the ancient quarries. The largest masses of the common kind in Rome are the eight grand old Corinthian columns which form the portico of the Temple of Antoninus Pius and Faustina in the Forum. The height of each shaft, which is composed of a single block, is forty-six feet, and the circumference fifteen feet. The pillars look very rusty and weather-worn, and are much battered with the ill-usage which they have received.

One of the most beautiful and highly-prized marbles of ancient Rome was the species which is familiar to every visitor under the name of Giallo antico. It must have existed in immense quantities in the time of the emperors, for fragments of it are found almost everywhere, and it is the variety that is most frequently picked up and converted into ornamental articles. It is easily recognised by its deep brownish-yellow colour, resembling somewhat the yellow marbles of Siena and Verona, though invariably richer and brighter. All the varieties are traversed more or less by veins and blotches of a darker yellow or brownish hue, which give them a charming variety. The texture is remarkably fine and close-grained. In this respect giallo antico can be distinguished from every other marble by the touch. When polished it is exquisitely smooth and soft, looking like ivory that has become yellow with age. No fitter material could be employed for the internal pavements or pillars of old temples, presenting a venerable appearance, as if the suns of many centuries had stained it with their own golden hue. From the fact that it was called by the Romans Marmor Numidicum, we are led to infer that this marble was quarried in Numidia, and was brought into Rome when the region was made a Roman province by Julius Cæsar. It was probably known to the Romans in the time of Jugurtha; but the age of luxury had not then begun, and Marius and Sulla were more intent upon the glories of war than upon the arts of peace. The quarries on the slopes of the Atlas, worked for three hundred years to supply the enormous demand made by the luxury of the masters of the world, were at last supposed to be exhausted; and the idea has long prevailed that the marble could only be found among the ruins of the Imperial City. But four or five years ago, the sources from which the Romans obtained some of their most precious varieties of this material have been rediscovered in the range of mountains called Djebel Orousse, north-east of Oran in Algeria. All over an extensive rocky plateau in this place numerous shallow depressions plainly indicate the existence of very ancient quarries. A large company has been formed to work and export the marble, which may now be had in illimitable quantity. The largest specimens of giallo antico existing in Rome are the eight fluted Corinthian pillars, thirty feet high and eleven feet in circumference, with capitals and bases of white marble, which stand in pairs within the niches of the Pantheon. In consequence of the fires of former generations, the marble has here and there a tinge of red on the surface. In the Church of St. John Lateran there is a splendid pair of fluted columns of giallo antico, which support the entablature over a portal at the northern extremity of the transept. They are thirty feet in height and nine feet in circumference, and were found in Trajan's Forum. In the Arch of Constantine are several magnificent giallo antico columns and pilasters, which are supposed to have belonged to the triumphal arch of Trajan. They are so damaged in appearance, and so discoloured by the weather, that it is not easy, without close inspection, to tell the material of which they are composed. For pavements and the sheathing of interior walls giallo antico was used more frequently than almost any other kind of marble; hence it is mostly found in fragments of thin slabs, with the old polish still glistening upon them.

It is difficult to describe, so as to identify it, the species of marble known as Africano. It has a great variety of tints, ranging from the clearest white to the deepest black, through yellow and purple. Its texture is very compact and hard, frequently containing veins of quartz, which render it difficult to work. Its ancient name is Marmor Chium, for it was brought to Rome from a quarry on Mount Elias, the highest summit in the island of Chios—the modern Scio—which contested the honour of being the birthplace of Homer. It received its modern name of Africano, not from any connection with Africa, but from its dark colour. It enters pretty frequently into the decoration of the Roman churches, though it is rare to see it in large masses. It seems to have been much in fashion for pavements, of which many fragments may be seen among the ruins of Trajan's Forum. The side wall of the second chapel in the Church of Santa Maria della Pace in the Piazza Navona is sheathed with large slabs of remarkably fine Africano, "with edges bevelled like a rusticated basement." In the Belvedere Cortile in the Vatican is a portion of an ancient column of this marble, which is the most beautiful specimen in Rome; and the principal portal of the portico of St. Peter's is flanked by a pair of fluted Roman Ionic columns of Africano, which are the largest in the city.

Closely allied to this marble is an ancient species which puzzles most visitors by its Protean appearance. Its tints are always neutral, but they vary in depth from the lightest to the darkest shade, and are never mixed but in juxtaposition. Dirty yellows, cloudy reds, dim blues and purples, occur in the ground or in the round or waved blotches or crooked veins. It has a fine grain and a dull fracture. This variety of Africano is known by the familiar name of Porta Santa, from the circumstance that the jambs and lintel of the first Porta Santa—a Holy Door annexed by Boniface VIII. to St. Peter's in the year 1300—were constructed of this marble. The Porta Santa, it may be mentioned, was instituted in connection with a centenary jubilee, but afterwards the period of formally opening it was reduced to fifty years, and now it is shortened to twenty-five. On the occasion of the jubilee, on Christmas Eve, the Pope knocks three times with a silver hammer against the masonry with which it is filled up, which is then demolished, and the Holy Door remains open for a whole twelvemonth, and on the Christmas Eve of the succeeding year is closed up in the same manner as before. A similar solemnity is performed by proxy at the Lateran, the Liberian, and the Pauline Basilicas. In all these great churches, as in St. Peter's, the jambs and Lintel of the Holy Door are of Porta Santa marble. This beautiful material was brought from the mountains in the neighbourhood of Jassus—a celebrated fishing town of Caria, situated on a small island close to the north coast of the Jassian Bay. From this circumstance it was called by the ancient Romans Marmor Jassense. Near the quarries was a sanctuary of Hestia, with a statue of the goddess, which, though unprotected in the open air, was believed never to be touched by rain. The marble, the most highly-prized variety of which was of a blood-red and livid white colour, was used in Greece chiefly for internal decoration. It was introduced in large quantity into Rome, and there are few churches in which the relics of it that existed in older buildings have not been adapted for ornamental purposes. Among the larger and finer masses of Porta Santa may be enumerated two columns and pilasters which belong to the monument of Clement IX., in the Church of Santa Maria Maggiore, and which are remarkable for their exceedingly fine texture and the unusual predominance of white among the other hues; four splendid Corinthian pillars, considered the finest in Rome, in the nave of Sta. Agnese; the pair of half columns which support the pediment of the altar in the Capella della Presentazione in St. Peter's; and the basin of the handsome fountain in front of the Pillar of Marcus Aurelius in the Piazza Colonna, constructed by the architect Giacoma della Porta out of an enormous mass of Porta Santa found lying on the ancient wharf.

Frequent specimens of a beautiful marble known as Fior di Persico, from the resemblance of the colour of its bright purple veins on a white ground to that of the blossom of the peach, may be found in the Roman churches. It was much used for mouldings, sheathings, and pedestals, and also for floors. In the Villa of Hadrian large fragments of slabs of this marble may be found, which lined the walls and floors of what are called the Greek and Latin Libraries. The Portuguese Church in Rome has several columns of Fior di Persico supporting the pediments of altars in the different chapels; especially four pairs of fluted ones which adorn the two altars at the extremity of the nave, which are among the largest and finest in Rome. But the most splendid specimens of all are a pair of columns in the Palazzo Rospigliosi. The dado, eight feet in height, in the gorgeous Corsini chapel in the Church of St. John Lateran, is formed of large tablets of highly-polished Fior di Persico, and the frieze that surrounds the whole chapel is composed of the same beautiful material, whose predominance over every other marble is the peculiarity of this sanctuary. The ancient name of this marble was Marmor Molossium, from a region in Epirus—now Albania—which was a Roman province in the time of Pompey. It is associated with the celebrated campaigns in Italy of Pyrrhus, king of Epirus, in which Greece was for the first time brought into contact with Rome. The region in which the quarries existed was the most ancient seat of Pelasgic religion.

The infinite hues and markings of the coloured marbles have all been painted by Nature with one material only, variously proportioned and applied—the oxide of iron. The varieties of marble are mainly caused by the different degrees in which this substance has pervaded them. They are variable mixtures of the metamorphous carbonates of protoxide of iron and lime. And it is an interesting fact that there is a distinct relation between deposits of magnetic iron ore and the metamorphoses of limestones into marbles; so that this substance not only gives to the marbles their colouring, but also their texture. Even the whitest saccharoidal or statuary marble, which it has not coloured, it has created by the crystallisation of the limestone associated with it. And the marbles of the entire province of the Apuan Alps owe their existence to the large quantities of iron ore disseminated throughout them, which have exercised a great influence on the molecular modification they have undergone. The same changes have been produced on the limestones of Greece and Asia Minor by veins containing iron ore running through them.

And of the marbles thus produced, one of the most beautiful is that which is known in Rome by the name of Pavonazzetto, from its peacock-like markings. The ground is a clear white, with numerous veins of a dark red or violet colour, while the grain is fine, with large shining scales. It resembles alabaster in the form and character of its veins, and in its transparent quality. It is a Phrygian marble, and was known to the ancients under the name of Marmor Docimenum. The poet Statius notices the legend that it was stained with the blood of Atys. It was a favourite marble of the emperor Hadrian, who employed it to decorate his tomb. It was brought to Rome when Phrygia became a Roman province, after the establishment of Christianity in Asia Minor. At first the quarry yielded only small pieces of the marble, but when it came into the possession of the Romans they developed its resources to the utmost; numerous large monolithic columns being wrought on the spot, and conveyed at great expense and labour to the coast. Colonel Leake supposes that the extensive quarries on the road from Khoorukun and Bulwudun are those of the ancient Docimenum. Hamilton, in his Researches, says that he saw numerous blocks of marble and columns in a rough state, and others beautifully worked, lying in this locality. In an open space beside a mosque lay neglected a beautifully-finished marble bath, once intended, perhaps, for a Roman villa; and in the wall of the mosque, and of the cemetery beside it, were numerous friezes and cornices, whose elaborately-finished sculptures of the Ionic and Corinthian orders proved that they were never designed for any building on the spot, but were in all probability worked near the quarries for the purpose of easier transportation, as is done in the quarries of Carrara at the present day. Pavonazzetto is thus associated in an interesting manner with the Phrygian cities of Laodicea and Colosse. When St. Paul was preaching the Gospel through this part of Asia Minor, the architects of Rome were conveying this splendid marble from the quarries of the Cadmus, to adorn the palatial buildings of the Imperial City. No marble was so highly esteemed as this, and no other species is so frequently referred to by the Latin poets.

The high altar of the subterranean church, under which the relics of St. Ignatius and St. Clement are supposed to lie, is covered by a canopy supported by elegant columns of pavonazzetto marble; while the high altar of the upper church is similarly surmounted by a double entablature of Hymettian marble, supported by four columns of pavonazzetto. The extramural church of St. Paul's had several splendid pillars of Phrygian marble, taken by the emperor Theodosius from the grandest of the law courts of the Republic; but these were unfortunately destroyed during the burning of the old basilica about sixty years ago. We see in the flat pilasters of this purple-veined marble, now erect against the transepts of the restored church, the vestiges of the magnificent Æmilian Basilica in the Forum, of whose celebrated columns Pliny spoke in the highest terms. Specimens of pavonazzetto are to be seen in almost every church in Rome. In the interesting old Church of Sta. Agnese there are two columns of this marble, the flutings of which are remarkable for their cabled divisions. The gallery above is supported on small columns, most of which are of pavonazzetto spirally fluted. In the Church of Santa Maria degli Angeli there is also a remarkably fine specimen; while there is a grand pair of columns in the vestibule of St. Peter's between the transept and the sacristy. Fourteen fluted columns of Phrygian marble have been dug up from the site of the Augustan Palace on the Palatine; while the one hundred and twenty employed by the emperor Hadrian, in the Temple of Juno and Jupiter erected by him, have been distributed among several of the Roman churches. The side walls of the splendid staircase of the Bracchi Palace are sheathed with a very rare and beautiful variety, remarkable for the delicacy of its veins and its brilliant polish. The veneer was produced by slicing down two ancient columns discovered near the Temple of Romulus Maxentius in the Forum, converted into the Church of SS. Cosma e Damiano. But the finest of all the pavonazzetto columns of Rome are the ten large ones in the Church of San Lorenzo outside the walls. In the volute of the capital of one of them a frog has been carved, which identifies it as having formerly belonged to the Temple of Jupiter or Juno, within the area of the Portico of Octavia. Pliny tells us that both temples were built at their own expense by two wealthy Lacedæmonian artists, named Sauros and Batrakos; and, having been refused the only recompense they asked — the right to place an inscription upon the buildings, — they introduced into the capitals of the pillars, surreptitiously, the symbols of their respective names, a lizard and a frog.

The most precious of the old marbles of Rome is the Rosso antico. Its classical name has been lost, unless it be identical, as Corsi conjectures, with the Marmor Alabandicum, described by Pliny as black inclining much to purple. For a long time it was uncertain where it was found, but recently quarries of it have been discovered near the sea at Skantari, a village in the district of Teftion, which show traces of having been worked by the ancients. From these quarries the marble can only be extracted in slabs and in small fragments. This is the case, too, with all the red marbles of Italy, which, in spite of their compact character, scale off very readily, and are friable, vitreous, and full of cleavage planes, in addition to which they are usually only found in thin beds, which prevents their being used for other purposes than table-tops and flooring-slabs. The predominance of magnetic iron ore, to which they owe their vivid colour, has thus seriously affected the molecular arrangement of the rocks. It is probable that rosso antico, like the Italian red marbles, belongs to one or other of the Liassic formations, which, in Italy as well as in Greece and Asia Minor, constitutes a well-marked geological horizon by its regular stratification and its characteristic ammonite fossils. The quantity found among the Roman ruins of this marble is very large; many of the shops in Rome carving their models of classical buildings in this material. But the fragments are comparatively small. When used in architecture they have been employed to ornament subordinate features in some of the grander churches. The largest specimens to be seen in Rome are the double-branched flight of seven very broad steps, leading from the nave to the high altar of Santa Prassede. Napoleon Bonaparte, a few months before his fall, had ordered these slabs of rosso antico to be sent to Paris to ornament his throne; but fortunately the order came too late to be executed. The cornice of the present choir is also formed of this very rare marble; while large fragments of the old cornice of the same material, which ran round the whole church, are preserved in the Belvedere Cortile of the Vatican. Tradition asserts that the pieces which have been converted to these sacred uses in the church once belonged to the house of Pudens, the father of its titular saint, in which St. Peter is supposed to have dwelt when in Rome. The entrance to the chamber of the Rospigliosi Palace, which contains the far-famed "Aurora" of Guido Reni on the ceiling, is flanked by a pair of Roman Ionic columns of rosso antico, fourteen feet high, which are the largest in Rome, although the quality of the marble is much injured by its lighter colour, and by a white streak which runs up each shaft nearly from top to bottom. In the sixth room of the Casino of the Villa Borghese the jambs of the mantelpiece are composed of rosso antico in the form of caryatides supporting a broad frieze of the same material wrought in bas-relief.

This marble seems to have been the favourite material in which to execute statues of the Faun; for every one who has visited the Vatican Sculpture Gallery and the Museum of the Capitol will remember well the beautiful statues of this mythic being in rosso antico, which are among their chief treasures, and once adorned the luxurious Villa of Hadrian at

Tivoli. This marble is admirably adapted for such sculpture, for it gives to the ideal of the artist the warm vividness of life. And it seems a fit colour, as Nathaniel Hawthorne has said, in which to express the rich, sensuous, earthy side of nature, the happy characteristics of all wild natural things which meet and mingle in the human form and in the human soul; the Adam, the red man formed out of the red clay, in which the life of the animals and the life of the gods coalesce. In the Gabinetto of the Vatican, along with a large square tazza of rosso antico, is kept a most curious arm-chair of this marble, called sedia forata, found near the Church of St. John Lateran, upon which, in the middle ages, the Popes were obliged to sit at their installation in the presence of the Cardinals. This custom, which was practised as late as the coronation of Julius II. in 1503, arose from a desire to secure the throne of St. Peter from being intruded upon by a second Pope Joan—whether there ever really was such a personage, or whatever gave rise to the curious myth. The chair is like an ordinary library chair, with solid back and sides, sculptured out of a single block, and perforated in the seat with a circular aperture. Rosso antico is not what might strictly be called a beautiful marble. Its colour is dusky and opaque, resembling that of a bullock's liver, marked with numerous black reticulations, so minute and faint as to be hardly visible. But the grain is extremely fine, admitting of the highest polish.

Of black marbles—in the formation of which both the animal and vegetable kingdoms have taken part, their substance being composed of the finely-ground remains of foraminifera, corals, and shells, and their colour produced by the carbonaceous deposits of ancient forests—few kinds seem to have been used by the ancient Romans. The nero antico was the species most esteemed, on account of its compact texture, fine grain, and deep black colour, marked occasionally with minute white short straight lines, always broken and interrupted. It is the Marmor Tænarium of the ancients, quarried in the Tænarian peninsula, which forms the most southerly point in Europe, now called Cape Matapan. The celebrated quarries which Pliny eloquently describes, but for which Colonel Leake inquired in vain, were under the protection of Poseidon, whose temple was at the extremity of the peninsula. They attracted, on account of the sanctuary which the temple afforded, large numbers of criminals who fled from the pursuit of justice, and who readily found work in them. Very fine specimens of this marble may be seen in a pair of columns in the obscure Church of Santa Maria Regini Coeli, near the Convent of St. Onofrio, on the other side of the Tiber; in a pair in the church of Ara Coeli; and also in a pair in the third room of the Villa Pamphili Doria, which are extremely fine, and are probably as large as any to be met with. In consequence of the quantity used in the inscriptional tablets of monuments, for which this seems to be the favourite material, nero antico is extremely scarce in modern Rome. The bigio antico is a grayish marble, composed of white and black, sometimes in distinct stripes or waves, and sometimes mingled confusedly together. It was the Marmor Batthium of the ancients, and two of the large columns in the principal portal of the Church of Santa Croce in Jerusalemme are remarkably fine specimens of it, probably taken from the Villa of Heliogabalus, in whose gardens, called the Horti Variani, the church was built.

Another species is the bianco e nero antico, the Marmor Proconnesium of antiquity, obtained from the celebrated quarries of Proconnesos, an island in the western part of the Propontis. Many of the towns of Greece were decorated with this marble. The internal part of the famous sepulchre erected by Artemisia, the widow of Mausolus, king of Caria, to her husband, and after whom all grand tombs ever since have received the name of mausoleum, was built of this marble. So celebrated were the quarries of Proconnesos that the ancient name of the island was changed to Marmora, and the whole of the Propontis is now called the Sea of Marmora. Although so highly esteemed in Greece, this marble does not seem to have been extensively used in Rome; the finest relics being the four columns supporting the marble canopy, in the form of a Gothic temple, which surmounts the high altar of St. Cæcilia, which is among the most ancient of all the churches of Rome. They were probably derived from some old Roman palace, and are remarkable for the clearness and brilliancy of the white blotches on a black ground. There are different varieties of this marble: one kind in which the blotches or veins are pure black on a pure white ground, and another in which the blotches or veins are pure white on a black ground. In these varieties, however, the black and the white are more confused together, but remain notwithstanding distinct and separate, so that if the veins are white the ground is sure to be black, and vice versâ. The ancient Marmor Rhodium, or the giallo e nero, had golden-coloured veins on a black ground, and, owing to its compact texture, was capable of receiving a high polish. It is very like the celebrated marble of Portovenere, a modern Italian species obtained from the western hills of the Gulf of Spezia, where the formation passes into that of the ammonitiferous limestones of the Lias and of the palæozoic rocks. A beautiful highly-polished specimen of Rhodian marble exists in the mask in front of the tomb of Paul III. in the tribune of St. Peter's, sculptured by Della Porta in 1547, long previous to the discovery of the quarries of Portovenere. It may be remarked that the grain of the latter species is such that it will not keep its polish without extreme care; a circumstance which distinguishes it from the Rhodian marble, whose tenacity in this respect renders it eminently adapted for the more costly class of decorative works.

The marbles we have been hitherto considering belong to the older calcareous formations of Italy, Greece, Asia Minor, and Egypt, and go down to the upper triassic and muschel-kalk limestones, and perhaps even to those of an older period. But there is a class of ancient marbles in Rome of much more recent geological origin—belonging indeed to the Miocene epoch—which are called Lumachella, from the Italian word signifying snail, on account of the presence in all the species of fossil shells. They vary in colour from the palest straw to the deepest purple. Some of them are exceedingly beautiful and valuable, and they are nearly all more or less rare, being found chiefly in small fragments of ancient pavements. Their substance is formed of the shells of the common oyster in bluish gray and black particles on a white ground, as in the Lumachella d' Egitto; of the cardium or cockle, assuming a lighter or deeper shade of yellow, as in the Lumachella d' Astracane; of the ammonite, as in the L. Corno d' Ammone; of the Anomia ampulla in the L. occhio di Pavone, so called from the circular form of the fossils whichever way the section is made; of encrinites, belemnites, and starfish, showing white or red on a violet ground, as in the L. pavonazza; and "of broken shells, hardly discernible, together with very shining and saccharoid particles of carbonate of lime," as in the Marmor Schiston of the ancients—the brocatello antico of the Italians, so named from its various shades of yellow and purple, resembling silk brocade. The most important specimens of Lumachella marbles are the pair of very fine large columns of L. rosea on the ground-floor of the Schiarra Palace, the balustrade of the high altar of St. Andrea della Valle, two columns in the garden of the Corsini Palace of L. d' Astracane, and a pair of large pillars which support one of the arches of the Vatican Library, formed of L. occhio di pavone. Specimens of brocatello may be found in several churches and palaces, forming mouldings, sheathings, and pedestals.

The most interesting of the Lumachella marbles is the bianca antica, the Marmor Megarense of the ancients, composed of shells so small as to be scarcely discernible, and so closely compacted that the substance takes a good polish. The well-known Column of Trajan—the first monument (columna cochlæa) of this description ever raised in Rome, and far superior to the Antonine Column—is composed of Lumachella marble from Megara. It presents, in twenty-three spiral bands of bas-reliefs, winding round thirty-four blocks of stone, the history of the victories of Trajan over the Dacians, and, without reckoning horses, implements of war, and walls of cities, is said to consist of no less than two thousand five hundred figures, each about two feet two inches high. It is a strikingly suggestive thought, that this majestic pillar—which produced so deep an impression upon the minds of posterity that, according to the beautiful legend, Pope Gregory the Great was moved to supplicate, by means of masses in several of the Roman churches, for the liberation of him whom it commemorated from purgatory — should be composed of the relics of sea-shells.

"Memorial pillar! 'mid the wreck of Time,
Preserve thy charge with confidence sublime,"

said Wordsworth; but this sublime charge is committed to frail keeping. It is itself a sepulchre of the dead; and the tragedies of the Dacian war are inscribed upon tragedies that took place long ages before there was any human eye to witness them. The historic sculptures that so deeply move our pity for a conquered people, are based upon the immemorial sculptures of creatures whose sacrifice in whole hecatombs touches us not, because it is part of the order of the world by which life forms the foundation of and minister to life. It is strange how many of the grandest monuments are wrought out of the creations of primeval molluscs. The enduring pyramids themselves are formed of the nummulitic limestone studded with its "Pharaoh's beans," the exuviæ of shell-fish that perished ages before the Nile had created Egypt.

Of the breccias there is a great variety among the relics of ancient Rome. A breccia is a rock made up of angular pebbles or fragments of other rocks. When the pebbles are rounded the conglomerate is a pudding-stone. Marble breccias are formed of angular pieces of highly crystalline limestone, united together by a siliceo-calcareous cement, containing usually an admixture of a hornblendic substance, and which is due to a particular action of adjacent masses or veins of iron ore. The hornblendic cement, with its iron or manganese base, produces the variegated appearance which may be seen in specimens from different localities. As may be imagined from their composition, these rocks are as a rule extremely unalterable by ordinary atmospheric agencies, and are susceptible of a high degree of polish, which they retain with the utmost tenacity. They were favourite materials with the ancient Roman decorators; but they do not occur in large masses in the city. A beautiful pair of Roman Ionic columns under the pediment of the altar of the third chapel in the Church of Ara Coeli are made of a valuable breccia called Breccia dorata, distinguished by its small light-golden fragments on a ground of various shades of purple. The high altar of Santa Prisca on the Aventine is supported by one column of Breccia corallina of remarkably fine quality, in which the fragments are white on a ground of light coral-red. In the second chapel of St. Andrea della Valle there are two Corinthian columns of Breccia gialla e nera, which is an aggregate mass of yellow and black fragments: the yellow in its brilliant golden hue surpassing that of all other marbles, and forming a striking contrast to the long irregular black fragments interspersed throughout it. In the first chapel of the same church there are four fluted Corinthian columns of breccia gialla, containing small and regular blotches, of which the prevailing tint is orange, each fragment edged with a rim of deeper yellow that surrounds it like a shadow. A most beautiful variety of Breccia gialla e nera forms the basin of holy water at the entrance of the Church of St. Carlo di Catinari, in which "the colours resemble a golden network spread upon a ground of black"; and an exceedingly lovely urn is seen underneath the altar in one of the chapels of the Portuguese Church, in which white fragments are imbedded in a purple ground which shines through their soft transparency.

Not the least attractive objects in the chamber of the Dying Gladiator in the Museum of the Capitol area portion of a large column of very beautiful and extremely valuable Breccia tracagnina, in which golden-yellow, white, red, and blue fragments occur in very nearly equal proportions, and two large pedestals of Breccia di Sete-Bassi — so called from the discovery of the first specimens near the ruins of the Villa of Septimus Bassus on the Appian Way — containing very small purple fragments of an oblong shape, which is the characteristic peculiarity of all the varieties of this species of marble. Probably the most beautiful of all the ancient breccias is that called Breccia della Villa Adriana, from its occasional occurrence in the ruins of Hadrian's Villa, and also Breccia Quintilina, from its having been found in the grounds of the magnificent Villa of Quintilius Varus, commemorated by Horace, at Tivoli, now occupied by the Church of the Madonna di Quintigliolo. The prevailing colour of the fragments is that of a dark brown intermixed with others of smaller size, of red, green, blue, white, purple, bright yellow, and sometimes black, all harmonising together most beautifully. The comparatively small pieces found at Tivoli now adorn the Churches of St. Andrea della Valle, famous for its rich varieties of breccias, St. Domenico e Sisto and Santa Pudenziana, where they appear among the marble sheathing of the walls. In the chapel of the Gaetani in the last-mentioned church, the wall is incrusted with the richest marbles, especially Lumachella and Brocatello, and large tablets of Hadrian's breccia setting off the splendid sarcophagus of Breccia nera e gialla dedicated to Cardinal Gaetani.

Along with the breccias which I have thus incidentally noticed, but to which a whole essay might be devoted on account of their beauty, rich variety, and great value and rarity, should be classified a kind of "breccia dure," called Breccia d' Egitto. It is not, however, a true breccia, but a pudding-stone, composed, not of calcareous but of siliceous fragments; and these fragments are not angular, as in the true breccias, but rounded, indicating that they had been carried by water and consequently rounded by attrition. The connected pebbles must have been broken from rocks of great hardness to have withstood the effects of constant abrasion. In the Egyptian breccia are found very fine pebbles of red granite, porphyry of a darker or lighter green, and yellow quartz, held together by a cement of compact felspar. It has a special geological interest, inasmuch as it represents an ancient sea-beach flanking the crystalline rocks of Upper Egypt, where the cretaceous and nummulitic limestones end. The pebbles were derived from the central nucleus of granite from beyond Assouan to the upper end of the Red Sea, round which are folded successive zones of gneiss and schist pierced by intrusive masses of porphyry and serpentine. The pair of beautiful Grecian Ionic columns, and the large green tazza—eighteen feet in circumference—the finest specimen of Egyptian breccia to be seen in Rome, both in the Villa Albani, and the vase of the same material in the chamber of Candelabra in the Vatican, in which the prevailing green colour is crossed by several stripes of pure white quartz, may thus have been sculptured out of a portion of littoral deposit formed from the ruins of the crystalline rocks of the mountain group of Sinai. There is something extremely interesting and suggestive to the imagination in the twofold origin of these conglomerate ornaments of the palaces of Rome. Around them gather the wonderful associations of ancient human history, and the still more awe-inspiring associations of geological history. They speak to us of the conquests of Rome in the desolate tracts of Nubia and Arabia, from which the spoils that enriched its palaces and temples were derived; and of the existence of coast-lines, when Egypt was a gulf stretching from the Mediterranean to the Mountains of the Moon, which became silted up by slow accumulations. Their language, in both relations, is that of ruin. They are survivors both of the ruins of Nature and of Man, and are made up of the wrecks of both. Older far than the marbles which keep them company in the sculptor's halls and churches of Rome, and whose human history is equally eventful, their materials were deposited along the shore of a vanished sea, when the mountains that yielded these marbles lay as calcareous mud in its depths.

Alabasters, of which there are numerous varieties, from pure diaphanous white to the deepest black, were favourite decorative materials with the ancient Romans. The different kinds were used for the walls of baths, vases, busts, pillars, and sepulchral lamps, in which the light shining through the transparent sides had an agreeable softness. Cornelius Nepos, as quoted by Pliny, speaks of having seen columns of alabaster thirty-two feet in length; and Pliny says that he himself had seen thirty huge pillars in the dining-hall of Callistus, the freedman of Claudius. One such column still exists in the Villa Albani, which is twenty-two and a half feet in height. The ancients obtained large blocks of alabaster from quarries in Thebes in Egypt, in the neighbourhood of Damascus, and on Mount Taurus. They imported some kinds also from Cyprus, Spain, and Northern Africa. They obtained varieties nearer home, in different parts of Italy, such as the beautiful Alabastro di Tivoli, employed by Hadrian in his villa, and which appears to have been brought from Terni, where it still exists in abundance. From the quarry near Volterra the Etruscans obtained the alabaster for their cinerary urns. The European alabasters are accumulated masses of stalactite and stalagmite, formed by the slow dropping of water charged with sulphate of lime, to which circumstance they owe the parallel stripes or concentric circles with which they are marked, while the rich and delicate varieties of colouring are produced by the oxides of iron which the water carries with it in its infiltration through the intervening strata. They are very soft and perishable, and consequently are very rarely found among the ruins of ancient Rome. The Oriental alabasters, on the other hand, which are distinguished from the European by their superior hardness and durability, are in reality not sulphates, but carbonates of lime. Their hardness is quite equal to that of the best statuary marbles. The ancient quarries on the hill—the modern Mount St. Anthony—near the town of Alabastron, in Middle Egypt, from which the material got its name, have only recently been re-opened, but blocks of large size and perfect beauty have been obtained. Owing to the facility with which alabaster can be reduced by fire to lime, very few large examples of it in Rome have escaped the ruthless kilns of the middle ages. The most interesting specimens of ancient alabaster are the very beautiful vase of Alabastro cotognino, prolate in form, and in colour white, streaked with very light pink, which contained the ashes of Augustus, found in the ruins of his mausoleum, and now in the Vatican; the bust of Julius Cæsar, made of the variety tartaruga, from the resemblance of its brownish-yellow markings to tortoise-shell, in the Museum of the Capitol; and the two large blocks of alabastro a pecorella, brought from the Villa of Hadrian, in the fourth portico of the Vatican, the largest and most beautiful specimens of this very rare alabaster in Rome, distinguished by white circular blotches, like a flock of sheep huddled together, on a deep blood-red ground. In the churches there are numerous specimens of all the varieties, forming the columns and sheathings of altars, memorial chapels, and monuments; the incrustations of alabaster on the walls of the Borghese chapel, in Santa Maria Maggiore, being conspicuous for their splendid effect. The baldacchino above the high altar of St. Paul's is supported by four splendid columns of Oriental alabaster presented to Gregory XVI. by

Mehemet Ali, the viceroy of Egypt. An interesting collection of beautiful and valuable varieties of alabasters may be made in connection with the building operations still carried on in the unfinished façade of the basilica fronting the Tiber.

The well-known Verde antico is not a marble, but a mixture of the green precious serpentine of mineralogists and white granular limestone. It may also be called a breccia, for it is composed of black fragments, larger or smaller, derived from other rocks, whose angular shape indicates that they have not travelled far from the spots where they occur. The ancient Romans called it Lapis Atracius, from Atrax, a town in Thessaly, in the vicinity of which it was found. It can hardly be distinguished, except by experts, from the modern green marbles of Vasallo in Sardinia, and Luca in Piedmont. It occurs somewhat abundantly in Rome, having been a favourite material with the old Romans for sheathing walls and tables. Magnificent columns of it were introduced into the temples and triumphal arches. We find relics of these in the older churches. Four splendid fluted Corinthian columns of Verde antico, with gilded capitals, support the pediment of the high altar in Sta. Agnese, in the Piazza Navone, which formerly belonged to the Arch of Marcus Aurelius in the Corso. A pair of very fine columns of this precious stone flank each of the niches, containing statues of the twelve apostles, in the piers which divide the middle nave from the side ones in the Church of St. John Lateran. These twenty-four columns are remarkable for the clearness of the white, green, and black colours that occur in them. They are supposed to have been taken from the Baths of Diocletian. Two of the splendid composite columns which support the pediment of the altar in the Corsini chapel of this church are of this marble, and were also taken from the Arch of Marcus Aurelius in the Corso. One most magnificent column of Verde antico has been found, along with seven others of different marbles, in the wall of the narthex of the subterranean Church of San Clemente. A small portion of it is polished to show the beauty of the material, while the rest is dimmed and incrusted with the grime of age.

Very different from this is the ancient serpentine or ophite of Sparta called the Lapis Lacedæmonius, found in different hills near Krokee, or in Mount Taygetus in Lacedæmon, where the old quarry has recently been opened. It has a base of dark green with angular crystals of felspar of a lighter green imbedded in it. It is a truly eruptive rock, occurring in intrusive bosses, or in beds interstratified with gneiss and mica-schist, and owes its various shades of green to the presence of copper. Owing to its extraordinary hardness, this stone was seldom used for architectural purposes; and the lapidary will charge three times as much for working a fragment of this material into a letter-weight as for making it of any other stone. A pair of fluted Roman Ionic columns, supporting the pediment of the altar of the chapel of St. John the Baptist, in the Baptistery of St. John Lateran, are the only examples of ophite pillars in Rome. Next to these the largest masses are a circular tablet, forming part of the splendid sheathing of one of the ambones in the Church of San Lorenzo; and two elliptical tablets, still larger, engrafted upon the pilasters in front of the high altar of St. Paul's.

The principal use to which this stone was devoted in Rome was the construction of mosaic pavements. The emperor Alexander Severus introduced into his palaces and public buildings a kind of flooring composed of small squares of green serpentine and red porphyry, wrought into elegant patterns, which became very fashionable, and was called after himself Opus Alexandrinum. The infamous Heliogabalus had previously paved some of the courts of the Palatine with such intarsio work, but his cousin Alexander Severus, following his example, adorned with it all the terraces and walks around, and the pavements within, the isolated villas called Diætæ, dedicated to his mother Mammæa, which he added to the Palatine buildings. We have examples of this beautiful kind of tesselated pavement in some of the chambers of the Baths of Caracalla; and it is highly probable that the Opus Alexandrinum in the transept and middle nave of the Church of Santa Maria in Trastevere is in part at least contemporaneous with Alexander Severus, who conceded the ground on which the original oratory stood to Pope Calixtus I. in 222, for the special use of the Christians. If this be so, we have in this first place of Christian worship established in Rome the first instance of the application of Opus Alexandrinum to the decoration of a church. In the middle ages the fashion was beautifully imitated by artists of the Cosmati family and their school; and the mosaic pavements of this kind in the medieval churches of Rome are no older than this period. But we have reason to believe that the Opus Alexandrinum in two of the chapels of Santa Maria degli Angeli was taken from the Baths of Diocletian; while the splendid pavement of the whole church, naves, transept, and choir of Santa Croce in Jerusalemme, formed originally part of the decorations of the Sessorian Palace of Sextus Varius, the father of Heliogabalus, after whom the church is sometimes called the Sessorian Basilica. The flooring of the whole upper church of San Clemente was transferred from the older subterranean church, which derived its pavement from some of the ruins of the Palatine or the Forum; and the serpentine fragments, which enter very largely into the composition of the curious old mosaic floor of Ara Coeli must have had a similar origin as far back as the time of its founder, Gregory the Great.

The Lapis Lacedæmonius must have been very abundant in Rome during the time of Alexander Severus—judging from the quantities that are made up into mosaics in the churches, and the heaps of broken fragments that are found on the Palatine and at the Marmorata. The circular space around the obelisk in the Piazza of St. Peter's to a considerable extent is paved with it; and specimens of it frequently occur among the ordinary road-metal in the city and neighbourhood.

Sicilian jaspers, so called, though really marbles, and purely calcareous, because of their resemblance in colour and form of the blotches to jasper, were wrought in great variety in the quarries in the neighbourhood of the celebrated Taormina, and were transported in the form of columns to Rome. Siliceous jaspers, obtained from the crystalline rocks of Asia Minor, Egypt, and Northern Italy, were also used for columns; and their brilliant red, green, and yellow hues, highly polished, contrasted beautifully with the white marbles of the interiors of the palaces. An even more sumptuous material called Murrha was employed, which has been identified with fluor-spar, a translucent crystalline stone marked with blue, red, and purple, similar to the beautiful substance found near Matlock in Derbyshire. Of this fluor-spar were formed the celebrated murrhine cups which were in use in Rome in the days of Pliny among the richest people, and for which fabulous prices were paid. Several blocks of this material were found some years ago at the Marmorata which had been originally imported from Parthia in the reign of Hadrian. One of them was employed by the Jesuits, when cut up into thin slices, in ornamenting the principal altar in the church of Il Gesu. One of the chambers in the Baths of Titus was paved with slabs of the finest lapis lazula—the Lapis Cyanus of the ancients—derived from the spoils of the Golden House of Nero, and originally procured by order of the luxurious tyrant from Persia and the neighbourhood of Lake Baikal. We can trace fragments of this exquisite pavement in the decoration of the chapel of St. Ignatius in the Church of the Jesuits. The globe, three feet in diameter, over the altar, beneath which repose the remains of Ignatius Loyola, is sheathed with this most precious stone, whose brilliant blue, contrasting with the white marble of the group of the Trinity—one of whose members holds it in His hands—has a splendid effect. The rare and costly marbles with which the Church of Il Gesu is profusely adorned were mostly taken from the ruins of the Baths of Titus by Cardinal Farnese in 1568. From the same source came also the magnificent sarcophagus, sheathed with lapis lazula, under the altar of St. Ignazio, which holds the body of St. Luigi Gonzaga.

But it is impossible, within the limits of this chapter, to describe fully the relics of other precious and beautiful stones which may be found among the ruins of ancient Rome, or among the churches to which they have been transferred. Profuse as were the ancient Romans in their general expenditure, upon no objects did they lavish their wealth so extravagantly as upon their favourite marbles and precious stones for the decoration of their public buildings and their private houses. No effort was spared that Rome might be adorned with the richest treasures of the mineral kingdom from all parts of the world. Slaves and criminals were made to minister to this luxury in the various quarries of the Roman dominions, which were the penal settlements of antiquity. The antiquary Ficoroni counted the columns in Rome in the year 1700, and he found no less than eight thousand existing entire; and yet these were but a very small proportion of the number that must once have been there. The palaces and modern churches of Rome owe, as I have said, all their ornaments to this passion of the ancients. There is not a doorstep nor a guardstone at the corner of the meanest court in Rome which is not of marble, granite, or porphyry from some ancient building. Almost all the houses, as Raphael said, have been built with lime made of the costly old marbles. The very streets in the newly-formed parts of the city are macadamised with the fragments of costly baths and pillars. I took up one day, out of curiosity, some of the road-metal near the Church of Santa Maria Maggiore, and I identified in the handful no less than a dozen varieties of the most beautiful marbles and porphyries from Greece, Africa, and Asia. And when we remember that all these foreign stones were brought into Rome during the interval between the end of the Republic and the time of Constantine—a period of between three hundred and four hundred years—we can form some idea of the extraordinary wealth and luxury of the Imperial City when it was in its prime.

CHAPTER XI - THE VATICAN CODEX

Among the numberless objects of interest to be seen in Rome, a very high place must be assigned to the Codex Vaticanus, probably the oldest vellum manuscript in existence, and the richest treasure of the great Vatican Library. This famous manuscript, which Biblical scholars designate by the letter B, contains the oldest copy of the Septuagint, and the first Greek version of the New Testament. In addition to the profound interest which its own intrinsic value has inspired, it has been invested with a halo of romance seldom associated with dry palæographical studies—on account of the unreasonable jealousy and capricious conduct of its guardians. For a long time it was altogether inaccessible for study to Biblical scholars, and few were allowed even to see it. These restrictions, however, have now happily to a considerable extent been removed; and provided with an order, easily obtained from the Vatican librarian, or from the Prefect of the sacred palaces, in reply to a polite note, any respectable person is permitted to inspect it.

The first feeling which one has in the Vatican Library is that of surprise. You might walk through the Great Hall and adjoining galleries without suspecting the place to be a library at all; for the bookcases that line the lower portion of the walls are closed with panelled doors, painted in arabesque on a ground of white and slate colour, and surrounded by gilded mouldings, and not a single book is visible. The vaulted ceiling of the rooms is glowing with gold and ultramarine; the walls are adorned with beautiful frescoes representing the different Councils of the Church; and magnificent tables of polished Oriental granite, and of various precious marbles, vases of porphyry, malachite, and alabaster, and priceless candelabra of Sevres china—the gifts of kings and emperors—occupy the spaces between the pillars and pilasters, and cast their rich shadows on the gleaming marble pavement. A vast variety of objects of rare beauty, artistic value, and antique interest arrest the attention, and would amply reward the study of weeks.

The nucleus of the present magnificent collection of books and manuscripts was formed in the Lateran Palace in the year 465 by Bishop Hilary; and, augmented by succeeding pontiffs, the accumulated stores were transferred in 1450 by Pope Nicholas V., the founder of Glasgow University, to the Vatican. What Nicholas began was completed by Sixtus IV. The library was classified according to subjects and writers, and Demetrius Lucensis, under the direction of Platina, made a catalogue of it which is still in existence. During this period Vatican MSS. were lent out to students, as attested by authentic registers containing the autographs of those who enjoyed the privilege. A little later the celebrated Vatican printing press was annexed to the library; and the office of correctors or readers for the accurate printing of ancient books which were wanting in the library was instituted. Pope Sixtus V. erected the present splendid edifice, and used every effort to increase the great collection. Several valuable accessions were made to it after this date, including the library of the Elector Palatine of Germany, the library of the Dukes of Urbino, the libraries of Christina, Queen of Sweden, of the Ottoboni, commenced by Pope Alexander VIII., and of the Marquis Capponi, and the MSS. taken from the convent of S. Basilio at Grotta Ferrata. Under Innocent XIII. in 1721 an attempt was made to prepare for the press a full catalogue of all the MSS. in every language. It was edited by Joseph Simon Assemani and Stephen Evodius, and three volumes were published. But the task was found too great for any one's strength, and was given up finally on account of the political disturbances of the time.

The library is a vast unexplored mine of wealth. Unknown literary treasures are contained in the closed cabinets. Among the thirty thousand manuscripts may be hid some of the ancient classical and early Christian treatises, which have been lost for ages, and whose recovery would excite the profoundest interest throughout the civilised world. A large number of these manuscripts had once belonged to the library of the famous Monastery of Bobbio, in the north of Italy, founded in the year 614 by the Irish St. Columbanus. The Irish and Scotch monks who inhabited this monastery were in the dark ages the most zealous collectors of manuscripts in Europe. At the close of the fifteenth century the convent was impoverished and deserted by its lawful occupants; and the Benedictine monks who succeeded them gave away their literary treasures partly to the Ambrosian Library at Milan and partly to the Vatican Library. Cardinal Angelo Mai, who discovered more lost works and transcribed more ancient manuscripts than any one else, found among these treasures in Milan and Rome several most interesting treatises that had long passed into utter oblivion.

But though permission is freely granted to duly accredited visitors who may be desirous of consulting manuscripts, the labour of searching among the huge bewildering piles would be overwhelming, and the thought of it would at once paralyse effort. There is no proper catalogue of the printed books; and the list of manuscripts is so deficient as to be altogether worthless. During six months, from November till June, the library is open for study every day, except Thursday and the numerous saints' days, whose recurrence can be easily ascertained beforehand so as to prevent disappointment. I cannot imagine a greater privilege to a student. It is the highest luxury of learning to explore the literary wealth of these princely apartments, that seem to have a climate of their own, like the great Basilica close at hand — the climate of eternal spring — and whose atmosphere breathes the associations of much that is grandest and most memorable in human history. To the charms of some of the noblest productions of human genius working by pen, or pencil, or chisel — adorning roof, and wall, and floor — and vanishing down the long vista in a bright perspective of beauty — Nature adds her crown of perfection. For nothing can exceed the loveliness of the views from the windows of the Papal gardens outside, with their gay flowery parterres, sparkling fountains, depths of shadowy glades and half-hidden sculptured forms of rarest beauty; and, beyond, a purple mountain range, summits old in story, closing up the enchanted vista through the ruddy stems and deep green foliage of tall stone-pines; the whole glowing in the brilliant sunshine and the exquisite violet transparency of the Roman sky. How delightful to spend whole days there and forget the commonplace present in converse with the master minds of the ages, and in dreams of the heroic past; the half-closed shutters and drawn curtains producing a cool and drowsy atmosphere, in delicious contrast with the broiling sun without! Learning, however, would be too apt to fall asleep, and be shorn of its strength on the Delilah lap of such splendid luxury.

A few of the most interesting books and manuscripts are now contained in two handsome cabinets placed in the centre of the Great Hall of the library. These cabinets have two cases, an outer and an inner one, and are carefully double-locked. The librarian opened them for me, and displayed their contents, which are usually seen only through a thick plate of protecting glass. In the one cabinet were a manuscript of the Latin poet Terence, of the fourth and fifth century; the celebrated palimpsest of Cicero de Republica, concealed under a version of St. Augustine's Commentary on the Psalms, the oldest Latin manuscript in existence; the famous Virgil of the fifth century, with the well-known portrait of Virgil; the Homilies of St. Gregory of Nazianzum; the folio Hebrew Bible, which was the only thing that Duke Frederico of Urbino reserved for himself of the spoil at the capture of Volterra in 1472, and for which the Jews in Venice offered its weight in gold; a sketch of the first three cantos of the Gerusalemme Liberata in the handwriting of Tasso; a copy of Dante in the handwriting of Boccaccio; and several of Petrarch's autograph sonnets. In the other cabinet is the great gem and glory of the Library—the Codex Vaticanus, in strange association with a number of the love-letters of Henry VIII. and Anne Boleyn, in French and English. This curious correspondence—which, after all that subsequently happened between the English monarch and the Papal Court, we are very much surprised to see in such a place—is in wonderful preservation. But though perfectly legible, the archaic form of the characters and the numerous abbreviations make it extremely difficult to decipher them. The tragic ending of this most inauspicious love-making invests with a deep pathos these faded yellow records of it that seem like the cold, gray ashes of a once glowing fire. In the same cabinet is seen another and altogether different production of this royal author—namely, the dedication copy of the "Assertio Septem Sacramentorum adversus Martinum Luther," written in Latin by Henry VIII. in defence of the seven Roman Catholic Sacraments against Luther, and sent to Leo X., with the original presentation address and royal autograph. The book is a good thick octavo volume, printed in London, in clear type, on vellum, with a broad margin. Only two copies are in existence, one in the Bodleian Library at Oxford, and the other in the Vatican. For this theological dissertation Henry VIII. received from the Pope the title of "Defender of the Faith," which has descended to the Protestant monarchs of England ever since, and is now inscribed on our coinage. Luther, several of whose manuscripts are in the Library, published a vigorous reply, in which he treated his royal opponent with scant ceremony. The author himself had no scruple in setting it aside when his personal passions were aroused. And Rome has put this inconsistent book beside the letters to Anne Boleyn, as it were in the pillory here for the condemnation of the world.

But deeply interesting as were these literary curiosities, I soon turned from them and became engrossed with the priceless manuscript of the Greek Scriptures. I had very little time to inspect it, for I was afraid to exhaust the patience of the librarian. In appearance the manuscript is a quarto volume bound in red morocco; each of the pages being about eleven inches long, and the same in breadth. This is the usual size of the greater number of ancient manuscripts, very few being in folio or octavo, and in this particular resembling printed books. Each page has three columns, containing seventeen or eighteen letters in a line. It is supposed that this arrangement of the writing was borrowed directly from the most primitive scrolls, whose leaves were joined together lengthwise, so that their contents always appeared in parallel columns, as we see in the papyrus rolls that have recently been discovered. This peculiarity in the two or three manuscripts which possess it, is regarded as a proof of their very high antiquity. The writing on almost every page is so clear and distinct that it can be read with the greatest ease.

What astonishes one most is the admirable preservation of this Codex, notwithstanding that it must be nearly sixteen hundred years old. It has quite a fresh and recent look; indeed many manuscripts not fifty years old look much more ancient. No one, looking at the faded handwriting of Tasso, Petrarch, and Henry VIII., beside it, would imagine that they were newer by upwards of twelve hundred years. This peculiarity it shares in common with the architectural remains of imperial Rome, which time has dealt so tenderly with that they appear far more recent than the picturesque ruins of our medieval castles and abbeys. This singular look of freshness in the Vatican manuscript is owing to three causes. In the first place, the vellum upon which it is written is exceedingly fine and close-grained in texture, and therefore has resisted the dust and discoloration of centuries, just as the thin and close-grained Roman brick has withstood the ravages of time. Every one is struck with the wonderful beauty of this vellum, composed of the delicate skins of very young calves. And this feature is a further proof of the high antiquity of the Codex, for the oldest manuscripts are invariably written on the thinnest and whitest vellum, while those of later ages are written on thick and rough parchment which speedily became discoloured. In the second place, we have reason to believe that the manuscript was for many ages almost hermetically sealed in some forgotten recess of the Lateran and Vatican Libraries, and thus unconsciously guarded from the attacks of time. In the third place, a careful scrutiny of the individual lines reveals the curious fact that the whole manuscript, six or seven centuries after it had been written, was gone over by a writer, who, finding the letters faint and yellow, had touched them up with a blacker and more permanent ink.

It is a strange circumstance that none of the facsimile representations of the pages of the manuscript that have been published give a correct idea of the original, with the exception of that of Dean Burgon in 1871. Not only do the number of lines in a given space in all the so-called facsimiles differ from that of the manuscript, but the general character of the letters is widely different. The importance of seeing the original, therefore, for purposes of study, is apparent. The uncial letters are very small and neat, upright and regular, and their breadth is nearly equal to their height. They are very like those in the manuscript rolls of Herculaneum. Originally the manuscript had no ornamental initial letters, marks of punctuation, or accents; a small interval of the breadth of a letter at the end of particular sections serving as a simple mode of punctuation. The number of such divisions into sections is very considerable, — one hundred and seventy occurring in St. Matthew; sixty-one in St. Mark; one hundred and fifty-two in St. Luke; and eighty in St. John, — and in this respect the Vatican Codex is unique. Where these divisions do not occur, the writing is continuous for several consecutive pages. Thus, while each of the beatitudes, each of the parables, and each of the series of generations in the genealogies of our Lord, are marked off into separate paragraphs by the small empty spaces referred to, there is no break in the text from the twenty-fourth verse of the seventeenth chapter of the Gospel of St. Matthew to the seventeenth verse of the twentieth chapter. So much has space been economised, that when the writer finished one book he began another at the top of the very next column; and throughout the manuscript there are very few breaks, and only one entire column left blank. This empty space is very significant; it occurs at the end of the eighth verse of the sixteenth chapter of St. Mark's Gospel, — thus omitting altogether the last twelve verses with which we are familiar. That this was done purposely is evident, for it involved a departure from the writer's usual method of continuous writing. The blank column testifies that he knew of the existence of this gap at the end of the Gospel, but did not know of any thoroughly trustworthy material with which to fill it up. And acting upon this authority our Revisers have printed the passage that has been supplied as an appendix, and not as a portion of the original Gospel of St. Mark. The only attempt at ornamentation in the Vatican manuscript is found at the end of Lamentations, Ezekiel, St. John's Gospel, and the Acts of the Apostles, where "an arabesque column of crossed lines, with dots in the intersections at the edge," and surmounted by the well-known monogram of Christ, so frequent in the inscriptions of the Catacombs, composed of the letter P in a cruciform shape, has been delicately and skilfully executed by the pen of the scribe. Most of the books have also brief titles and subscriptions.

Such was the original state of the Codex, but the critic of the ninth or tenth century already referred to introduced a great many changes. Not only did he deepen the colour of the ink; he, as Dean Burgon tells us, also accentuated the words carefully throughout, marking all the initial vowels with their proper breathings. He also placed instead of the small initial letter of each book an illuminated capital six times the size of the original uncial, painted in bright red and blue colours which have still retained nearly all their old brilliancy. At the top of the column, whenever a new book commenced, he also placed a broad bar painted in green, with three little red crosses above it. Nor was this all; he exercised his critical judgment in revising the text, and marking his approval or disapproval by certain significant indications. "What he approved of he touched up anew with ink, and added the proper accents; what he condemned he left in the faded brown caligraphy of the original and without accentuation." In this way the Codex may be called a kind of palimpsest, in which we have some portions of the original manuscript, and the rest overlaid with the later revision. We must discriminate carefully between these two elements; for it is obvious that it is the oldest portion that is most interesting and suggestive.

The Codex consists of upwards of one thousand five hundred pages, of which two hundred and eighty-four are assigned to the New Testament. Originally it contained the whole Bible, and also the Apocrypha and the Epistle of St. Clement to the Corinthians; which last was so much esteemed by the early Christians that it was regularly read in the churches, and bound up with the Scriptures — to which circumstance, indeed, we are indebted for its preservation to our own time. At present the greater part of Genesis and a part of the Psalms are missing from the old Testament; while, in the New Testament, the Epistle to Philemon, the three Pastoral Epistles, the latter part of the Epistle to the Hebrews, and the Apocalypse, in the original handwriting, are lost; their place having been supplied, it is said, in the fifteenth century, from a manuscript belonging to Cardinal Bessarion. From the evidence of its materials — arrangement and style of writing — the very high antiquity of this Codex may be inferred. It is generally supposed to have been written in the beginning of the fourth century. Vercellone, who edited Cardinal Mai's version of it, argues, from the remarkable correspondence of its text with that used by Cyril of Alexandria in his Commentary on St. John, that it must have been written at Alexandria, where there was a band of remarkably skilful caligraphists. He believes that it was one of the fifty manuscript copies of the Holy Scriptures which Eusebius, by order of the emperor Constantine the Great, got prepared in the year 332 for the use of the Christian Church in the newly-formed capital of Constantinople. And a circumstance that seems to corroborate this opinion is, that the Vatican Codex does not contain, as has already been mentioned, the last twelve verses of St. Mark's Gospel, a peculiarity which Eusebius says belongs to the best manuscripts of the Gospels. On this supposition, the Vatican Codex would be the very first edition of the Bible that had the seal of a sovereign authority.

But it may be of even older date than the time of Constantine, for its marginal references do not correspond with the Eusebian canons; and this fact would seem to imply that it belonged to the third century. Its only rival in point of antiquity is the famous Sinaitic Codex, known by the Hebrew letter [Hebrew: alef], discovered in a most romantic way by Tischendorf in the Convent of St. Catherine on Mount Sinai. Tischendorf has pronounced a decided opinion, not only that this manuscript is of the same age as the Vatican one, but that the Vatican manuscript was written by one of the four writers who, he infers from internal evidence, must have been employed upon the Sinaitic Codex. This opinion, however, has been disputed by other scholars; and it seems improbable, for the Sinaitic Codex has four columns to the page, whereas the Vatican Codex has only three. Its uncial letters are also much larger and plainer than those of the Vatican manuscript; and it has the Ammonian sections and Eusebian canons written in all probability by the original hand.

There can be little doubt that the Vatican manuscript goes, if not farther, at least as far back in date as the Council of Nice, and is the oldest and most valuable of extant monuments of sacred antiquity. It may have been transcribed directly from some Egyptian papyrus, or through the medium of only one intervening prototype. Perhaps it was a single copy saved from the fate of many surrendered to be burned by the class of Christian renegades called traditores, who averted the martyr's death in the great Diocletian persecution by giving up the sacred books of their religion to their enemies. For this pagan emperor endeavoured not only to deprive the Christian Church of its teachers, like his predecessors, but also to destroy the sacred writings upon which the faith of the Church was founded, and whose character and claims were beginning at this time to be generally recognised. The Alexandrine Codex—which is placed first on the list of uncial manuscripts, and therefore distinguished by the letter A—belongs undoubtedly to a more recent time. It is said by tradition to have been written by a noble Egyptian martyr named Thecla about the beginning of the fifth century, and was sent as a present to Charles I. by Cyrillus Lucaris, patriarch of Constantinople, who brought it from Alexandria. It is now one of the greatest treasures of the British Museum. The voice of tradition is confirmed by internal evidence, for it has only two columns in a page, while capital letters of different sizes abound, and vermilion is frequently introduced — all marks of the period indicated.

How or when the Codex Vaticanus was brought to the Vatican Library is a matter that is altogether involved in obscurity. It probably formed part of the library in the Lateran Palace, which goes nearly as far back as the time of Constantine, and was transferred along with the other contents of that library to the Vatican in 1450 by Pope Nicholas V. We first hear of it distinctly in a letter written to Erasmus in 1533 by Sepulveda; although there is a somewhat obscure reference to it a few years earlier in the correspondence of the Papal librarian Bombasius with Erasmus. A Roman edition of the Septuagint portion based upon the Vatican MS. appeared in 1587. After that period to 1780 it was several times collated; among others, by Bartolocci, the Vatican librarian; by Bentley, who employed for the purpose the Abbate Mico and Rulotta; and by Birch of Copenhagen, who travelled under the auspices of the King of Denmark. Along with many of the best sculptures and most valuable art-treasures of the Vatican, the precious Codex was taken to Paris in 1810 by order of Napoleon Buonaparte, that unscrupulous robber of foreign palaces and churches for the aggrandisement of his own capital; and while there it was carefully examined by the celebrated critic, J.L. Hug, who was the first to determine, from the nature of its materials and its internal evidence, its very great antiquity. When it was restored, along with the other spoils of the great Roman Palace, it was sealed up by its jealous possessors, and could no longer be consulted for critical purposes. In 1843 Tischendorf could only see it for two days of three hours each. Tregelles, who went to Rome in 1845 for the special purpose of consulting the Codex, provided with a strongly-recommendatory letter of introduction from Cardinal Wiseman, was only permitted to see it, but not to transcribe any of its readings. His pockets, as he himself tells us, were searched, and his pen, ink, and paper taken away, before he was allowed to open it; and if he looked at a passage too long the manuscript was snatched rudely from his hands by the two prelates in watchful attendance. When Dean Alford, in 1861, made use of the manuscript for four days, his labours of collation were carried on in the face of much opposition from the librarian, who insisted that the order of Antonelli permitted him only to see the manuscript, but not to verify passages in it.

The reason alleged to the scholars of Europe for this childish jealousy was that the authorities of the Vatican were themselves preparing to publish a thorough collation, and they did not wish the glory of the achievement to pass away from Rome. Cardinal Mai began, indeed, to prepare an edition for publication in 1828; but it did not appear till 1857, three years after the cardinal's death, under the learned editorship of Vercellone. There was a rumour copied into the Edinburgh Review from Sir Charles Lyell's work on the United States, that the cardinal was prevented from publishing his work by Pope Gregory XVI., on account of its variations from the Vulgate, which had been solemnly sanctioned by the decrees of the Council of Trent and the Church's claims to infallibility. It was further asserted that he finally obtained permission to publish his edition on condition that he inserted within brackets the celebrated text 1 John v. 7, which was wanting in the manuscript. Whether this was true or not, it is certain that what the learned cardinal gave to the world was more an edition, a critical recension of the text, than a faithful transcript of the Vatican Codex. Although he had the MS. with him at his residence in the Palazzo Altieri—a circumstance which gave rise to the belief at the time that it had disappeared during the French occupation of Rome—he could only bestow upon the arduous task the scanty leisure available from more engrossing duties. The work was therefore so imperfectly done that the cardinal himself was reluctant to publish it; and the learned and honest Barnabite under whose editorial auspices it appeared was obliged to append a formidable list of errata, and to make a gentle apology in his preface for his friend's inaccuracies. But, with all its defects, the five quarto volumes of the cardinal's reprint has added largely to our critical knowledge of the Codex; and it derives a special interest from the circumstance that it was the first time the Greek Scriptures had ever been published in Rome.

Since then Tischendorf, during his second visit to the Eternal City, had an audience of Pope Pius IX., and offered to bring out at his own expense an edition of the Vatican Codex similar to that which he had prepared, under the auspices of the Russian emperor, of the Sinaitic Codex. This request the Pope refused, under the old pretext that he wished to publish such an edition himself. Tischendorf, however, was allowed to use the manuscript more freely than on the former occasion; though several times it was taken away from him, and his labours interrupted, because of alleged breaches of faith on his part. The result of this unusual privilege was that the great Textuary has issued by far the most accurate and satisfactory edition which we possess at present. Pius IX. carried out his intention of publishing a Roman edition in five volumes, printed by the famous press of the Propaganda. The New Testament instalment appeared under the editorship of Vercellone and Cozza in 1868; but Vercellone dying soon after, the subsequent volumes were prepared under less able supervision. The famous manuscript therefore labours under the disadvantage of uncertainty, there being no guarantee that any reading is really that of the original. And while the Alexandrine Codex has been reproduced by photography, and the Sinaitic Codex has been faithfully published, the exact palæography, or the genuine text as it stands, of the Vatican Codex is still a desideratum among scholars.

The total disappearance of all manuscripts previous to the Vatican Codex is a matter of surprise, for it has been calculated on sufficient evidence that many thousands of copies of the Gospels were circulated among Christians at the end of the second century. The loss may be attributed to the fact that the older manuscripts were written on less enduring materials. Previous to the second century the principal writing material was paper made of papyrus, a plant found at one time not only in Egypt, but also in the north of Palestine and various parts of southern Italy and Sicily, although now almost extirpated; and we have reason to believe, from one or two incidental notices in St. John's writings, that it was the material employed by the apostles themselves. This papyrus paper was of a very perishable nature, and manuscripts written on it, apart from the wear and tear of continual use, would succumb to the process of decay in a comparatively short period. We are indebted for the preservation of all the papyrus manuscripts that have come down to us from a remote antiquity to the fact of their having been kept in exceptionally favourable circumstances, as in the hermetically-sealed interiors of Egyptian tombs. Those exposed to the air have all disappeared ages ago. In the second century parchment was brought into common use as a writing material, and papyrus paper gradually fell into disuse. And with the change of material the shape of manuscripts was changed; the ancient form of the papyrus-roll giving place, in manuscripts written on parchment, to the form of books with leaves. How we should value the original rolls which contained the handwriting of the evangelists and apostles! With what profound interest should we gaze upon the signature and salutation of St. Paul affixed to the Epistles which he dictated to an amanuensis on account of his defective eyesight! How we should prize the apostolic autograph of the Epistle to the Galatians, of which the writer says, "Ye see how large a letter I have written unto you with mine own hand." What a thrill would pass through us at the sight of those two pastoral Epistles, at the close of which St. John says, — "I had many things to write, but I will not with pen and ink write unto thee"! Our legitimate veneration, however, would be apt to pass over into idolatrous superstition. We should worship such precious documents as the early Christians worshipped the relics of the saints. It was, therefore, a wise providential arrangement that such a temptation should have been taken out of the way. All the original manuscripts of the sacred writings disappeared, on account of the fragile character of their materials, probably in a few years after the death of the writers, no special care having been taken to preserve them; and, as Dr. Westcott has remarked, not a single authentic appeal is made to them in the religious disputes regarding the exact words of certain passages in the Gospels and Epistles in the writings of the second century.

But though the Vatican Codex is the oldest manuscript of the New Testament in existence, it does not follow from that circumstance that it is the most reliable. Widely different views of its critical value are entertained by scholars. By some it has been accepted as the most authoritative of all versions, while others have regarded it as one of the most corrupt and imperfect. Indeed the conjecture has been hazarded that the very circumstance of its continued preservation during so many centuries is a proof that it was an unreliable copy long laid aside, and therefore exempt from the wear and tear under which genuine copies of the same date have long ago perished. These extreme views, however, are unjust. While it is not free from many gross inaccuracies and faults, it presents upon the whole a very fair idea of the Greek Vulgate of the early Church, and is worthy of as much respect at least as any single document in existence. The chief peculiarity of the Codex is the large number of important omissions in it; so that, as Dr. Dobbin says, it presents an abbreviated text of the New Testament. A few of these omissions were wilfully made, while the large majority were no doubt caused by the carelessness of the writer in transcribing from the copy before him; for there are several instances of his having written the same words and clauses twice over. On the supposition of the MS. being one of the fifty prepared at Constantine's order, the extreme haste with which such a task would be executed would account for the multitude of clerical errors. Besides the last verses of the Gospel of St. Mark already alluded to, and no less than three hundred and sixty-four other omissions in the same Gospel of greater or less moment, the doxology at the end of the Lord's Prayer, in Matthew vi. 13, is wanting; as also the description of the agony of the Saviour and the help of the angel in Luke xxii. 43, 44; the important clause, "For he was before me," in John i. 27; the miraculous troubling of the water in the Pool of Bethesda in John v. 3, 4; the narrative of the adulterous woman in John vii. 53 to viii. 11; the question of Philip and the answer of the Ethiopian eunuch in Acts viii. 37; the significant and affecting incidents in Paul's conversion mentioned in Acts ix. 5, 6; and the well-known disputed text of the Three witnesses in Heaven, in 1 John v. 7. These omitted passages, which, from internal evidence, apart from the external testimony of the largest number of critical documents, we must acknowledge to be genuine, are the most serious of the lacunæ, amounting altogether to the extraordinary number of two thousand four hundred and fifty-six. They give the document a very distinctive character; while even the less striking disappearances from the text, which can only be apprehended on a close collation, more or less affect the sense. German critics have stamped several of these omissions with their approbation, especially those referring to the supernatural, owing to their well-known repugnance to the miraculous element in Scripture.

There are other peculiarities of the Codex which greatly interested me; but the discussion of them would require me to go too much into critical details. I must mention, however, the occasional use in the manuscript of a Latinised orthography. The name of Silvanus, for instance, mentioned in 1 Peter v. 12, is rendered into the Latinised Greek Silbanou, instead of Silouanou, the common Greek form; and in 2 Peter iii. 10, instead of the last word of the verse, katakaêsetai, "shall be burned up," occurs the singular word eurethesetai, — which means, "shall be found." The Syriac and one Egyptian version have the reading "shall not be found"; and either the "not" was accidentally omitted when the Vatican Codex was copied from an earlier exemplar that had that reading, or the writer had some confused idea of the Latin word urerentur, "shall be burnt up," in his mind, and adopted the word eurethesetai from its resemblance to it — as a Latin root with a Greek inflection. Some curious examples of Latin forms and constructions might be given; and this circumstance has led to the hypothesis that the origin of the Vatican manuscript might, after all, have been Italian, and not Alexandrian as is commonly supposed. The Codex has also been accused of theological bias; for in John i. 18, "only begotten God" is substituted for "only begotten Son." This is considered by some to be a reference to the polemics of the fourth century regarding the Arian doctrines; although this supposition would make it of later date. The order of the books of the New Testament in the Codex is different from that with which we are familiar. The Catholic Epistles from James to Jude follow the Acts, according to the order of the ancient Greek Church; then come the Pauline Epistles; and the Epistle to the Hebrews comes in between the Second Epistle to the Thessalonians and First Timothy. Its sections, however, are numbered as if it had originally been placed between the Epistles to the Galatians and Ephesians; thus showing that this was the arrangement in the older document from which the Codex was copied. One of the Moscow manuscripts, it may be mentioned in connection with this novelty in location, places the Epistle to the Hebrews in a position as abnormal as in the Vatican manuscript — namely, before the Epistle to the Romans.

In the formation of the Received Text of our New Testament, the Vatican manuscript was not employed. The basis of the early printed editions—the Elzevir and those of Robert Stephens the celebrated Parisian printer—was the Greek New Testament of Erasmus, published in 1516, compiled with the aid of such manuscripts as he found at Basle, and the Complutensian Polyglot—so called after Complutum, the modern Alcala, in Spain, where it was printed in 1522, under the patronage of Cardinal Ximenes, whose text was said to have been formed from manuscripts sent from the Papal Library at Rome—the Vatican Codex certainly not being among the number, as abundantly appears from internal evidence. But though the Vatican manuscript was not employed in the construction of our Authorised Version, it has recently been used as the chief authority by the New Testament Revisers. Drs. Westcott and Hort have built up their Greek text with special deferential regard to it; and this exclusive devotion has been severely condemned by several critics, such as Dean Burgon, who regard it as an endeavour to balance a pyramid upon its apex. But apart from the contradictory views of such textuaries, there can be no doubt that the Vatican Codex has been of the greatest service in these later days in correcting the Authorised Version, and helping to restore the sacred text as nearly as possible to the purity of the original autographs. And it has added its most valuable testimony to that of the many other ancient manuscripts of the Sacred Writings in existence, that, notwithstanding unimportant variations of readings naturally caused by the great multiplication of copies, the sacred text from the time when it first appeared to the present has been preserved substantially uncorrupt; so that we have the same divine truth presented to us that was presented to the Christians of the ages immediately succeeding the time of the apostles.

With all these remarkable associations and points of interest connected with the Vatican manuscript, it is not to be wondered at that I should gaze upon it with a species of veneration. It transported me in imagination to a period when the canon of the New Testament was as yet in a state of flux. The evidence of the Muratorian fragment in the Ambrosian Library at Milan shows to us that the separate books of the New Testament had indeed been collected into one; and a belief in their Divine inspiration equally with the Old Testament Scriptures had begun to be entertained. But there was as yet no prevailing unanimity of opinion as to what books should be admitted into the Canon and what books should be excluded. No formal attempt had as yet been made to reconcile conflicting testimonies; or, if made, the recensions undertaken did not meet with general acceptance. Even a good many years afterwards, as late as at the Council of Laodicea in 361, doubts were still expressed as to the claims of the Apocalypse to canonicity. This book was not originally included in the Vatican Codex; for the manuscript copy of it bound up in the volume is of much later date, and in a different handwriting. And this hesitation regarding the full recognition of certain books, proves the great care that was exercised, and the deep sense of responsibility that was felt, in the collection of the other books. The formation of the sacred Canon was done gradually and imperceptibly; but the result to every thoughtful mind is more suggestive of the inspiration of that Spirit whose operation is like the wind that bloweth where it listeth, and thou hearest the sound thereof, but canst not tell whence it cometh and whither it goeth—than if the process had been more formal and conspicuous.

CHAPTER XII - ST. PAUL AT PUTEOLI

The Gospel first came to Europe in circumstances similar to those in which it came into human history. Through poverty, shame, and suffering — through the manger, the cross, and the sepulchre — did our Saviour accomplish the salvation of the world; through stripes and imprisonment, through the gloom of the inner dungeon and the pain and shame of the stocks, did Paul and Silas declare at Philippi the glad tidings of salvation. Out of the midnight darkness which enveloped the apostles of the Cross, as they sang in the prison, came the marvellous light that was destined to illumine all Europe. Out of the stocks which held fast the feet that came to the shores of the West shod with the preparation of the gospel of peace, to proclaim deliverance to the captives, sprang that glorious liberty which has broken every fetter that bound the bodies and souls of men throughout Christendom. After the earthquake that shook the prison walls and released the prisoners came the still, small voice of power, which overthrew the tyrannies and superstitions of ages, and remade society from its very foundations.

Very similar were the circumstances in which the apostle landed at the quay of Puteoli. A weary, worn-out prisoner, accused by his own countrymen, on his way to be judged at the tribunal of the Roman emperor, associated with a troop of malefactors, St. Paul disembarked, on the 3d of May of the year 59, from the ship Castor and Pollux, after having gone through storm and shipwreck, and first touched the shore of the wonderful land destined afterwards to be the scene of the mightiest triumphs of the Gospel, and the most enlightened centre for its diffusion throughout the world. Like the birth of Rome itself, whose obscure foundation, according to the beautiful myth, was laid by the outcast son of a Vestal Virgin, the kingdom of the despised virgin-born Jesus of Nazareth that cometh not with observation, stole unawares, amid the meanest circumstances, into the very heart of the Roman world. Momentous events were taking place at the time throughout the Roman Empire, attracting all eyes, and engaging the attention of all minds; but the unnoticed landing at Puteoli of the humble Jewish prisoner, judging by its marvellous results, was by far the most important. It marked a new era in the history of the world. And there was something significant in the coincidence that St. Paul should have come to the Italian shore in the ship Castor and Pollux, the names not merely of the patrons of sailors, but also of the saviours of Rome. The mighty empire which human tyranny had established has crumbled to pieces, and we walk to-day amid its ruins; but the kingdom of peace and righteousness which Paul came to inaugurate has spread from that coign of vantage over all the earth, and in a world of death and change has impressed upon the minds of men with a new force the idea of the eternal and the unchangeable.

Earth holds no fairer scene than that which met the apostle's gaze as he entered the bay of Puteoli. "See Naples, and die," is the cuckoo cry of the modern tourist who visits this enchanted region; and such a vision is indeed worthy to be the last imprinted upon a human retina. It is called by the Italians themselves "Un pezzo di cielo caduto in terra," a piece of heaven fallen upon earth. Shores that curve in every line of beauty, holding out arm-like promontories, into whose embrace the tideless sea runs up; mountain-ranges whose tops in winter are covered with snow, and whose sides are draped with the luxuriant vegetation of the South; a large city rising in a series of semicircular terraces from the deep azure of the sea to the deep azure of the mountains, whose eastern architecture flushes to a vivid rosy hue in the afternoon light like some fabled city of the poets; and dominating the glorious horizon the double peak of Vesuvius forming the centre in which all the features of landscape loveliness are focussed — crowned by its pillar of cloud by day and of fire by night. Such is the picture upon which travellers crowd from the ends of the earth to gaze.

Nor was the view different in its most important elements in the days of the apostle. The same great forms of the landscape met the eye; and the same magic play of light and colour, the same jewel-points flashing in the waters, the same gleams of purple and crimson wandering over town, and vineyard, and wood, transfigured the scene then, which gives it more than half its loveliness now. But its human elements were different. Swarming with life as are these shores at the present day, they were even more populous then. Where we now wander through picturesque ruins and silent solitudes, prosperous towns and villages stood; and temples, palaces, and summer houses of patrician magnificence crowded upon each other to such an extent that the sea itself was invaded, and an older Venice rose from the waters along the curves of its bays. The shores of Baiæ were the very centre of Roman splendour. The emperor and his court spent a large part of the year there; and noble families, that elsewhere had domains miles in extent, were there satisfied with the smallest space upon which they could build a house and plant a garden. Pompeii and Herculaneum, in all their reckless gaiety, lay, unconscious of danger, at the foot of Vesuvius, then a grassy mountain wooded to the summit with oak and chestnut, and known from time immemorial as a field of pasture for flocks and herds. The Bay of Misenum, now so solitary that the scream of the sea-fowl is almost the only sound that breaks the stillness, was crowded with the vessels of the Roman fleet, commanded by Pliny; and its waters were alive with the pleasure-boats of the patrician youths, filling the air with the music of their laughter and song. Puteoli, or, as it is now called, Pozzuoli, a dull and stagnant fourth-rate town, was then the Liverpool of Italy, carrying on an immense trade in corn between Egypt and the western provinces of the Roman Empire. It rivalled Delos in magnificence, and was called the Little Rome. It had a splendid forum and harbour, and was guarded by fortifications which resisted the repeated attacks of Hannibal. In this region almost every famous Roman of the later days of the Republic and the earlier days of the Empire had his sea-side villa to which he retired from the noise and bustle of the Imperial City. It was the Brighton or more properly the Bath of Rome; for though it was frequented during the burning heats of summer for the sake of its comparative coolness, it was principally chosen as a winter retreat to escape from the frosts and snows of the north. Lucullus carried here the gorgeous luxury and extravagance of his city life; here Augustus and Hadrian had their palaces erected on vast piers thrown out into the sea, whose waters still murmur over their remains; while Cicero built here his Puteolanum, delightfully situated on the coast, and surrounded by a shady grove, which he called his Academy, in imitation of Plato, and where he composed his "Academia" and "De Fato." Hardly an inch of the soil but is full of fragments of mosaic pavements. The common stones of the road are often rich marbles, that formed part of imperial structures; and the very dust on which you tread, if analysed, would be found to be a powder of gems and precious stones.

But alas! in some of the fairest spots of earth man has been vilest; and like the ancient Cities of the Plain, which stood in a region of Edenic loveliness, the shores of the Bay of Naples were inhabited by a race corrupted with the worst vices of Roman civilisation. Some of the most dreadful crimes that have disgraced humanity were committed on that radiant shore. Yonder sleeps in the azure distance the enchanted isle of Capri, haunted for ever by dreadful memories of the unnameable atrocities with which the Emperor Tiberius had stained its peaceful bowers. On the neighbouring heights of Posilipo are traces of the villa of Vedius, and of the celebrated fish-ponds where he fed his murenæ with the flesh of his disobedient slaves. On the shore of Puteoli the apostle might have seen the remains of one of the maddest freaks of imperial folly—the floating-bridge of Caligula, stretching across the bay for nearly three miles, and decorated with the finest mosaic pavements and sculpture. Over this useless bridge the insane emperor drove in the chariot and armour of Alexander the Great, to celebrate his triumph over the Parthians; and from it, on his return, he ordered the crowd of inoffensive spectators to be hurled into the sea. By withdrawing for the construction of this bridge the ships employed in the harbour, the importation of corn was put a stop to, and a grievous famine, felt even in Rome, was the result. And near at hand was Bauli, where Nero—the very Cæsar to whom it is startling to remember that St. Paul appealed, and before whom he was going to be judged,—only two years before attempted the murder of his own mother, Agrippina, which failed because of her discovery of the plot, but which was most ruthlessly accomplished very soon afterwards. Here too Marcellus was poisoned by Livia, that Tiberius might ascend the throne of Augustus; and Domitian by Nero, that he might enjoy the wealth of his aunt. Here Hadrian, a few days before his own miserable end, compelled his beautiful and accomplished wife, Sabina, to put herself to death, that she might not survive him in such a wretched world. And in the cities at the foot of Vesuvius have been revealed to us, after nature had kindly hidden them for eighteen centuries, tokens of a depravity so utter, that we cannot help looking upon the fiery deluge from the mountain, that soon after St. Paul's visit swept them out of existence, as a Divine judgment like that of Sodom and Gomorrha. And darker even than these monstrosities of wickedness was the divine worship paid on these shores to the Roman emperors. It was a pitiable spectacle when the sailors of an Alexandrian ship, coming into the harbour of Puteoli, gave thanks for their prosperous voyage to the dying Augustus, whom they met cruising on the waters vainly in search of health, and offered him divine honours, which the gratified emperor accepted, and rewarded with gifts. But what shall we think of the worship of the god Caligula and the god Nero? Surely a people who could raise altars and offer sacrifices to such unmitigated monsters must have lost the very conception of religion. Not only virtue, but the very belief in any source of virtue, must have been utterly extirpated in them. When Herod spoke, the people said it was the voice of God; and he was smitten with worms because he gave not God the glory. And surely the superhuman wickedness of the Cæsars may be regarded as a punishment, equally significant, of the fearful blasphemy of the worshipped and the worshippers.

No wonder that the shores of Baiæ now present a picture of the saddest desolation. Where man sins, there man suffers. The relation between human crime and the barren wilderness is still as inflexibly maintained as at the first. Until all recollection of the iniquities of the place has passed away it is fitting that these silent shores should remain the desert that they are. We should not wish the old voluptuous magnificence revived; and these myrtle bowers can never more regain the charm of virgin solitudes untainted by man. Italy, like Palestine, has thus an accursed spot in its fairest region—a visible monument to all ages, of the great truth that the tidal wave of retribution will inevitably overwhelm every nation that forgets the eternal distinctions of right and wrong.

St. Paul was a man of keen sensibilities and strong imagination. He must therefore at Puteoli have been deeply impressed at once with the loveliness of nature and the wickedness of man. The contrast would present itself to him in a very painful manner. As at Athens—where his spirit was moved within him when he saw the city wholly given up to idolatry—so here he must have had that noble indignation against the iniquities of the place—the outrages committed on the laws of God, and the dishonour done to the nature of man made in the Divine image—to which David and Jeremiah, and all the loftiest spirits of mankind, have given such stern and yet patriotic utterance. What others were callous to, filled him with keen shame and sorrow. He who could have wished that himself were accursed from Christ for his brethren, his kinsmen according to the flesh, must have had a profound pity for these wretched victims of profligacy, who were looking in their ignorance for salvation to a brutal mortal worse than themselves,—"the son of perdition, sitting in the temple of God, showing that he was God." And to this feeling of indignation and sorrow, because of the wickedness of the place, must have been added a feeling of personal despondency. From the significant circumstance that the apostle thanked God, and took courage, when he met the Christian brethren at Apii Forum, we may infer that he had previously great heaviness of spirit. He would be more or less than human, if on setting his foot for the first time on the native soil of the conquerors of his country, and the lords of the whole world, and seeing on every side, even at this distance from the imperial city, overwhelming evidences of the luxury and power of the empire, he did not feel oppressed with a sense of personal insignificance. Evil had throned itself there on the high places of the earth, and could mock at the puny efforts of the followers of Jesus to cast it down. Idolatry had so deeply rooted itself in the interests and passions of men which were bound up in its continuance, that it seemed a foolish dream to expect that it would be supplanted by the preaching of the Cross, which to St. Paul's own people was a stumbling-block and to all other nations foolishness. And who was he that he should undertake such a mission—a weak and obscure member of a despised race, a prisoner chained to a soldier, appealing to Cæsar against the condemnation of his own countrymen. We can well believe, that notwithstanding the sustaining grace that was given to him, the heart of the apostle must have been very heavy when he stood in the midst of the jostling crowd on the quay of Puteoli, and took the first step there on Italian soil of his journey to Rome. He felt most keenly all that a man can feel of the shame and offence of the Cross; but nevertheless he was not ashamed of the Gospel of Christ. And his presence there on that Roman quay—a despised prisoner in bonds for the sake of the Gospel—is a picture, that appeals to every heart, of the triumph of Divine strength in the midst of human weakness; and a most striking proof, moreover, that not by might, but by the Spirit of love, does God bring down the strongholds of sin.

But God furnished a providential cure for whatever despondency the apostle may have felt. No sooner did he land than he found himself surrounded by Christian brethren, who cordially welcomed him, and persuaded him to remain with them seven days. Such brotherly kindness must have greatly cheered him; and the week spent among these loyal followers of the Lord Jesus must have been a time of bodily and spiritual refreshment opportunely fitting him for the trying experiences before him. Doubtless these brethren were Jewish converts to the Christian faith; for that there were Jewish residents at Puteoli, residing in the Tyrian quarter of the city, we are assured by Josephus; and this we should have expected from the mercantile importance of the place and its intimate commercial relations with the East. How they came under the influence of the Gospel we know not; they may have been among "the strangers of Rome" who came to Jerusalem at Pentecost to keep the national feasts in obedience to the Mosaic Law, and who were then brought to the knowledge of the truth by the preaching of St. Peter; or perhaps they were converts of St Paul's own making, in some of the numerous places which he visited on his missionary tours, and who afterwards came to reside for business purposes at this port. We see in the presence of the Jewish brethren at Puteoli one of the most striking illustrations of the providential pre-arrangements made for the diffusion of the Gospel throughout all nations. The Jews had a more than ordinary attachment to their native land. Patriotism in their case was not only a passion, but a part of their religion; and their love of country was entwined with the holiest feelings of their nature. In Jerusalem alone could God be acceptably worshipped. And yet it was divinely ordered that those who had been for ages the hermits of the human race should become all at once the most cosmopolitan, when the time for imparting to the world the benefits of their isolated religious training had come. And the Jews thus scattered abroad preserved amid their alien circumstances their national worship and customs, and thus became the natural links of connection between the missionaries of the Cross and the Gentiles whom they wished to reach. Through such Jewish channels the Gospel speedily penetrated into remote localities, which otherwise it would have taken a long time to reach. We are struck with distinct traces of the Christian faith in the time of St. Paul in the most unexpected places. For instance, in the National Museum at Naples I have seen rings with Christian emblems engraved upon them, which were found at Pompeii; proving beyond doubt that there had been followers of Jesus even in that dissolute place, who, unlike Lot and his household, were overwhelmed in the same destruction with those whose evil deeds must have daily vexed their righteous souls. The same symbols which we find in the Roman Catacombs, — the palm branch, the sacred fish the monogram of Jesus, the dove, are unmistakably represented on these rings. Some of them are double, indicating that they were used by married persons: one has the palm branch twice repeated; another exhibits the palm and anchor; a third has a dove with a twig in its bill; and one ring has the Greek word elpis — hope — inscribed upon it.

St. Paul at Puteoli may be said to have dwelt among his own people. Not only was he with his own countrymen and fellow-disciples, but he was in the midst of associations that forcibly recalled his home. The apostle was a citizen of a Greek city, and the language in which he spoke was Greek; and here, in the Bay of Naples, he was in the midst of a Greek colony, where Roman influence had not been able to efface the deep impression which Greece had made upon the place. The original name of the splendid expanse of water before him was the Bay of Cumæ; and Cumæ was absolutely the first Greek settlement in the western seas. Neapolis or Parthenope was the beautiful Greek name of the city of Naples, testifying to its Hellenic origin; and Dicæarchia was the older Greek name of Puteoli, a name used to a late period in preference to its Latin name, derived from the numerous mineral springs in the neighbourhood. The whole lower part of Italy was wholly Greek; its arts, its customs, its literature, were all Hellenic; and its people belonged to the pure Ionic race whose keen imaginations and vivid sensuousness seemed to have been created out of the fervid hues and the pellucid air of their native land. Everywhere the subtle Greek tongue might be heard; and all, so far as Greek influence was concerned, was as unchanged in the days of the apostle as when Pythagoras visited the region, and adopted the inhabitants as the fittest agents in his great scheme of universal regeneration. St. Paul therefore, at Puteoli, might have imagined himself standing on the very soil of classic Hellas, and felt as much at home as in his own native city of Tarsus. This wide diffusion of the Greek language throughout the West as well as the East at this time is another of the remarkable providential pre-arrangements which prepared the way for the preaching of the Gospel throughout the world. A Gentile speech, by a series of wonderful events, was thus made ready over all the world to receive and to communicate the glorious Gospel that was to be preached to all nations.

The remains of the ancient pier upon which St. Paul landed may still be seen. Indeed, no Roman harbour has left behind such solid memorials. No less than thirteen of the buttresses that supported its arches are left, three lying under water; all constructed of brick held together by that Roman cement called pozzolana, after the town of Pozzuoli, whose extraordinary tenacity rivals that of the living rock. You can plant your feet upon the very stones upon which the apostle must have stood. And if you happen to be there on the 3d of May you will see a solemn procession of the inhabitants of the decayed town, headed by their priests, celebrating the anniversary of this memorable incident. The first conspicuous object upon which the eye of the apostle would rest on landing would be the Temple of Neptune, of which a few pillars are still standing in the midst of the water. Here Caligula, in his mad passage over his bridge of boats, paused to offer propitiatory sacrifices. Here, too, Cæsar, before he sailed to Greece to encounter the forces of Antony at Actium, sacrificed to Neptune; and here the crew of every ship presented offerings, in order to secure favouring winds and waves when outward bound, or in gratitude when returning home from a successful voyage. Beyond this he would see in all its splendour the famous bathing establishment built over a thermal spring near the sea, which has since been known as the Temple of Serapis, an Egyptian deity, whose worship had spread widely in Italy. Three tall columns of cipollino marble, belonging to the portico of this building, are still standing, with their bases under water; and they have acquired a world-wide interest, especially to geologists, as records of the successive elevations and depressions of the coast-line during the historical period; these changes being indicated on their shafts by the different watermarks and the perforations of marine bivalves or boring-shells well known to be living in the Mediterranean Sea. In the upper part of the town, on a commanding height, he would behold the Temple of Augustus, built for the worship of the deified founder of the Roman Empire. A Christian cathedral dedicated to St. Proculus, who suffered martyrdom in the same year with St. Januarius, containing the tomb of Pergolesi, the celebrated musical composer, now occupies the site of the pagan shrine, and has six of its Corinthian pillars, that looked down upon the apostle as he landed, built into its walls. A temple of Diana and a temple of the Nymphs also adorned the town, from which numerous columns and sculptures have been recently recovered. On every side the apostle would see mournful tokens that the city was wholly given up to idolatry, — to the worship of mortal men and an ignoble crowd of gods and goddesses borrowed from all nations; and yet he had equally sad proofs that the idolatry was altogether a hollow and heartless pretence, — that the superstitious creed publicly maintained by the city had long ceased to command the respect of its recognised defenders.

I walked up from the town along the remains of the Via Campana, a cross-road that led from Puteoli to Capua and there joined the famous Appian Way. Along this road the apostle passed on his way to Rome; and it is still paved with the original lava-blocks upon which his feet had pressed. One of the principal objects on the way is the amphitheatre of Nero, with its tiers of seats, its arena, and its subterranean passages, in a wonderful state of preservation, richly plumed with the delicate fronds of the maiden-hair fern, which drapes with its living loveliness so many of the ruins of Greece and Italy. It was here that Nero himself rehearsed the parts in which he wished to act on the more public stage of Rome. The sands of the arena were dyed with the blood of St. Januarius, who was thrown to the wild beasts by order of Diocletian, and whose blood is annually liquefied by a supposititious miracle in Naples at the present day. Behind the amphitheatre the apostle would get a glimpse of the famous Phlegræan Fields so often referred to in the classic poets as the scene of the wars of the gods and the giants.

This is the Holy Land of Paganism. All the scenery of the eleventh book of the Odyssey and of the sixth book of the Æneid spreads beneath the eye. At every step you come upon some spot associated with the romantic literature of antiquity. From thence the imaginative shapes of Greek mythology passed into the poetry of Rome. There everything takes us back far beyond the birth of Roman civilisation, and reminds us of the legends of the older Hellenic days, which will exercise an undying spell on the higher minds of the human race down to the latest ages. It is the land of Virgil, whose own tomb is not far off; and under the guidance of his genius we visit the ghostly Cimmerian shores, now bathed in glowing sunshine, and stand on spots that thrilled the hearts of Hercules and Ulysses with awe. There the terrible Avernus, to which the descent was so easy, sleeps in its deep basin, long ago divested by the axe of Agrippa of the impenetrable gloom and mysterious dread which its dark forests had created; its steep banks partly covered with natural copsewood bright with a living mosaic of cyclamens and lilies, and partly formed of cultivated fields. During my visit the delicious odour of the bean blossom pervaded the fields, reminding me vividly of familiar rural scenes far away. Yonder is the subterranean passage called by the common people the Sibyl's Cave, where Æneas came and plucked the golden bough, and, led by the melancholy priestess of Apollo, went down to the dreary world of the dead. It was the general tradition of Pagan nations that the point of departure from this world, as well as the entrance to the next, was always in the west. We find the largest number of the prehistoric relics of the dead on the western shores of our own country. The cave of Loch Dearg—at first connected with primitive pagan rites and subsequently the traditional entrance to the Purgatory of St. Patrick—is situated in the west of Ireland, and corresponds to the cave of the Sibyl and the Lake of Avernus in Italy. Indeed the word Avernus itself bears such a close resemblance to the Gaelic word Ifrinn—the name of the infernal regions, and to the name of Loch Hourn, the Lake of Hell, on the north-west coast of Scotland—that it has given rise to the supposition that it was the legacy of a prehistoric Celtic people who at one time inhabited the Phlegræan Fields. On the other side of Lake Avernus is the Mare Morto, the Lake or Sea of the Dead, with its memories of Charon and his ghostly crew, which now shines in the setting sun like a field of gold sparkling with jewels; and beyond it are the Elysian Fields, the abodes of the blessed, the rich life of whose soil breaks out at every pore into a luxuriant maze of vines and orange trees, and all manner of lovely and fruitful vegetation. Still farther behind is the Acherusian Marsh of the poets, now called the Lake of Fusaro, because hemp and flax are put to steep in it; and the river Styx itself, by which the gods dare not swear in vain, reduced to an insignificant rill flowing into the sea. It is most interesting to think of the apostle Paul being associated with this enchanted region. His presence on the scene is necessary to complete its charm, and to remind us that the vain dreams of those blind old seekers after God were all fulfilled in Him who opened a door for us in heaven, and brought life and immortality to light in the Gospel.

St. Paul must have noticed—though Scripture, intent only upon the unfolding of the religious drama, makes no reference to it—the crater of Solfatara, one of the most wonderful phenomena of this wonderful region, for it lay directly in his path, and was only about a mile distant from Puteoli. This was the famous Forum of Vulcan, where the god fashioned his terrible tools, and shook the earth with the fierce fires of his forge. On account of its gaseous fumaroles, and the flames thrown out with a loud roaring noise from one gloomy cavern in its side, this volcano may still be considered active. Its white calcined crater is clothed in some places with green shrubs, particularly with luxuriant sage, myrtle, and white heather; but an eruption took place in it so late as 1198, during which a lava current, a rare phenomenon in this district, flowed from its southern edge to the sea, destroying the ancient cemetery on the Via Puteolana, and forming the present promontory of Olibano. The ground sounds hollow beneath a heavy tread, reminding one unpleasantly that but a thin crust covers the fiery abyss which might break through at any moment. With the exception of Vesuvius, this is the only surviving remnant of the fierce elemental forces which have devastated this coast in every direction. The whole region is one mass of craters of various sizes and ages, some far older than Vesuvius, and others of comparatively recent origin. They are all craters of eruption and not of elevation; and in their formation they have interfered with and in some cases almost obliterated pre-existing ones. Some of them are filled with lakes, and others clothed with luxuriant vineyards, and wild woods fit for the chase, or encircling cultivated fields. To one looking upon it from a commanding position such as the heights of Posilipo, the landscape presents a universally blistered appearance. Hot mineral springs everywhere abound, often associated with the ruins of old Roman baths; and the soil is a white felspathic ash, disposed in layers of such fineness and regularity that they look as if they had been stratified under water, the sea and the shore having alternately given place to each other. Of the white earth abounding on every side, which has given to the place the old name of Campi Leucogæi, and is the result of the metamorphosis of the trachytic tufa by the chemical action of the gases that rise up through the fumaroles, a very fine variety of porcelain—known to collectors as Capo di Monti—used to be made on the hill behind Naples, and it has been supposed that the china clays of Cornwall and other places have been produced from the felspars of the granites in a similar way. The whole of the Solfatara crater has been enclosed for the purpose of manufacturing alum from its soil. On the hillside to the north there are several caverns, called stufe, from whence gas and hot steam arise, and these are used by the inhabitants as admirable vapour baths. So late as the year 1538 a terrible volcanic explosion, accompanied with violent earthquakes, happened not far from Puteoli, which threw up from the flat plain on which the village of Tripergola stood, a mountain called Monte Nuovo, four hundred and forty feet high and a mile and a half in circumference, consisting entirely of ashes and cinders, obliterating a large part of the celebrated Leucrine Lake, elevating the site of the temple of Serapis sixteen feet, and then depressing it, and generally changing the old features of this locality. This eruption gave relief to the throes of Lake Avernus, which henceforth ceased to send forth its exhalations, and became the cheerful garden scene which we now behold.

Here on a small scale, in the very neighbourhood of man's busiest haunts, occur the cosmical cataclysms which are usually seen only in remote solitudes, and which during the unknown ages of geology have left their indelible records on large portions of the earth's surface. Here we are admitted into the very workshop of Nature, and are privileged to witness her processes of creation. In the neighbourhood of Rome the volcanoes are long extinct. Nature is dead, and there is nothing left but her cold gray ashes. But here we see her in all her vigour, changing and renewing and mingling the ruins of her works in strange association with those of man—the ashes of her volcanoes with the fragments of temples and baths and the houses of Roman senators and poets. The whole region lies over a burning mystery, and one has a constant feeling of insecurity lest the ground should open suddenly and precipitate one into the very heart of it. Naples itself, strange to say, a city of more than five hundred thousand inhabitants, is built in great part within an old broken-down volcanic crater, and the proximity of its awful neighbour shows that it stands perilously on the brink of destruction, and may share at any time the fate of Pompeii and Herculaneum. Were it not for the safety-valves of Vesuvius and Solfatara, the whole intermediate region, with its towns and villages and swarming population, would be blown into the air by the vehement forces that are struggling beneath. It was this elemental war—fiercer, we have reason to believe, in classic times than now—that gave rise to the religious fables of the poets. The gloomy shades of Avernus, the tremendous battles of the gods, the dark pictures of Tartarus and the Stygian river, were the supernatural suggestions of a fiery soil. To the fierce throes of volcanic action we owe the weird mythology of the ancients, which has imparted such a profound charm to the region, and also, strange as it may seem, the surpassing loveliness of Nature herself. The fairest regions of the earth are ever those where the awful power of fire has been at work, giving to the landscape that passionate expression which lights up a human face with its most impressive beauty.

The visit of the apostle to Puteoli served many important purposes. He who had sent his people Israel into Egypt and Babylon that they might be benefited by coming into contact with other civilisations, sent St. Paul to this famous region where Greece and Rome—which, geographically and historically, were turned back to back, the face of Greece looking eastward, the face of Italy looking westward—seemed to meet and to blend into each other, in order that his sympathies might be expanded by coming into contact with all that man could realise of earthly glory or conceive of religion. We can trace the overruling Hand that was shaping the destinies of the Church in the course which he was led to take from Jerusalem to Damascus, and thence to Asia Minor, Corinth, Athens, Philippi, Puteoli, and Rome; gathering as he went along the fruits of all the wide diversity of experience and culture characterising these places, to equip him more thoroughly for his work for the Gentiles. And we see also how the doctrines of the Gospel were becoming more clearly and fully unfolded by this method of progression; how questions were settled and principles carried out which have shown to us the exceeding riches of Divine grace in a way that we could not otherwise have known. Like the lines and marks of the chrysalis which appear on the body of the butterfly when it first spreads out its wings to fly—like the folds of the bud which may be seen in the newly-expanded leaf or flower—so Christianity at first emerged from its Jewish sheath with the distinctive marks of Judaism upon it. But as it passed westward from the Holy City, it slowly extricated itself out of the spirit and the trammels of Judaism into the self-restraining freedom which Christ gives to His people. The teaching of the Gospel was fully developed, guarded from all possible misinterpretation, and practically applied to all representative circumstances of men, through its coming into contact with the events, persons, and scenes associated with the wonderful missionary journeyings of the apostle Paul, which began at Jerusalem and terminated at Rome. When the Gospel reached the Imperial City, its relations to Jews and Gentiles, bond and free, were fixed for ever, its own form was perfected, and the conditions for its diffusion matured; and its history henceforth, like that of Rome itself, was synonymous with the history of the world.